Microcomputers and Applications

The Scott, Foresman Series in Computers and Information Systems

Thomas H. Athey, Consulting Editor

INTRODUCTION TO COMPUTERS AND INFORMATION SYSTEMS, 2E
Athey and Zmud

COMPUTERS AND END-USER SOFTWARE
Athey, Day, and Zmud

MICROCOMPUTERS AND APPLICATIONS
Day, Athey, and Zmud

PFS: FIRST CHOICE WORKBOOK AND DOCUMENTATION
(WITH OR WITHOUT PFS: FIRST CHOICE SOFTWARE)
Day and Software Publishing Corporation

USING LOTUS 1-2-3, SUPERCALC4, WORDPERFECT, WORDSTAR, AND DBASE III PLUS
Warrner and Werner

USING LOTUS 1-2-3
Werner and Warrner

USING LOTUS 1-2-3, WORDSTAR, AND DBASE III PLUS
Warrner and Werner

QUICKBASIC
Scott

MANAGING INFORMATION AS A CORPORATE RESOURCE
Tom

MICROCOMPUTERS IN BUSINESS
Day

STRUCTURED COBOL PROGRAMMING
Pierson and Horn

INFORMATION SYSTEMS IN ORGANIZATIONS
Zmud

BASIC PROGRAMMING
Zmud and Eagle Software, Inc.

THE PC-PROFESSOR BASIC PROGRAMMING SOFTWARE TUTORIAL FOR THE IBM PC (BASICA)
Eagle Software, Inc.

Microcomputers and Applications

■ ■ ■ ■ ■ ■ ■ ■ ■

John C. Day
Ohio University

Thomas H. Athey
California State Polytechnic University at Pomona

Robert W. Zmud
Florida State University

Scott, Foresman/Little, Brown College Division
Scott, Foresman and Company
Glenview, Illinois
Boston
London

▪▪▪▪▪▪▪▪▪

A *Study Guide to Accompany Microcomputers and Applications* has been prepared to help you master the concepts discussed in your text. The *Guide* contains chapter summaries; detailed annotated chapter outlines; drill sections made up of multiple-choice, true/false, fill-in-the-blank, matching, and essay questions; as well as practice tests made up of true/false and multiple-choice questions. Page-referenced answers are provided for all questions. If the *Guide* (ISBN 0-673-38117-X) is not available in your bookstore, your bookstore manager will be able to order it for you.

▪▪▪▪▪▪▪▪▪

QA
76.5
.D34
1988

Acknowledgments follow the index, constituting a legal extension of the copyright page.

Library of Congress Cataloging-in-Publication Data

Day, John C. (John Charles)
   Microcomputers and applications.

   (Scott, Foresman series in computers and information systems)
   Study guide available.
   Includes index.
   1. Microcomputers.   I. Athey, Thomas H.   II. Zmud,
Robert W.   III. Title.
QA76.5.D34   1988   004.16   87-28508
ISBN 0-673-38109-9

Copyright © 1988 Scott, Foresman and Company.
All Rights Reserved.
Printed in the United States of America.
1 2 3 4 5 6 -VHJ- 92 91 90 89 88 87

PREFACE

Students today are increasingly aware of the importance of microcomputers in their education, in their careers, and even in their leisure-time activities. The need for knowledge of the microcomputer and its applications is growing as fast as the number of computer hardware and software products. *Microcomputers and Applications* is our response to the demand for a practical, application-oriented course for students who want to learn to use the microcomputer in various ways to improve their lives.

Two of our other books, *Introduction to Computers and Information Systems* and *Computers and End-User Software,* are aimed at students who wish to become intelligent consumers of computer technology and information systems. Our goal with this textbook is similar—helping students achieve computing literacy—but is more focused on the needs of those who plan to work with microcomputers rather than with larger computer systems. We have thus concentrated on the microcomputer and its uses:

1. *The microcomputer*. Microcomputers and their applications are the basis of discussion and illustration in every chapter. We also provide practical advice for students planning to buy a microcomputer in "Selecting a Microcomputer" (Appendix B).

2. *End-user computing*. The person interacting directly with the microcomputer through software, the end-user, is the crucial element in effective use of the microcomputer. This key interaction is covered in eight chapters, which are devoted to software packages designed for end-users and to ways end-users can develop their own computerized applications.

Each topic in this textbook is presented in understandable language and appropriate depth. We have made every effort to concentrate on the information students need to be able to simplify and improve their lives with microcomputers.

A generous, full-color illustration program is interwoven with the text to explain and clarify every topic. Numerous study aids emphasize and reinforce important concepts: chapter outlines, boldfaced key terms, chapter summaries with key terms, and end-of-chapter review questions.

THE SUPPLEMENT PROGRAM

We are also aware that a good book alone is not enough, given the demands of today's teaching environment. Understanding microcomputers and their uses can be challenging for both instructor and student. Instructors must keep abreast of developments and trends, as well as offer students opportunities for hands-on experience through computer exercises that reflect real-world applications. Thus, our text provides a full range of supplements designed to meet the needs of both instructors and students. These supplements include innovative software teaching aids, outstanding paper-based supplements, and the *CIS Profiles in Excellence* newsletter that showcases outstanding CIS programs around the nation.

Software and Paper-Based Teaching and Learning Aids

1. PFS: First Choice Software and Workbook. PFS: First Choice is the easy-to-use integrated software program from Software Publishing Corporation designed specifically for businesspeople and students who are new to computers. First Choice combines the four applications that owners of personal computers use most often in their work: a versatile word processor with a built-in spelling checker, a flexible file manager, a powerful spreadsheet, and easy-to-use electronic communications. Complete documentation prepared by Software Publishing Corporation, as well as a workbook that guides students through the use of the PFS: First Choice program, are available from Scott, Foresman and Company in one publication entitled *PFS: First Choice Workbook and Documentation*. The full version of the PFS: First Choice software will be made available to users of this text free of charge for duplication and distribution to their students. PFS: First Choice software is also available for student purchase packaged with the text. For additional details, contact your Scott, Foresman/Little, Brown sales representative or call (312) 729-3000 and ask for either Susan Dollman or Jim Boyd.

2. Using Lotus 1-2-3, SuperCalc4, WordPerfect, WordStar, and dBase III Plus by Thomas W. Warrner and D. Michael Werner of InfoSource, Inc., is a detailed, hands-on guide to these four software packages. Educational versions of SuperCalc4, WordPerfect, and dBase III Plus software are available to users of this text free of charge for duplication and distribution to their students. This software is also available for student purchase packaged with the text.

3. Using Lotus 1-2-3 by D. Michael Werner contains introductory and advanced material on Lotus 1-2-3. Two demonstration diskettes that illustrate the key features and functions of the program and one diskette with prebuilt student work files are provided to users of the guide.

4. Using Lotus 1-2-3, WordStar, and dBase III Plus by Thomas W. Warrner and D. Michael Werner is a detailed, hands-on guide to these three software packages. It is also available with demonstration diskettes and prebuilt student work files.

5. TRIO, for the Apple IIe and IIc, is an integrated spreadsheet, word processing, and data base management software package available now.

6. An electronic classroom management system, **DIPLOMA,** consists of four programs that assist instructors in testing, grading, and course management. DIPLOMA operates on IBM, Apple IIe and IIc, and compatible microcomputers.

EXAM provides almost 2000 true/false and multiple-choice questions keyed to our text. In addition, EXAM lets instructors create and edit questions, allowing them to develop personalized test files. EXAM accommodates an unlimited number of multiple-choice, true/false, matching, and short-answer/essay questions. Fourteen test-printing options can be used to leave space for figures or graphs, set margins, minimize page count, insert page headings, number pages, scramble questions and/or answers, generate answer keys, and provide student answer sheets.

GRADEBOOK, an electronic grade book, provides a work area that looks like the familiar grid of traditional paper grade books. In addition, GRADEBOOK offers these four advantages: (1) Student records can be located by name or ID number and can be sorted using combinations of four sorting options. In addition, comments about students, tests, or classes can be entered. (2) GRADEBOOK automatically calculates running averages for both students and tests and can be tailored to display letter grades, percentage averages, GPA, or points earned. (3) Tests can be given independent weights and curved using a variety of options. The program automatically generates and displays a test's bell curve during curving operations. (4) Graphic report screens monitor the effectiveness of a test or a student's progress.

PROCTOR allows students to take tests generated by EXAM at a computer. As with tests given on paper, students can browse, skip difficult questions, and review or alter their answers. Upon completion, PROCTOR will grade each test and present results in the form of graphs that depict overall performance, as well as performance by subtopic.

CALENDAR is a free-form scheduling tool that allows instructors to enter up to nine events or messages for any particular date. Messages can be easily entered, edited, saved, and displayed, while a transfer feature allows recurring events to be entered for several dates without retyping. The program can be set up to automatically load and save information.

7. Instructor's Manual provides an overview and summary of each text chapter, lecture outlines, ideas for lecture and discussion, answers to in-text review questions, class projects and activities, additional essay and review questions, and abstracts from popular and academic literature.

8. Test File contains approximately 30 true/false and 70 multiple-choice items for each chapter. These same questions are available through the DIPLOMA classroom management software.

9. One hundred twenty-five full-color **Transparency Acetates** have been prepared to enhance classroom lectures.

10. Study Guide includes chapter summaries; detailed annotated chapter outlines; drill sections made up of multiple-choice, true/false, fill-in-the-blank, matching, and essay questions; and practice tests made up of true/false and multiple-choice questions. Page-referenced answers are provided for all questions.

11. The **Scott, Foresman *CIS Profiles in Excellence* Newsletter,** published three times annually, showcases outstanding CIS programs in two-year, undergraduate, and graduate schools around the nation, allowing readers to see how their colleagues have coped with the challenges of establishing curricula, developing courses, choosing hardware and software, and obtaining the funding for such programs.

ACKNOWLEDGMENTS

To Our Publisher and Families

It is a rare experience for authors to work with a team of professionals who are committed to excellence in everything that they do. We have been privileged to become part of the Scott, Foresman team.

More important, we all have had the understanding and support of our families: Ruth Day and children Elizabeth and Sam; Nancy Athey and children Tim, Jay, and Carol; and Jo Anne Zmud and children Danny and Jana. Their contributions have been invaluable.

To Our Colleagues

We owe a special debt to the many colleagues who have reviewed our books and manuscripts and given us valuable feedback. We also want to thank Kate Kaiser, University of Wisconsin at Milwaukee, for her contribution to "Selecting a Microcomputer."

James Adair	*Bentley College*
Virginia Bender	*William Rainey Harper College*
Richard Bernardin	*Cape Cod Community College*
Kathy Blicharz	*Pima Community College*
Ronald R. Bush	*Austin Community College*
James Buxton	*Tidewater Community College*
Frank E. Cable	*Pennsylvania State University*
Geoffrey Crosslin	*Kalamazoo Valley Community College*
Mary J. Culnan	*American University*
Branston DiBrell	*Metropolitan State College*
Richard Fleming	*North Lake College*
M. H. Goldberg	*Pace University*
Thomas M. Harris	*Ball State University*
Jean Margaret Hynes	*University of Illinois at Chicago*
Peter L. Irwin	*Richland College*
Durward P. Jackson	*California State University, Los Angeles*

Richard Kapperman	*El Camino College*
James Kasum	*University of Wisconsin, Milwaukee*
Richard Kerns	*East Carolina University*
James Kho	*California State University, Sacramento*
Lyle Langlois	*Glendale Community College*
Jeffrey I. Mock	*Diablo Valley College*
Christopher W. Pidgeon	*California State Polytechnic University*
Janet Pipkin	*University of South Florida*
Leonard Presby	*William Patterson College*
Herbert F. Rebhun	*University of Houston-Downtown*
Linda Rice	*Saddleback College*
Tom Richard	*Bemidji State University*
Leonard C. Schwab	*California State University, Hayward*
Fred Scott	*Broward Community College*
Sumit Sircar	*The University of Texas at Arlington*
Vince Skudrna	*Baruch College (CUNY)*
Glenn Smith	*James Madison University*
Tim Sylvester	*College of Dupage*
Bob Tesch	*Northeast Louisiana University*
James Wynne	*Virginia Commonwealth University*
Ron Yates	*Orange Coast College*
Robert F. Zant	*North Texas State University*

John C. Day
Thomas H. Athey
Robert W. Zmud

OVERVIEW

PART ONE   **THE INFORMATION SOCIETY**
- Chapter 1 Welcome to the Information Society
- Chapter 2 Computers in Business

PART TWO   **COMPUTER HARDWARE**
- Chapter 3 The Central Processing Unit
- Chapter 4 Input, Output, and Secondary Storage

PART THREE   **END-USER COMPUTING**
- Chapter 5 Microcomputer Operating Systems
- Chapter 6 Word Processing
- Chapter 7 Introduction to Electronic Spreadsheets
- Chapter 8 Advanced Spreadsheets
- Chapter 9 Graphics
- Chapter 10 Microcomputer Data Bases
- Chapter 11 Data Communication
- Chapter 12 Advanced End-User Software

APPENDICES
- Appendix A The History of the Computer
- Appendix B Selecting a Microcomputer

CONTENTS

PART ONE THE INFORMATION SOCIETY

Chapter 1
WELCOME TO THE INFORMATION SOCIETY 1

COMPUTING LITERACY IN AN INFORMATION SOCIETY 2
- Computing, Not Computer, Literacy
- The Purpose of This Text

WHAT A COMPUTER IS 9
- Hardware
- Software
- People

WHAT A COMPUTER DOES 14
- Inputs Data
- Processes Data
- Stores and Retrieves Data and Information
- Outputs Information
- Summarizing the Computer's Basic Capabilities

SUMMARY 22

REVIEW QUESTIONS 22

Chapter 2
COMPUTERS IN BUSINESS 23

WHY BUSINESS COMPUTER USE IS GROWING 24
- Advances in Computer Systems
- Progress in Achieving Computing Literacy

COMPUTERS IN BUSINESS 26
- What Doing Business Involves
- How Business Uses Computers
- How Information Systems Interact

PERSONAL COMPUTING IN BUSINESS 35
- Electronic Spreadsheets
- Word Processing
- Business Graphics

File Management
Communications Software
Integrated Software Packages

DECIDING WHEN COMPUTERS SHOULD BE USED   41
Analyzing the Task
Weighing the Benefits and Costs

SUMMARY   46

REVIEW QUESTIONS   46

PART TWO   COMPUTER HARDWARE

Chapter 3
THE CENTRAL PROCESSING UNIT   47

PROBLEM SOLVING WITH COMPUTERS   48

COMPUTER PROCESSING OVERVIEW   49

CODING DATA FOR COMPUTER USE   51
The Binary Number System
Data Encoding Schemes

MICROCOMPUTER ARCHITECTURE   56
Semiconductor Chip Technology
Primary Memory Chips
Microprocessor Chips
Support Units

SUMMARY   62

REVIEW QUESTIONS   62

Chapter 4
INPUT, OUTPUT, AND SECONDARY STORAGE 63

COMPUTER INPUT DEVICES 64
  Keyboard
  Alternatives to the Keyboard

COMPUTER OUTPUT DEVICES 69
  Visual Display
  Print

SECONDARY STORAGE DEVICES 77
  Magnetic Disks
  Optical Disks
  Cartridge and Cassette Tapes

SUMMARY 85

REVIEW QUESTIONS 86

PART THREE END-USER COMPUTING

Chapter 5
MICROCOMPUTER OPERATING SYSTEMS 87

THE ROLE OF SYSTEM SOFTWARE 88

MICROCOMPUTER OPERATING SYSTEMS 89
  De facto Standard Operating Systems
  Using a Microcomputer Operating System

COMMANDS 94
  The FORMAT Command
  The Directory Command

The TYPE Command
The ERASE Command
The RENAME Command
The CHKDSK Command
The COPY Command
The PRINT Command

ADVANCED OS FEATURES 100
    Menu-Driven Operating Systems
    Editors
    Startup Files
    Subdirectories
    Hard Disks and Backup

SOFTWARE PORTABILITY 103

SUMMARY 104

REVIEW QUESTIONS 104

Chapter 6
WORD PROCESSING 105

CREATING A DOCUMENT 106

DOCUMENT EDITING 107
    The Cursor
    Moving the Cursor
    Word Wrap
    Correcting a Document
    Deleting Text
    Block Moves
    Searching

DOCUMENT FORMATTING 113
    Margins
    Indenting
    Centering
    Justification

DOCUMENT PRINTING 117

DOCUMENT MANAGEMENT 117

CHOOSING A WORD PROCESSOR   119

SUMMARY   122

REVIEW QUESTIONS   122

Chapter 7
INTRODUCTION TO ELECTRONIC SPREADSHEETS   123

INTERACTING WITH A SPREADSHEET   124
    Moving Around
    Windows

CREATING A SPREADSHEET   126
    The Control Panel
    Labels, Numbers, and Formulas
    Entering Labels and Numbers
    Entering Formulas
    Automatic Recalculation
    Ranges
    Built-In Functions

EDITING A SPREADSHEET   133
    Editing Cells
    Adding and Removing Rows and Columns
    Moving Cells

FORMATTING THE SPREADSHEET   135
    Formatting Labels
    Formatting Numbers
    Changing Column Widths

SPREADSHEET COMMANDS   137
    Menus
    The HELP Facility
    Global Versus Range Commands
    Printing a Spreadsheet
    Saving and Retrieving

SUMMARY   141

REVIEW QUESTIONS   142

Chapter 8
ADVANCED SPREADSHEETS 143

    COPYING FORMULAS 144
        Adjustment of Relative Formulas
        The COPY Command
        Absolute Versus Relative Addresses

    ADVANCED BUILT-IN FUNCTIONS 149
        The LOOKUP Function
        The IF Function
        The CHOOSE Function

    TEMPLATES 152
        Designing a Template
        Cell Protection
        Hidden Cells

    KEYBOARD MACROS 154

    CHOOSING AN ELECTRONIC SPREADSHEET 155

    SUMMARY 156

    REVIEW QUESTIONS 156

Chapter 9
GRAPHICS 157

    DATA-DRIVEN GRAPHICS 158
        Spreadsheet Graphics
        Dedicated Graphics
        Selecting a Graphics Program

    ILLUSTRATION GRAPHICS 170

    PRESENTATION GRAPHICS 171

DESKTOP PUBLISHING   173
    Creating Publications
    Manipulating Text
    Manipulating Graphics
    Page Layout

SUMMARY   176

REVIEW QUESTIONS   176

Chapter 10
MICROCOMPUTER DATA BASES   177

THE ROLE OF DATA MANAGEMENT SOFTWARE   178

THE MICROCOMPUTER DBMS   179

CREATION AND UPDATING   180

RETRIEVAL   182
    Projecting
    Selecting
    Joining
    Sorting
    Performing Calculations

MICROCOMPUTER DBMS FEATURES   187
    Data Dictionary Features
    Restructuring the Data Base
    Data Base Programming
    Forms
    Natural Language Interfaces
    Report Generators
    Backup and Recovery Features
    Integration with Other End-User Tools

CHOOSING A DBMS   196

SUMMARY 197

REVIEW QUESTIONS 198

Chapter 11
DATA COMMUNICATION 199

DATA COMMUNICATION FUNDAMENTALS 200
External Data Paths
Telecommunication Fundamentals

LOCAL AREA NETWORKS 206
Topology

ROLE OF COMMUNICATION SUPPORT SOFTWARE 209

USING A MICROCOMPUTER IN DATA COMMUNICATION 210
Terminal Emulation
Sending and Receiving Files
Accessing Information Utilities

USING CROSSTALK TO COMMUNICATE WITH THE SOURCE 214

CHOOSING A COMMUNICATION PROGRAM 216

SUMMARY 218

REVIEW QUESTIONS 218

Chapter 12
ADVANCED END-USER SOFTWARE 219

END-USER COMPUTING 220
A Crisis in Business Computing
The Solution: Very High-Level Languages and Microcomputers

MULTIPURPOSE TOOLS 221
  Integrated Software
  Software Integrators
  Desktop Organizers

ADVANCED END-USER TOOLS 226
  QUERY Facilities
  Report Generators
  Financial Modeling
  Statistical Analysis
  Project Management

PROMOTING AND MANAGING END-USER COMPUTING 231
  Information Center
  Personal Computer Support Center

SUMMARY 234

REVIEW QUESTIONS 234

APPENDICES 235

APPENDIX A   THE HISTORY OF THE COMPUTER 237

APPENDIX B   SELECTING A MICROCOMPUTER 255

GLOSSARY/INDEX 269

PART ONE — The Information Society

CHAPTER 1 ■ Welcome to the Information Society

COMPUTING LITERACY IN AN INFORMATION SOCIETY
    Computing, Not Computer, Literacy
    The Purpose of This Text

WHAT A COMPUTER IS
    Hardware
    Software
    People

WHAT A COMPUTER DOES
    Inputs Data
    Processes Data
    Stores and Retrieves Data and Information
    Outputs Information
    Summarizing the Computer's Basic Capabilities

SUMMARY

REVIEW QUESTIONS

We live in an age in which computers now outnumber the people living on Earth. This fact may scare someone who does not understand what computers are, what they do, or how they do it. The sheer number of computers now in use is a bit surprising, even for those of us who have been working with and around computers for more than twenty years. The overpowering fact is that we are seeing just the beginning of the surge. How will they all be used? How will their use affect people, businesses, and society? And, perhaps most importantly, how might computers affect you and your career?

While no text can fully answer all of these questions, this one can give you the information you need to understand and deal effectively with the growing number of computers in your personal and professional life. In this chapter, you will begin by learning to do the following:

1. Define the term *information society* and explain its meaning within the world of work.
2. Define the term *microelectronics* and describe three major impacts of microelectronic technology.
3. Define the term *computing literacy* and describe its five levels.
4. Define the term *information system* and describe the three basic elements that make up an information system.
5. List and describe the four stages of the *information processing cycle*.

COMPUTING LITERACY IN AN INFORMATION SOCIETY

Throughout this text we will be highlighting issues that will affect you as a business professional, even if you do not go on to become a computer professional. We'll begin by focusing on the information society. Are you aware that our society has been transformed from an industrial society into an information society? In fact, in this **information society,** collection, processing, and distribution of information have actually replaced the manufacture of goods as the primary source of wealth and work.

For most of the twentieth century, economic growth has been fueled by "heavy" manufacturing industries, such as the steel and auto industries. These industries transformed basic raw materials, such as iron, coal, and oil, into a wide range of products for markets around the world. Beginning in the 1970s, however, intense worldwide competition in these markets led many experts to believe that some of the leading industrialized nations, such as the United States, were losing their world economic leadership.

But these experts overlooked two things. First, the demand for one "product"—the knowledge being accumulated by workers, technicians, scientists, and managers—increased more than ever. Information had become and continues to be America's primary business. Second, the 1960s witnessed the birth and growth of a major new American industry, the microelectronics industry.

Microelectronics refers to the miniaturization of electronic circuits and components. These devices process information. The most obvious use of microelectronics is, of course, the computer. A key aspect of today's computers is that they can process information in all of its forms—words, numbers, voice, and pictures. As we can see in Appendix A, many years of effort went into the development of this fast, reliable, and relatively inexpensive way to process information using electricity instead of human labor.

Much of this technology has been developed in Silicon Valley, around Palo Alto, California. This area, home of Stanford University and Hewlett-Packard Corporation, became a haven for innovative engineers during the late 1950s and the 1960s. The engineers major accomplishment has been the development of the **integrated circuit,** also called a **microchip** or simply a **chip.** Over the years, engineers have perfected the means by which thousands of complete electronic circuits are contained on a single sliver of silicon. And, while the chip's size and cost have dropped, its power has increased. For example, consider the following:

The prices of electronic devices have been cut in half every two to three years.

The speed of electronic devices has doubled every two to three years.

The **microprocessor,** a "computer on a chip," did not exist in 1974, cost about $400 to manufacture in 1975, about $30 by 1976, $3 by 1977, and less than $1 today. Some of today's microprocessors are more powerful than some of the large computers of the early 1960s.

The most powerful electronic devices in 1980 performed around 5 million operations a second and occupied a cubic yard of space. By the late 1980s, the most powerful devices will likely perform 100 million operations a second, but will occupy less than a 6-inch cube of space.

This technological progress is illustrated by the increasing complexity of the integrated circuits (see Exhibit 1.1).

These advances in microelectronics have had three major effects. First, microelectronic technology has "liberated" the computer, that almost mystical machine of the 1950s and 1960s. The electronic circuitry of the early computer was awkward, delicate, and expensive. For this reason, the computer was used primarily in large organizations, was usually locked

EXHIBIT 1.1
Integrated circuit technology began the process of combining multiple components within a single piece of silicon material (left). Modern microelectronic technology allows hundreds of thousands of electrical components and wiring to be imprinted on a single "chip" (right).

EXHIBIT 1.2
Recent Sales of Personal Computers in North America

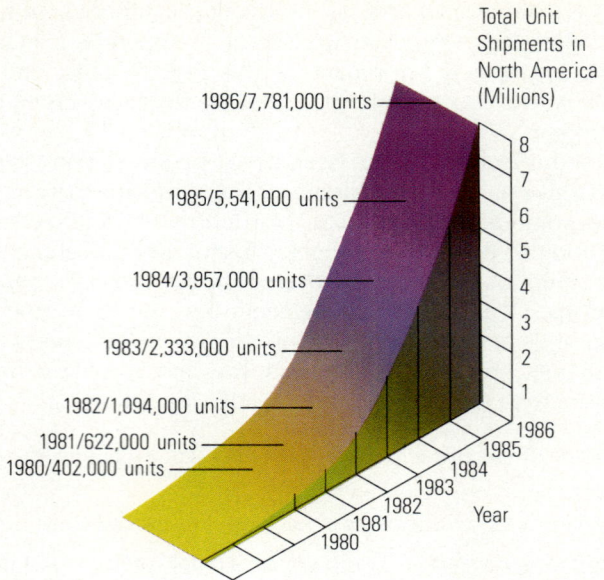

away in rooms with carefully controlled environments, and was operated only by specialists. With microelectronics, the computer became much smaller, more powerful, more durable, less expensive, and much easier to use. A variety of businesses and employees at many levels are using computers today.

Today, the fastest growing segment of the computer industry involves **personal computers,** or computers meant to be used by an individual. Other terms for these computers are **microcomputers,** a reference to the microchips that enable these computers to function, and **desktop computers,** a reference to their usual location. Exhibit 1.2 is a chart showing recent sales trends in North America for personal computers.

By bringing the computer down in scale, personal computer manufacturers allowed people to hold it, prod it, and play with it. As a result, it is common to find people without formal training in computers improving their professional and personal lives by using personal computers, which can liberate them from much of their work's monotony and tedium.

The second major impact of microelectronics involves its role in creating the information society. The economies of many nations are becoming increasingly dependent on the processing of information. The need to create, collect, store, and dispense this information has launched many new industries. Consulting firms, public and private information services, and research organizations, as well as public relations firms, represent just a few examples. Older industries have been affected as well. For example, insurance and banking are, first and foremost, information processing businesses. Insurance companies process vast amounts of customer and claim information, while banks process vast amounts of data describing the financial transactions of their customers. Even in government and the more traditional manufacturing, retail, and service industries, the movement of information is fast becoming the lifeblood of business and management. Thus, industries directly supporting information processing, such as communications, transportation, and office equipment, are growing. None of this would have been possible without microelectronics.

The third major impact of microelectronics finds these tiny and inexpensive devices being used to control a variety of other products. When connected to a sensing device, a microprocessor can capture and then process information to "control" the product within which it has been inserted. Microprocessors, in particular, seem to be able to improve the performance of almost anything, anywhere.

- A microwave oven can vary cooking time and temperature depending on what is being cooked.
- A videocassette recorder can be scheduled to tape a series of television shows in the middle of the night.
- A cardiac pacemaker, perhaps the ultimate *personal* computer, maintains the functions of a sick or aging heart.
- A sewing machine automatically handles a number of complex stitching operations.
- A camera automated by a microprocessor allows an amateur photographer to take excellent pictures easily.

Adding **intelligence**—the apparent capability to act in an informed manner—to consumer products not only makes them more sophisticated, but it also makes them easier to use.

We all use computers on a daily basis—they make life more convenient and more enjoyable. The consumer products within the average American household contain over forty microprocessors. Think of your own house, apartment, or dormitory room. How many microprocessors do you own? This use of microprocessors means that you may be more familiar and comfortable with computers than you realize.

Computing, Not Computer, Literacy

What impact does the information society have on you? It primarily affects the career options open to you. In 1976, white-collar workers outnumbered blue-collar workers for the first time. Today, "information occupations" represent over 60 percent of the American work force. Some examples include programmers, teachers, clerks, secretaries, accountants, stockbrokers, managers, salespeople, lawyers, bankers, and engineers. Not only are you likely to find yourself in an "information occupation," but the odds favor your working with computers in that occupation.

You are probably already aware of the key role computers play in today's world of work. The news media are constantly running stories about computers and about the need to educate people to fill meaningful and productive roles in an information society. Computers in education, computer camps, computer magazines, computers on "Sesame Street"—the list goes on and on (see Exhibit 1.3). In the business world, computer training has become a major new industry. It is estimated, for example, that in 1986 $3 billion of the $14 billion to be spent on personal computers in the United States will go toward computer training seminars and workshops.

EXHIBIT 1.3
Computer education and training, in all of its forms, has become a growth industry. People of all ages are using computers at home, at school, and in the work place.

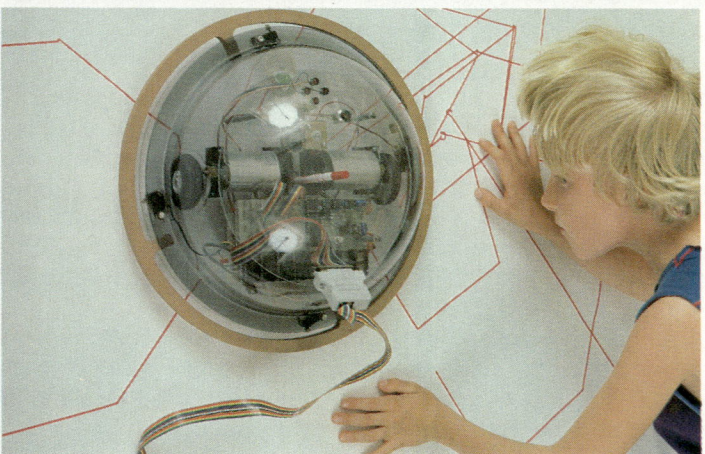

Some debate exists today regarding the type of computer education, or **computer literacy,** people need to function in an information society. Must everyone become a computer expert? More directly, what should you learn in order to be able to benefit from computers? The answer, as you might suspect, depends on how you intend to use computers.

Computer professionals certainly need to understand how computers work. Few computer users, however, really need to understand all of the technology that makes up today's computers. Fortunately, you can take advantage of most of a computer's capabilities without knowing how electrical circuits function or even how to program—the process of developing the instructions, or **programs,** that direct a computer in its information processing. On the other hand, you may find computer technology interesting and computer programming fun; learning these skills may even be useful in your career.

What most computer users need is an understanding of what computers can do and an ability to feel comfortable when using a computer. You need to develop the same sense of command and confidence toward computers that you have toward automobiles. While you do not need to be an engineer to drive a car, you do need to know the "rules of the road" and to feel at ease while driving. **Computing literacy** is the ability to use the computer as a tool to enrich your personal and professional life. Computing literacy—not computer literacy—should be the educational goal for most students.

Yet even with that understanding, there are levels of computing literacy (see Exhibit 1.4). These levels reflect the fact that people differ in their involvement with computers. As this involvement grows, a deeper and broader understanding of computers is needed. These five levels of computing literacy also indicate the variety of ways you are likely to become involved with computers:

1. *You develop a good-enough understanding of the basic roles that computers serve in an information society to overcome any fear of computer use.* The computer will touch even those people who never come into physical contact with it. It is unlikely that a person with a true fear of computers will be able to cope in such a world. This first level must be acquired by all members of an information society.

2. *You become comfortable with the use of computers as machines.* This involves the use of computers in handling everyday tasks that have been automated. Examples include banking, shopping, health-care, and education tasks, as well as information-search tasks in libraries and government agencies. People not acquiring this second level of computing literacy will find they are not taking advantage of many of the services and conveniences of an information society.

3. *You develop a willingness and an ability to use computers as tools to support routine business activities.* This includes using the computer for typing tasks, clerical tasks, and other tasks involved in the collection, storage, and retrieval of information. An inability to reach this third level will exclude an applicant from many kinds of jobs.

4. *You understand the strengths and weaknesses of computers, as well as the tasks being performed with computer support, in order to identify new ways of improving work performance.* Business and professional success is increasingly being tied to the innovative use of computers.

EXHIBIT 1.4
The Staircase of Computing Literacy

Employees not acquiring this fourth level of computing literacy may be bypassed for promotions and other professional rewards.

5. *You design a computer application by specifying what the computer is to do and how it will do it, and perhaps you do some of the programming.* While these activities are usually performed by computer specialists, computer technology is so advanced that most employees can be trained to develop some computer applications. People reaching this fifth level of computing literacy do not have to depend on others to meet their computing needs.

What is fascinating about this list is that none of these literacy levels requires a detailed knowledge of the inner workings of computers. Only the people who will go on to become full-time computer professionals will need to attain higher levels of computing literacy.

The Purpose of This Text

The topics covered in this text will help you achieve each of these five levels of computing literacy. Part One, "The Information Society," introduces you to the computer's capabilities and its uses in business. Part Two, "Computer Hardware," explains the information processing devices that make up modern computers. Part Three, "End-User Computing," describes the software typically used in business applications and their capabilities that are available to end-users. An **end-user** is simply anyone who uses the information generated by a computer. Appendix A introduces you to the history of computers and Appendix B provides you with information on selecting a microcomputer.

It takes very little time to get started in developing your computing literacy, particularly with today's personal computers or microcomputers. Personal computer hardware and software are fairly easy to understand, are simple to use, and can provide immediate practical benefits to anyone willing to learn about them. Since your first contact with computers is likely to be with a microcomputer, this text will focus on the microcomputer and its uses from the perspective of an end-user. But before beginning, you need to recognize that simply reading about computer use and computer technology will not move you up many of the levels of computing literacy; you must use computers if you wish to gain any kind of familiarity with them. Computing literacy can only be achieved through practice. Acquiring computing literacy requires both an investment of your time and a willingness to make mistakes and learn from them. As you'll see, though, this learning need not be all hard work.

This text will start you on your progress up the ladder of computing literacy. How far you go and what you do with this knowledge, however, depends on your willingness to experience computer technology on a firsthand basis. The remaining sections of this chapter help you begin by taking a closer look at both computers and computing.

WHAT A COMPUTER IS

We have been using the term **computer** as if it refers to a single electronic device, but computers are actually composed of many electronic and electromechanical devices. **Electromechanical devices** contain both electronic and mechanical parts; all of these devices together are referred to as computer **hardware.** Hardware is the focus of Part Two of this text.

However, hardware by itself is useless. Hardware must be directed in its information processing by programs, and all of these programs are collectively referred to as computer **software.** Software is the focus of Part Three.

When people refer to "a computer," they are usually referring to a set of hardware and software used as a single unit. In fact, it is more correct to use the phrase **computer system.** A wide variety of computer systems exist. The common link of all of these computer systems, however, is that they are composed of the same basic set of hardware and software components.

The primary purpose of this text is not to study the computer as an end in itself, but rather as a means to an end—the productive use of computers in business. When a computer system serves a practical use in a business, the application is termed an **information system.** An information system processes data to produce information. The term **data** refers to symbols used to represent facts, events, or things. **Information** is the meaning given to a set of data.

Information systems are actually made up of three components: hardware, software, and people. People both build and use information systems. In the rest of this section we will discuss the ways in which hardware, software, and people interact.

EXHIBIT 1.5
The four basic hardware components are the computer processor, input devices, output devices, and secondary storage devices. As data and information are processed, they flow between these components.

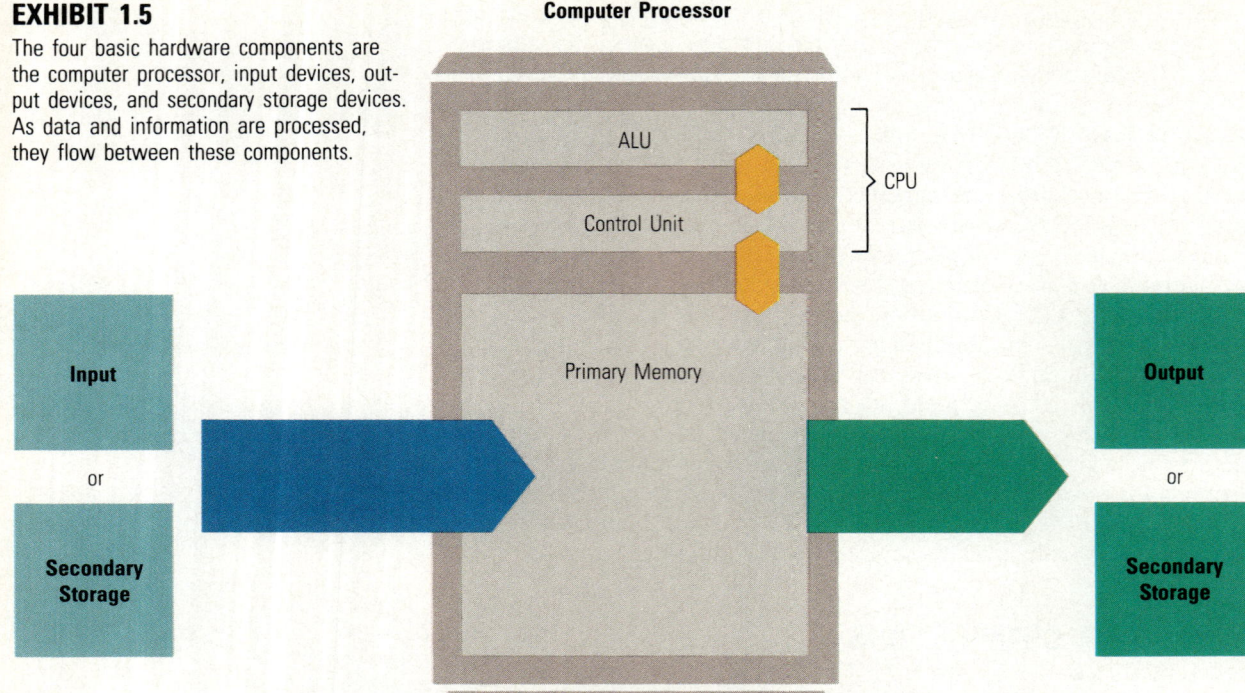

Hardware

Hardware refers to the devices that physically enter, process, store and retrieve, and deliver data and information. All computer systems contain four types of hardware components: a computer processor, input devices, output devices, and secondary storage devices. These components are diagrammed in Exhibit 1.5. Occasionally input, output, and secondary storage devices are called **peripheral devices** to reflect the fact that they are added on to the computer processor.

Computer Processor

The **computer processor** is made up of two parts: primary memory and the central processing unit. **Primary memory** provides temporary storage for all of the data and information being processed, as well as the software directing this processing. The most crucial hardware component, however, is the **central processing unit (CPU).** It is there that all processing operations take place.

The CPU is made up of an arithmetic-logic unit and a control unit. The **arithmetic-logic unit (ALU)** contains the electronic circuits that actually perform the data processing operations. Data items flow between primary memory and the ALU as this processing occurs. A **control unit (CU)** contains electronic circuits that direct and coordinate these processing activities. A complete description of how these computer processor components function together is given in Chapter 3, "The Central Processing Unit." Generally, the more primary memory available in the computer processor and the more numerous and complex the ALU and CU circuits, the more powerful the computer system.

Input and Output Devices

Input and **output devices** are used to move data and information, respectively, into and out of the primary memory. The most common type of input device is the computer keyboard, which is similar to that of an electric typewriter.

Other input devices use **media,** or special kinds of material. When you take notes in class, you are placing your thoughts on paper, perhaps the most common medium. The most common input device involving a special medium on a microcomputer is a **disk drive.** A disk drive uses a diskette as its input medium. A "floppy," or flexible, diskette looks like a small 45 rpm record. Just as a record "stores" sound on its surface, a diskette stores data on its surface. A diskette reader, then, picks up these data from the diskette's surface, translates them into electrical signals, and transmits them to the primary memory.

A variety of devices are capable of producing computer output:

A **microcomputer** displays data and information on the monitor screen. Output can be displayed on a monitor very quickly. However, once information leaves the screen, it is gone. To produce **hard copy,** a permanent form of the information, a printer or plotter can be used along with the microcomputer.

A **printer** uses paper as its output medium. A printer is very similar to a typewriter except that electrical signals from the computer processor, rather than a typist, direct the printing.

A **plotter** also uses paper as its output medium. By following the electrical signals from the processor, a plotter can produce detailed graphics.

A **disk drive** can be used as an output as well as an input device. Data can be transferred from primary memory to a diskette, where it is stored permanently.

Secondary Storage Devices

It is relatively costly to store data, information, and programs in primary memory. Furthermore, if a computer system's power source is turned off, anything stored in primary memory will probably be lost. As a result, most of the data, information, and programs used within a computer system are kept in **secondary storage** until they are needed. It takes longer to store data on or retrieve data from secondary storage devices because these devices use mechanical as well as electronic parts, but secondary storage is less expensive than primary memory storage. More importantly, data placed in secondary storage are not lost when a computer system's power is cut.

The most common secondary storage medium is the **magnetic disk.** Disks can be flexible (a floppy disk) or rigid (a **hard disk**). **Secondary storage devices** are the hardware that places (or "outputs") data onto and reads (or "inputs") data from these media. Once data and information are stored on disk, secondary storage devices can also serve as input devices.

Exhibit 1.6 shows some of these hardware components in the type of microcomputer system with which you may already be familiar.

EXHIBIT 1.6

Input and output devices are used to move data and information, respectively, into and out of primary memory. The microcomputer has a keyboard for entering data and a televisionlike monitor on which the data appear. To the left of the microcomputer is a printer, an output device that uses paper as its medium. The businessman pictured here is holding a secondary storage medium called a diskette, or floppy disk.

What a Computer Is

Software

Software refers to the programs, or sets of instructions, that direct the information processing operations performed by hardware. There are two types of software: applications software and systems software.

Applications Software

The general term for programs that perform specific user-oriented tasks is **applications software** (see Exhibit 1.7). These tasks can range from playing chess to solving business problems. Some of the first business applications software was written to handle such basic business tasks as payroll, accounting, and customer billing.

Applications software is normally acquired in one of two ways. First, it can be "customized," or created especially for a specific business. Second, it can be bought in a ready-made, or "packaged," form.

Systems Software

Coordinating the flow of data, information, and programs within a computer system is a complex task. Today, most of these functions are performed by **systems software**—the general term for programs that direct hardware-related tasks. Exhibit 1.8 illustrates the relationship between computer hardware, systems software, and applications software.

The most important systems software is the **operating system.** This set of programs supervises all of the activity that takes place within a computer system. For now, think of the operating system as an office

EXHIBIT 1.7
One of the driving forces behind the surge in the use of microcomputers is the ready availability of applications software.

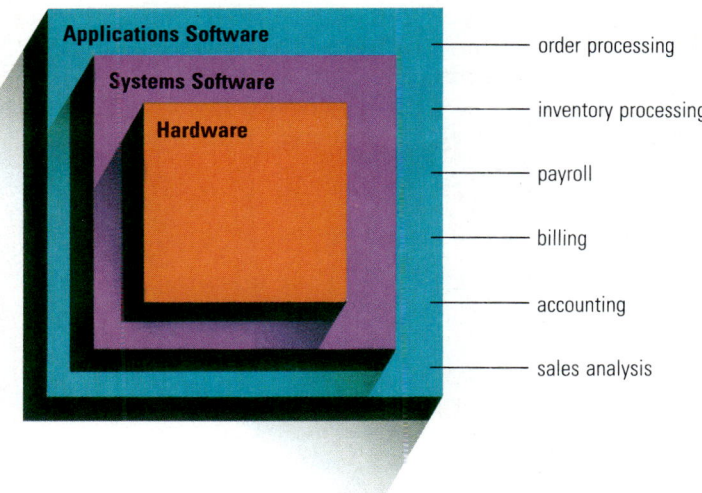

EXHIBIT 1.8
Systems software allows applications software to handle user-oriented problems rather than the details of directing the hardware.

manager who assigns work to a computer system's different components and who also helps with the more important and difficult tasks. Chapter 5 discusses microcomputer operating systems and how to use them.

People

People, most simply, "breathe life" into an information system. People play two major roles in information systems: information system user and information system creator.

User Role

Almost all of the data used by information systems must be either directly put into the computer or placed on a computer-readable medium by a person. Most information system outputs are sent to a person, who then makes use of the information. Without these users, there would be no data to process and no reason to create or use information systems.

Creator Role

Before an information system can be used effectively, it must be brought into a business. For this to occur, systems analysis, systems design, and programming activities must take place. Systems analysts do the following:

Determine whether an information system is needed.

Describe the business activities to be computerized.

Specify the exact nature of the needed information system.

Systems designers perform specific tasks:

Design the information system.

Decide whether applications software needs to be customized.

Decide whether additional hardware is needed.

Programmers have a single goal:

Create a customized program.

Often, computer specialists perform all or most of these creation activities. Three of the most common occupations found in an information systems department are **systems analyst, systems designer,** and **programmer.** These computer specialists must work closely with an information system's eventual users to create a truly useful information system (see Exhibit 1.9).

WHAT A COMPUTER DOES

EXHIBIT 1.9
A programmer works closely with an information system user to create a customized program.

On the surface, computers may seem to have mysterious and limitless powers. The computer applications pictured in Exhibit 1.10 include some of the sophisticated uses of computers. With these or any other computer applications, however, the computer is merely processing information. But what exactly do we mean by "processing information"? When people process information, they receive data from the environment, interpret that data by comparing it to data already stored, and, if necessary, produce a response. Consider what happens when you approach a red stop light in a car. You receive (input) data concerning the color of the light. You retrieve stored information that you have concerning the meaning of the red light. Based on your interpretation of the signal, you produce a response: you apply the brake.

The stages of input, processing, storage and retrieval, and output activities are exactly what a computer does when it processes information and are referred to as the **information processing cycle.** Exhibit 1.11 portrays these stages for a relatively simple business information processing task, the processing of a customer order by a mail-order book firm. We will be looking at this example throughout the rest of this chapter.

Inputs Data

Both people and computers "take in" data. People capture data through their senses of sight, hearing, touch, smell, and taste; most people, however, do not realize that their sensory organs are much more sophisticated than are a computer system's input devices. Much of the data they capture is in its original form. The computer is not so flexible. It must have data prepared in special ways and must be instructed, through a program, to look for and collect these data. The computer then "translates" the data into a pattern of electrical signals it can process. We will discuss this series of activities in greater detail in Part Two.

The book order form has been enlarged in Exhibit 1.12. To process the order, the computer will need to do the following:

1. Read the customer name and address.
2. Read the identification number, title, author, quantity, and price of each book being ordered.
3. Read the total cost of the order.

Notice that this set of input data includes both letters and numbers. Both are easily captured by computers. However, it is unlikely that the com-

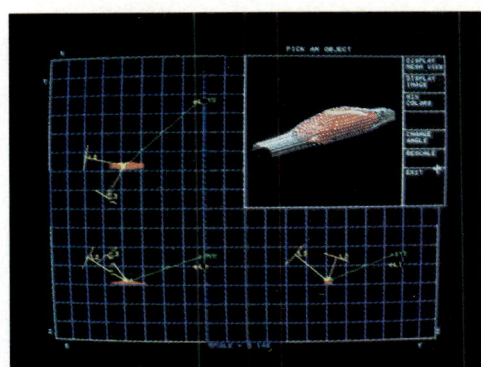

EXHIBIT 1.10
Many of today's computer applications seem to go far beyond our human capabilities to meet diverse needs. Examples include (clockwise from top) auto design, air-traffic control, sculpture, computerization of artificial limbs, control of factory equipment, and athletic performance analysis.

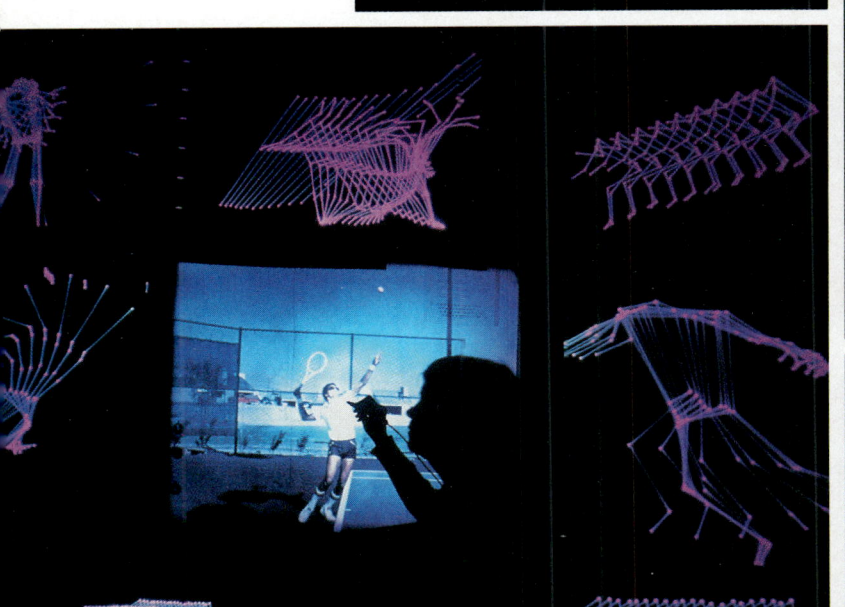

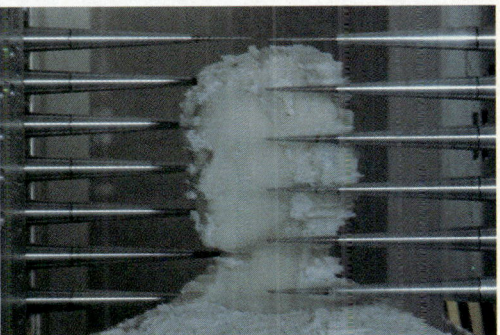

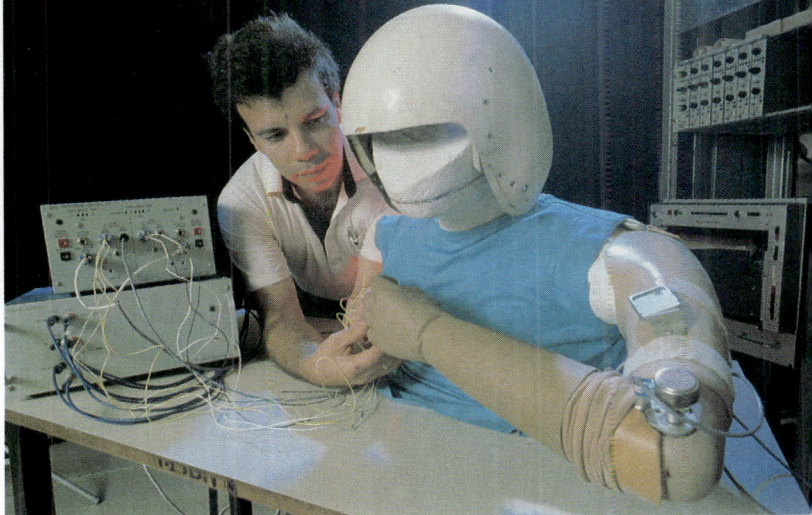

What a Computer Does

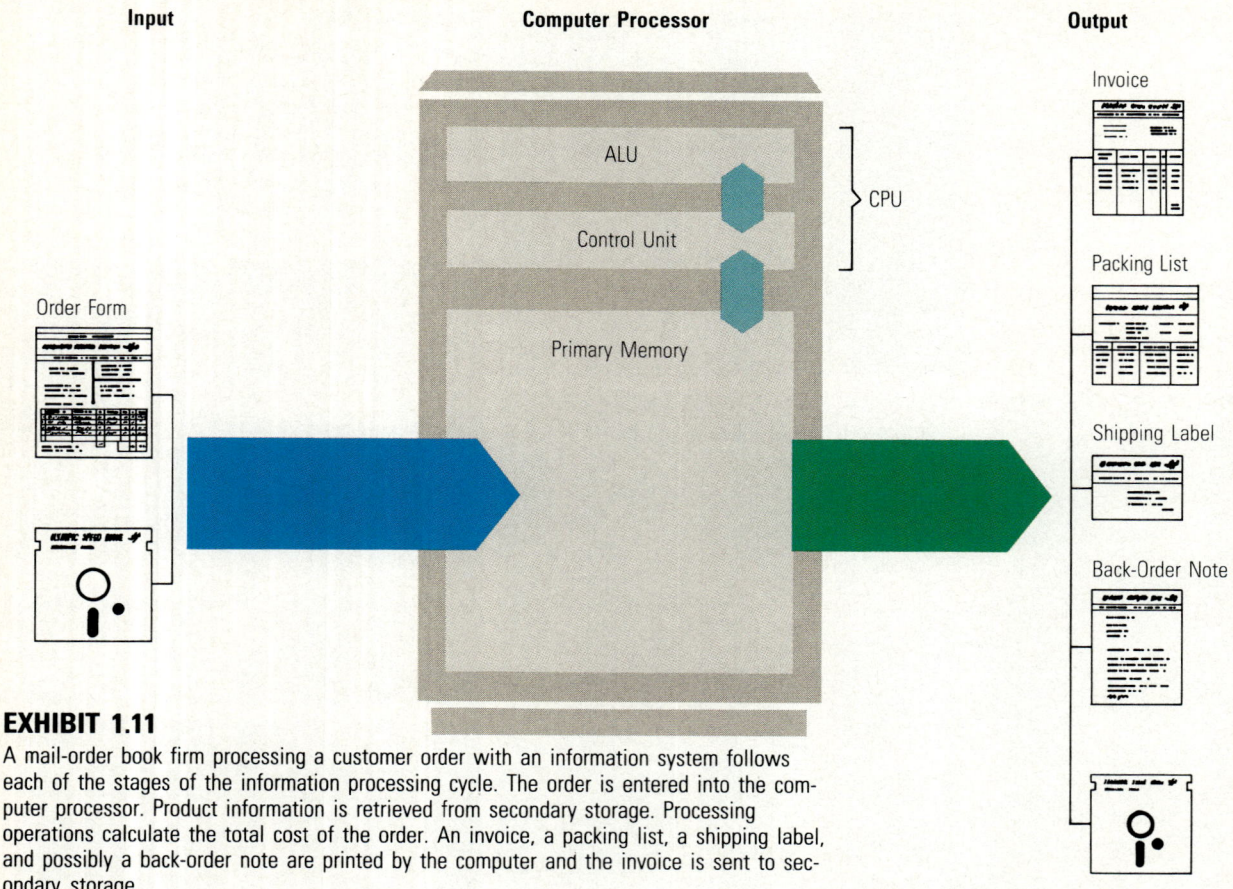

EXHIBIT 1.11
A mail-order book firm processing a customer order with an information system follows each of the stages of the information processing cycle. The order is entered into the computer processor. Product information is retrieved from secondary storage. Processing operations calculate the total cost of the order. An invoice, a packing list, a shipping label, and possibly a back-order note are printed by the computer and the invoice is sent to secondary storage.

puter will be able to enter this data directly from the handwritten order form. Instead, a clerk will prepare the data for entry, perhaps using a keyboard.

Given these limitations, you may wonder why computers are used as much as they are. The answer lies in the computer's speed and reliability. Once the order data are organized and entered in a form that the computer can handle, termed a **computer-readable form,** the data can be captured and processed in a fraction of the time it would take a person to read the data items.

While this speed may be of little benefit when processing a single book order, the benefit is significant when there are thousands of orders each day. Not only can all of these orders be processed in a short period of time, but the cost of processing the orders is far less than if they were done by hand. Furthermore, it is unlikely that the computer will make any errors in processing the data. People, in contrast, are prone to typing mistakes and mathematical errors. Finally, once the order data have been entered into the computer, they become available for further computer-based information processing. The advantages of this will become clearer as the remaining stages of the information processing cycle are discussed.

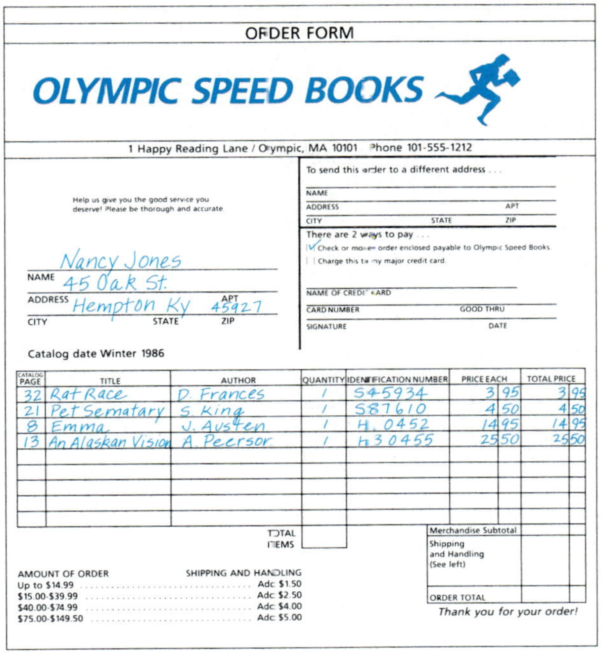

ORDER FORM

OLYMPIC SPEED BOOKS

1 Happy Reading Lane / Olympic, MA 10101 Phone 101-555-1212

Help us give you the good service you deserve! Please be thorough and accurate.

NAME: Nancy Jones
ADDRESS: 45 Oak St.
CITY: Hempton STATE: Ky ZIP: 45927
APT

To send this order to a different address . . .
NAME
ADDRESS APT
CITY STATE ZIP

There are 2 ways to pay . . .
[✓] Check or money order enclosed payable to Olympic Speed Books.
[ ] Charge this to my major credit card.

NAME OF CREDIT CARD
CARD NUMBER GOOD THRU
SIGNATURE DATE

Catalog date Winter 1986

CATALOG PAGE	TITLE	AUTHOR	QUANTITY	IDENTIFICATION NUMBER	PRICE EACH	TOTAL PRICE
32	Rat Race	D. Frances	1	S45934	3 95	3 95
21	Pet Sematary	S. King	1	S87610	4 50	4 50
8	Emma	J. Austen	1	H 0452	14 95	14 95
13	An Alaskan Vision	A. Peersor	1	h30455	25 50	25 50

TOTAL ITEMS

Merchandise Subtotal
Shipping and Handling (See left)
ORDER TOTAL

AMOUNT OF ORDER	SHIPPING AND HANDLING
Up to $14.99	Add $1.50
$15.00-$39.99	Add $2.50
$40.00-$74.99	Add $4.00
$75.00-$149.50	Add $5.00

Thank you for your order!

EXHIBIT 1.12
Handwritten Book Order Form

Processes Data

Both people and computers process data. People, in fact, possess some very sophisticated information processing capabilities. Our ability to work with incomplete sets of data and to generalize meanings across sets of data is very powerful. Most important, however, is our ability to create. When we are faced with a new problem, we are often able to arrive at a solution by piecing together prior experiences, sketchy facts, and human intuition.

Computers, on the other hand, have extremely limited data processing capabilities. They are limited to a few rather basic processing operations:

Computers perform simple **arithmetic operations,** such as addition, subtraction, multiplication, and division.

Computers perform simple **text manipulation operations,** such as inserting or deleting characters and moving characters, words, and longer pieces of text.

Computers perform simple **logic operations,** such as comparing the values of two numbers or determining whether two words contain the same letters.

Furthermore, computers must be directed in a step-by-step fashion to perform these operations.

Given these limitations, why should we use computers? Again, the computer's speed and reliability prove to be key factors. Today's computers can perform thousands of error-free processing operations in the time it takes a person to perform one operation. Most computers perform their operations in **milliseconds,** one thousandth of a second, **microseconds,** one millionth of a second, and **nanoseconds,** one billionth of a second. These speeds are so great they are difficult to comprehend. How long does it take you to add two numbers in your head? One second? A computer might take one nanosecond to perform the same addition. The computer, then, is about 1,000,000,000 (one billion) times faster than you are. Just how much faster is this? You may have a better idea if you consider that a commercial jet liner is about 100 times faster than your walking speed, a jet fighter about 400 times faster, the space shuttle about 4000 times faster, and the speed of light about 150,000,000 times faster.

The speed of today's computer systems enables them to process vast amounts of data very quickly. As a result, the overall cost of processing large sets of data is far less than it would be if people did the data processing. Some tasks, such as processing today's U.S. Census, would be virtually impossible to complete without the processing power of computer systems.

The fact that computer systems can perform only very simple arithmetic, text manipulation, and logic data processing operations turns out to be a fairly minor limitation. Computer programs can be developed to handle just about any information processing task. The limit to what can be done with computer systems lies not in the computer, but rather in our skill in using the computer's capabilities.

The data processing operations required in processing the book order described in Exhibit 1.11 are fairly simple. In fact, most of the resulting information is the same data that were entered into the computer: customer name and address; book identification numbers, titles, and authors; quantities and prices; and total cost of an order. As a double check, the computer will probably calculate the total price charged the customer.

The process becomes a bit more complex when a book is out of stock. In this case, the applications program will direct the information system to perform two additional tasks. First, the computer system will recalculate the amount due. Second, the computer system will print a back-order notice to be sent to the customer. Producing this back-order notice is easy, since much of the message remains the same whenever it is written. What changes from note to note are data items that come directly from the order form: the customer's name and address and the identification numbers, titles, authors, and prices of the out-of-stock books.

Stores and Retrieves Data and Information

Both people and computers store and then retrieve data and information. Your mind, in fact, can hold more data than the largest of today's computers. Just think about it. The "data" stored in your memory include all of your past experiences, all of the facts and concepts that you ever learned, and all of the ideas that ever occurred to you. Your ability to retrieve data from your memory also turns out to be far more sophisticated than that available with computer systems.

Why, then, are computers used so extensively in storing data and information? Again, we come back to the computer's speed and reliability. If information is stored in an organized manner within a computer, it can be retrieved quickly and accurately when it is needed. *Organizing* a set of data means storing it in a way that fits the data retrieval operations to be performed. Also, the cost of storing a large quantity of data within a computer system has become much less than the cost of storing these same data in file cabinets.

In the book order-processing example, data are retrieved from a data file. A **data file** refers to an organized set of related data items. In this case, data describing all of the books offered by the mail-order firm are kept in a book file (see Exhibit 1.13). All of the data for a particular book are stored in a **data record** within this book file. Each of the data items that describes a feature of a book is termed a **data field**.

When the data file is organized in this way, retrieving the record for a particular book becomes easy—just search through the book file until a match is found between the identification number of a book being ordered and the "identification number" field of a particular record. When a match occurs, the correct data record, or book in this case, has been found.

Notice that the operations to be performed in processing a book order may be affected by this retrieved information. What if no match was found in the book file for an ordered book? Or, what if a match is found but the book's title, author, or price does not agree with what is on the book order? In such cases, it may be best to return the order form to the customer with a polite form letter—generated by the information system.

EXHIBIT 1.13

Organizing the book file in a systematic manner makes it fairly easy for the information system to locate the record for a particular book. Once located, the data stored in this data record can be retrieved for use in processing a book order.

What a Computer Does

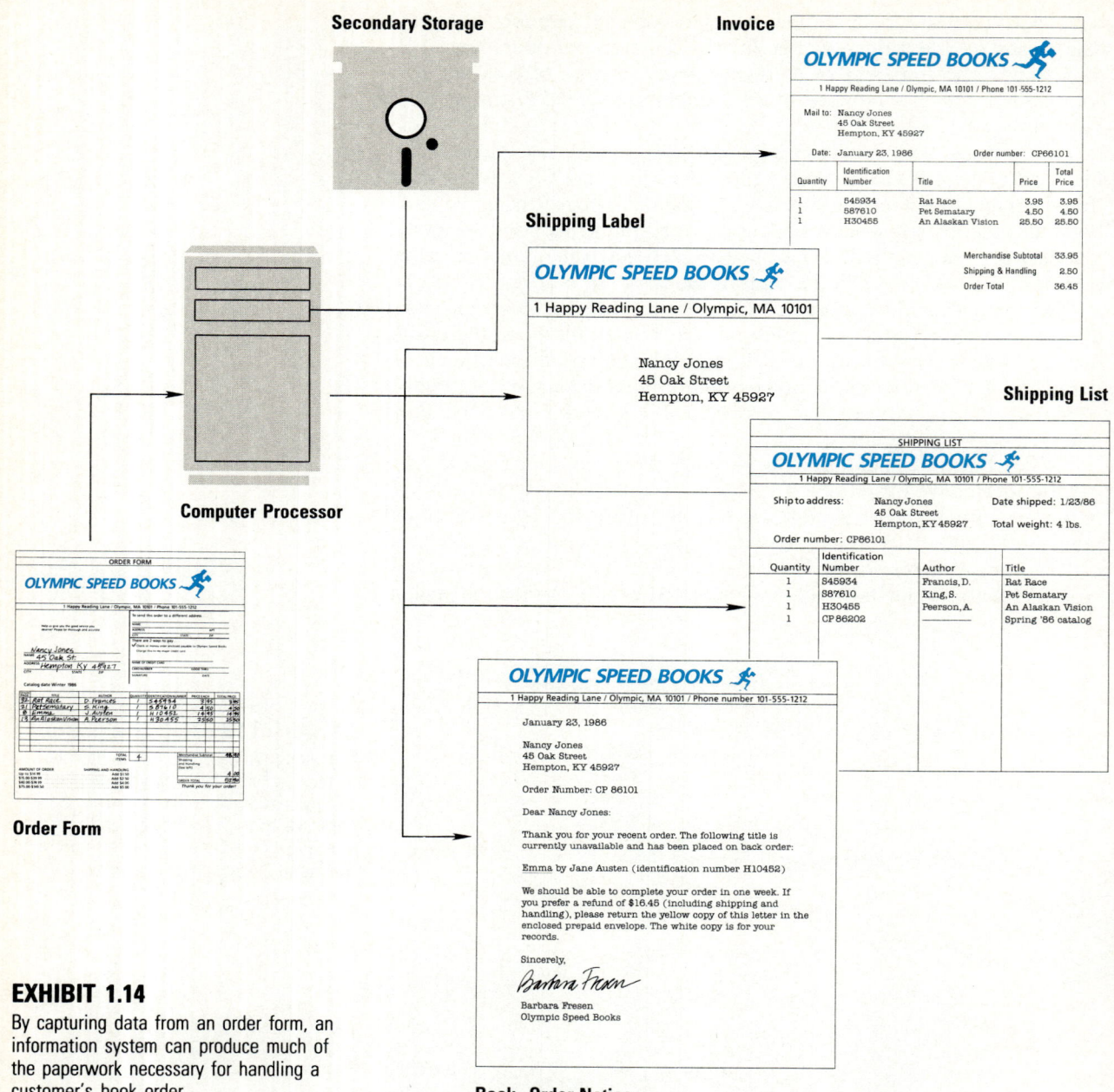

EXHIBIT 1.14

By capturing data from an order form, an information system can produce much of the paperwork necessary for handling a customer's book order.

Outputs Information

Both people and computers communicate information. People, however, are much more versatile than computers in expressing their information. They have developed sophisticated abilities to transmit quite different messages with only slight changes in the information being communicated. Have you ever said one thing while indicating just the opposite through your tone or facial expression? Computers simply do not have the versatility or sophistication that people have when communicating.

What computers provide, not surprisingly, is the ability to produce information quickly, accurately, and inexpensively. An obvious benefit is the ability to process the large number of outputs, such as the shipping lists, shipping labels, back-order notices, and invoices needed by the mail-order book company each month. A more detailed view of these outputs is illustrated in Exhibit 1.14. It is common, as shown, to find that a few input data items "trigger" a number of information system outputs.

Another benefit of computer-based information processing is the ability to vary easily the form of an information output. Exhibit 1.15, for example, shows the same information in three different forms—table, graph, and chart. Each form might be useful for different situations. In producing these "user-oriented" outputs, each information item is translated from the electrical signals used to represent it within the computer to the symbols used to print it on paper.

Summarizing the Computer's Basic Capabilities

What, then, does a computer do?

1. Both numbers and letters can be entered into a computer. These data items can then be stored within a data file and can be produced from the computer in this original form.
2. New data items can be created by performing arithmetic operations on numbers and by changing or rearranging text. These newly created data can also be stored within a data file or communicated from the computer. Also, any of the data items currently being processed can be used to determine the information processing operations to be performed.
3. Data or information previously stored within the computer can be retrieved for processing (numerical operations or text manipulations) or for output. Often, these retrieved data are combined with data that have just been entered in order to create still other data items.
4. Information produced by earlier input, processing, and storage and retrieval operations can be generated in a number of forms.

The real advantage of computer-based information processing, however, is that these operations can be performed more quickly, more reliably, and less expensively by a computer than by people. You will begin to learn in Chapter 2 how to spot situations where these advantages are likely to arise.

Finally, it is important to recognize exactly how computer-based information processing supports people in doing work. The computer does not do any of the physical labor involved in sending shipments of books to customers. However, it does perform the following activities:

The computer processes the "paper" that goes along with shipping a book order.

The computer provides to the people performing specific tasks associated with shipping a book order the information that helps them perform their tasks.

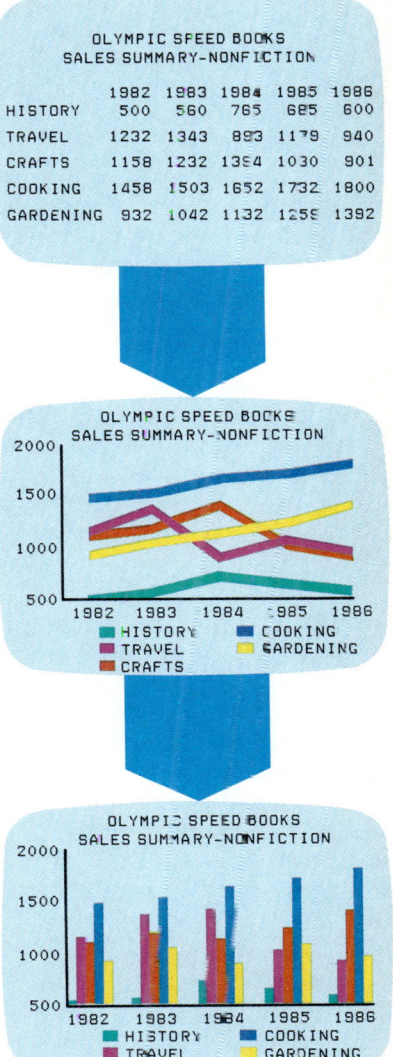

EXHIBIT 1.15
The same information can appear in different forms on a computer system. Information outputs can thus be tailored to meet the information user's needs.

What a Computer Does

Summary

In an *information society*, the collection, processing, and distribution of information have become the primary source of wealth and work.

The 1960s witnessed the birth and growth of the microelectronics industry. *Microelectronics* refers to the miniaturization of electronic circuits and components used to process information.

The major microelectronic device is the *integrated circuit*, also called a *microchip* or *chip*. The *microprocessor* is a computer on a chip. Microprocessors are being used to add *intelligence*, the apparent ability to act in an informed manner, to a variety of familiar products.

In the future, most workers will probably work in "information careers" using computers. Some debate exists about the type of computer education, or *computer literacy*, people need to function in an information society. Computer professionals need to understand computer technology and how to write *programs*, or computer instructions. Most people, however, need *computing literacy*, the ability to use the computer as a tool to enrich their personal and professional lives.

Computers are made up of electronic and electromechanical devices. *Electromechanical* devices contain both electronic and mechanical parts. Another term for computer devices is *hardware*. Hardware is useless without *software*, the programs that direct information processing. Hardware and software used as a single unit make up a *computer system*. An *information system*, a computer system that serves a practical business purpose, is made up of hardware, software, and people.

Information systems process data to produce information. The term *data* refers to symbols used to represent facts, events, or things. *Information* is the meaning given to a set of data.

The four types of hardware components are computer processors, input devices, output devices, and secondary storage devices. The computer processor is made up of primary memory and the central processing unit. *Primary memory* provides temporary storage for data and programs. The *central processing unit (CPU)* is made up of the *arithmetic-logic unit (ALU)*, which performs arithmetic, data manipulation, and logical processing operations, and the *control unit (CU)*, which directs and coordinates all processing.

Input and *output devices* move data into and out of the computer processor. The most common input device is the keyboard. Diskette readers use diskettes as input media. Common output devices include the *monitor screen, printers, plotters,* and *diskettes. Hard copy,* a permanent copy of computer output, is produced by printers and plotters.

Because primary memory is relatively expensive, it is used only for temporary storage of data. Most data and programs are stored on *secondary storage*. Common secondary storage media are magnetic tape and magnetic disk.

Applications software, the general term for practical computer applications, can be customized or bought ready-made in the form of a *software package. Systems software* are programs that coordinate the flow of data, information, and programs within a computer system. The most important systems software is the *operating system,* which functions as an office manager for the computer system.

In an information system, people act as both users and creators. A *systems analyst* recognizes that an information system is needed, describes the business activities to be computerized, and specifies the exact nature of the needed information system. A *systems designer* designs the information system, decides whether applications software needs to be customized, and decides whether additional hardware is needed. A *programmer* creates customized software.

Computers transform data into information through an *information processing cycle* made up of input, processing, storage and retrieval, and output stages.

Computers can be used to produce quickly and accurately the paperwork associated with routine business tasks. Computers can also be used to produce information.

Review Questions

1. What is the difference between information and knowledge?

2. Identify and discuss four ways in which the computer has had an impact on your life.

3. What is the difference between computer literacy and computing literacy?

4. List and briefly describe the five levels of computing literacy.

5. Differentiate between hardware and software. Which is more important to computer users? Explain.

6. Identify the four basic types of hardware and describe their functions.

7. Differentiate between the two basic types of software.

8. Briefly describe the steps contained in the information processing cycle.

9. What two advantages does the computer offer over human information processing? Under what conditions do these advantages become most important?

10. Evaluate the following statement: "The computer is overrated—it is not as creative as a human being, cannot accept as wide a range of inputs, cannot store as much data, and is not as flexible in presenting the results of its efforts."

CHAPTER 2 ■ Computers in Business

WHY BUSINESS COMPUTER USE IS GROWING
Advances in Computer Systems
Progress in Achieving Computing Literacy

COMPUTERS IN BUSINESS
What Doing Business Involves
How Business Uses Computers
How Information Systems Interact

PERSONAL COMPUTING IN BUSINESS
Electronic Spreadsheets
Word Processing
Business Graphics
File Management
Communications Software
Integrated Software Packages

DECIDING WHEN COMPUTERS SHOULD BE USED
Analyzing the Task
Weighing the Benefits and Costs

SUMMARY

REVIEW QUESTIONS

A major factor contributing to success in business today is the use of computers to solve business problems. The ability to identify situations where computers can be used in business is an extremely valuable one, and this chapter will help you begin to develop that skill. You will learn to do the following:

1. List and explain the two major forces behind the increasing use of computers in business.
2. Describe what a business does and the three types of computer-based information systems used in business.
3. List and describe the six most popular "personal computing" applications in business.
4. List and discuss the two major factors to be considered in deciding whether to use a computer-based information system.

WHY BUSINESS COMPUTER USE IS GROWING

As Exhibit 2.1 shows, the use of computers in businesses of all sizes has grown rapidly since 1976. There are two reasons for this growth. First, advances in microelectronics have increased the power and reduced the cost of business computing. Second, many employees have achieved the levels of computing literacy needed to allow their firms to benefit from computer use.

Advances in Computer Systems

Stated simply, today's hardware provides more capability for less money. For example, the IBM PC/AT, a common fixture on many managers' desks, can be purchased today for about $4000. In terms of processor speed and primary memory, this personal computer is equivalent to the System/360 series computer system offered by IBM in the 1960s. Yet, the price of a comparable System/360 computer at that time was over $1 million. In addition, System/360 computer systems also required large, costly computer staffs. Given the expense and inconvenience, it isn't surprising that only large and wealthy corporations could justify frequent computer use. As hardware prices have dropped, however, more and more businesses are able to afford a computer system.

While hardware advances prompted this surge in business computing, software is now the driving force. Hardware provides a tool for solving business problems, but software puts this tool to use. Why has software become such a key factor in today's world of business computing?

The growing number of businesses owning computer systems has created a thriving market for software packages that perform standard business applications. And, as more specialized software packages become available, even more businesses become convinced that they can benefit from computer use.

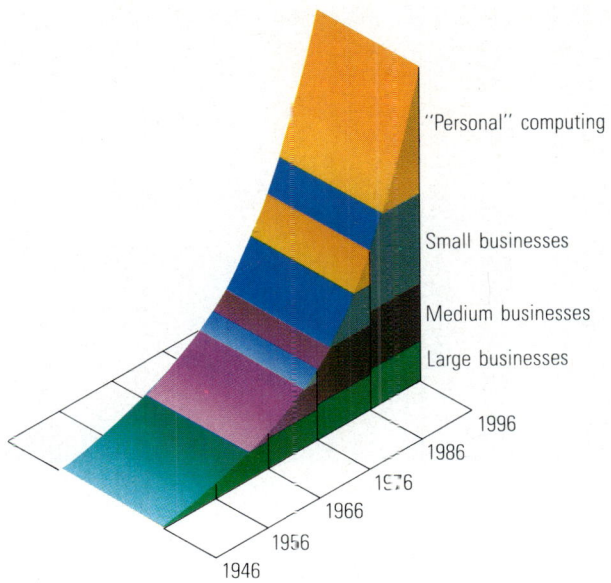

EXHIBIT 2.1
The Growth of Business Computing

The attraction of "ready-made" software packages is not hard to understand. When you take a trip, you don't draw your own map, because you can buy very good maps at low prices. The same reasoning applies to standard business software. Why should a firm develop its own programs when it can buy them from a software company, which spreads the development cost over a large sales volume?

Improvements in today's hardware allow programmers to develop software that is far more powerful and far simpler to use than software developed only a decade ago. Sophisticated and easy-to-use business software requires large amounts of primary memory and secondary storage as well as fast processing and data retrieval. Much of the success of today's popular microcomputer software packages, such as Lotus 1-2-3, is traced to the fact that the software packages are very capable and convenient to use (see Exhibit 2.2).

As we will see in Chapter 4, "Input, Output, and Secondary Storage," today's computer users are gaining the ability to interact with software in very natural ways. Managers at Filene's department store in Boston, for example, are using the Intellect software package to retrieve information from their computer system's data files in the following way:

Show me all the salespeople in Region 5 who have exceeded their sales quotas by 20 percent or more.

Software that works in this manner requires a very powerful central processor unit.

The result of these advances in information systems is a spiral of computer use. As hardware becomes more advanced and less expensive, more businesses use computers. With more computer systems in place, the cost of sophisticated, easy-to-use software decreases, prompting even more business computing.

Why Business Computer Use Is Growing

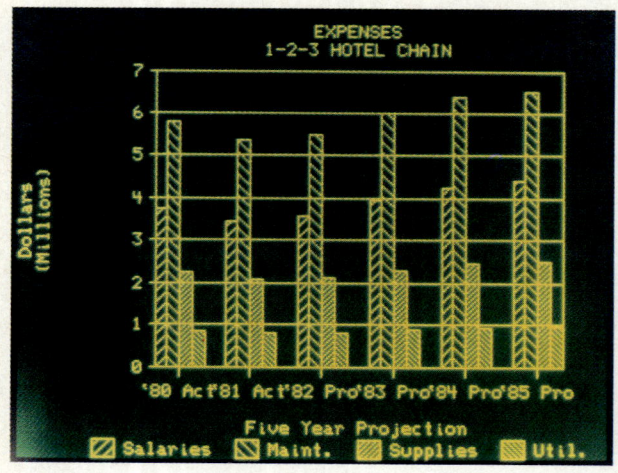
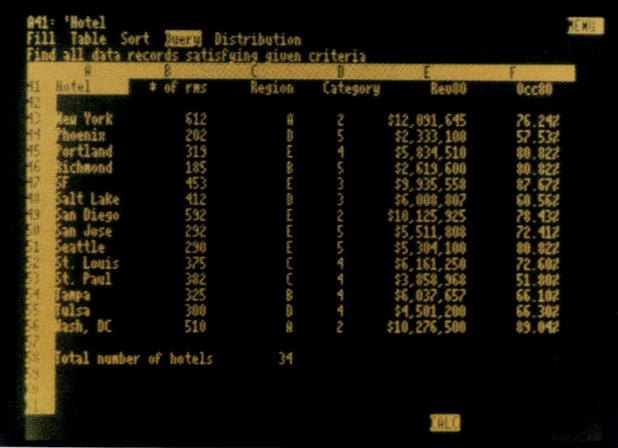

EXHIBIT 2.2
The Lotus 1-2-3 microcomputer software package offers users a variety of features, including display graphics and a spreadsheet.

Progress in Achieving Computing Literacy

Successful business computing requires the efforts of many employees in user and creator roles. Users must minimally attain literacy level 3, using computers as business tools, and creators need to attain literacy level 4, identifying new computer applications, or level 5, designing information systems, depending on the role being performed.

Many employees today have already attained these levels of computing literacy. Exhibit 2.3 shows the results of a recent study of employee attitudes toward computing. Two groups of people were surveyed. First, middle managers were questioned about their attitudes toward computers. Second, the firms' computer trainers were asked to predict the middle managers' responses. The computer trainers were surprised to find that these middle managers had more positive attitudes about using computers than expected.

COMPUTERS IN BUSINESS

By now, you may have an appreciation of the importance of computers in business. In this section, we want to discuss, in general terms, some facets of business operations, the types of information systems used in business, and how these information systems interact.

What Doing Business Involves

Businesses produce goods and services and they buy and sell them, and all of this necessitates a great deal of clerical work in handling and controlling these functions.

Manufacturing

If you have ever assembled anything, you probably have a basic understanding of the work activities involved in manufacturing. People who work in manufacturing must do the following:

Determine whether the products can be built. (Are there enough materials in stock? Are there enough workers and machinery available?)

Schedule the steps involved in making the products. (How can we best use the available workers and machinery? Will all of the parts needed be available at the proper time?)

Perform each of the tasks required to make the product.

Deliver the completed products to a finished goods storage area.

The general term for these activities, **manufacturing,** requires careful coordination. Similar needs for planning and monitoring also exist in businesses such as law firms and advertising agencies, where services, rather than manufactured goods, are provided.

EXHIBIT 2.3

The computing literacy level within many firms is often higher than computer professionals realize. In this study, computer trainers, labeled *corporate policy,* underestimated the computing literacy of the middle managers, labeled *end-users.*

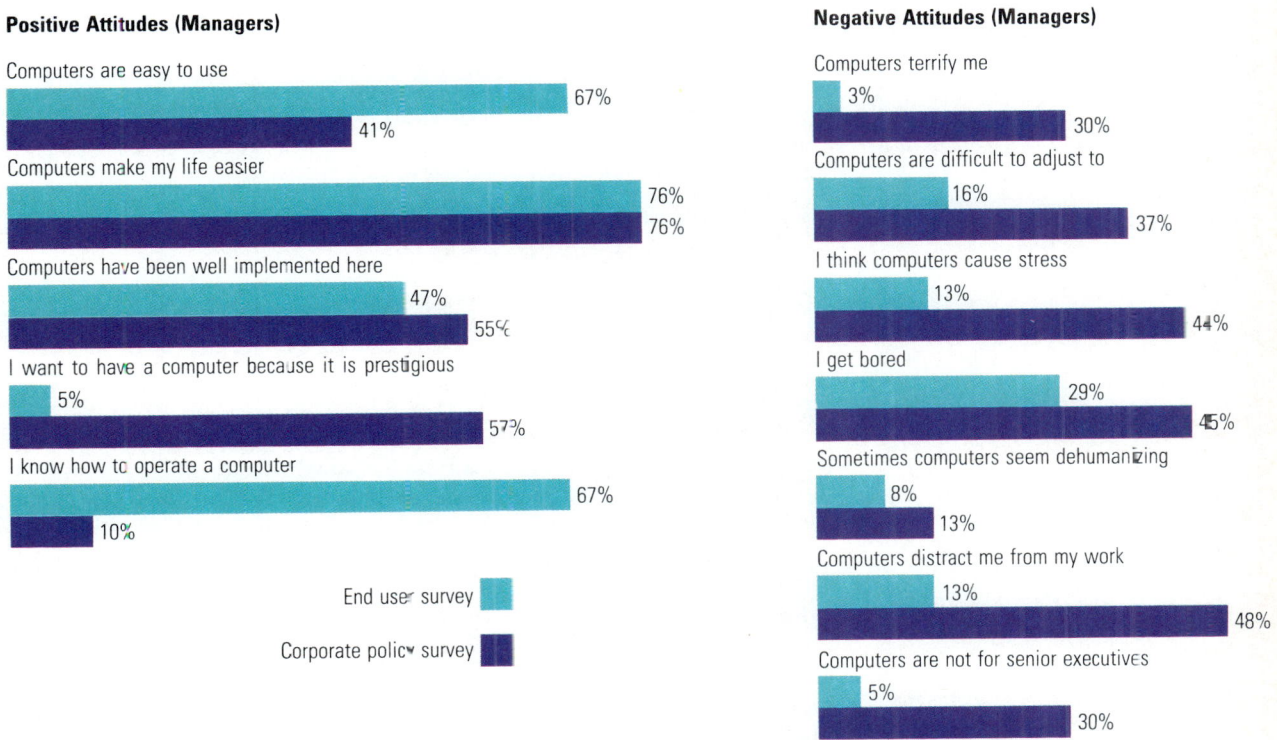

Reprinted from the June issue of *Modern Office Technology,* and copyrighted 1984 by Penton/IPC, subsidiary of Pittway Corp.

Computers in Business

Buying and Selling

Other important aspects of business operations include, of course, buying and selling. You might be surprised to learn that business buying behaviors are very similar to your own behaviors as a consumer. For example, a business must do the following:

Assess needs. (What stock levels are low? How many units do we need to purchase?)

Set purchase rules. (Is quick delivery more important than low price? Is a 3-percent rejection rate for "bad" supplies too high?)

Evaluate the goods offered by suppliers. (Is the higher quality of Product A worth its higher price?)

Make the purchase.

Receive the purchased goods.

Examine the quality of the received goods.

Pay for the purchase.

A general term for this business function is **purchasing.** The business activity of paying suppliers is termed **accounts payable.**

The other side of the coin is business selling. Here, the considerations are somewhat different. A business must make specific decisions and implement them.

In order to maximize its potential for profit making, a business must consider every aspect. It must make decisions about the following:

Decide what goods it will offer to others.

Create a demand for its products.

Maintain a sufficient inventory of its products to meet customer demand. (How many do we expect to sell this week?)

Accept a customer order.

Process the customer order.

Deliver the goods the customer ordered.

Bill the customer.

Receive and process customer payments.

Deciding what products to offer and creating a demand for those products is the general responsibility of **marketing,** while selling and delivering goods is the responsibility of **sales.** The business activity of receiving and processing customer payments is **accounts receivable.**

Buying, manufacturing, and selling are the obvious activities of doing business that occur to most of us. What might not be so obvious, however, is the crucial link between buying and manufacturing and between manufacturing and selling. This link is provided by **inventory,** a supply of goods held in reserve. As seen in Exhibit 2.4, inventory acts as a buffer for a business' manufacturing, buying, and selling activities. Without this buffer, manufacturing, buying, and selling would have to be perfectly coordinated. Imagine how difficult that would be. Monitoring inventory is important, particularly because inventory is a major business expense. Too little inventory means the company runs the risk of being unable to fill impor-

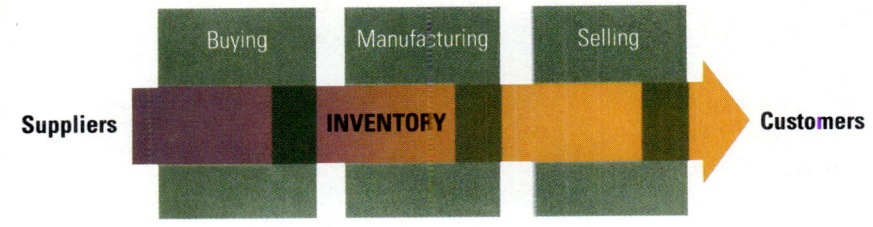

EXHIBIT 2.4

Product inventories serve as a buffer between a business' buying and selling activities.

tant customer orders. Too much inventory means that company money is tied up in unneeded products stored in a warehouse.

Accounting

Most business activities involve the exchange of valuable resources. The financial aspects of such an exchange must be accurately and promptly handled and reported. This is the responsibility of the **accounting** function. All of these financial accounts are kept in a **general ledger system,** from which are produced a business' financial statements, such as the **income statement** and the **balance sheet** (see Exhibit 2.5). In a fashion similar to that of inventory, the general ledger system serves as a financial link between the different parts of a business (see Exhibit 2.6).

Office Work

Do you want an office job? *Office* is a term people use every day. It's no wonder—a majority of the labor force works in offices. Even people who do not have "office" jobs spend a great deal of their time in offices. What types of work do office jobs entail? There is surprising variety in answers to this question.

A common view of the **office** sees it as those parts of a business that handle the paperwork that keeps a business going. Most of this paperwork falls into one of four categories:

1. Accounting—the financial transactions involved with business activities
2. Various sets of administrative records, such as payroll, personnel, and equipment records
3. General management activities, such as planning, budgeting, evaluating employee and department performances, and evaluating major investment decisions
4. General "office work" that occurs throughout all businesses, such as typing, document copying, and company mail

How Business Uses Computers

Our simplified description of what a business does may give you some idea of the vast amount of data processing that is involved in everyday business activities. Computer information systems provide a fast and accurate way of handling and controlling these data. They can also be a powerful tool for the managers responsible for setting and meeting the goals of a business. Information systems that are used for managerial support are called **management information systems,** or **MIS.**

Computers in Business

EXHIBIT 2.5
Two Types of Accounting Reports

INCOME STATEMENT
($ thousands)

Total Revenues	$1737
Cost of Goods Sold	808
Gross Profit	929
Research & Development	154
Marketing	264
Administration	209
Total Operating Costs	627
Earnings Before Interest and Taxes	302
Interest	6
Earnings Before Taxes	296
Taxes	143
Net Income	$153

BALANCE SHEET
($ thousands)

ASSETS	
Cash	$189
Accounts Receivable	371
Inventories	356
Other Current Assets	36
Total Current Assets	952
Property and Equipment	721
Depreciation	245
Net Fixed Assets	476
Other Assets	34
Total	$1462
LIABILITIES	
Notes Payable	$85
Accounts Payable	71
Short-Term Loans	259
Total Current Liabilities	415
Long-Term Loans	10
Bonds	35
Total Long-Term Liabilities	45
Stock	276
Retained Earnings	726
Total	$1462

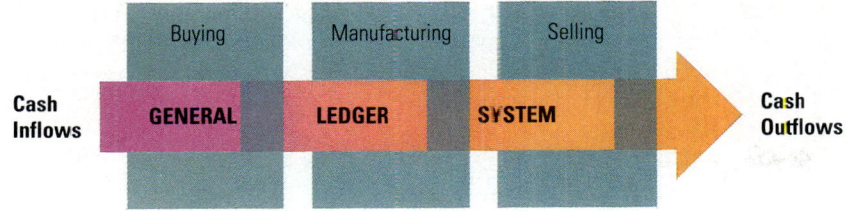

EXHIBIT 2.6
Linking Role of General Ledger System
The general ledger system tracks the cash inflows and outflows associated with business' buying, manufacturing, and selling activities.

There are three categories of management information systems: transaction processing systems, information reporting systems, and decision support systems. Each type of information system serves a distinct information processing role. Brief discussions of these three types of information systems will be given here.

Transaction Processing Systems

A **transaction** is a single business event, such as taking an item out of or adding it to inventory, making a sale, making a purchase, or paying a bill. **Transaction processing systems** are used to record, process, and manage data from these everyday business activities. Often, many of these basic business tasks, such as entering orders, paying bills, maintaining accounting ledgers, and keeping track of the flow of supplies and materials into and out of inventories, are the responsibility of the business' accounting department. Historically, the earliest, and still one of the heaviest, users of business information systems is the accountant.

Exhibit 2.7 illustrates the standard inputs and outputs normally associated with a transaction processing system. The input data describe a business transaction, such as ordering supplies. The transaction is then recorded in secondary storage. In this example, the data are placed in an "open purchase" file. The firm now has a permanent record that it ordered these supplies on this date. A business document, in this case a purchase order, may be printed. Usually in processing transactions, data also need to be retrieved from other data files. In printing a purchase order, for example, the computer may be instructed to read the supplier's name and address from a "supplier" file.

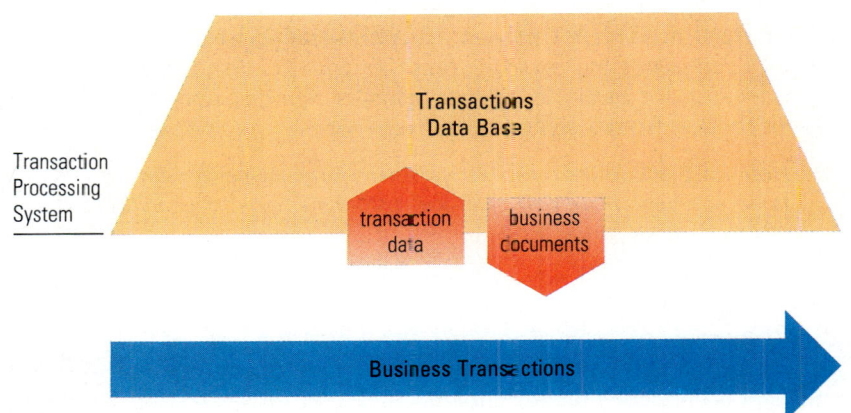

EXHIBIT 2.7
A Transaction Processing System
Transaction processing systems support the day-to-day activities of a business. In this example, business purchases are processed and recorded.

Computers in Business

A key point to note is that transaction processing systems build and maintain data files. The data contained in these files provide a detailed description of a firm's business activities. The term **data base** is often used when referring to such a computerized pool of business data.

Information Reporting Systems

While transaction processing systems help a business carry out its day-to-day activities, they do not provide much support to mid- and upper-level managers. To do their jobs well, these managers need more general types of information—what should be done, what was done, and how well it was done. The data available in transaction processing systems are just too detailed and, thus, not very useful for most managers. **Information reporting systems** process these raw data to produce summary reports that are useful to managers.

For example, a sales manager is not interested in knowing how many wrenches Joe Smith sold to the Acme Company on April 15 or how much Joe spent on a business lunch that day. What the sales manager needs to know, however, are answers to questions such as:

> *Has Joe Smith met his sales quota yet?*
> *Is the overall sales goal for wrenches on schedule?*
> *Are the department's travel expenses within budget?*

To answer these questions, previously stored data about sales and travel transactions need to be analyzed and presented in a summary report to the sales manager at regular intervals. Information reports such as this help managers keep abreast of important issues.

Exhibit 2.8 illustrates the inputs and outputs that are found in an information reporting system. Raw data are retrieved from data files, transformed into meaningful information, and distributed in the form of **management reports.** The information produced for one report can also be stored in the data base. Then, this information can become the data for yet another management report.

Decision Support Systems

While an information reporting system informs managers about the general well-being of their departments, it is often not helpful when a manager must make a specific decision. Then the manager turns to a **decision support system,** which allows him or her to produce management reports in an *ad hoc* fashion. The phrase *ad hoc* means that the need for a specific set of information could not have been anticipated.

Consider, for example, a plant manager who receives the following urgent request from a senior executive:

> *How long would it take to manufacture and deliver a rush order to a new customer? If we can meet the customer's request, we will get more of this business in the future.*

How useful are the following reports: a weekly status report on inventory levels (three days old), a monthly sales forecast (two weeks old), and a daily status report on all customer orders (twelve hours old)? While each of these reports provides the plant manager with some picture of how well the plant is operating, they are not much help in answering the executive's question.

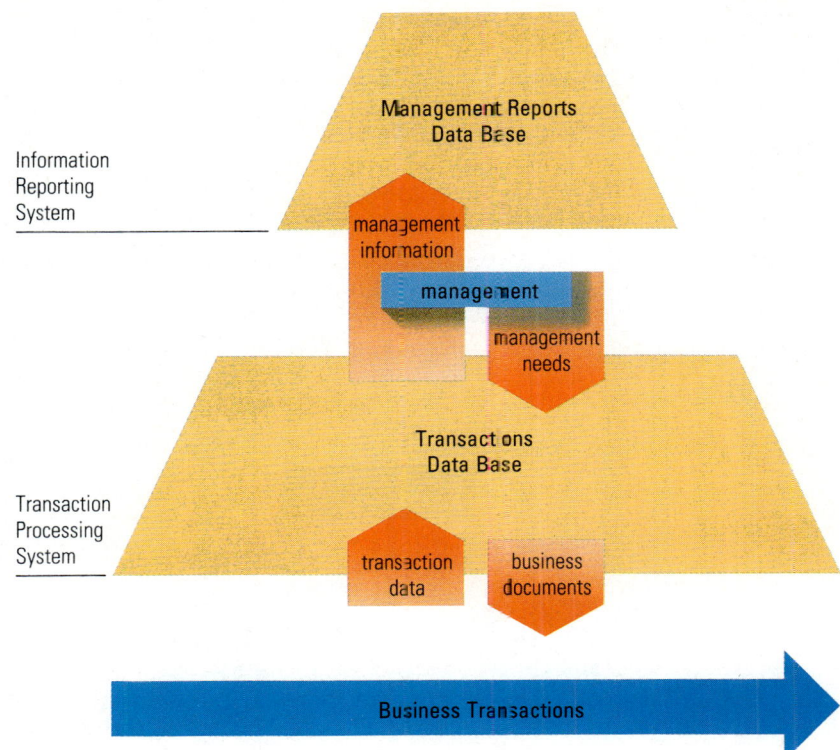

EXHIBIT 2.8
An Information Reporting System
Information reporting systems provide managers with the information they need to keep a business performing at a productive level.

What the plant manager needs is some way to pull together current data on inventory levels, manufacturing operations, and order priorities so that he or she can determine whether it would be possible to rearrange manufacturing schedules for this rush order. Decision support systems provide this type of *ad hoc* information reporting.

Exhibit 2.9 illustrates the inputs and outputs normally found within a decision support system. A manager can directly interact with this information system to indicate which data are needed and what processing operations are to be performed. The decision support system then retrieves the requested data from the data base, sets up the needed processing operation, processes the data, and produces the results. The phrase *decision support* is used because these information systems support managers in making decisions.

How Information Systems Interact

Transaction processing systems, information reporting systems, and decision support systems fill three levels of business computing needs (see Exhibit 2.10). These levels reflect two ideas:

1. Information systems at higher levels make use of data stored by information systems at lower levels. Information reporting systems "feed" off of transaction processing systems, and decision support systems "feed" off of both transaction processing systems and information reporting systems.

Computers in Business

2. Information systems at higher levels tend to serve higher business needs. Recall that transaction processing systems primarily support a firm's day-to-day activities. Information reporting systems are chiefly used by the managers responsible for making sure these day-to-day activities can be performed and are being performed well. Managers responsible for a firm's major business decisions depend on decision support systems for vital information to give them a broad picture backed up by and based on specific details.

Did you notice that we moved from talking about information systems that support business activities to information systems that support individual managers in a business? This dual nature of many business information systems emphasizes the key role that people play in an effective information system.

EXHIBIT 2.9
A Decision Support System
Decision support systems allow managers to interact with an information system and define *ad hoc* information reports.

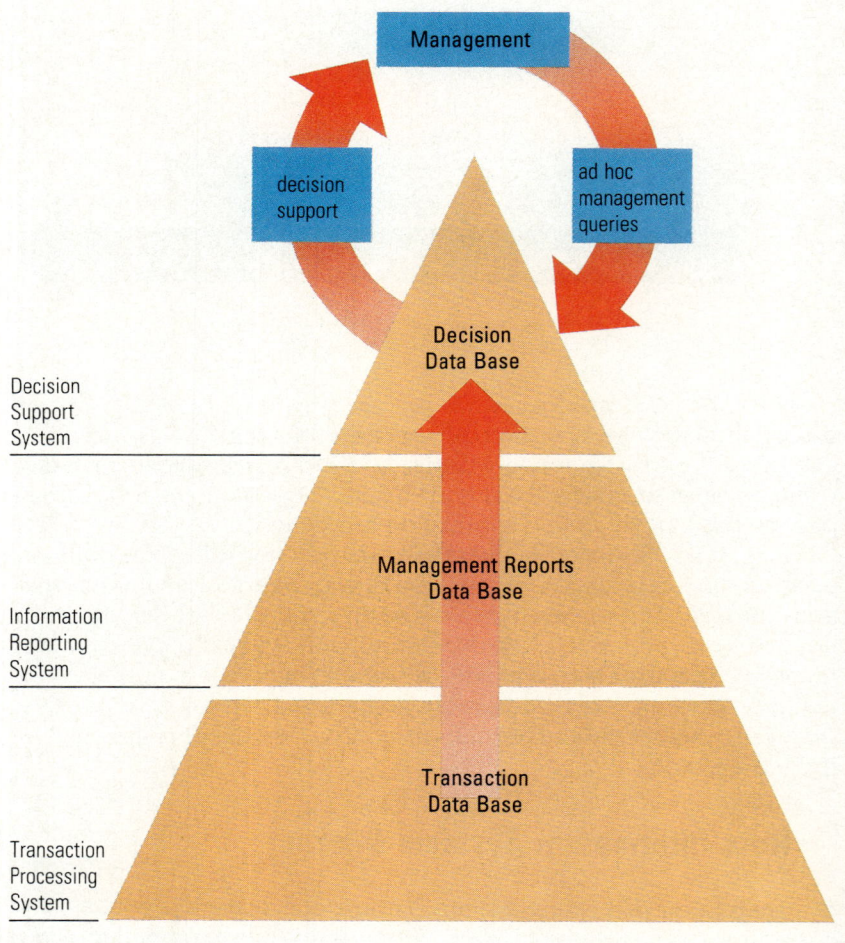

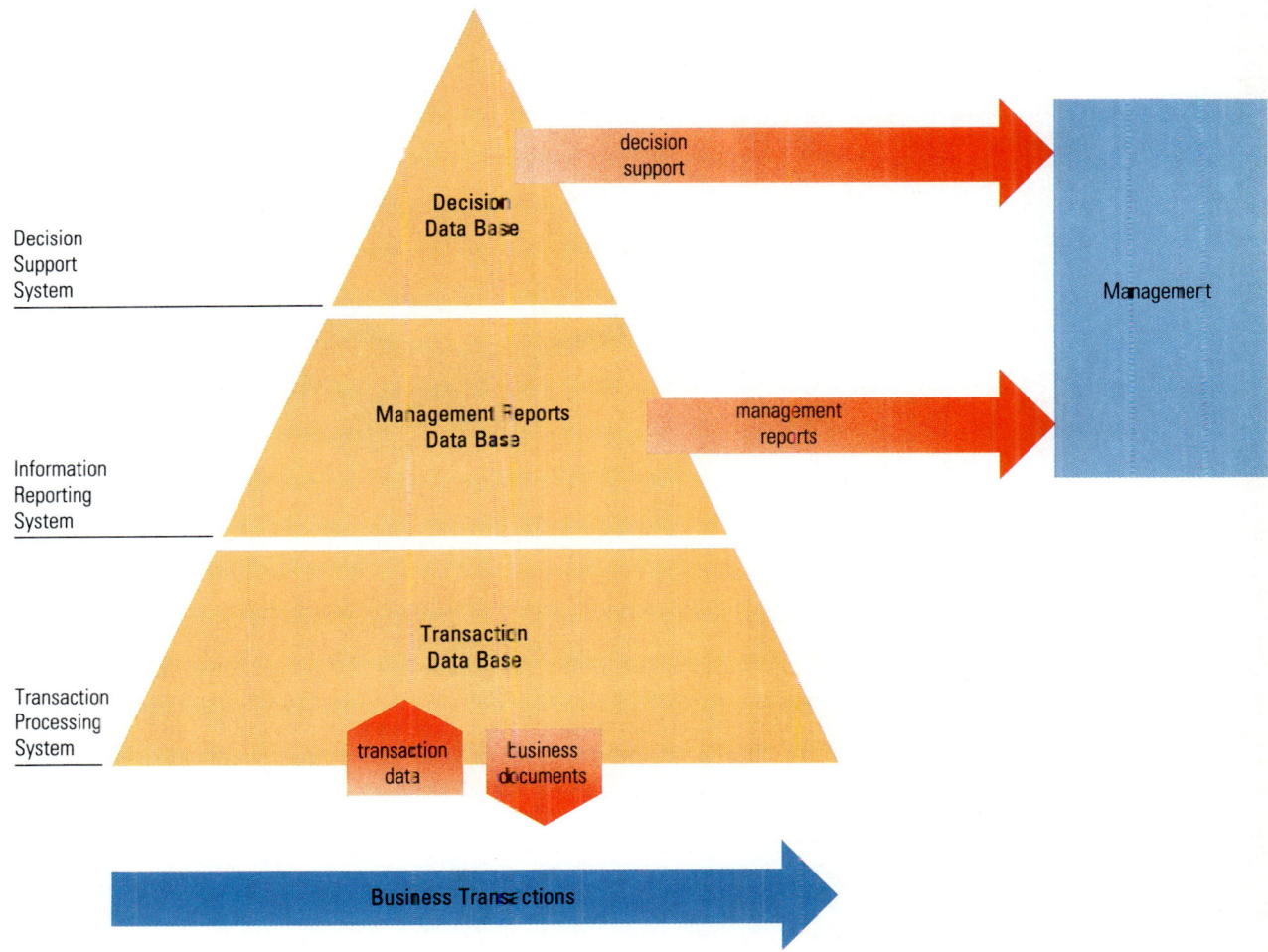

EXHIBIT 2.10
The Triangle of Management Information Systems
Transaction processing systems, information reporting systems, and decision support systems tend to serve three distinct levels of business computing.

PERSONAL COMPUTING IN BUSINESS

The most recent addition to the world of business computing is the microcomputer. **Personal computing,** or the use of personal computers to directly support business professionals in their work, is the main force behind the explosive business demand for microcomputers (see Exhibit 2.11). A **business professional** is an employee who holds an information occupation that requires judgment, such as a manager, planning analyst, legal specialist, or engineer.

Professional employees spend a great deal of their time processing data. The typical professional seems constantly to be sifting through mail, memos, magazines, technical documents, reports, and books or preparing memos, letters, reports, and presentations. Through these work activities, business professionals use their experience, knowledge, judgment, and creativity to create and communicate information.

EXHIBIT 2.11
Predicted Total Personal Computer Units Installed in the United States, 1981–91

Adapted from Figure 3 in "Personal Computers in the Eighties" by Greggory S. Blundell, *BYTE*, January 1983, p. 171. Copyright © 1983 McGraw-Hill, Inc., New York, 10020. All rights reserved. Reprinted by permission.

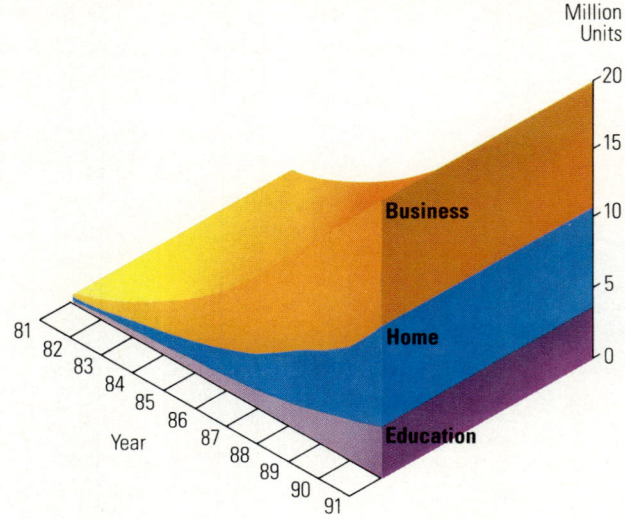

The microcomputer can relieve much of the time-consuming frustrations of the business professional's job. It's the low cost of microcomputers that makes them affordable—a $4000 expense item can be squeezed into most office budgets without too much trouble.

Personal computing software has been successful for two major reasons. First, it is aimed at a set of tasks performed by all business professionals. Second, it handles these tasks in much the same manner that business professionals perform them. As a result, most business professionals realize almost immediate benefits once they begin using a software package. The personal computing tools introduced here represent the most popular personal computing software applications. These applications are discussed in detail in Part Three of this text.

Electronic Spreadsheets

What if you had studied engineering rather than business, history, or psychology? What if you had gone to Europe instead of buying a car? Questions like these tantalize us largely because we can't answer them. In the business world, however, "what if" questions often determine a firm's profit—or even its survival.

Electronic spreadsheets, software that divides a microcomputer screen into a table of rows and columns, provide business professionals with a quick and accurate means of performing the mathematical calculations involved in answering "what if" questions. These packages provide the following capabilities.

Text can easily be inserted into the spreadsheet to form report titles and row and column headings.

Data can quickly be entered into a spreadsheet's **cells,** the points of intersection between rows and columns.

The spreadsheet's cells can then be related to one another, through arithmetic and logical formulas representing business rules, to create business information; whenever data are changed, the software instantly calculates the effects of the change on all cells and displays the results.

These spreadsheets can easily be printed onto paper.

Once a spreadsheet has been built, it is simple to store on a floppy disk so that it can be retrieved later to be used again, and again. . . .

A recent survey found that a remarkable 90 percent of the businesses questioned used their microcomputers for spreadsheet software applications. Exhibit 2.12 pictures a display screen for a typical electronic spreadsheet package.

Word Processing

Have you ever handed in a report late because you realized at the last moment it could be improved? Have you ever had to retype a full page or more of text simply because you made a typing error or left out a word or whole sentence? These are the kinds of annoying delays business professionals frequently encounter.

Word processors, software that transforms a microcomputer screen into "sheets of paper" to be electronically written on, provide quick and accurate ways to create and revise business documents. These packages have the following capabilities:

Text can easily be written onto an electronic document.

Any part of the document, whether a letter, word, sentence, paragraph, page, or group of pages, can be instantly changed or moved elsewhere in the document.

EXHIBIT 2.12
This spreadsheet allows a user to make monthly mortgage payment comparisons.

Personal Computing in Business

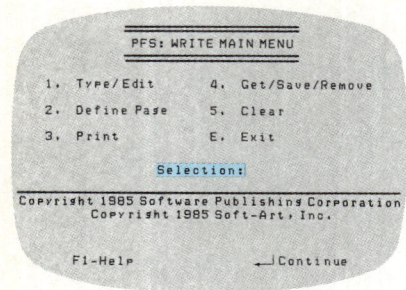

EXHIBIT 2.13
A word processing package makes preparing business reports a simple and convenient process. As the menu shows, this package can perform a number of useful tasks, including editing and proofreading.

A document's **format,** such as margins, spacing, page numbers, and headings can be set automatically and easily adjusted.

A partially completed document can be stored on a floppy disk to be retrieved later for completion.

Once completed, a document can be stored on a floppy disk and then retrieved later for printing or revisions.

The complete document, or perhaps just a portion of it, can be retrieved from secondary storage and inserted anywhere within another document.

Exhibit 2.13 pictures the display screen for a word processing package.

Business Graphics

In writing a report or preparing an oral presentation, have you ever wished you were a good enough artist to express yourself visually as well as with words? Even people with the talent to produce quality art or graphics often don't have the time needed to prepare such presentation materials.

Business graphics, software that transforms primary memory into an electronic drawing board, provide business professionals with a quick and accurate means of creating quality presentation graphics. These packages have impressive capabilities:

Tables of raw data can easily be represented in bar chart, pie chart, and line graph forms.

When data values change, the graphics displays can instantly reflect the changes.

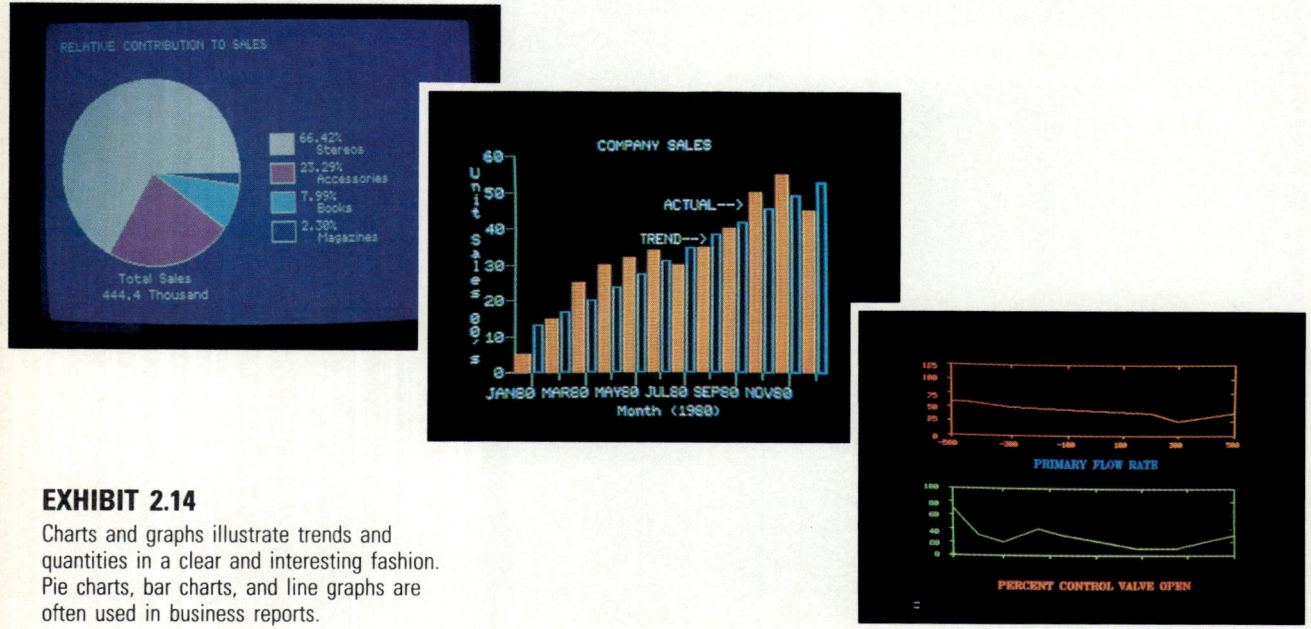

EXHIBIT 2.14
Charts and graphs illustrate trends and quantities in a clear and interesting fashion. Pie charts, bar charts, and line graphs are often used in business reports.

Text, including headings, titles, and legends, can easily be inserted into charts and graphs.

Color can be used to improve the meaning and visual appeal of a chart or graph.

A graph or chart can easily be printed on paper, or even on a 35mm slide.

Once a graph or chart has been created, it can be stored on a floppy disk to be retrieved later for printing, for revision, or to become part of an automated slide show.

Exhibit 2.14 shows examples of the presentation materials that can be produced with business graphics software.

File Management

Where do you keep important names and addresses? Can you find them when you need them? Is your personal filing system organized? Can you find notes, memos, tables of figures, important dates, or reports when you want them? Most business professionals spend a lot of time organizing, storing, and then locating the information their work requires.

File management is software that transforms secondary storage into an electronic filing cabinet, providing business professionals a quick and accurate way to organize, store, and retrieve the information that they depend on in doing their jobs. These packages have the following capabilities:

Numbers and text can easily be organized as a data file and then stored on a floppy disk.

Automatic retrieval cues for retrieving these numbers and text are simple to establish.

Data stored previously can quickly be located, retrieved, and changed.

Reports making use of stored data can be designed and then displayed on a microcomputer screen or printed onto paper.

Exhibit 2.15 shows a data record that a typical file manager package has retrieved from secondary storage and displayed.

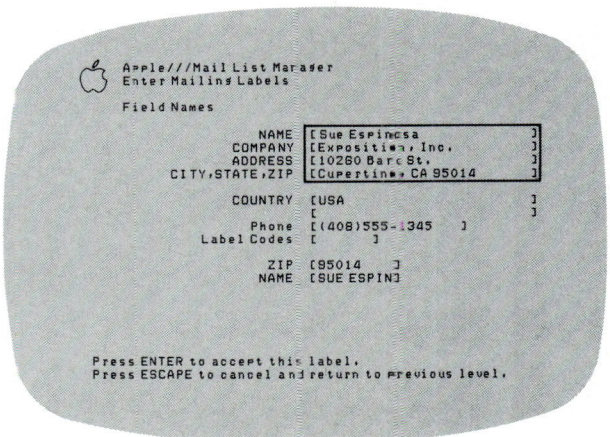

EXHIBIT 2.15

This is a data record from a typical file management package.

Personal Computing in Business

Communications Software

Have you ever been working on a report and suddenly realized that a piece of information you need is missing? Worse, you know where to find it—at a library or at a friend's home or office—but don't have the time to go get it. This is another of the frustrating problems that tend to plague business professionals.

Communications software, software that electronically links a personal computer to another computer system, provides a way to quickly and accurately communicate with distant sources of information. These packages have the following capabilities:

A personal computer can easily be linked to a friend's or co-worker's personal computer so that messages, programs, or data can be exchanged.

A personal computer is easily linked to a larger computer system so that data or programs stored on the larger computer can be transferred, or **downloaded,** to the personal computer.

Exhibit 2.16 illustrates some options offered by a typical communications package.

Integrated Software Packages

Once business professionals began to use these personal computing wonders, they soon wanted the convenience of combining the capabilities of several software packages. In preparing a report, for example, a manager might want to insert a graph without having to create the text with a word processing program, create the graph with a graphics program, and then manually cut and paste the two pieces together. Instead, business professionals wanted to be able to use—at any time—combinations of

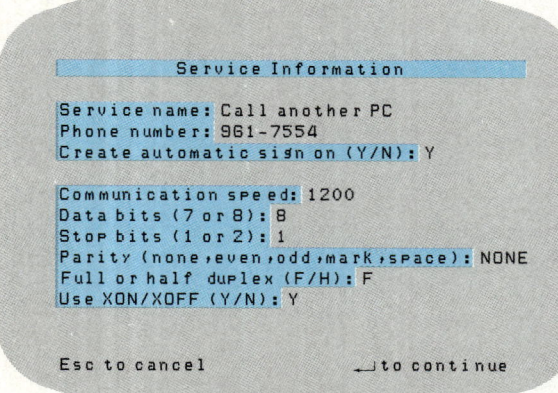

EXHIBIT 2.16
Communications software links one personal computer to another computer system.

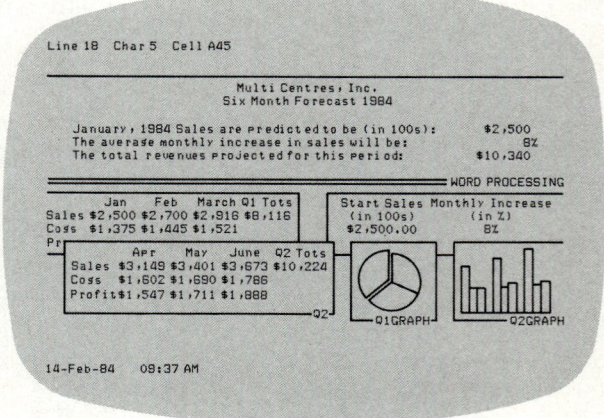

EXHIBIT 2.17
This is a sales forecast prepared with integrated software.

electronic spreadsheets, word processing, graphics, file management, or communications.

Integrated software combines a number of these personal computing tools into one software package. An integrated package provides the following capabilities:

- A user can easily switch back and forth among the software tools made available in the package.
- Data entered via one tool, such as a spreadsheet, are automatically available to the other tools, such as graphics.
- Documents displaying data and text in multiple forms are easily created with electronic "cut and paste" commands.

One of the most popular integrated software packages is Lotus 1-2-3, which combines software for an electronic spreadsheet with graphics and file management. Exhibit 2.17 pictures an example of the type of business documents that can be created with integrated packages.

DECIDING WHEN COMPUTERS SHOULD BE USED

Two major questions need to be answered in deciding to computerize a business task. First, do the information processing characteristics of the task match the information processing strengths of a computer system? Second, do the benefits of computer use outweigh the costs? Answering the first question provides a quick means of identifying likely computer applications. A yes answer here, however, is not a guarantee that a firm should computerize the task. Business investments need to produce economic benefits. If this rule isn't followed, a business won't be around for very long! Decisions to computerize should only follow yes answers to *both* questions.

Analyzing the Task

We looked at some of the advantages of computer-based information processing in Chapter 1 and at the beginning of this chapter. Exhibit 2.18, which summarizes these discussions, can serve as a checklist of task characteristics favorable to computer use. Let's examine this checklist in detail.

Input
A task in which a large amount of data needs to be entered is usually a good candidate for computerization. Entering large amounts of data by computer will probably cost less per data item, and data entry will certainly be completed a lot sooner. Computerized data input, however, requires that special equipment be used and that the data be in computer-readable form. If only a small amount of data needs to be entered, it might be best to do so manually. A factory having to enter the number of hours worked for each of 3500 workers is sure to benefit from putting its payroll on a computer. A factory with 15 employees would not.

EXHIBIT 2.18
Checklist: Task Characteristics Favorable to Computerization

	YES	NO
Input: Does a *large volume* of data need to be entered? Is the data *already stored* in a computer system? Can the data be easily converted to *computer-readable form*?		
Processing: Do a *large number* of calculations need to be performed? Do *complex* calculations need to be performed? Can a *clear set of rules* be stated that define the processing operations to be performed? Will these rules *remain fixed* for the foreseeable future? Are these processing operations performed on a *frequent basis*?		
Storage and Retrieval: Does a *large volume* of data need to be stored? Does stored data need to be retrieved *frequently*?		
Output: Does a *large volume* of data need to be printed?		
Overall Task Needs: Is *accuracy* important? Is *speed* important? Are *current* data needed?		

Processing

The computer is well suited for tasks that involve many complex calculations. In planning each day's work, for example, a factory supervisor might have to determine the best way to process eighty orders for six different products through three or four manufacturing steps. Figuring out by hand the best of all possible schedules would be a very time-consuming task. Performing this task with a computer would seem a far better solution.

A scheduling program, however, must exist to perform this task. Can the factory supervisor list all of the decisions he or she makes in putting together a daily work schedule? Are all of these steps clearly defined, are they somewhat ambiguous, or do they vary? Without a clear set of processing rules, it will be difficult for a programmer to develop the needed program. Even if a clear set of rules can be defined for the scheduling task, it might take a long time and cost a lot of money to develop the program.

Storage and Retrieval

If a large amount of data needs to be stored, such as the parts inventory for a Boeing 747, it will probably be less expensive to store the data in a computer system than in filing cabinets. If only a small amount of data needs to be stored, however, such as warranty information on three company cars, it makes little sense to computerize. What about storing a medium amount of information? The answer may depend on how often the data items need to be retrieved.

Consider the following two situations:

A purchasing clerk must refer to a list of 1500 supplier names and addresses one day each month in order to mail out about 15 purchase orders.

Another purchasing clerk must constantly refer to another list of 1500 supplier names and addresses in mailing out about 60 purchase orders per day.

In the first case, computer use is probably not needed. In the second case, it would be extremely helpful.

Output

As with data input, a task that requires a large amount of data output is a good candidate for automation. Preparing 3900 paychecks by hand would take a great deal of time but could be done quickly and inexpensively by a computer. Typing 15 paychecks would probably cost less than printing the paychecks on a computer.

Overall Task Needs

This final set of issues can be critical for task success—the accuracy, speed, and currentness of information processing. Accuracy and speed are a computer's primary advantages. Whenever task accuracy or speed are important, computer use should be considered. The need for high levels of accuracy in a firm's financial records is one reason accounting applications are usually one of the first information systems used in most businesses; and the speed with which travel agents need to access airline schedules makes this an extremely important computer application for travel agencies.

The speed of computers can also result in very current data files. If it is crucial that information outputs are "up-to-date," then computer use might be appropriate. When an important customer demands to know when an order is to be delivered, a salesperson would naturally want access to the most current data possible from the manufacturer so that he or she can get the information back to the customer quickly and control a potential problem.

Weighing the Benefits and Costs

As you might imagine, assigning dollar values to information system benefits and costs can be very difficult. Performing these calculations also requires more information about computer hardware and software than this text has presented so far. For now, Exhibit 2.19 introduces you to the major categories of benefits and costs.

Benefits

There are four categories of information system benefits. With some proposed computer applications, only one of the categories may apply. With other applications, all may be pertinent.

EXHIBIT 2.19
The Decision to Computerize: Benefits and Costs

BENEFIT CATEGORIES	COST CATEGORIES
Reducing Costs labor equipment materials	**Hardware** purchase installation maintenance
Avoiding Future Costs labor equipment materials	**Software** development purchase maintenance
Products or Services improvements new	**People** training use
Management Information improvements new	**Operations** data preparation overhead

When Computers Should Be Used

The most common information system benefit occurs when *costs are reduced* with computer use. The costs normally affected are labor costs, equipment costs, and materials costs. An inventory control application, for example, may have the following impacts:

Inventory clerks no longer need to work overtime.

Two, rather than three, warehouses are needed.

The amount of inventory kept in stock is reduced by 40 percent.

Another common information system benefit is that computer use *avoids some future costs.* Again, labor, equipment, and supplies costs are typically involved. By replacing an old accounts-receivable information system with one using newer technology, the following benefits might arise:

Clerks in the accounting department can handle increased work loads without working overtime.

The cost of the computer equipment needed to process these customer payments is cut in half.

The cost of office supplies is reduced by 20 percent.

A less common, but very important, benefit is realized when the information system allows a firm to offer its customers *new products and services* or *improved products and services.* Examples of these benefits include:

New Product	A savings and loan institution offers its customers a combination savings/checking account, in which savings are automatically transferred into the checking account when the checking account balance is low.
New Service	A bank offers its business customers the service of managing the excess cash in these customers' checking accounts.
Improved Product	An information system helps an automobile manufacturer turn out engines with fewer defects.
Improved Service	A mail-order firm reduces the time it takes to process a customer's order.

The final category of information system benefits, *management information,* is common but often very difficult to state in dollar terms. A new marketing information system, for example, may provide the marketing staff with customer surveys that previously were not available, as well as with more current sales information on competitors' products.

Costs

There are four categories of information system costs: hardware, software, people, and operating expenses. All four cost categories usually apply to all information systems.

The most obvious cost category involves *hardware* costs. The cost of new hardware, such as microcomputers, is a major factor in estimating the cost of a proposed information system. Hardware costs also include installation and maintenance costs. **Hardware maintenance** refers to the technical work involved in repairing or servicing equipment.

Another cost category that is usually considered is *software* costs. New information systems always require investment in computer programs. Software costs include the price of a software package, the labor costs involved with any software development, and software maintenance costs. **Software maintenance** involves fixing software errors and keeping the information system up-to-date.

A third cost category, and one often overlooked, is *people* costs. Computer use may take employees away from other tasks they need to perform, particularly when an information system is first introduced. Also, all computer users require training if they are to make good use of an information system.

The final set of information system costs are those directly associated with the *day-to-day operation of an information system*. Data input often requires that data first be placed in computer-readable form and then entered into a computer system. Also, the overhead costs and any supplies involved with input, processing, storage and retrieval, and output activities must also be considered as part of an information system's costs.

Summary

The use of computer systems by business is increasing at a rapid rate. Two major forces behind this growth are the remarkable advances in computer technology and the progress made in increasing the computing literacy levels of business employees.

While hardware prompted the surge in business computing, advances in computer software are now the driving force. This is due to the ready availability of powerful and easy-to-use business software packages.

Information systems serving managers are called *management information systems,* or *MIS.*

There are three categories of management information systems. *Transaction processing systems* record, process, and manage data about everyday business activities. Much of the data processed by transaction processing systems is placed in a *data base,* all of the data files stored on a business' computer systems. *Information reporting systems* process the raw data kept in this data base to produce *management reports. Decision support systems* allow managers to access this data base in an *ad hoc* fashion to obtain information needed to make specific decisions.

Personal computing, using microcomputers to directly support business professionals in their work, is the main force behind the growing use of microcomputers in business. A *business professional* is an employee who holds an information occupation requiring the use of judgment. Personal computing can relieve much of the time-consuming and frustrating aspects of business professionals' jobs.

The five most popular personal computing software applications are *electronic spreadsheets, word processors, business graphics, file managers,* and *communications.*

Tasks that are good candidates for computerization have the following characteristics: large amounts of data are entered; many complex calculations are required; the rules to follow can be stated in a clear and precise manner; a large amount of data needs to be stored; stored data are frequently retrieved for use; large amounts of data are output; and accuracy, speed, and currentness are important for task success.

There are four categories of information system benefits. First, labor, equipment, and materials costs can be reduced. Second, future labor, equipment, and materials costs can be avoided. Third, better or improved products and services can be provided to a business' customers; and fourth, better or improved information can be provided to business managers.

There are four categories of information system costs: the cost of acquiring, installing, and maintaining hardware; the cost of developing and maintaining software; the training and related "people" costs that occur when introducing an information system; and the costs associated with the day-to-day operation of an information system.

Review Questions

1. Explain why software has become the driving force in computing today.

2. Briefly list and discuss the activities performed in a typical manufacturing process. How can the computer be applied?

3. Briefly list the major activities involved in a typical purchasing process. How can the computer be applied?

4. What activities are required in the sales function? How can the computer be applied?

5. Briefly describe the three categories of management information systems.

6. What is a business professional? How has the computer revolution aided these employees?

7. Assume that the corporation for which you work knows that computerization of its operations is feasible. How can the firm decide whether it *should* computerize?

PART TWO — Computer Hardware

CHAPTER 3 ■ The Central Processing Unit

PROBLEM SOLVING WITH COMPUTERS

COMPUTER PROCESSING OVERVIEW

CODING DATA FOR COMPUTER USE
   The Binary Number System
   Data Encoding Schemes

MICROCOMPUTER ARCHITECTURE
   Semiconductor Chip Technology
   Primary Memory Chips
   Microprocessor Chips
   Support Units

SUMMARY

REVIEW QUESTIONS

Computers are becoming an important part of modern society. Yet many people interact with computers without learning how they actually work and miss an exciting and valuable part of the computing experience.

In this chapter, we introduce you to the functioning of the central processing unit, the computer's "brain." This knowledge will take the mystery out of the way a computer works. Too often, people think computers are capable of magic; in this chapter, you'll learn how and where the so-called *magic* happens. Also, understanding how a computer works can help you evaluate the relative merits of various computer models. This knowledge will be critical if you are faced with the responsibility of choosing a computer for a specific business application. In this chapter, you will learn to do the following:

1. Describe the process used by a computer in solving a problem.
2. Describe the architecture of the central processing unit and explain the function of each part.
3. Define the technology used for the major functions in microcomputers.

PROBLEM SOLVING WITH COMPUTERS

The reason computers are becoming so widely used in business, in government, at school, and at home is that they help users solve problems. To process information, the computer needs very specific instructions that explicitly state what is to be done. There is no room for vagueness. Like a mathematical formula, the step-by-step instructions given a computer must make no assumptions and must lead to the same result every time. Precise instructions such as these are called **algorithms.** Algorithms are used as the basis of computer programs or software.

To see how this concept is applied, consider the simple payroll example in Exhibit 3.1. John Avery worked 40 hours last week, and he gets paid $7 per hour. What is his gross pay? Even without your calculator, you know that the answer is $280. But how did you figure this out? More importantly, what list of instructions would a computer need to execute in order to calculate the gross pay for all employees of this company? Keep in mind that the computer cannot do anything beyond your instructions. The step-by-step instructions might be the following:

EXHIBIT 3.1
The Payroll Problem-Solving Process

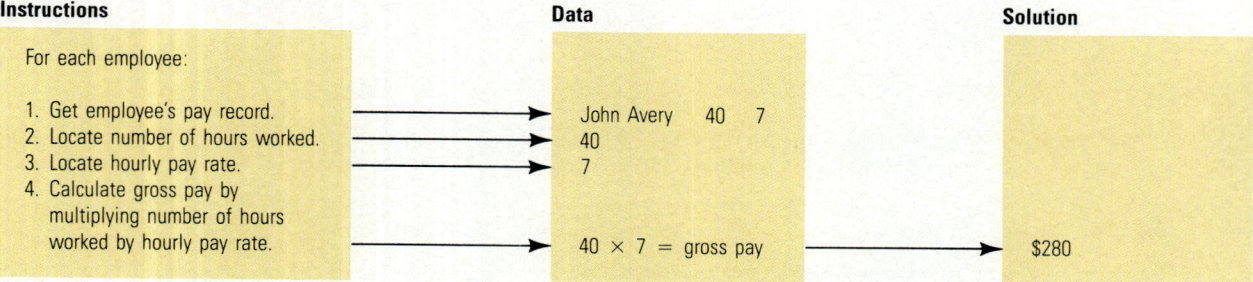

EXHIBIT 3.2
The Major Components of a Microcomputer System

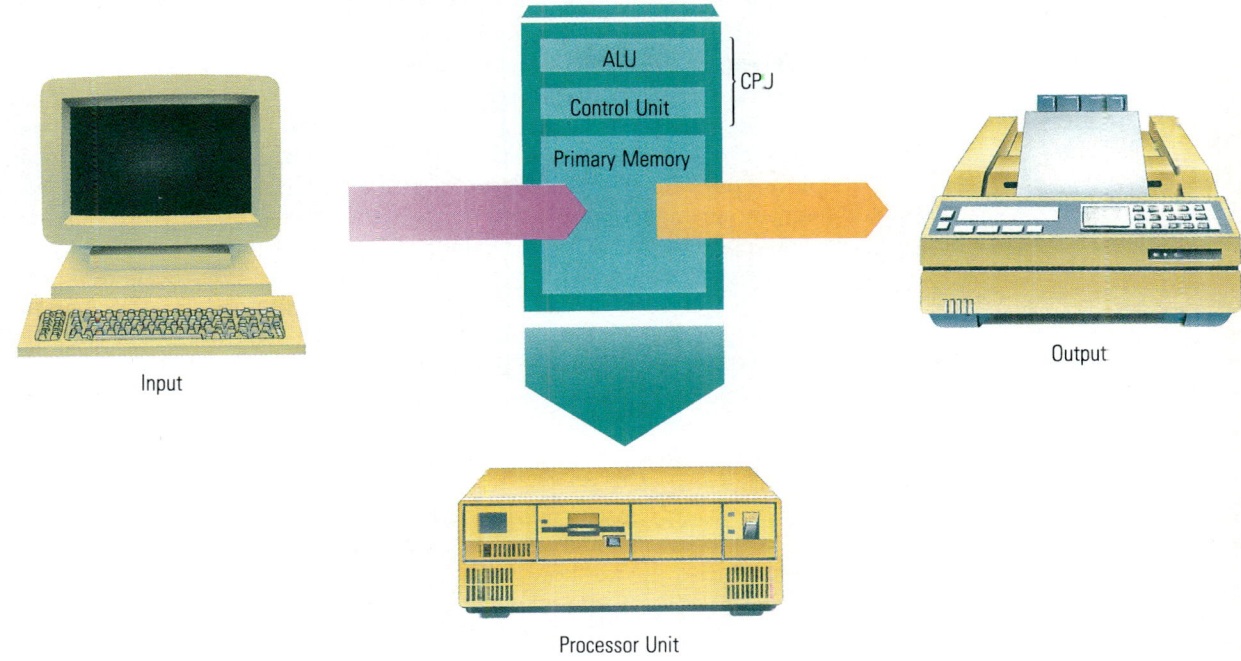

For each employee:
1. Get employee pay record.
2. Locate number of hours worked.
3. Locate hourly pay rate.
4. Calculate gross pay by multiplying number of hours worked by hourly pay rate.

This set of instructions would be an algorithm for calculating gross pay. The problem-solving process would apply the instructions to a set of data. In John Avery's case, the resulting solution would be $280.

COMPUTER PROCESSING OVERVIEW

Let's take the payroll problem-solving steps and see how a computer could be used to determine the solution. A simplified version of the computer system will be used so that we may highlight the main concepts and not be overloaded with complex details at this point.

The major components of a computer system are the input and output devices, primary memory, and the central processing unit (CPU). The CPU contains the control unit and the arithmetic-logic unit (ALU). Generally, the CPU and primary memory are housed in the computer processor (see Exhibit 3.2).

The first step in using a computer system to solve a problem is to enter, or **load,** the appropriate instructions into primary memory. In Exhibit 3.3, the control unit will show which events are being processed. The red arrows indicate the sequence of steps being carried out. After the instructions are loaded (see Exhibit 3.3a), the data records are loaded into primary memory (see Exhibit 3.3b).

This process instructs a part of the control unit to go to primary memory and select the first instruction, which in this case is "Get employee pay record." To carry out this instruction, the control unit sends a signal to primary memory and retrieves the pay record for John Avery. The completion of this task (see Exhibit 3.4a) signals the control unit to start processing the second instruction in memory, which is "Locate number of hours worked." The control unit copies the value of "hours" from the record for John Avery and places that value (40) in the arithmetic-logic unit for later use in the calculation of gross pay (see Exhibit 3.4b). The control unit then continues to execute the next instruction in sequence. Instruction 3 is "Locate hourly pay rate." John Avery is paid $7 per hour. A copy of this value is put into the arithmetic-logic unit by the control unit (see Exhibit 3.4c).

The fourth instruction is "Calculate gross pay." To carry out this instruction, recall that the formula to be used was "multiply the number of hours worked by the hourly pay rate." The control unit sends a signal of "multiply" to the arithmetic-logic unit. The ALU multiplies the two values it contains (40 times 7). The result of the calculation equals 280. At this point all instructions of the Gross Pay Algorithm have been carried out (see Exhibit 3.4d).

One additional major point that needs to be covered is the statement "for each employee" in the Gross Pay Algorithm. After the instructions have been carried out for one employee, this statement would reset the control unit to cycle through the algorithm for the next employee. This cycling would continue until all employee records had been processed (see Exhibit 3.4e).

But the algorithm didn't state a way to get the information, gross pay, out of the computer and display it for use. To do this, we would have to add several instructions to the algorithm. These would involve storing the result of the ALU calculation in primary memory as Gross Pay and associating it with the employee name, John Avery. For convenience we will skip showing these steps and proceed to a final instruction, which would order the printing of the employee name and gross pay amount (see Exhibit 3.4f).

While this payroll problem is very straightforward and the complex workings of the computer have been greatly simplified, it is helpful for understanding the following key points about computer processing:

> Instructions, in the form of an algorithm, must provide a step-by-step procedure leading to the desired result.
>
> Instructions and data must be loaded into the computer's primary memory to be processed.
>
> The control unit sequences the events within the computer system according to the instructions of the program.
>
> All calculations and logic comparisons take place in the ALU or the CPU.
>
> The set of instructions within the algorithm are applied to one case and then recycled as necessary.

EXHIBIT 3.3

(a) In using a computer system to solve a problem, the first step is to enter, or load, instructions into primary memory.

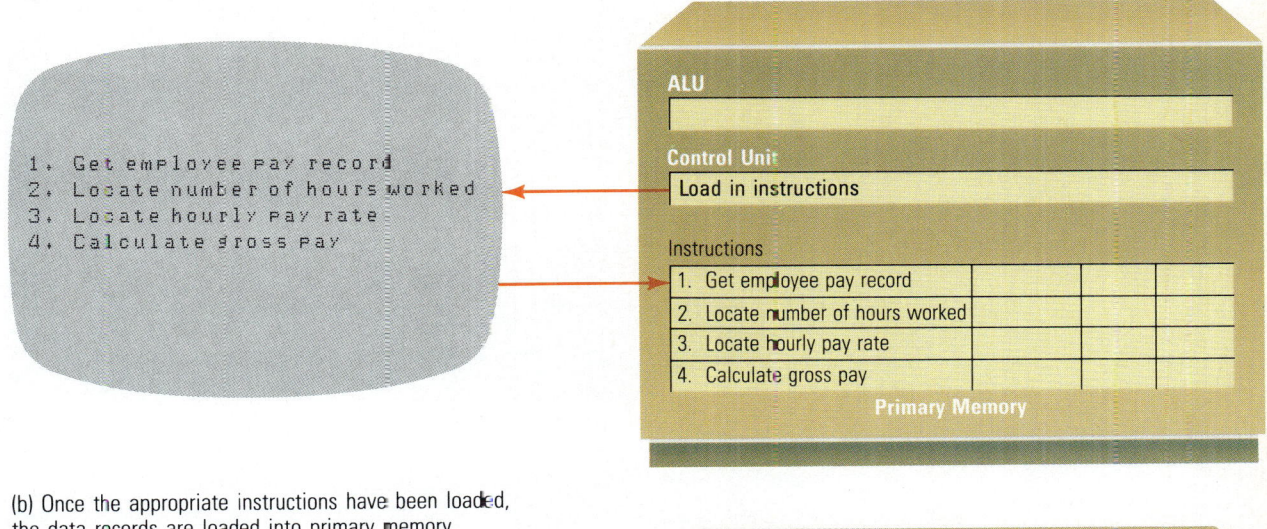

(b) Once the appropriate instructions have been loaded, the data records are loaded into primary memory.

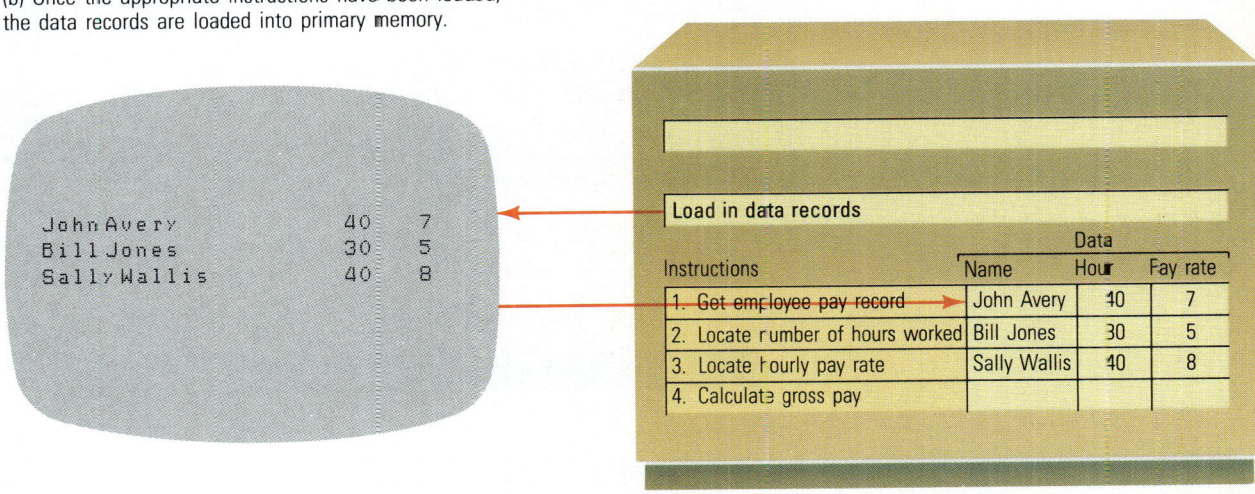

In order to see the results of computer processing, the solution must be displayed by means of an output device (printer or video display terminal).

CODING DATA FOR COMPUTER USE

Although computers are very complex electronic devices, they work on a very simple principle. Data can be represented by two states. For example, an electrical current is either flowing or not flowing; a particle is either magnetized or it isn't; a voltage is either high or low. These two "on/

EXHIBIT 3.4
Process first instruction: "Get Employee Pay Record."

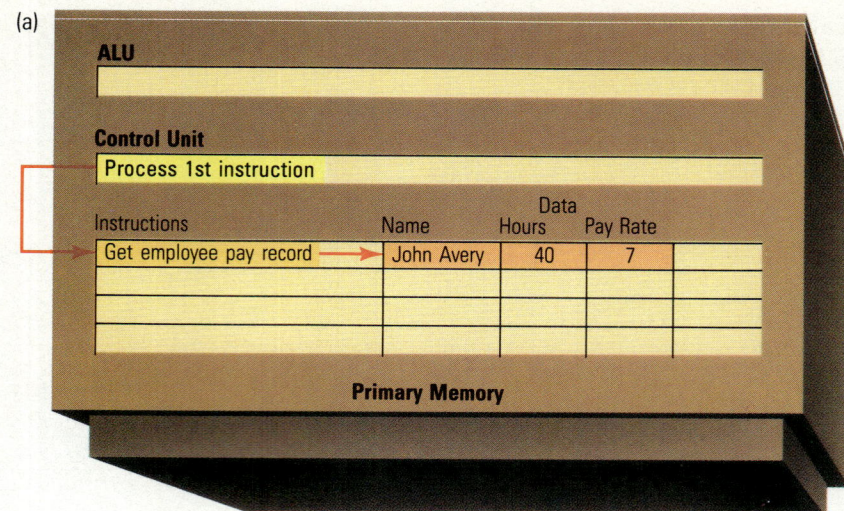

Process second instruction: "Locate Number of Hours Worked."

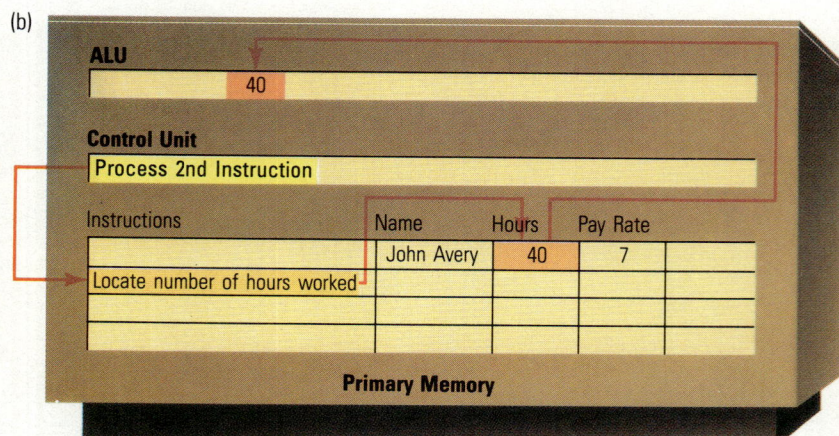

Process third instruction: "Locate Hourly Pay Rate."

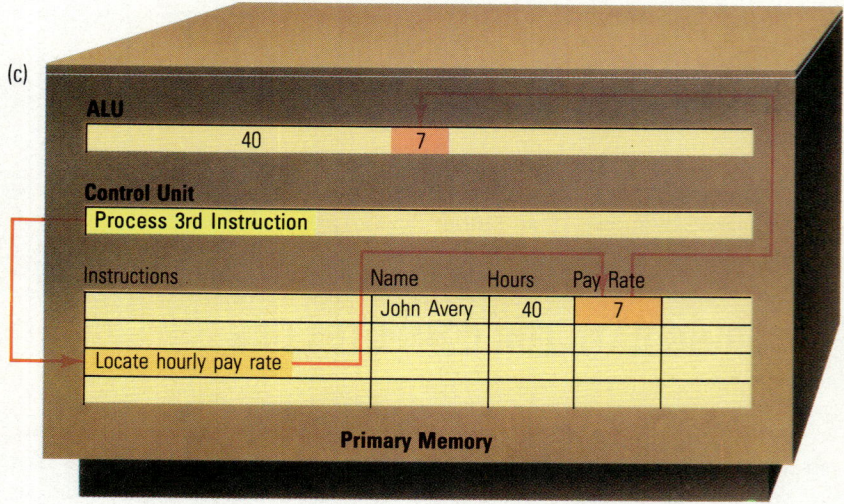

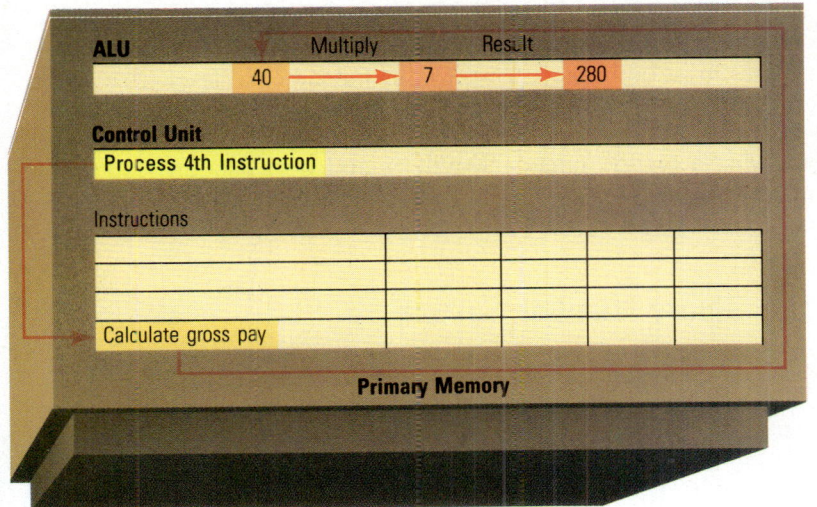

(d) Process fourth instruction: "Calculate Gross Pay."

(e) Start sequence over.

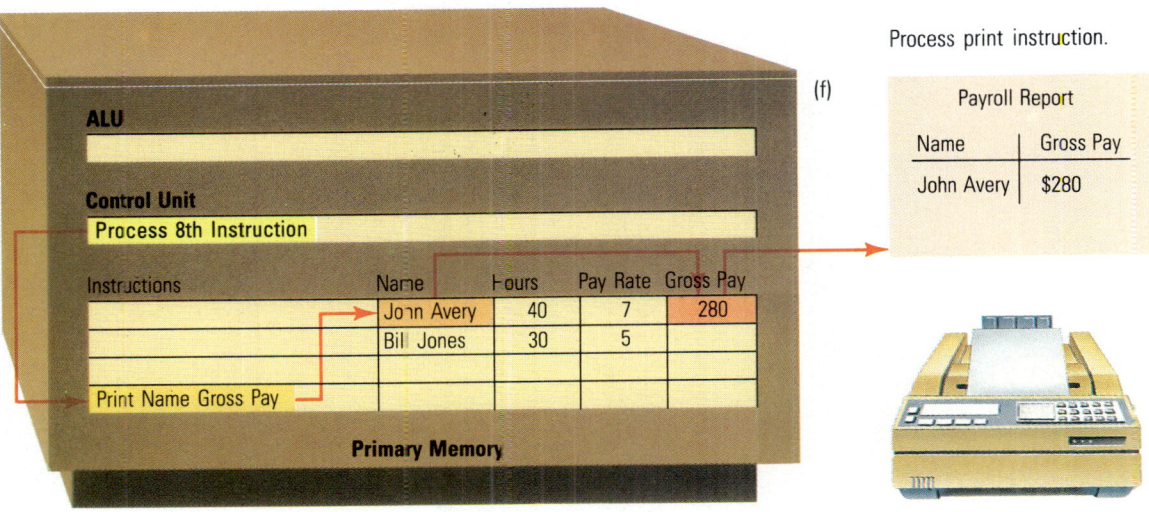

(f) Process print instruction.

Coding Data for Computer Use

off" or "high/low" states are the basis for everything the computer does. Thus all computer problems such as payroll calculations, word processing, or graphics must be broken down to this fundamental level. That is, all data, program instructions, and arithmetic-logic operations must be represented in the binary system of 1s and 0s. To see how this works, let's discuss what a binary number system is, and how data are coded for computer use.

The Binary Number System

A **number system** is simply a way of representing numbers. The number system we commonly use is the base 10, or decimal, system. In base 10, there are 10 symbols 0 through 9. Numbers higher than 9 are represented through the use of place values. Each place value is represented by a digit. For example, the number 185 is made up of three digits and could also be represented as shown in Exhibit 3.5. In the notation 10^n, 10 represents base 10 and the exponent n indicates the place value. Any number with an exponent of zero equals 1. Because it is familiar, we usually don't bother to break each number down to its place values. This knowledge is useful, however, when dealing with number systems with bases other than 10.

In the binary, or base 2, system the symbols used are limited to 1 and 0, which correspond to the two-state nature of computer systems. Higher numbers are shown by using place values. Each place value is called a binary digit, or **bit.** A bit is the smallest piece of data. The binary number 10111001 would be equivalent to 185 in the decimal system.

EXHIBIT 3.5

In the binary, or base 2, system, the symbols used are limited to 1 and 0, which correspond to the two-state nature of computer systems.

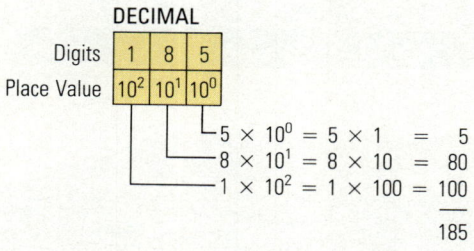

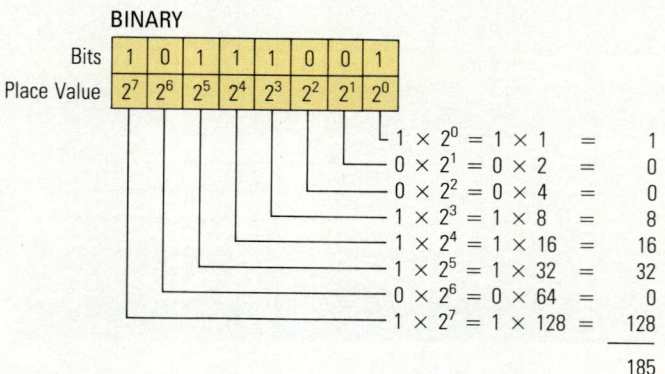

EXHIBIT 3.6
Selected ASCII-8 Binary Codes

Uppercase Alpha		Lowercase Alpha		Special Characters		Numeric	
A	10100001	a	11100001	!	01000001	0	01010000
B	10100010	b	11100010	"	01000010	1	01010001
C	10100011	c	11100011	#	01000011	2	01010010
D	10100100	d	11100100	$	01000100	3	01010011
E	10100101	e	11100101	%	01000101	4	01010100
F	10100110	f	11100110	&	01000110	5	01010101
G	10100111	g	11100111	(	01001000	6	01010110
H	10101000	h	11101000	)	01001001	7	01010111
I	10101001	i	11101001	*	01001010	8	01011000
J	10101010	j	11101010	+	01001011	9	01011001

Any decimal number can be converted to its binary equivalent and vice versa. It is also true that other number systems such as base 8 (octal) and base 16 (hexadecimal) are used with computer systems.

Data Encoding Schemes

How are alphabetic letters, such as *A* or *j*, or special characters, such as $ or !, represented in computer systems? What about numbers used as characters in ZIP codes, phone numbers, or mechanical part numbers? A modification to the pure binary number system has been developed for encoding alphabetic letters, special characters, and numbers.

Two popular coding schemes are the Extended Binary Coded Decimal Interchange Code (EBCDIC) and the American Standard Code for Information Interchange (ASCII). IBM developed and uses EBCDIC on large mainframe computers, as do several other computer manufacturers. ASCII was developed by the American Standards Institute, and it is used on almost all microcomputers, including IBMs. Software is available to translate from one code to the other.

For our purposes, the importance of these codes is that each letter, special character, and number is given a unique code that is made up of a fixed number of bits. For example, in the ASCII system, the digit 1 would be coded as 01010001, the uppercase letter *J* would be 10101010, and special character $ is 01000100 (see Exhibit 3.6).

The combination of bits that may be used to represent a character is called a **byte.** An eight-bit coding scheme allows up to 256 unique symbols to be defined. This is more than enough for representing all digits; lower- and uppercase letters; and a variety of special characters, graphic symbols, and data communication codes.

An important aspect of these coding schemes is the change they make in the way numbers are represented. Under normal circumstances, base 2 would require four bits—1111—to represent the decimal number 15. In a similar way, base 2 would require eight bits—10111001—to represent the decimal number 185. The problem is that base 2 requires a different number of bits to represent different decimal numbers. ASCII avoids this problem by converting each digit individually. Thus, the decimal number 15 would be encoded as two bytes of eight bits each, 01010001 (the 1) and 01010101 (the 5).

EXHIBIT 3.7
Many components, chips, boards, and peripherals are necessary to build a microcomputer.

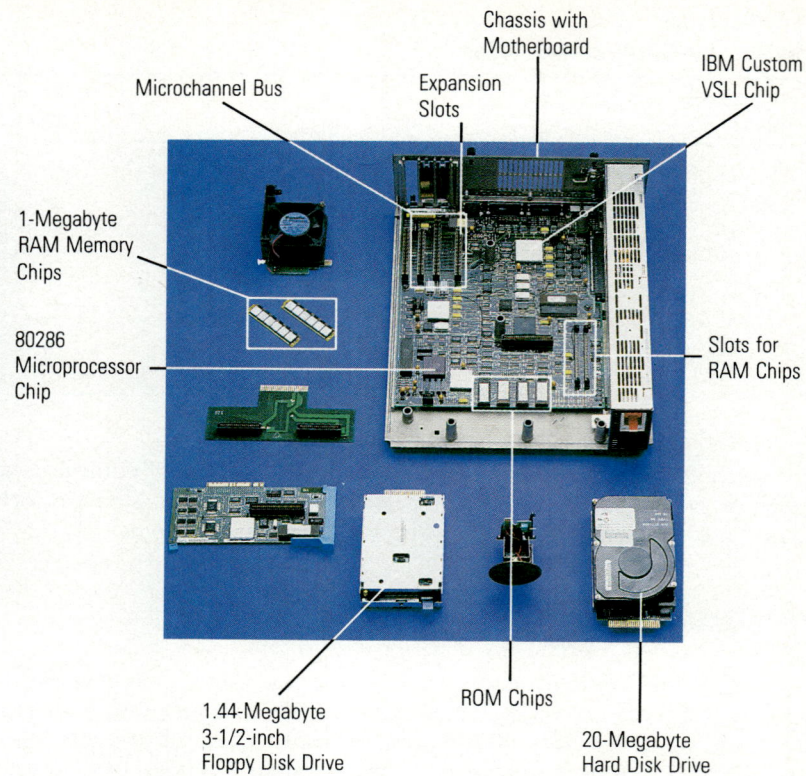

MICROCOMPUTER ARCHITECTURE

If we took the lid off of a computer, we might think we were looking at a science fiction city, with clusters of low buildings connected by superhighways. In fact, the engineers who design modern computers often play the role of architects in planning the layout and design of these computer "cities." The microcomputer system in Exhibit 3.7 is typical of what you might see the next time you go to a computer store or visit a computer lab; and what you have learned thus far has given you a good foundation for understanding what it all means.

Semiconductor Chip Technology

The basic building blocks of this computer system are semiconductor chips. These chips are composed of anywhere from several thousand to hundreds of thousands of transistors.

Transistors are electronic components that function as semiconductors. Solid materials, such as copper or silver, can serve as conductors, meaning they will always transmit electricity. Other solid materials, such as plastic or rubber, will never transmit electricity, and are classified as insulators. A transistor is made up of silicon (a product of sand, which acts as an insulator or nonconducting material) that has been injected with small amounts of conducting materials. The result is a **semiconductor,** a device that can be made to serve as a conductor or as an insulator, depending on conditions. Thus, a transistor can be made to represent a 1 (conductor) or a 0 (insulator). The transistor is highly reliable, requires little power, and can be manufactured very inexpensively. In addition, unlike vacuum tubes, which have to have air-conditioned environments in order to function, transistors give off very little heat.

Individual transistors can be combined to encode and store information, or they can be used to carry out arithmetic or logic operations. Semiconductor chips are used for the CPU, for primary memory, and for the interface devices between various hardware components. **Interface devices** are used to coordinate the flow of electrical signals between two hardware units.

As shown in Exhibit 3.7, a collection of chips is mounted on printed circuit boards to perform particular functions, such as connecting a printer or disk drive to a microcomputer. The largest circuit board, called the **motherboard,** generally contains the central processing unit. Other boards are used to adapt the microcomputer to a particular user's needs. Add-on boards for increasing primary memory or connecting a graphics monitor can be plugged into **expansion slots,** built-in brackets for holding additional circuit boards. With this overview, let's study the major parts in more detail.

Primary Memory Chips

In explaining how the computer could be used to process employee gross pay, we saw the importance of using primary memory as a storage area. The two main types of memory chips used in primary memory are called RAM and ROM.

RAM stands for **Random Access Memory,** which means that instructions or data can be written into this form of primary memory as needed. These instructions or data can also be read out of memory as needed and transferred to the CPU for processing. Thus, RAM is sometimes referred to as **read/write memory.**

On the other hand, **Read Only Memory,** or **ROM,** can only be used to read data or instructions that have been permanently loaded onto the chip. Nothing can be written into this memory by the computer user. It is common, for example, to put a software language, such as BASIC, in ROM. This makes the language readily available to translate programming instructions and still protects it from users who might accidentally order the computer to write over this valuable information. Software that is stored in ROM hardware is called **firmware.**

RAM primary memory is used for temporarily storing a user's program instructions and data. A programmer using a high-level language, such as BASIC or COBOL, can refer to data as "hours" or "pay rate" and not be concerned with knowing exactly where data are physically stored within primary memory. Instead, the control unit will handle the task of finding that information.

To do this, the control unit maintains a map of primary memory in much the way that streets are mapped. As shown in Exhibit 3.8, both maps and memory chips are made of grids formed by the intersection of horizontal and vertical lines. Each intersection is assigned a set of coordi-

EXHIBIT 3.8
Primary memory is mapped in a way analogous to street maps. Horizontal and vertical coordinates are used to directly find a specific location. For RAM chips, these would be memory addresses, which contain data or instructions.

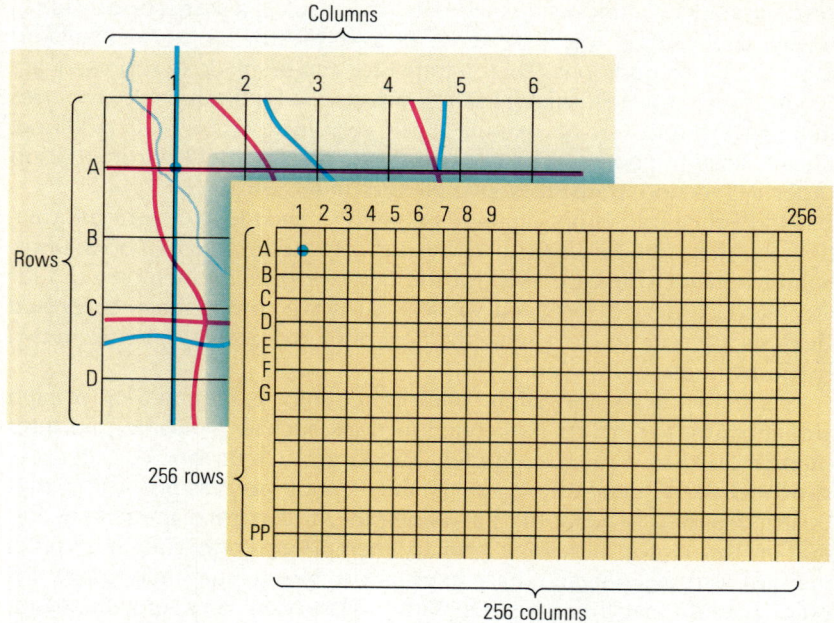

nates. If you look up the entry South Street in the map index, for example, its coordintes would be A1. To find this location, you would look down the left side of the map until you located sector A. Then you would proceed horizontally until you reached sector 1. Primary memory addressing works in a similar fashion. Assume, for example, that our computer has 64K of primary memory. **K,** or **kilo,** is an abbreviation for kilobyte, or 2^{10}, or 1024 bytes. A 64K memory would be arranged in a grid of 256 rows by 256 columns. Each address, or intersection on this grid, could be found by using two coordinates, one for the particular row and one for the particular column.

In computers that have larger amounts of primary memory, the RAM chips are arranged in banks, and the bank number is added to the address. This is similar to using a set of maps to represent a large area. For example, the map for a large city might give the address of South Street as page 17, coordinates A1.

The major disadvantage of the type of RAM memory chips most commonly used today is that whenever electric power is turned off, the contents of RAM are lost. This is known as **volatile** RAM. To keep this from happening accidentally during temporary power outages, a backup power supply must be used. ROM uses a different storage technology which is nonvolatile and is not affected by power problems.

ROM's major advantage—its ability to protect valuable information by storing it permanently—is also a disadvantage when that information needs to be changed. However, ROM chips have been developed that can be modified. Ultraviolet light is used to erase information stored on the chips. These types of chips are called **Erasable Programmable ROM,** or **EPROM.** They can be recognized by the clear glass window built into the chip package to absorb the ultraviolet light. To change the EPROM, it must be removed from the computer. After the chip is cleared, it can be reprogrammed.

A more recent advancement has been the **EEPROM,** the **Electrically Erasable Programmable ROM.** This chip can be used for applications that require an occasional updating of the program or data being stored. The big advantage of EEPROM chips is that their contents can be changed without removing them from the computer. Rather, electrical signals can be sent to the chip, and changes can be made on a byte-by-byte basis. EEPROMs are being used to hold price lists in **point-of-sale terminals,** the electronic cash registers used in many stores. EEPROMs can be updated on a selective basis by sending signals over telephone lines. Their disadvantage is that they cost three to four times more than regular ROM chips. Exhibit 3.9 shows some of the chips currently used in primary memory.

Microprocessor Chips

We have seen that the key element of the computer is the central processor unit. A CPU that has been implemented on a single silicon chip is called a **microprocessor.** This chip would contain at least the control unit and the arithmetic-logic unit. In more advanced designs, the chip could also include RAM, ROM, and other support devices.

Microprocessor chips use many different internal designs, and the chips vary in appearance and capability. For example, microprocessors differ in the type of transistor technology used, the range of instructions they are capable of executing, the speed of their machine cycles, and their physical packaging. The most popular microprocessors are MOS Technology from Zilog, INTEL, and Motorola. As shown in Exhibit 3.10, the Apple IIe uses the 6502; the IBM PC uses the 8088; and Apple Macintosh uses the 68000. Examples of the newest generation of microprocessor chips from INTEL are the 80286 and the 80386, which are used in the IBM Personal System/2 microcomputers. The Motorola 68020 chip is used in the Apple Macintosh SE.

When you visit the computer store or read ads in your local newspaper, you will often see microcomputers referred to as using 8-, 16-, or 32-bit processors. "Eight-bit" is a measure of a computer's dataword length. **Dataword length** refers to the number of bits of data that can be retrieved from memory each machine cycle. In a computer with an 8-bit microprocessor chip, 8 bits, or 1 byte, would be retrieved or processed each machine cycle. Each byte would contain one character, such as a $ or 4 or c. An 8-bit machine would therefore require four machine cycles to fetch four characters. A 32-bit machine could perform this same task in a single cycle. Thus, dataword length is an important indicator of a computer's power, somewhat akin to the way horsepower is an overall indication of the power of a car's engine.

In this simple comparison, it is important to stress first that the 8-bit processor can do any job the 32-bit processor can but at a much slower rate. This slower rate may be unacceptable for certain time-dependent applications, however. Second, computers with 32-bit processors are faster

EXHIBIT 3.9
Typical Microelectronic Chips Used in Computer Systems

Microcomputer Architecture

EXHIBIT 3.10
Popular Microprocessor Chips
The 68000 computer chip shown here contains 70,000 transistors.

Microprocessor Chip	Manufacturer	Dataword Length	I/O Bus Width	Microcomputers Using This Chip
6502	MOS Technology	8	8	Apple IIe Atari 800 Commodore 64
Z-80A	Zilog	8	8	Radio Shack TRS-80 Osborne 1
8088	INTEL	16	8	IBM PC/XT COMPAQ Portable HP 150 (touch screen)
80286	INTEL	16	16	IBM PC/AT AT&T PC 6300 Plus IBM Personal System/2 Model 50
68000	Motorola	32	16	Apple Macintosh Plus
80386	INTEL	32	32	COMPAQ DeskPro 386 IBM Personal System/2 Model 80
68020	Motorola	32	32	Apple Macintosh SE Sun Microcomputer

than computers with 16-bit processors, but not twice as fast. Many other variables affect overall computer speed. Third, 32-bit processors are much more complex to design and build than 8- or 16-bit chips, and they cost more.

Support Units

To perform its tasks, the control unit needs the support of a variety of devices. One support device is a **clock,** which plays an important part in the computer's performance. Each event in a computer needs to be sequenced, and many things need to go on simultaneously. To orchestrate this, the control unit needs to set a certain beat. This beat is established by the timing signal of the clock and is measured in Mega-Hertz, or millions of cycles per second. Typical microcomputer clocks are 5, 8, or 16 MHz. Therefore, with an 8 MHz clock, events could be sequenced 8 million times per second!

If you looked inside a microcomputer, you could see sets of tiny lines connecting the various chips. These electronic highways, called **buses,** are used to send electrical signals between functional units. Some microcomputers contain one main bus for all internal communication, while other systems use separate buses for control, for address, and for data communication.

The control unit also needs the support of interface devices to enter data by means of a keyboard or joystick or to display data from the computer on a peripheral device, such as a printer, disk drive, or video monitor. Frequently, a separate interface device is required for each input and output device. Interface devices are needed for two reasons. First, there are often tremendous differences in the rates at which the processor, primary memory, and peripherals can transfer data. The interface device adjusts these rates so that various devices can communicate. Second, not every equipment vendor uses the same standards for electronic voltage levels, and the physical connections may even differ. In addition, vendors may use different methods for encoding data. This is especially true when a computer system is made up of equipment from different vendors, as is so common with microcomputers. Interface units overcome these obstacles.

Summary

To process information, a computer needs step-by-step instructions that lead to the same result every time. Called *algorithms,* they are used as the basis for computer programs.

The computer processor unit is made up of a CPU and primary memory. The *CPU* contains the arithmetic-logic unit (ALU) and a control unit. *Primary memory* is used to hold data and program instructions.

A *number system* is simply a way of representing numbers. The number system we commonly use is the base 10, or decimal, system. In the binary, or base 2, the symbols used are limited to 1 and 0, which correspond to the binary nature of computer systems. Higher numbers are shown by using place values. Each place value is called a binary digit, or *bit.*

A modification to the pure binary number system has been developed for encoding alphabetic letters, special characters, and numbers. Microcomputers use the ASCII coding scheme. The combination of bits referring to a complete character is called a *byte.*

A basic building block of modern computer circuitry is the semiconductor chip. A *semiconductor* is a solid-state device that can be made to conduct electricity under certain conditions and act as an insulator inhibiting electrical flow at other times. Semiconductor chips are used for the CPU, for primary memory, and for interface devices. *Interface devices* are used to coordinate the flow of electrical signals between two hardware units.

Primary memory chips are designed as RAM or ROM. *RAM* stands for *Random Access Memory* and is sometimes referred to as *read/write memory.* The type of RAM chips most commonly used today are *volatile,* meaning that the memory contents will be lost when the electrical power is turned off.

ROM, or *Read Only Memory,* can only be used to read permanently loaded instructions or data. Software that is stored in ROM hardware is called *firmware.* ROM uses storage technology that is nonvolatile and, thus, is not affected by loss of power.

Erasable Programmable ROM or *EPROM* chips have been developed in which ultraviolet light can be used to erase the information stored on the chip. *EEPROM* or *Electrically Erasable Programmable ROM* chips can be used in situations where selected bytes of information need to be changed electronically.

A CPU that has been implemented on a single silicon chip is called a *microprocessor.* Microprocessor chips use many different internal designs, and the chips vary in appearance and capability. One of the specific ways in which they vary is in *dataword length.*

Several devices are used to support the microprocessor. One is the *clock* used by the control unit to establish the precise timing for the sequencing of computer events. *Buses* are electronic highways that are used to send electrical signals between functional units.

Review Questions

1. How do computer algorithms differ from the general instructions we use in everyday life?

2. What is the CPU? What are its major components? Where is the CPU housed?

3. Briefly describe the components and functions of the control unit.

4. Briefly explain the binary system and describe its role in the operation of the computer. Convert 01000110 (binary) to its decimal equivalent.

5. How can letters, special characters, and numbers be encoded into binary code?

6. What is a semiconductor? Why is it important to the operation of a computer?

7. Compare RAM/ROM memory.

8. What is meant by the term *volatile?* How can volatility be overcome in RAM?

9. What is a microprocessor? How is the computer's microprocessor related to its power?

10. What are interface devices? Why are they needed?

CHAPTER 4 ■ Input, Output, and Secondary Storage

COMPUTER INPUT DEVICES
Keyboard
Alternatives to the Keyboard

COMPUTER OUTPUT DEVICES
Visual Display
Print

SECONDARY STORAGE DEVICES
Magnetic Disks
Optical Disks
Cartridge and Cassette Tapes

SUMMARY

REVIEW QUESTIONS

The foundation of computer processing is data. Data are so important to the basic operations of organizations that many managers now regard data as a corporate asset in the same way that money, buildings, and people are considered to be assets. Accessing, organizing, updating, and checking data are, therefore, essential and frequently performed tasks. In this chapter, we will concentrate on the fundamental devices and techniques used to collect data, enter them into a computer system for further processing, and display the results.

You will learn to do the following:

1. Explain the methods that have been used to automate the collection of data at their source.
2. Describe the way people presently communicate with computers, and understand how this is progressing to a more natural human approach.
3. Describe three different ways to classify computer output.
4. Use three primary factors to differentiate the dozen or so technologies used with printers.
5. Describe available magnetic disk technologies and compare their capabilities and limitations.
6. Identify the unique characteristics of optical disks.

COMPUTER INPUT DEVICES

People are able to deal with data in a wide variety of forms. Computers require data that have been coded in very specialized forms. In order to input data into a computer, people must translate that data into a form that the computer can understand. The **human-computer interface** refers to the basic problem that arises when people have to communicate with machines. What is best and most comfortable for an individual is not always the most efficient use of the machine.

When any technology is new, it is costly and awkward to use. Moreover, at the beginning, people are forced to adapt to the machine when they perform their tasks. As the technology reaches a certain level of

EXHIBIT 4.1
Variety of Keyboard Designs
Keyboard designs reflect the nature of users and their purposes. Shown here are keyboards used in graphics design (left) and bookkeeping (right).

EXHIBIT 4.2
The Dvorak Keyboard Layout

maturity, it can then be designed in a cost-effective manner to meet its users' needs more efficiently and conveniently.

For much of the history of computing, people have been limited to using some form of keyboard as the primary way to enter data or give commands to the computer. Alternative ways, including touchscreens, "mice," and voice, have emerged as more natural human interactions with the computer.

Keyboard

Keyboard designs reflect the nature of users and their purposes. Note that, in the keyboards shown in Exhibit 4.1, there are significant differences in the number, placement, and function of the keys.

The main body of the keyboards shown in Exhibit 4.1 is very similar to the keyboard arrangement of a standard typewriter. The history of the **QWERTY** keyboard goes back to the early days of the typewriter, in the late 1800s. To keep the closely spaced mechanical arms from tangling, the keyboard was designed so that the arms for frequently typed characters would be far apart.

Since computer systems use electronic keyboards, it would seem that the keyboard should be rearranged to increase productivity rather than continue the tradition of the early mechanical typewriters. An alternate keyboard arrangement has been proposed by **Dvorak** (see Exhibit 4.2). His philosophy is that people can increase their typing speeds if the most frequently used keys were put in the home row and arranged to make better use of both hands. The home row includes the vowels under the fingertips of the left hand and the most common consonants under the fingertips of the right hand.

Computer Input Devices

Studies have shown increased productivity in typing speeds of between 10 and 50 percent over standard keyboards. Many computer manufacturers now offer Dvorak keyboards. The chances that his approach will displace the QWERTY keyboard seem limited, however. First, it would require retraining millions of people; second, alphabetic letters are really only a small part of computer input; and third, keystroke speed is less important than having a keyboard that is familiar and easy to use.

Until ten years ago, the standard keyboard was sufficient for keying in data or entering programming instructions in various computer languages. However, as computer systems became more interactive, ordinary users, not computer experts, needed to be able to select functions from a menu. What was needed was an enhanced keyboard to simplify word processing, spreadsheet analysis, and data queries.

A **numeric keypad,** a set of numeric keys similar to those on a calculator keyboard, was added to the regular typewriter keyboard. These keys allowed faster entry of numeric data. (Recall that, on a standard typewriter keyboard, numbers are in the top row.) **Arrow keys** were added to facilitate the movement of the cursor. **Function keys** were added to provide a way to command certain common tasks in one step, rather than making several keystrokes to accomplish the same thing. For example, a function key could be defined for activities such as HELP, PRINT, GRAPH, and END.

Even though the enhanced keyboard can provide more efficiency, it has several important drawbacks for people using the computer interactively. Many people who don't know how to type feel uncomfortable with a keyboard system. And there are those who don't want to use a keyboard—regardless of its convenient design. Some executives consider keyboarding to be clerical work and are concerned about loss of status. Using a keyboard is also slow and often requires you to split your attention between the screen and the keyboard to find special keys.

Alternatives to the Keyboard

There are several alternatives to the keyboard that allow a user to point to options or functions on the screen. Instead of actual function keys to press, the screen will display boxes that contain the names of functions or a menu of options. Selections are made by touching a light pen to a specific area on the screen. Touching the screen at a particular location with the light pen causes a change in electrical potential, which signals the computer to perform specific actions. Another method allows the user to interact with the computer through the touch of a finger (see Exhibit 4.3).

In these different methods for selecting functions or moving data to different locations on the screen, the functions have been specified in words such as LOAD, DISPLAY, and EXIT. The next advancement for making the human-computer interface more natural is the use of **icons.** These are graphic symbols for functions. There are symbols for new document creation, application tools, and documents in computer storage.

In 1984, Apple introduced several microcomputers. The one having the greatest impact is the Macintosh, which uses the icon approach and is priced around $2000. In its first year, Macintosh sales were $500 million. The Macintosh is being used in small, medium, and large organizations. One of the largest single purchases was by the University of Texas at

EXHIBIT 4.3
With the Hewlett-Packard Touchscreen, a user can interact with the computer simply by touching a fingertip to the screen.

Austin, which bought 13,000 Macintosh microcomputers for educational and administrative uses.

Apple's concept in developing the Macintosh was to make the screen layout resemble a desktop and to allow the user to function as he or she normally would at a desk. That is, the user would select documents from the file folders, use a calculator to do arithmetic, write letters and file them, and throw away waste in the trash can.

With the Macintosh, the user selects functions by moving the cursor over the icon. The movement of the cursor is controlled with a hand-sized box called a **mouse.** As the mouse moves around the desktop, the cursor moves accordingly on the screen. For example, if the mouse moves to the left, the cursor moves to the left on the screen. To select an item, the user simply positions the cursor on it and pushes the button on the top of the mouse (see Exhibit 4.4).

One of the newer technologies for automating data entry is voice recognition. In **voice recognition** systems, a microphone converts the spoken word into electrical signals. The signal patterns are processed to extract a set of identifying features, which are then compared to a set of voice templates stored in machine memory. The templates form the vocabulary of words the machine can recognize.

EXHIBIT 4.4
The Icon Interface
Apple's Macintosh screen layout resembles a desktop, complete with calculator and file folders. Moving the mouse around a desktop causes the cursor to move accordingly on the screen.

Computer Input Devices

A technological obstacle to voice recognition devices is the consistency of the spoken word and its relationship to the stored template. An individual will say the same word differently at different times, depending on his or her energy level, mood, and health. Both colds and allergies, for example, can change voice quality. Even more variability occurs when different speakers say the same word. Physiology, age, sex, and geographic origin all contribute to this variation.

To reduce variability, speaker-dependent voice recognition systems have been developed. In this case, a specific individual "trains" the voice recognition machine by speaking a word a number of times. The resulting signal patterns are averaged, and a template is developed for the word. This process is repeated for each word that is to be recognized.

Texas Instruments has a voice recognition unit that has been used successfully with, for example, spreadsheet applications on microcomputers. This type of application is not constrained by speaker-dependent voice systems, which can recognize only a limited number of word sounds. A spreadsheet program would generally be used by one executive on his or her personal computer. The individual functions are specified by

EXHIBIT 4.5
The Raster Scan Process
(a) A beam of electrons sweeps across a CRT horizontally in raster scan. (b) Pixels are selectively turned on to form characters. (c) Red, green, and blue are the three primary colors that are "electronically" mixed to produce other colors. A spectrum of color is generated by turning on different combinations of the RGB electron guns on a triad of phosphor dots.

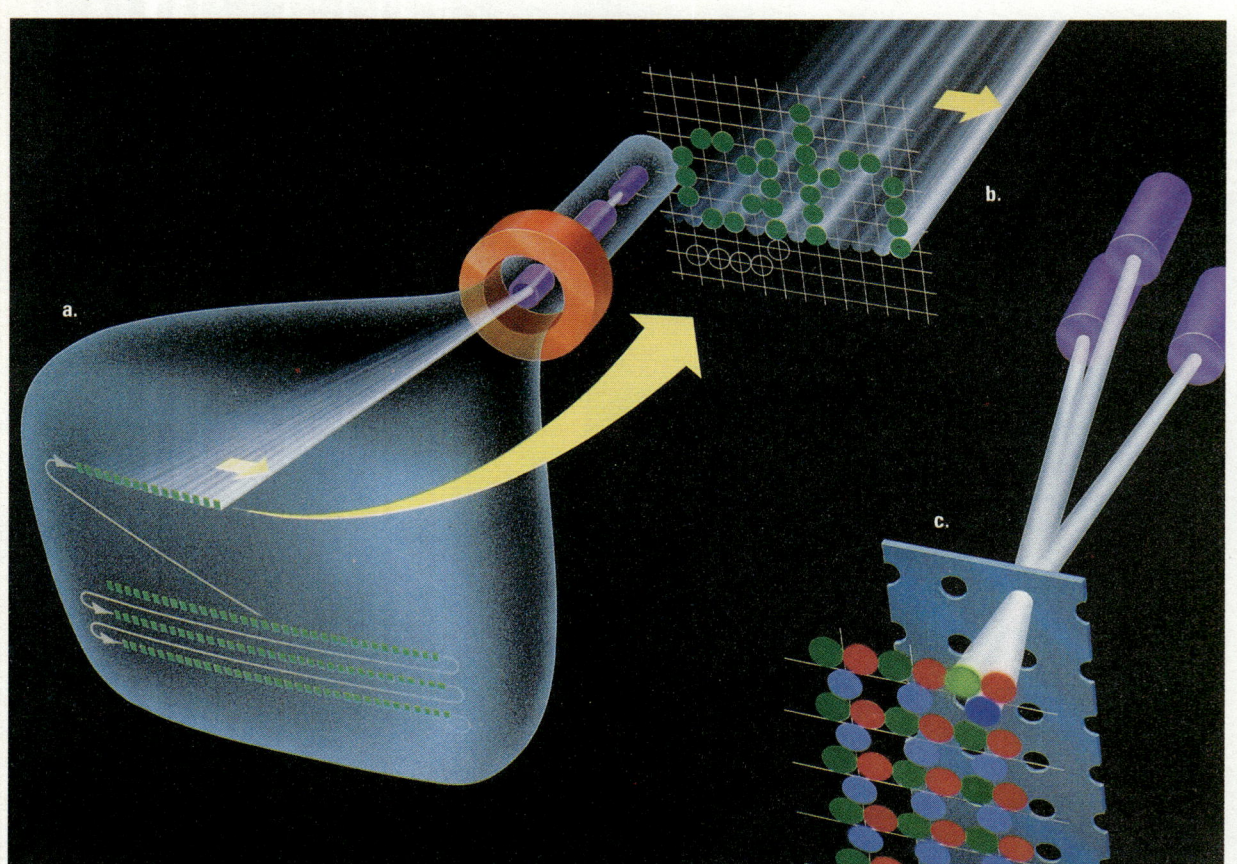

Reprinted with permission, *High Technology* Magazine, February, 1985. Copyright © 1985 by Infotechnology Publishing Corporation, 214 Lewis Wharf, Boston, MA 02110.

speaking one or two words, such as *worksheet, column width, move, copy,* and *add*. Numbers would be communicated in the same manner.

We have discussed the keyboard; pointing devices that are used with text, or icons; and voice input as ways of interacting with the computer. The dominant technology is the keyboard, and most experts believe it will continue to be for the foreseeable future because the pointing devices don't do away with the keyboard; they are a complementary input means, primarily useful for selecting functions. Any applications requiring substantial data or text input can be done faster with the keyboard.

COMPUTER OUTPUT DEVICES

Useless. That's what even the most sophisticated computer would be if it couldn't present data in a form that people could understand. For some users, printed output is adequate, while others prefer graphic displays, or even voice output. Historically, printed output was the only means for showing the results of computer processing. Though paper remains the primary medium for computer output, a variety of alternative means to communicate information has emerged.

Computer output can be classified in several different ways. **Hard copy** output, such as paper printouts, provides the user with a permanent record. **Soft copy** output, such as the visual display on a microcomputer screen or computer voice output, provides a temporary record. Both hard and soft copy output can be understood by human users, whereas the electronic data stored on magnetic tape or disk are computer-readable only. Information presented in the form of letters, numbers, and special characters is termed **alphanumeric.** In contrast, **graphics** are pictures or graphs depicting information. In the next section, we will discuss the technology and capabilities of visual display and print.

Visual Display

Visual display of information is one of the most effective means for communicating the results of computer processing. The primary technologies for producing and displaying the images on the monitor screen are the cathode-ray tube and the flat-panel.

Cathode-Ray Tube Displays

For many years, the primary technology used to create a visual image on the terminal screen has been the **cathode-ray tube (CRT).** In fact, this technology has become so dominant that computer terminals are often called CRTs. CRTs, like television picture tubes, electronically paint characters on a screen. Inside the tube, an electronic "gun" shoots a beam of electrons on the back of the phosphor-coated glass face of the screen. The movement of the beam creates images on the face of the screen.

In a CRT using **raster scan,** a beam of electrons sweeps back and forth horizontally across the screen. As the beam moves across the screen, the electrical current is increased or decreased to create brighter (on) or darker (off) points. These are **pixels,** or picture elements. This sequence is continued for each line of the screen (see Exhibit 4.5).

The color of the phosphor coating on the glass face of the screen determines whether the characters displayed are green, amber, or some other color. As the beam of electrons passes across the screen, the phosphors emit light instantaneously and then decay (go dark) quickly. This means that an image must be constantly refreshed. Typically, the whole screen is repainted at least thirty times per second. The advantage of the fast decay rate is that screen displays can be changed rapidly. The disadvantage is that, to the viewer's eye, the display may seem to flicker slightly. The intensity of the electron beam determines the brightness of the image on the screen. This is regulated by varying the voltage applied to the electron gun.

CRTs are used in monochrome and color monitors. **Monochrome monitors** display one color, such as green or amber, on a black background. Each pixel is represented by a green or amber phosphor dot. A single electron gun directs the beam to each dot (see Exhibit 4.6).

Color monitors use a triad, or trio, of dots to form a pixel. The three phosphor dots are red, green, and blue. In a **composite video monitor,** one electron gun is used to turn on the appropriate colors within each triad. In contrast, **RGB** (red, green, and blue) **monitors** use three electronic guns—one for each color. This results in sharper graphical images than are possible with composite video monitors because of the finer control allowed by using three electron beams.

Another major factor affecting display screens is the number of addressable locations on a screen that is being used. In a **bit-map,** or **dot-addressable display,** each individual pixel is addressable (see Exhibit 4.7). Only blocks of pixels can be addressed or manipulated in **character-addressable displays.** The major advantage of the character-addressable approach is that it requires much less memory capacity. The number of locations is specified by the number of characters that can be displayed on a row and the number of rows on the screen. Typically, CRT screens can display 80 characters per row and have 24 or 25 rows. **Resolution** is a measure of the number of pixels that can be addressed on the screen.

EXHIBIT 4.6
Monochrome Monitors

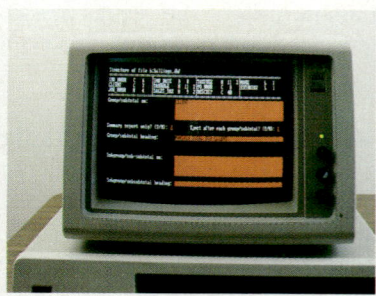

Flat-Panel Displays

A new technology is emerging to challenge the CRT as the primary means of displaying alphanumeric and graphical images. It is the flat-panel display. Plasma and liquid crystal are two of the primary technologies used with it.

The CRT has several disadvantages. One is that the screen-painting approach has a strobe light effect. The flicker causes many people who interact with a computer for hours at a time to develop eye fatigue. Second, the shooting of electrons against the phosphors causes radiation, as well as light, to be given off. Studies seem to indicate that the levels of radiation are too low to be dangerous, but many people are still concerned. Third, displays using CRTs have a large footprint, a reference to the amount of desk space occupied by the monitor. The culprit is the electronic gun. For a typical CRT with a 12-inch display screen, the gun measures approximately 6 inches long from front to back. To accommodate the gun, most CRTs are about 1 foot deep and 1 foot wide and weigh as much as a 12-inch TV. The flat-panel display, a possible successor to the CRT, does not have these disadvantages.

The flat-panel display shown in Exhibit 4.8 is a computer terminal using plasma technology. The display is only 3 inches thick, is lightweight, and has a resolution rivaling that of a photograph. Here is how the plasma display works. An ionized gas (plasma) is held between two glass plates. A set of horizontal wires is embedded in one of the glass plates, and a set of vertical wires is embedded in the other glass plate. These wires form a grid or matrix in which each intersection is a pixel. A particular pixel can be turned on by sending current through the appropriate horizontal and vertical wires. The current at the intersection excites the plasma—a neon-argon gas mixture—between the plates, and this produces orange light at that pixel. Flat-panel displays create a screen image by illuminating discrete dots to display alphanumeric data, graphics, and video images.

High resolution and steadiness of flat-panel displays yield high-quality results. CRTs using raster scan to refresh the screen sometimes produce images with a wavy quality. In contrast, plasma display images are stable, with each pixel emitting a steady glow until it is turned off. Though the plasma flat-panel display technology has many exciting advantages, the terminals cost significantly more than CRTs. This high price tag will slow

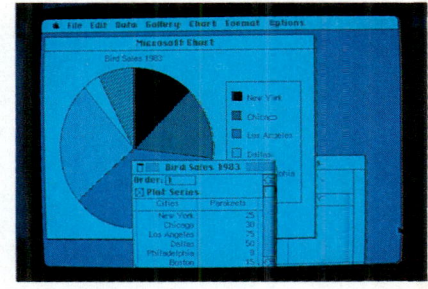

EXHIBIT 4.7
A Macintosh Bit-Map Screen
The Macintosh computer uses bit-map display and special software to provide pull-down windows, text, graphic displays, and icons for selecting functions.

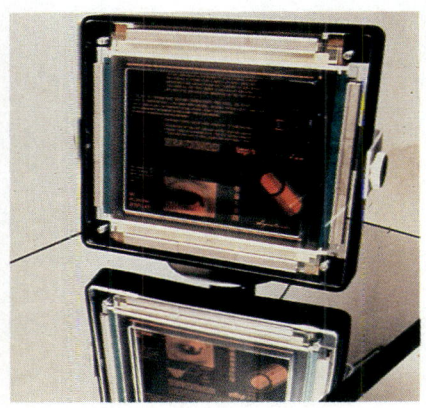

EXHIBIT 4.8
A Flat-Panel Display
Glowing neon-argon gas produces a high-resolution, flicker-free image.

Computer Output Devices

market penetration. This type of display requires a great deal of power and gives off a large amount of heat, which are further disadvantages.

To meet the needs of people who want to use their computers in the office, at home, and on business trips, the portable computer was developed. The initial entry was the Osborne 1, which used CRT technology to drive a 5-inch display screen. The complete computer was designed to fold up small enough to fit under an airplane seat. Companies such as COMPAQ took this concept one step further by developing a portable computer system with a larger, more workable 9-inch display screen. However, because these portables use the CRT technology, they are quite heavy, weighing around 20 to 30 pounds. Thus, they are more accurately described as "luggable."

Truly portable, lightweight computers with full-size screens became available with the introduction of Data General's DG/One. This briefcase-size computer weighs 10 pounds and has a flat-panel display using the liquid crystal display (LCD) technology (see Exhibit 4.9).

You may be familiar with LCD technology, as it is used in a variety of products, including pocket calculators and digital watches. A thin layer of liquid crystal molecules is put between two sheets of glass and separated into little squares. When a voltage is applied to the liquid crystal in an individual cell or square, the normally clear material will turn opaque and block light reflected from behind it. The result is a black square. The display screen is thus a pixel grid, which can be controlled so that characters can be shown by patterns of dots.

The major advantages of an LCD computer screen are that it doesn't give off radiation and it has no flicker. It also has a very low power requirement, so it can run off of a small battery pack for many hours before recharging is necessary.

One disadvantage of the LCD, however, has been the small screen display. Typically, this was a 40-character by 8-line display. The breakthrough with the DG/One allows a standard 12-inch screen with display dimensions of 80 characters by 24 rows, but the resolution and brightness of the LCD display for a standard-size screen are less than those of a CRT of

EXHIBIT 4.9
A Portable Computer
The Data General/One, introduced in 1984, had a full-size, flat-panel display using liquid crystal display (LCD) technology.

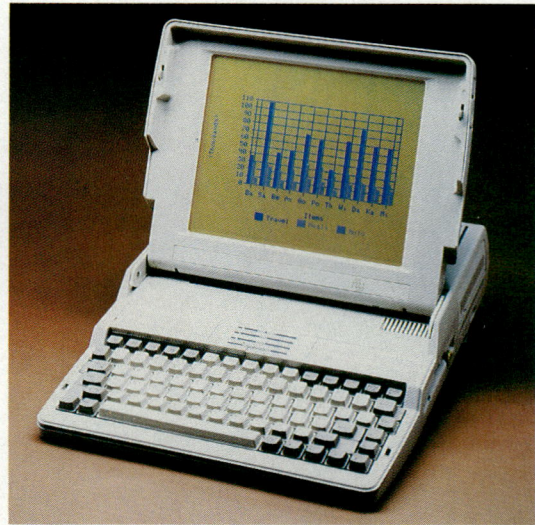

4 Input, Output, Secondary Storage

Character formation	Fully formed	Dot-matrix	Image
Character transfer	Impact		Nonimpact
Number of characters	Character		Page

EXHIBIT 4.10
Key Approaches to Printing Characters

comparable size. Another disadvantage is that the quality of the LCD picture is dependent on the ambient (surrounding) light. Under low light conditions, the screen is very hard to read. With proper lighting, the display is sharpest when viewed directly and loses resolution or crispness when viewed on an angle.

Print

Computer users need a form of output that not only can be read but can also serve as a permanent record of any transaction. The number and type of output forms used to communicate results will vary from situation to situation, of course, but paper has traditionally been the dominant form of output. In spite of all the talk about the concept of the "paperless office," it appears that paper will continue to be the major medium for communication documentation.

Historically, it is also true that alphanumeric data has been the primary information output. Thus, the computer printer, with its capability to print alphanumeric data on paper, has been the predominant means of generating hard copy output. More recently, the need for graphical displays has changed the type of printers that are in demand and has also encouraged the development of plotters.

In this first section, we will discuss the technology for computer printers that have been used primarily to print alphanumeric data. In the next section, printers and plotters used mainly for printing graphics will be described. Keep in mind that, generally, output devices that can print graphics can also print alphanumeric data. However, not all devices that print alphanumeric data can print high-quality graphics.

Alphanumeric Printers

The computer printer industry has not yet settled on a limited number of ways to print alphanumeric information. Rather, a dozen or so technologies are being used today. These technologies differ in three basic ways: the way in which characters are formed; the way in which characters are transferred to paper or another medium; and the number of characters that are printed at any one time (see Exhibit 4.10).

Character Formation. There are three methods for forming characters: fully formed, dot-matrix, and image. The old manual typewriters and the new electric ones both use the fully formed character approach. Both the striker arms on the manual style and the "golf ball" typing element on the electric model have permanently shaped, or fully formed, characters. The electric typewriter is more versatile because different type fonts can be used by changing the typing element.

EXHIBIT 4.11
Golf Ball, Daisy-Wheel, and Thimble Print Mechanisms

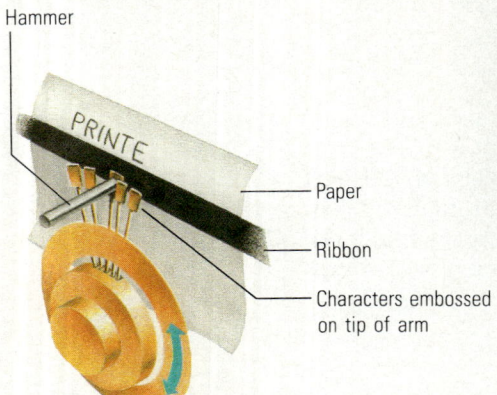

In computer printers, the fully formed character approach has been implemented by using either a **golf ball, daisy-wheel, thimble, band, belt,** or **chain** as the print mechanism (see Exhibit 4.11). In a daisy-wheel printer, each "petal" contains an embossed character. The wheel is rotated until the appropriate character is in place, and then a hammer presses the character against a ribbon, which transfers an impression onto the paper. A variation in which the petals appear to be folded back is called a thimble.

The dot-matrix approach has become the most widely used character formation method of computer printers. In dot-matrix printers, characters are formed by a pattern of dots. In a 5 × 7 dot matrix, the 5 refers to the number of horizontal dots and the 7 refers to the number of vertical dots. Selective pins are activated to form characters, as shown with the letter *T* in Exhibit 4.12.

The third way to form a character is by image. The dot-matrix approach uses a fixed block pattern of dots, such as 9 × 18 or 18 × 36, for each character. Image processing generates characters through a raster scan type of approach, in which selected dots are "turned on" on a line-by-line basis. When all lines have been scanned, the resulting image will show the characters in their appropriate positions. This method is used by laser printers, and we will discuss that particular technology later.

Character Transfer. Characters can be trasferred by either an impact or nonimpact method. The impact method of character transfer is widely used with computer printers. It works much like a typewriter, using an impression-making element to push a ribbon against paper. This transfers an ink impression in the color of the ribbon onto the paper. Daisy-wheel and thimble printers use this approach, as do belt, band, and chain printers. There is variation in whether the ribbon, paper, or fully formed character is struck first.

At one time, the impact method was limited to fully formed characters, but dot-matrix impact printers now make wide use of the impact method. Dot-matrix printers that form characters using columns of "dot hammers" are classified as impact printers.

The other major approach to character transfer is nonimpact. No physical hammering is used with this method. The character is transferred to the paper by means of heat, electrostatic charge, magnetism, or ink shot against selected parts of the paper. The nonimpact technique can be used with either the dot-matrix or image method of character formation. An application of this concept is shown with thermal and electrostatic dot-matrix printers. Each method forms characters on specially treated paper. Thermal printers use heated printheads to burn dots onto heat-sensitive paper. Electrostatic printers use electrically charged printheads to melt away dots in thin aluminum-coated paper.

Characters Printed at a Time. Most of the inexpensive printers print one character at a time. Thus, a line of text is generated as with a typewriter. Serial printers move the printhead from left to right, line by line. This is a relatively slow process, however. A modification used in many printers is **bidirectional printing,** or printing right to left and then left to right. This saves the time it takes the printhead to return from the end of one line to the beginning of the next one.

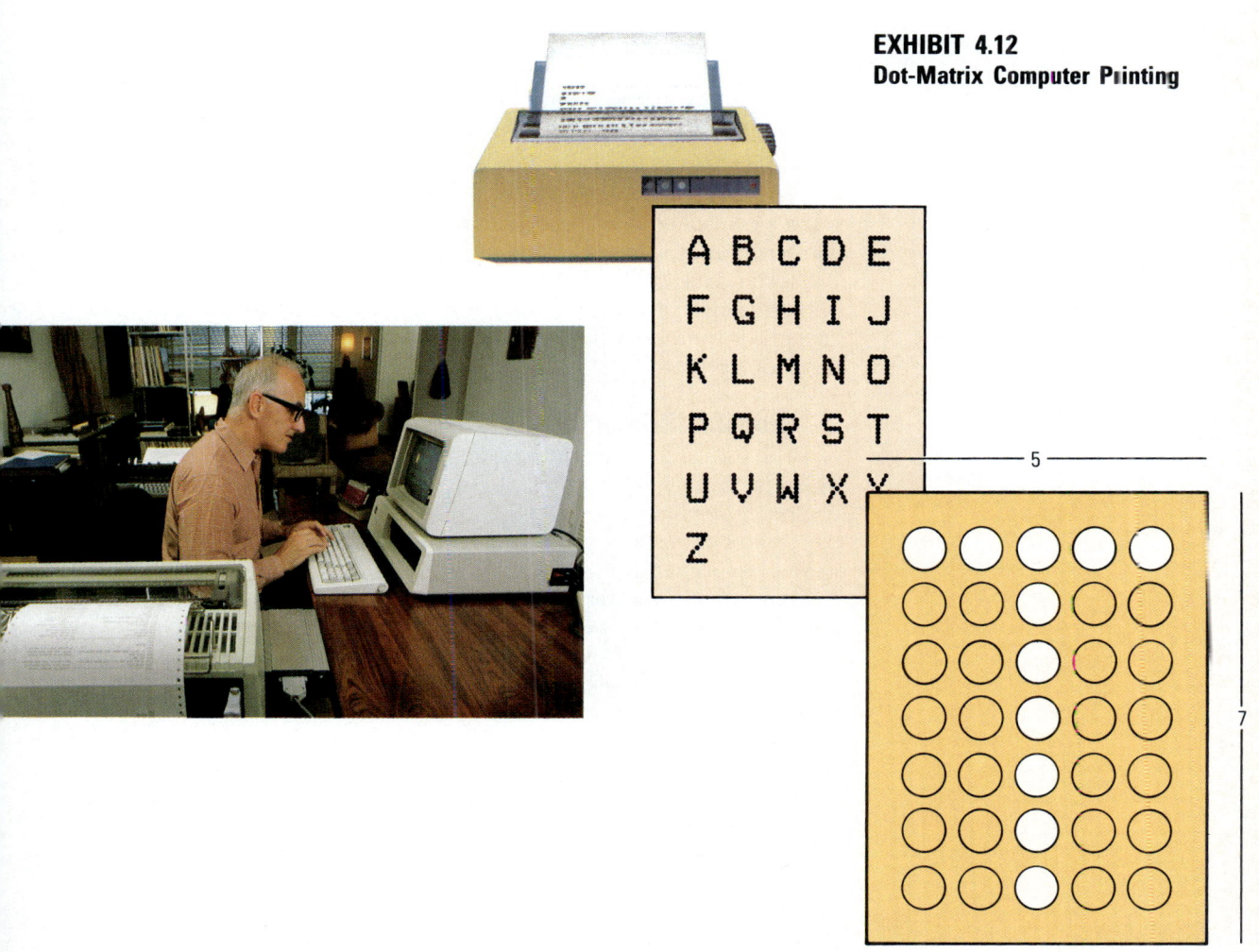

EXHIBIT 4.12
Dot-Matrix Computer Printing

Computer Output Devices

EXHIBIT 4.13
Ink-Jet Technology
Ink-jet printers using the drop-on-demand technology eject individual ink drops through a nozzle onto paper. Primary colors and black inks are used to produce high-resolution graphics.

EXHIBIT 4.14
Plotters
A plotter can produce high-resolution graphics at low cost. Computer plotters are used in a variety of applications.

The very-high-speed printers are page printers. Typical of this process is the electrophotographic approach used with laser printers, which use a combination of raster scan and xerographic copy machine technologies. The raster scan approach is used to trace an image of an entire page onto a photosensitive drum. The drum is rotated and the image, a pattern of charges, is transferred to a plain sheet of paper by attracting toner that is fused on by heat.

Graphics Printers and Plotters

The growing popularity of graphics terminals has been accompanied by an increasing need for hard copy of the graphics developed on the computer terminal. For a long time, the only option available was to use the printer to make a graphical representation. Thus, business graphics were first printed by plotting points using fully formed characters. For example, to show a trend line, a character was printed at specific points. The letter *P* could be used to represent profits and the letter *S* to represent sales. Some clever programmers developed quite impressive computer drawings of holiday greetings, calendars, and even centerfolds with patterns of characters such as *X*s and *O*s.

Dot-matrix printing improved on the quality of graphics that were possible with fully formed characters. The dot-matrix approach is used in multifunction dot-matrix impact printers, as well as in printers using nonimpact thermal and ink-jet technology. For example, low-cost text and graphics printers used with personal computers can print business graphics, such as bar graphs and pie charts.

Ink-jet technology is being used to generate higher-quality images. Fine-nozzle jets spray individual ink drops at the paper. By using multiple nozzles, several different colors of ink can be printed. This form of dot-matrix projection is useful for printing text and graphics. The nonimpact process is also used for printing on packages or odd-shaped objects. Exhibit 4.13 shows the excellent resolution possible with ink-jet technology. Flexibility in printing, color, and high resolution make this technology useful in a variety of areas, including engineering and business.

Very expensive laser printers offer the best quality in hard copy graphics. Because they make use of the raster scan method, higher resolution is possible. This form of image processing is so good that it is being used as the base technology for electronic publishing.

Plotters are output devices that are specialized to produce graphics. Plotters produce a picture made up of a series of straight lines. A pen plotter can only be programmed to move right, left, up, down, or diagonally. Curves are drawn as a series of very short lines. The quality of the outcome is a direct function of the fineness of the lines, the type of pen tips used, and the number of color pens available. This low-cost approach can give surprisingly high-resolution graphics (see Exhibit 4.14).

SECONDARY STORAGE DEVICES

The major function of secondary storage media is to hold data in a permanent form. To be processed, computer programs and data have to be loaded into primary memory; but the present primary memory technology has several major problems. One is that read/write primary memory, such as RAM, can only be used for temporary storage of information, since it is *volatile*. That is, when power to the computer is cut off, the information in RAM is lost. In contrast, secondary storage is *nonvolatile*. Tapes and disks use magnetic recording techniques that retain the data when the power is off.

A second problem is that primary memory has limited storage capacity. Often, the complete program and all data records needed cannot fit into primary memory at one time. This limitation can be overcome, in part, by special support software called an operating system, which can be used to bring in only the active portions of instructions and data records from secondary storage. This allows large programs and extensive data records to be run on smaller computer systems.

The medium that has come to dominate the secondary storage market is the magnetic disk. Another secondary storage device, the optical disk, is emerging as an important secondary storage medium. It is attractive because of its very large storage capacity and its ability to store high-quality video images. The optical disk will be discussed later in this chapter.

Magnetic Disks

There are two basic forms of magnetic disks—hard and floppy. **Hard disks** are rigid aluminum platters coated with a magnetic oxide. They come in a variety of physical sizes and have significantly different storage capacities. They can be further categorized in terms of being fixed or removable (see Exhibit 4.15). **Diskettes** (also called floppy disks) are made of a flexible Mylar plastic coated with magnetic oxide. These diskettes also come in several physical sizes, but all are designed to be removable.

EXHIBIT 4.15
Fixed and Removable Media
Removable media, such as floppy disks (right), allow almost unlimited storage capacity, as one set of data can be swapped for another. Fixed secondary storage media, such as hard disks (left), offer higher reliability and extensive storage capacity without operator intervention.

Before we consider the variety of disks available, let's see how they are designed to store and gain access to data. The disk itself is sometimes compared to a phonograph record, but there is a major difference. The disk has a series of invisible concentric circles called **tracks.** Note that this differs from a phonograph record, which has a single, visible groove that spirals toward the center of the record. Disk tracks are invisible, since they are simply composed of magnetically encoded data.

Along each track, data are encoded in the form of magnetic bit patterns. A read/write head is used to sense the magnetic direction of each bit or to change magnetic patterns in the appropriate place on a specific track. The magnetic bit pattern for the letter K, using an 8-bit ASCII code, is shown in Exhibit 4.16. To read or write data, the disk platter is mounted on a spindle, which rotates at a fixed speed.

The storage capacity of a disk is a function of the number of tracks per surface and the bit density (see Exhibit 4.17). The number of tracks per surface is influenced by the physical size of the disk and the technology used to record the data. Platter sizes are commonly either 5¼ or 3½ inches (see Exhibit 4.18). The number of tracks on a surface can range from 40 to 80.

Bit density is measured in terms of the number of bits per inch (bpi). The bpi measure is 2000 in diskette systems.

EXHIBIT 4.16
Encoding Data on a Magnetic Disk
Along each invisible concentric track, data are encoded in the form of magnetic bit patterns.

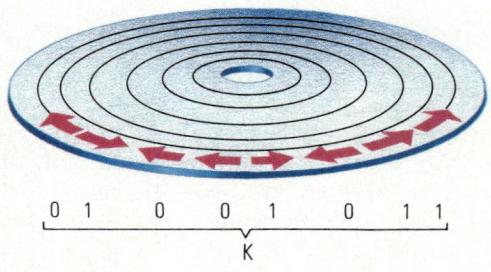

Overall, disk storage capacity ranges from less than 1 megabyte on the smaller diskette systems to over 100 megabytes on the newest hard disk systems. To read or write data, a read/write (r/w) head must be positioned over the appropriate track. An **actuator,** which contains the read/write head, swings in and out over the disk surface to locate the correct track. Once the r/w head is positioned, the needed data record is found by letting the disk rotate beneath the r/w head. Most disk drives allow data to be recorded on both sides of the diskette. To accomplish this, the drive contains two r/w heads, one for each side, or surface, of the diskette.

Each surface of a disk is logically divided into sectors (like slices of pie). Often, there are eight or more sectors on a surface. Data are then located by specifying the surface number, the sector, and the track number (see Exhibit 4.19).

The speed at which data can be found and retrieved is a function of access time. **Access time** is the amount of time it takes from the point of requesting data until the data are retrieved. With disks, access time is composed of seek, search, and data transfer time. **Seek time** is the time it takes to position the r/w head over the desired track. **Search time** is the time it takes for the requested data to rotate under the r/w head. This is directly related to the rpm of the disk drive.

Once located, how quickly can the data be transferred into primary memory? It depends on the **data transfer rate.** There is a significant difference in transfer rates between floppy and hard disk systems.

Hard Disks

The largest capacity magnetic disks have been the hard disk systems. To attain high storage capacities and quick access rates, very close tolerances are required between the r/w head and the surface of the disk. When the disk is at rest, the r/w head rests on the disk surface. As the disk starts to spin, the r/w head takes off like an airplane because of centrifugal force. The r/w head flies a fraction of an inch above the disk surface. Because the strength of the magnetic field diminishes quickly as vertical distance above the surface increases, the greatest storage capacities are gained when the head is as close as possible to the surface without touching it.

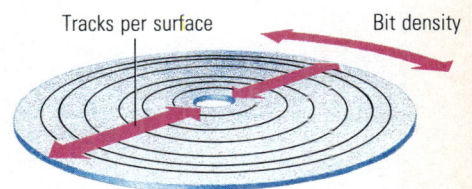

EXHIBIT 4.17
Disk Storage Capacity Factors
The storage capacity of a disk is a function of the number of tracks per surface and the bit density.

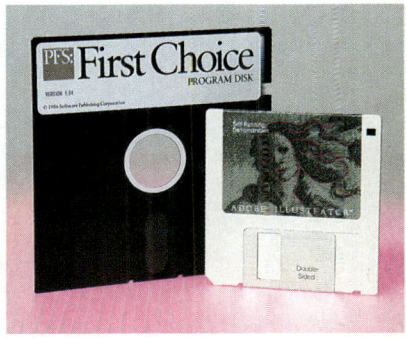

EXHIBIT 4.18
Diskettes come in a variety of sizes, including 5¼ and 3½ inches in diameter.

EXHIBIT 4.19
The disk surface is logically divided into sectors, or horizontal sections. Data are located by specifying surface number, sector, and track number.

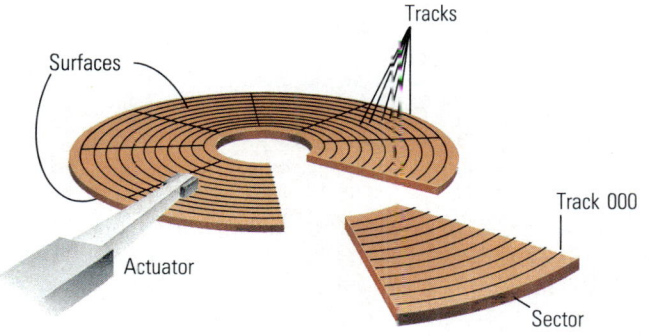

Secondary Storage Devices

EXHIBIT 4.20
Potential Causes of Disk Head Crashes

To attain high storage capacities and quick access rates, very close tolerances between the read/write head and the surface of the disk are necessary. Dust or a hair can cause the disk head to scratch the disk surface, resulting in the loss of data stored in those areas. Winchester technology helps prevent this by hermetically sealing the disk.

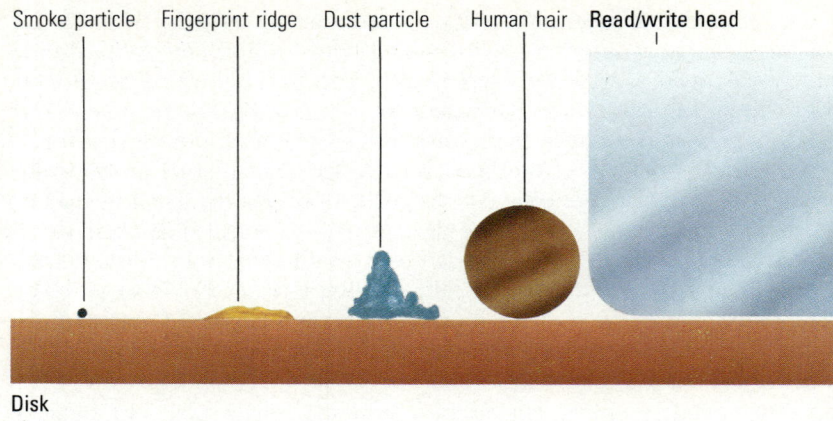

The tolerances are so close, any kind of dust or human hair can make the disk head crash (see Exhibit 4.20). A head crash causes the disk head to scratch the disk surface, resulting in loss of the data stored in those areas. To cope with the need for dust-free environments, the **Winchester technology** is used. Basically, this technology seals the disk inside a hermetic (airtight) container. This approach has greatly increased the reliability of hard disk systems. The major disadvantage has been that Winchester disks were not removable. However, removable Winchester disks have recently been developed.

For business applications, microcomputers primarily use 5¼-inch Winchester disks. Typically a 50 Mbyte hard disk would sell for several thousand dollars. For professional microcomputers, a 10 Mbyte hard disk has become quite common as part of the standard configuration. The newest IBM Personal Computers will have hard disks as large as 115 Mbytes.

Diskettes

Diskettes, or floppy disks, are used primarily with microcomputers in the business, professional, and home markets. The diskette market is rapidly approaching annual sales of a billion dollars.

A diskette resembles a 45 rpm record with a square jacket on it (see Exhibit 4.21). The most popular size diskette is 5¼ inches in diameter. It is made of Mylar plastic and is coated with a thin layer of metallic oxide particles. Diskettes vary in capacity from 100K to 2 Mbytes. Capacity depends on whether the diskette is **single, double,** or **quad density** and whether it is **single-** or **double-sided.** Advances in recording technology have allowed more bits per inch and more tracks per surface.

The actual amount of data that can be stored on a diskette is a function of how the data are formatted by the computer operating system. Often single-density disk systems have 40 tracks, each of which has 10 sectors that store 256 bytes of data. This results in a capacity of 100K bytes for a single surface.

Double-density disk systems can pack more than 500K bytes on a surface by using 80 tracks instead of 40, 16 sectors per track, and 512 bytes per sector. To increase the capacity even more, both sides of the disk can be used. Thus, a double-sided, double-density disk system could hold over 1 Mbyte.

The standard for diskettes is now the 5¼-inch size. The previous standard of 8-inch diskettes is slowly disappearing. The latest trend is toward smaller diameter diskettes called microfloppies, or **microdiskettes.** Four major groups of disk manufacturers are trying to set the standard for the market segment of microdiskettes under 4 inches. But 3½-inch disks designed by Sony seem to have the lead, since they are being used in leading microcomputer systems, such as the Macintosh, the Hewlett-Packard portable, and the new IBM Personal System/2.

A disk drive for a typical 5¼-inch diskette has a 2 Mbyte storage capacity and a transfer speed of 50,000 cps. It costs several hundred dollars, making it useful for personal and home computers where direct access is desired. Microfloppy disk systems provide around 1 Mbyte of storage for approximately two hundred dollars in a physically smaller package.

By their very nature, diskettes are a removable form of storage. The read/write head rides on the surface of the disk. This causes wear and tear, which eventually results in low reliability. To counter the limited online storage capacity and low reliability of diskette systems, removable hard disk cartridges are emerging. The rigid cartridge allows greater storage capacity, yet is more reliable and durable than the diskette because the removable disk is housed in an airtight plastic cartridge (see Exhibit 4.22).

Optical Disks

Optical technology used with laser disk systems is providing a very high capacity storage medium with the **optical disk,** also called a **videodisc** (see Exhibit 4.23). Videodiscs will open new applications, since they can be used to store data, text, audio, and video images.

Optical disk systems look like magnetic disk systems. Each has a rotating platter and a head mechanism to record information. However, optical systems differ because they use light energy rather than magnetic fields to store data. A high-powered laser beam records data by one of two methods. With the **ablative method,** a hole is burned in the disk surface

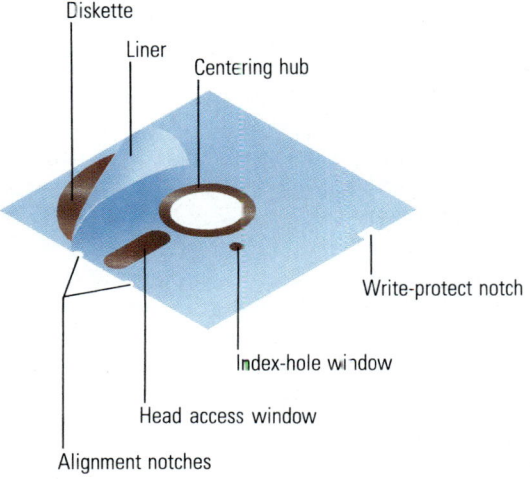

EXHIBIT 4.21
The Diskette in Its Protective Cover

EXHIBIT 4.22
A Removable Disk Cartridge
The Bernoulli Box is a disk cartridge-based system that offers the removability and low cost of floppy disks with the reliability and great storage capacity of hard disks.

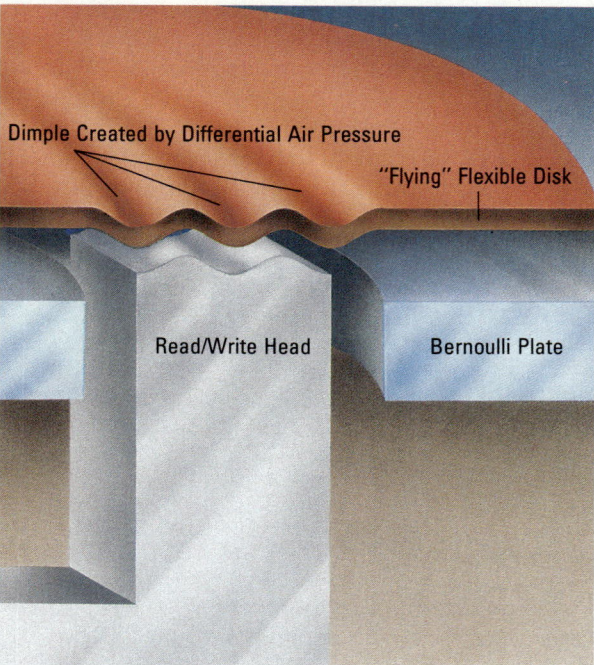

(see Exhibit 4.24). With the **bubble method,** the disk surface is heated until a bubble forms.

The laser beam, in a lower power mode, reads the data by sensing the presence or absence of holes or bumps. The light beam will be reflected at different angles from a flat or disfigured surface. A series of mirrors is used to reflect the light beam to a photodiode, which transforms the light energy into an electric signal. The photodiode process works like the automatic doors at your local supermarket. As you walk toward the door, you deflect a light beam, which signals the doors to open.

The optical properties of this device allow very high-density recordings so that an optical disk can store 100 times more than a magnetic disk of the same size.

As discussed previously, to achieve high storage capacity, the magnetic r/w heads have to be very, very close to the surface of the magnetic disk. This necessitates the dust-free environment of Winchester technology. The usual result is a hard disk that is not removable. With optical disks, however, high density can be achieved without these restrictions. Due to the levels of light energy used, the recording mechanism doesn't have to be as close to the disk surface as for a magnetic disk. Further, optical disks can be coated in plastic so that people can handle them freely without lessening their readability.

EXHIBIT 4.23
Optical Disk Systems
Optical disk systems use light energy rather than magnetic fields to store data. This allows storage densities one hundred times greater than the magnetic disk's and the ability to store high-quality video images and sounds.

Also, the optical disk doesn't wear out like a diskette does. To summarize, the optical disk is removable, has high storage capacity, and is very reliable.

In addition to having a large stoarge capacity, optical disks have another very important attribute. They can be used to store not only data and text, but also high-quality video images and sounds. Digitized patterns of images and sounds are stored in **frames**. A typical optical disk has 54,000 frames which can be used to store screen images or a 30-minute audio and video presentation.

Unfortunately, at present, optical disk systems do not have the capability to erase or rewrite data onto the disk. The ablative and bubble methods of recording data by deforming the disk surface provide only the capability to read data. However, Matsushita, a Japanese company, has recently produced a prototype erasable optical disk, which uses a combination of optical and magnetic properties to provide read/write capabilities.

Even as a read-only device, optical disks have great potential as a medium for archiving important records and documents for long-term storage. Organizations are often required by law to store documents from ten to twenty years, and sometimes even longer. To date, much of the archiving has been done on microfilm or microfiche, but overall, this micrographics approach has never really taken off. It is too expensive, people intensive, and awkward a method to use. Edward Rothchild, publisher of *Optical Memory Newsletter,* predicts that, in the near future, optical disk systems will make film-based document storage obsolete because optical disk systems will have the important advantages of lower costs and improved access time.

Cartridge and Cassette Tapes

With hard disks capable of storing more and more data, the loss of data due to a failure of the hard disk itself could be disastrous. If a hard disk contains valuable data, it is wise to backup, or make copies of that data to protect it from such a failure. With a microcomputer, diskettes are often

EXHIBIT 4.24
Encoding Data on an Optical Disk
The ablative method of recording data uses a high-power laser to burn holes in the disk surface. In a lower power mode, the laser beam reads the data by sensing the presence or absence of holes in the disk surface.

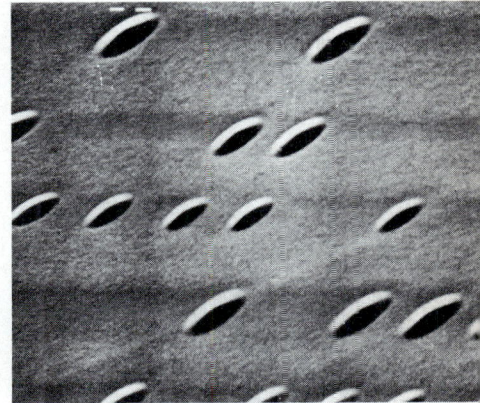

EXHIBIT 4.25
Data cartridge tapes can be used as a high-speed backup alternative to the diskette. These streaming tape units can store 60 megabytes of data and transfer it in 10 minutes.

used as a means of backup. The data on the hard disk are copied onto floppy disk and stored in a safe place. However, since a diskette can hold only a megabyte or so, 30 diskettes would be needed to backup a 30 Mbyte Winchester hard disk. This approach is expensive, awkward, and slow.

Magnetic tape vendors have developed ¼-inch-wide data cartridges as backup alternatives to the diskettes. Very small, inexpensive, and convenient, these units use the streaming concept. They can store up to 60 megabytes and can transfer this amount of data in 10 minutes (see Exhibit 4.25).

Cassette tapes have been used primarily for home computers as a means of entering programs and data. While this is a very inexpensive form of secondary storage, the overall results have been quite poor. Cassette tapes were designed for audio—not data—recording. They tend to be slow and have fairly high error rates. This market will probably be taken over by microfloppy systems, which can provide accurate results at a price in line with inexpensive microcomputers.

Summary

The foundation of computer processing is data. A major effort is expended in entering data in a computer-readable form.

The *human-computer interface* refers to the means of interaction between a human being and the machine. The basic problem that arises when people have to communicate with machines is that the best and most comfortable way for people is not always the most efficient use of a machine.

Keyboards are the primary means through which humans interact with computers. Keyboard designs differ significantly in terms of the number, placement, and function of the keys. A typical keyboard used with a microcomputer is very similar to the QWERTY keyboard arrangement of a standard typewriter. An alternate keyboard arrangement has been proposed by *Dvorak*, in which the home row includes the vowels under the fingertips of the left hand and the most common consonants under the fingertips of the right hand.

To simplify word processing, spreadsheet analysis, or data queries, users needed an enhanced keyboard. To the typewriter keyboard has been added a *numeric keypad*, which functions as a quicker way to enter numeric data than using the top row of the keyboard. *Arrow keys* were added to facilitate the movement of the cursor. *Function keys* were added to provide a way to command certain common tasks in one step, rather than making several keystrokes to accomplish the same thing.

Pointing devices are a complementary input means, primarily useful for selecting functions. A recent advancement that makes the human-computer interface more natural is the use of *icons*. These are graphic symbols for functions such as selecting documents, using a calculator, filing letters, and removing unwanted data. These functions are selected by the movement of the cursor, which is controlled with a hand-sized box called a *mouse*.

For computer-processed data to be of any value, they must be in a form that users can understand. Historically, printed output was the primary way of showing computer processing results. While paper is still the dominant output medium, there are now many other alternative ways to communicate information.

Computer output can be classified in several different ways. *Hard copy* output, such as paper printouts, provides the user with a permanent record. *Soft copy* output, such as the visual display on a monitor, provides a temporary record. These forms of output can also be understood by human users, whereas the electronic data stored on magnetic tape or disk are *computer-readable*. Information that is presented in the form of letters, numbers, and special characters is *alphanumeric*. In contrast, *graphics* are pictures or graphs depicting information.

Visual display of information is one of the most effective means for showing users the results of computer processing. The primary technology for producing and displaying the images on the terminal screen are the cathode-ray tube and the flat-panel.

Cathode-ray tubes (*CRTs*), like television picture tubes, electronically paint characters on a screen. In the *raster scan* process, a beam of electrons sweeps back and forth horizontally across the screen. As the beam moves across the screen, the current is increased or decreased to create brighter (on) or darker (off) points. These points are called *pixels*, or picture elements. *Resolution* is a measure of the number of pixels that can be addressed on the screen.

CRTs are used in monochrome and color monitors. *Monochrome monitors* display one color, such as green or amber, on a black background. *Color monitors* use a triad, or trio, of dots to form a pixel.

If each individual pixel is addressable, this is known as a *bit-map*, or *dot-addressable*, display. When only blocks of pixels can be addressed or manipulated in displays, this is known as *character-addressable* display.

A new technology is emerging to challenge the CRT. It is the *flat-panel* display. Plasma and liquid crystal are two of the primary technologies used with it. Flat-panel displays create a screen image by illuminating a pattern of discrete dots. The high resolution and steady image of flat-panel displays yield high-quality results.

The computer printer field has not settled on a limited number of ways of printing alphanumeric information. Rather, a dozen or so technologies are being used. These technologies differ in three basic ways: *character formation*, *character transfer* (to paper or another medium), and *number of characters printed at a time*. Character information options are fully formed, dot-matrix, and image. Characters, once formed, can be transferred by an impact or nonimpact method. The number of characters to be transferred at a time can range from one character to a complete page.

The growing popularity of graphics terminals has been accompanied by an increasing need for hard copy of the graphics developed on the computer screen. Business graphics use multifunction dot-matrix impact printers, as well as printers using nonimpact thermal and ink-jet technology.

Plotters are output devices that are specialized to produce graphics. Plotters produce a picture made up of a series of straight lines. Plotters come in a wide variety of sizes ranging from small desktop models to enormous devices used to draw full-scale airplane designs.

For secondary storage systems where there is a need for high reliability and extensive storage capacity, fixed hard-disk systems are used. Generally, these high-precision systems use the *Winchester technology,* in which the read/write heads and disk platters are sealed in an environment free from contaminants.

The *storage capacity* of a disk is a function of the number of tracks per surface, the bit density, and the number of recording surfaces. The speed with which data can be found and retrieved is a function of access time. *Access time* is the amount of time it takes from the point of requesting data until the data are retrieved.

Diskettes, or floppy disks, are made of a flexible Mylar plastic coated with a thin layer of metallic oxide particles. These diskettes also come in several sizes, and all are designed to be removable. Diskettes vary in storage capacity, depending on whether the diskette is single, double, or quad density and whether it is single- or double-sided.

Optical disk systems use light energy rather than magnetic fields to store data. A high-powered laser beam is used to record data by either burning a hole in the disk surface or heating the disk surface until a bubble forms. The optical disk is emerging as an important direct-access secondary storage medium. It is attractive because of its large storage capacity and its ability to store high-quality video images.

Cartridge or cassette tapes are often used to backup hard disk systems to protect valuable data from a failure of the hard disk itself.

Review Questions

1. How is communication with computers becoming more natural for people?

2. Briefly explain the advantages offered by a voice recognition system. What technological problems must still be overcome in order to fully utilize such a system?

3. Briefly describe the basic classifications of computer output. Why do some systems provide "redundant" outputs?

4. How does a CRT display work? What is meant by the term *raster scan?* What is *resolution,* and why is it important?

5. Compare flat-panel displays and CRT displays. What advantages does the flat-panel display offer?

6. Briefly summarize the text's conclusions regarding current printer technology. Which of the current technologies is the most flexible?

7. What factors influence the storage capacity of a disk?

8. Briefly describe the components of access time as applied to disks. Assuming that a firm requires the fastest possible access times, would diskettes or hard disks be more likely to be used?

9. What are *optical disks?* What advantages do such storage systems have? How are data recorded on optical disks?

PART THREE — End-User Computing

CHAPTER 5 ■ Microcomputer Operating Systems

THE ROLE OF SYSTEM SOFTWARE

MICROCOMPUTER OPERATING SYSTEMS
  De facto Standard Operating Systems
  Using a Microcomputer Operating System

COMMANDS
  The FORMAT Command
  The Directory Command
  The TYPE Command
  The ERASE Command
  The RENAME Command
  The CHKDSK Command
  The COPY Command
  The PRINT Command

ADVANCED OS FEATURES
  Menu-Driven Operating Systems
  Editors
  Startup Files
  Subdirectories
  Hard Disks and Backup

SOFTWARE PORTABILITY

SUMMARY

REVIEW QUESTIONS

Recent technological advances in producing high-powered, but inexpensive, microcomputers have combined with increased availability of low-cost, but powerful, software packages to usher in the era of end-user computing. An end-user, usually a business professional, interacts directly with the computer through the use of commercial software packages to develop his or her own computerized applications. In Part Three you will learn how to use these software packages for a variety of purposes, including financial analysis, electronic memos, information reports, presentation graphics, and file and data base management.

As explained in Parts One and Two of this textbook, a computer is directed by a series of program instructions. **System software** is a series of programs that has been written to act as an interface between application programs, which have as their focus the needs of end-users, and the computer itself. These are programs that perform such functions as starting the computer and storing files. The system software first interprets and then carries out the commands necessary to run an application program. This intermediary role allows users to be less concerned with the inner details of computer operations and provides for more efficient use of computer resources.

In this chapter we will concentrate on the operating system, which is the foundation of system software, and, in particular, the microcomputer OS. In this chapter you will learn to do the following:

1. Explain the different roles played by operating software and support software.
2. Identify which brands of operating systems are becoming predominant for use with microcomputers.
3. Understand some of the commands used with microcomputer operating systems.
4. Identify some of the advanced features associated with a microcomputer operating system.

THE ROLE OF SYSTEM SOFTWARE

When an application program is written, the programmer relies on the system software to interface with the computer hardware. The programmer can then concentrate his or her efforts on meeting the needs of the end-user when creating the application program.

System software is generally composed of an operating system, language translators and utilities, data management, and data communication systems. The overall function of the **operating system (OS)** is to control the activities of the computer system. It serves as the traffic cop, directing and managing computer events. To do this, the OS has a set of programs called a **supervisor.** (This set of programs is also called an executive or a monitor.) The supervisor handles the overall management of the many tasks that are being conducted by the computer system. The supervisor is concerned with making the computer resources, such as the CPU, primary memory, input/output devices, and support software, available in an efficient way.

Supplementing the OS are **language translators.** These are programs that translate the Englishlike program instructions of a high-level language, such as BASIC or COBOL, into the binary code of ones and zeros of machine language. **Utilities** are programs that have been written to accomplish common tasks such as sorting records or copying disk files on magnetic tape for backup.

In executing computer programs, data must be transferred between primary memory and peripherals. This involves providing data paths, interfacing with many different types of input and output devices, and often moving data over long distances through telephone networks and other telecommunication links. Exhibit 5.1 shows the varied roles of system software.

MICROCOMPUTER OPERATING SYSTEMS

Historically, operating systems for microcomputers have been developed in a different way from those for the large maxicomputer systems. The major difference has been the public orientation of microcomputer operating systems, as opposed to the proprietary single-vendor orientation of mini- and maxicomputer operating systems. For the large computer systems, an operating system is generally developed by the manufacturer for use only with its own computers. Developing the OS in this way allowed each computer manufacturer to tailor its OS to its own computer system characteristics.

However, because a manufacturer would not readily divulge detailed information on the internal workings of its OS, third-party hardware and software vendors couldn't easily design their offerings to "plug in" to these computer systems. The net result was that users were forced to select peripheral equipment and application software from the manufacturer only.

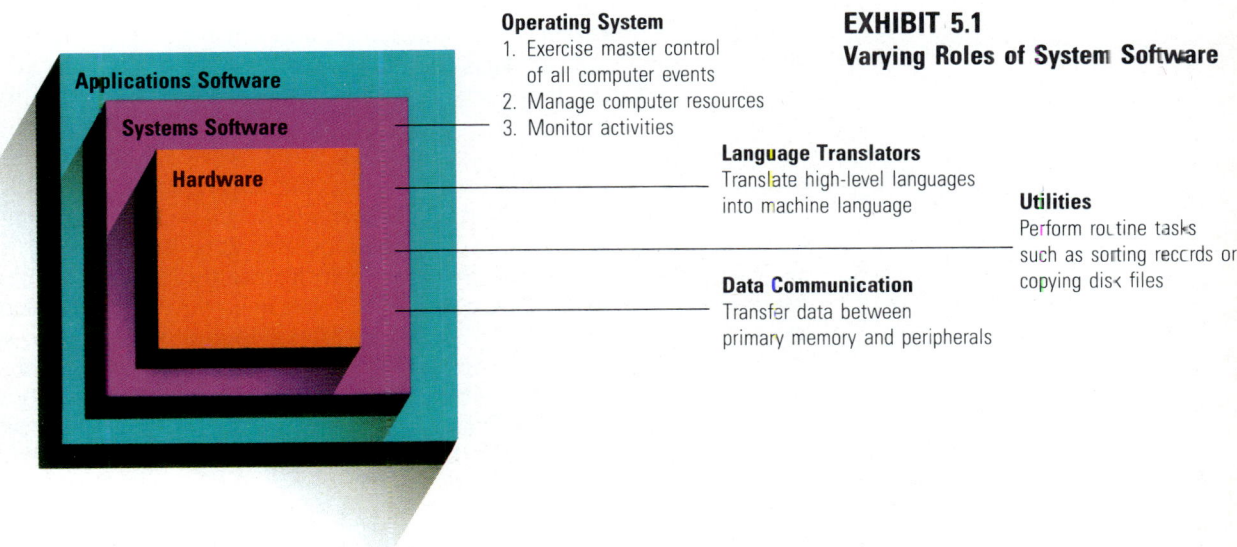

EXHIBIT 5.1
Varying Roles of System Software

Operating System
1. Exercise master control of all computer events
2. Manage computer resources
3. Monitor activities

Language Translators
Translate high-level languages into machine language

Utilities
Perform routine tasks such as sorting records or copying disk files

Data Communication
Transfer data between primary memory and peripherals

With microcomputers, the total orientation has been one of unbundling all facets of hardware, software, training, financing, and even maintenance. Often, the user will get a microcomputer manufactured by one vendor and the disks from another vendor. The OS will come from someone else and the word processing or decision support software from still other independent vendors. Thus, microcomputers are sold more like stereo equipment, where a system's components can each be produced by a different vendor. Unfortunately, there isn't yet any standard way to connect a microcomputer's hardware and software together, as there is with stereos (see Exhibit 5.2).

De facto Standard Operating Systems

Although an official committee has not specified standards, several de facto standards for microcomputer operating systems have developed. A **de facto standard** is one that vendors informally accept, generally because it has come to dominate a market segment of the business.

For microcomputers with 8-bit processors, the OS developed by Digital Research called CP/M (Control Program for Microcomputers) has become the de facto standard. It is a single-user interactive system and can process only one task at a time. This operating system is used on 100 different brands of microcomputers.

For the 16-bit microprocessors, the IBM PC has very quickly become a dominant force. The OS that IBM chose was the operating system developed by Microsoft. The IBM PC version is called PCDOS (Personal Computer Disk-Based Operating System) and is a variation of MS-DOS (Microsoft Disk Operating System) sold by Microsoft to computer vendors other than IBM.

MS-DOS is designed for the 8086 and 8088 16-bit microprocessors used in the IBM PC, DEC Rainbow, Televideo 1602, Wang PC, and Texas Instrument Professional Computer. This is a single-user interactive system that cannot do tasks concurrently. With many microcomputer systems, the user can't use the computer while the computer is printing. He or she has to wait until the print job is complete before using the CRT to do work on a spreadsheet program, for example. Operating systems that allow concurrent tasks are classified as **multitasking** (see Exhibit 5.3).

For those users who would like a multiuser environment for the IBM PC or some other 16-bit microcomputers, the Oasis-16 operating system has been developed. It is possible to have 32 concurrent users with this OS.

In the 32-bit microprocessor world, it is not clear yet what the dominant OS will be. Many experts believe that the leading candidate will be some version of the UNIX operating systems developed by AT&T. The UNIX operating system was developed by Bell Lab. Western Electric, another subsidiary of AT&T, was chosen to license the product to other vendors. A variation of UNIX, called XENIX, has been developed by Microsoft. This OS is used with Radio Shack's Model 16 and other microcomputers based on the 68000 microprocessor. These UNIX-type operating systems are multiuser time-sharing systems. A more likely candidate, however, is the new IBM OS/2 operating system. OS/2 runs on IBM's new Personal System/2 32-bit microcomputers, which are also multitasking systems.

Using a Microcomputer Operating System

Because of the popularity of the IBM PC, MS-DOS is perhaps the most commonly used microcomputer OS. Therefore, in our discussion of the features of a microcomputer OS, our examples will be in MS-DOS, although equivalent commands in other operating systems, like CP/M, will also be mentioned.

The OS allows a user to work with data stored in a **file**, a collection of related information. A file can contain a document from a word processor, a spreadsheet, or even a program. The OS provides commands for information about and maintenance of these files as well as the computer itself. In MS-DOS and most other microcomputer operating systems, a file is given a two-part name: an eight-character file name and a three-character file type (or extension). These two parts are joined by a period to form the complete file specification. For example, a document might be named LETTER.DOC. The file name is LETTER and the file type is DOC. The file type is typically used to indicate what the file is used for. A document might have a DOC (for document) or TXT (for text) extension, while a spreadsheet could have a WKS (for worksheet) extension.

In microcomputers, files are kept on diskettes or on hard disks, which serve as secondary storage. Microcomputers often have two disk drives, enabling users to work with files on two different diskettes at the same time. Exhibit 5.4 shows a microcomputer with two disk drives. The two drives are usually labeled A and B, although some microcomputers, such as the Apple IIe, use numbers as labels.

To begin working on a microcomputer, a user inserts a disk containing the operating system into the default disk drive. When the microcom-

EXHIBIT 5.2
Microcomputers are multivendor endeavors.

EXHIBIT 5.3

Multitasking operating systems allow a user to work concurrently on several different tasks.

puter has two drives, the **default drive** is the one referred to as drive A. In Exhibit 5.4, the drive on the left is the default drive.

When the microcomputer is turned on, it automatically looks for a diskette in the default drive. If one is found, the microcomputer looks for the OS on that diskette and loads it into primary memory. This process of loading the OS into primary memory from a diskette in the default drive is commonly referred to as **booting** the computer. On microcomputers with hard disks, the OS is typically placed on the hard disk, which serves as the default drive. This allows the computer to be booted from the hard disk as opposed to a floppy disk in one of the floppy disk drives.

The operating system usually consists of a small group of files with a special file type, such as COM or CMD, standing for *command*. Also there are sometimes some *hidden* files which are part of the OS. These files cannot be manipulated by the user but are used by the microcomputer to configure the keyboard and other parts of the computer so that they can be used. The computer can be booted with any diskette containing those files.

In the MS-DOS OS, the basic operating system consists of two hidden files (IBMBIO.COM and IBMDOS.COM) and the COMMAND.COM file. The hidden files contain the basic input/output operations (BIOS) part of the operating system and the DOS service routines. These parts of the OS lie between the software and the peripheral devices of the computer, such as the monitor, keyboard, and disk drives. When the user issues a simple OS command that requires access to a peripheral device, such as reading

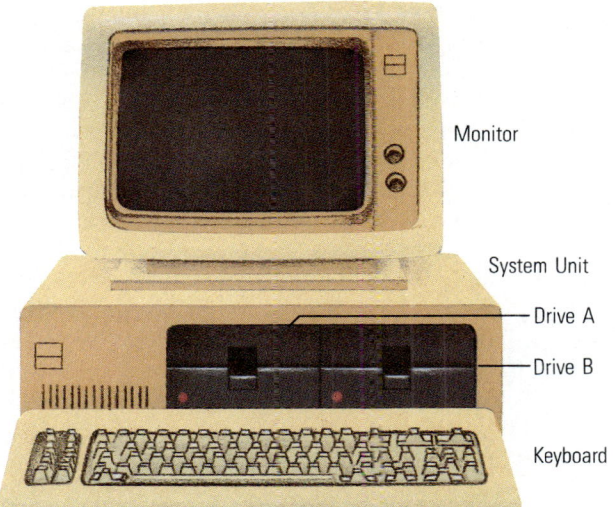

EXHIBIT 5.4
A Microcomputer with Two Disk Drives

something from a disk, these OS routines translate that command into all of the steps needed to make the computer perform that function. The COMMAND.COM file contains the routines that DOS uses to understand the commands users enter from the keyboard.

Once the OS is loaded into primary memory, the OS commands are available for manipulating files and maintaining a diskette. When the microcomputer is waiting for the user to indicate which command is to be executed, a **prompt** is displayed on the screen. In the MS-DOS and CP/M operating systems, the prompt is A>. This prompt indicates which disk drive is the default (A, in this case) and that the user can type any OS command on the line following the prompt. Exhibit 5.5 shows how the command to change the default drive from A to B is entered.

When the A> prompt appears, the user types B: and presses the return key. The **return** (or enter) **key** is used to tell the OS that the user is finished typing the command and that it should begin executing that command. This allows the user to indicate when a command is ready to be executed. If the user makes a mistake when typing a command, a **backspace key** can back up to the error and the correct command can be retyped. The OS will not begin executing the command until the user presses the return key.

EXHIBIT 5.5
Changing the Default Drive from A to B

The B: command tells the OS to change the default drive to B. Whenever the user wishes to instruct the OS to do something involving a particular disk drive, the letter of that disk drive is followed by a colon.

Once the B: command is executed, the OS displays the prompt again, indicating that the command is finished and it is again waiting for the user to enter a command. Note how the second prompt is B>. This indicates that the default drive is B instead of A, which is what the B: command instructed the computer to do. To return the default drive to A, the user can enter A:.

Since microcomputers usually have two disk drives, the user can manipulate files on either drive. When a command deals with a file on one of the disk drives, the name of that file must be preceded by the letter of that drive. Thus, if the LETTER.DOC file is on the disk in drive B, the file is identified as B:LETTER.DOC. If the file is in drive A, A:LETTER.DOC is used.

Having one of the disk drives designated as a default allows the user to omit the drive letter in front of a file name when that file is on the disk in the default drive. The default drive is also important when using a software package, such as a word processor, spreadsheet, or data base. When two drives are available, the software is placed in the default drive so that the OS can find the files containing the software programs without having to decide which drive contains those files.

COMMANDS

The commands provided by microcomputer OS allow a user to perform many different functions utilizing the files on diskettes and the diskettes themselves. The commands let an end-user obtain information about the files on a diskette and about the diskette itself. Using these commands, an end-user can also prepare a diskette for use by the operating system and examine the contents of a file.

The FORMAT Command

Before a file can be placed on a diskette, that diskette must be prepared to be used by the OS. The **FORMAT** command **initializes** a diskette by dividing it into sectors and tracks and creating a directory and file allocation table that will hold information about the files that will be stored. When a file is created, its name is entered into the directory, and the file allocation table is used to keep track of the sectors and tracks on which the file is stored.

An example of the FORMAT command is shown in Exhibit 5.6. Following the word FORMAT, the user types the letter of the drive containing the diskette to be initialized. The user can have the OS perform additional tasks during formatting. In this case, the /S (read *slash S*) has been specified. This tells the OS to transfer the OS files needed to boot the computer onto the blank diskette after it has been formatted. Another common parameter allowed by some operating systems is /V (slash V), which tells the OS to test all of the locations on the new disk to make sure they are readable. This is known as **verifying** the new diskette. Different operating systems will have different parameters associated with the FORMAT command.

```
A>FORMAT B:/S
Insert new diskette for drive B:
and strike ENTER when ready

Formatting...Format complete
System transferred

    362496 bytes total disk space
     62464 bytes used by system
    300032 bytes available on disk

Format another (Y/N)?N
A>
```

EXHIBIT 5.6
The FORMAT Command

After the user enters the FORMAT command and strikes a key, the OS formats the disk and then shows the user how much space is on the disk and how much is used by the system. In addition, if any bad spots exist on the disk, the FORMAT command will mark them as unusable and tell the user how many bytes are unusable. At the end of the FORMAT command, the user has the option of immediately formatting another disk or stopping the format process.

The Directory Command

A user can get a listing of the contents of a disk's directory with the DIR command (some computers also use CAT for CATALOG). The **DIR** command gives the user a list of the file names and file types of all of the files on the disk. Additional information, such as the size of each file (in bytes) and the last time and date that the file was modified, may be listed as well. Exhibit 5.7 shows an example of the DIR command used to list the files on a diskette in the B drive.

```
A>DIR B:

 Volume in drive B has no label
 Directory of  B:\

COMMAND   COM    17664   3-08-86   12:00p
INCOME    WKS     1008   1-01-85   12:52a
LETTER    DOC     3456   1-01-83   12:38a
RESUME    TXT     1408   1-01-83    1:10a
PROGRAM   BAS     7994   1-01-83   12:18a
BASIC     COM     3346   1-01-83   12:58a
       6 File(s)     302080 bytes free

A>
```

EXHIBIT 5.7
Using the DIR Command to Look At the Diskette in Drive B

Commands

EXHIBIT 5.8
Using a Wildcard in the DIR Command

```
A>DIR B:*.COM

 Volume in drive B has no label
 Directory of  B:\

COMMAND  COM    17664   3-08-86   12:00p
BASIC    COM     3346   1-01-85   12:58a
        2 File(s)    302080 bytes free

A>
```

Note how the B: is used after the word DIR to specify that the diskette is in drive B. If the user wanted a list of the files on a diskette in drive A, DIR A: could be used. Since A is the default drive, the user could have simply typed DIR and the OS would have assumed that the user wanted the list of files on drive A. Above the list of files returned by the DIR command is some information about the diskette itself. The word *volume* is a reference to the diskette, and the words *no label* indicate that this diskette has no label or title associated with it. After a diskette is formatted, an OS that allows diskettes to be labeled will ask the user to supply a title for that diskette. If the user does not give a title, the diskette will not have a label associated with it. Below the list of information for the files is some summary information which tells the user how many files are listed by the DIR command and how much free space is left on the diskette for new files.

Exhibit 5.8 shows how the DIR command can be used to list a subset of the files on a disk by substituting an asterisk (*) for the file name and entering the file type of the files to be listed. (This * is commonly known as a **wildcard** character and it can be used in the DIR command in place of either a file name, a file type, or both.) The DIR B:*.COM command lists all of the files on the diskette in drive B which have *any* file name and a COM file type.

EXHIBIT 5.9
An Example of the TYPE Command

```
A>TYPE B:LETTER.DOC
This is an example of what the contents of a text file will
look like when it is displayed on the screen with the TYPE
command.

A>
```

5 Microcomputer Operating Systems

```
A>ERASE B:INCOME WKS          Erases INCOME.WKS from
                              the diskette in drive B.

A>ERASE A:*.DAT               Erases all files with a DAT
                              extension from the diskette
                              in drive A.

A>ERASE B:*.*                 Erases all files from the diskette
ARE YOU SURE (Y/N)? Y         in drive B. User is asked to confirm
                              this type of deletion.
```

EXHIBIT 5.10
Three Examples of the ERASE Command

The TYPE Command

A user can display the contents of a file on the screen by using the **TYPE** command. This command will work only with files that contain text. Certain files, such as spreadsheet files, are stored in special formats. When they are typed on the screen, they are typically unreadable. Exhibit 5.9 shows an example of the TYPE command being used to display a small text file on drive B. As with the DIR command, the drive specification can be left off if the file is on the diskette in the default drive.

The ERASE Command

A user often finds that certain files on a diskette are no longer needed. An OS provides a command which allows a user to delete a file from a diskette's directory. This command is commonly called **ERASE** (or sometimes ERA or DELETE). It can be used to delete a single file, a group of files with a common file name or file type, or all of the files on a disk. Exhibit 5.10 shows three examples of the ERASE command. In the first example, a single file, INCOME.WKS is deleted from the diskette in drive B. In the second example, all of the files on the diskette in drive A with a file type of DAT are deleted. In the third example, all of the files on the diskette in drive B are deleted. Note how the OS makes the user confirm that he or she really intends to delete all of the files by making the user response Y to a second question.

The RENAME Command

An OS also allows users to change the name of files on diskettes. This command is usually **RENAME** or REN. Following the name of the command, the user must type the old name of the file and then the new name for the file. If the file is not on a diskette in the default drive, the letter of the drive must precede the file name. Exhibit 5.11 shows an example of the RENAME command. In this example, only the file name is being changed; the file type is left the same. A user can change either the file name, the file type, or both.

EXHIBIT 5.11
The RENAME Command

```
A>RENAME B:INCOME.WKS B:BUDGET.WKS
A>
```

The CHKDSK Command

A diskette is capable of holding only a certain number of files. At some point the diskette will become full and no additional files can be stored on it. A user can get information from the OS about how full a disk is by using the **CHKDSK** (check disk) command. The letters *chkdsk* are followed by the letter of the drive in which the diskette to be checked is stored. If the drive letter is omitted, the default drive will be used. Exhibit 5.12 shows an example of the CHKDSK command. The first four lines show the status of the diskette. The first line shows the total amount of space on the diskette, and the fourth line shows how much of that is free to be used by new files. On this particular diskette, about five sixths of the diskette is available. The second and third lines show how much of the diskette is used by the two categories of files: hidden files, which are used by the OS, and user files.

The fifth and sixth lines show the status of the primary memory of the microcomputer. This computer has 256K (256 kilobytes) of memory. The sixth line shows how much of that primary memory is available to be used.

The COPY Command

An OS allows a user to copy files from one diskette onto another or onto the same diskette. The command is commonly called **COPY,** although other names are sometimes used (CP/M uses PIP for *peripheral*

EXHIBIT 5.12
The CHKDSK Command

```
A>CHKDSK B:

  362496 bytes total disk space
   22528 bytes in 2 hidden files
   34816 bytes in 6 user files
  305152 bytes available on disk

  262144 bytes total memory
  237568 bytes free

A>
```

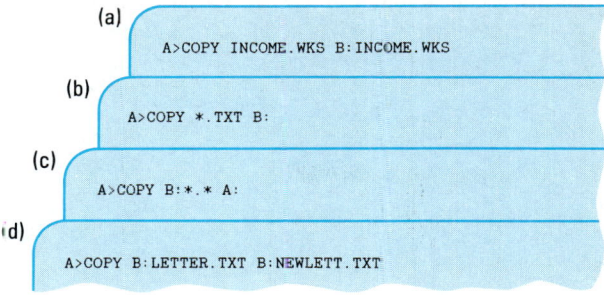

EXHIBIT 5.13
Four Examples of the COPY Command

interchange program, for example). The most common use of this command is in transferring files between diskettes. It is important to realize that copying a file does not destroy the original file; instead, the OS duplicates the original file.

The COPY command can be used to copy a single file, a group of files, or all of the files on a diskette. Exhibit 5.13 shows four examples of the COPY command. In all of them, the word *copy* is followed by two pieces of information: the original file and the new file to be created. (A notable exception to this format is in the CP/M OS, where the new file is given first, followed by an equal sign and then the original file.)

In Example a, a file is copied from a diskette in drive A (default is used) to drive B. Example b copies all files with a TXT file type from drive A to B. Note how there is no file name or file type following the B:. This indicates that the OS should use the original file names and file types from drive A when creating the new files on drive B.

Example c shows how all of the files on drive B can be copied to drive A. Again the new files will be named the same as the old ones, since after A: there is no file name or file type. An OS will often have a command called DISKCOPY, which can be used to copy all of the files on one diskette to another. This command would serve the same purpose as the COPY command in Example c.

Example d shows a special use of the copy command in which a file is copied to the same diskette that contained the original. Following the COPY command, the diskette in drive B will have two files on it which are exactly the same except that they will have different names. This command can be used to create a backup copy of a file in case something happens to the original file. When a file is copied onto the same diskette, the second file must be called something different from the first so that there are not two files on the same diskette with the same name.

The PRINT Command

Some operating systems have a **PRINT** command which is similar to the TYPE command, except that the display of the contents of the file go to a printer attached to the microcomputer rather than to the screen. The same constraints on typing files exist for printing. Files stored in special formats, such as spreadsheet files, cannot be printed by the OS. Instead, the software which works with these files has a PRINT command within it which handles output to a printer.

EXHIBIT 5.14
Sending a File to the Printer

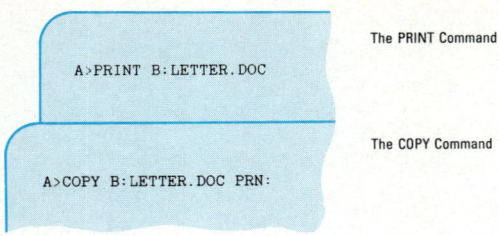

In an OS without a PRINT command, the COPY command can often be used to copy a file to the printer as if it were another disk drive. Exhibit 5.14 shows examples of these two forms of printing from an OS. In a COPY command, the printer is designated as PRN: (LST: in CP/M).

ADVANCED OS FEATURES

The OS commands discussed so far represent the most basic features of a microcomputer OS. There are often additional features included in an OS which give an end-user more complete control over the files on diskettes.

Menu-Driven Operating Systems

The MS-DOS operating system which was discussed earlier is an example of a **command-line OS.** To instruct the OS to carry out a task, the user types the instructions onto the line following the prompt. A potential disadvantage to this is that the user must remember the name of the command and must enter it perfectly for the OS to understand what is to be done. Menu-driven operating systems often use a mouse in place of a keyboard so that inexperienced users can interact with the OS.

Some operating systems use menus which allow users to pick which task is to be performed. Once a choice is made, the OS may ask for some additional information by showing the user a second menu or by asking the user to type in something. Exhibit 5.15 shows a menu from the Apple Macintosh OS. If the EDIT option is selected, the OS will then display a list of the files and ask the user to pick the one to be edited.

Editors

Most of the files on a diskette are used in conjunction with some type of software, such as word processors, spreadsheets, or data bases. When a user wants to alter the contents of one of these files, he or she simply uses the functions built into that software.

Occasionally a user wants to create files that are not associated with any particular software product. (The startup files discussed in the next section are an example of this.) An OS will usually contain a program, called an **editor,** which can be used to create and edit such files. An editor

EXHIBIT 5.15
An Example of a Menu-Driven Operating System from the Macintosh Microcomputer

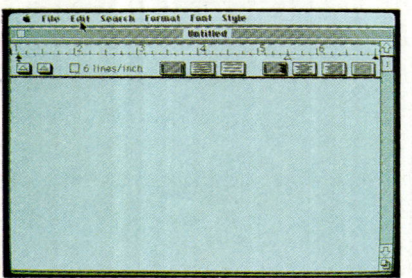

100 ■ 5 *Microcomputer Operating Systems*

is similar to a word processor and allows the user to enter information into a file or change its contents. Editors, however, do not contain as many features as word processors. Most editors are referred to as line editors, as word processors are usually full-screen editors. A **line editor** lets a user work on only one line of a file at a time, while a **full-screen editor** lets a user move through the file with the arrow keys on the keyboard.

Startup Files

Most operating systems allow the user to place a special file, called a **startup file,** on a diskette. This file is given a special name, and it contains certain OS commands which the user wants to have executed whenever the computer is booted with that diskette. During the booting of the computer, the OS is loaded and looks at the diskette to see if it can find this special file. If the file exists, the OS executes its commands before giving the user the prompt to indicate that the OS is ready.

In the MS-DOS OS this file is called AUTOEXEC.BAT. In other operating systems it may be called something different. A diskette containing software, such as a spreadsheet program, will often have a startup file which runs the software program. A user simply puts the diskette in the default drive and boots the computer, and the startup file puts the user directly into the spreadsheet program. This allows a user who knows nothing about the OS to use the software; it also reduces the number of keystrokes needed to get into an application program.

A user can create a startup file or alter its contents with an editor. The startup file can be tailored to perform any OS command the user needs executed when that diskette is used to boot the computer. Exhibit 5.16 shows an example of a startup file. Note how this file simply contains OS commands which the user can enter individually.

Subdirectories

Sometimes when disks contain more than 100 files, it becomes difficult for a user to locate a file. This is a common problem with a hard disk, which has storage space greater than 30 diskettes combined. A diskette always contains a single *root* directory, but some operating systems allow users to divide a disk into multiple directories. Exhibit 5.17 shows the structure of a diskette with **subdirectories.** Note how the directories form a tree structure similar to an organization chart of a business, with one directory at the top and many levels of subdirectories below. Below the ROOT directory are subdirectories for word processing files (WP), for spreadsheet files (SPREAD), and for data base files (DBASE). The WP directory has two subdirectories of its own, one for letters (LETTER) and one for memos (MEMO).

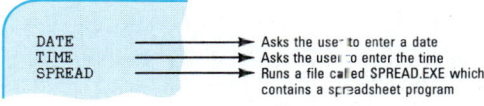

EXHIBIT 5.16
An Example of a Startup File

Advanced OS Features

EXHIBIT 5.17
A Sample Subdirectory Structure

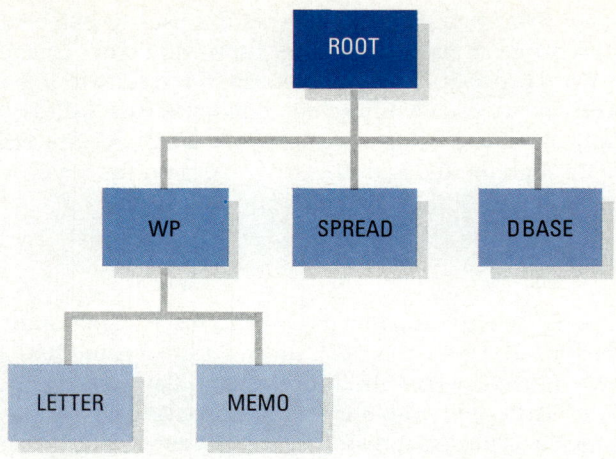

Hard Disks and Backup

Floppy disks can be particularly vulnerable to damage. It is easy for the exposed magnetic surfaces to be smudged with fingerprints, and users often spill things on them. Because of the fragile nature of floppy disks and the extreme value of the data which is stored on them, making backup copies of diskettes is an extremely important part of using a microcomputer and one which is often overlooked.

Hard disks give users greater speed and more storage space, but they are also vulnerable. Because a hard disk can store the equivalent of more than 30 floppy disks, a failure can be extremely costly. This increased storage capacity makes it more difficult to make backup copies, because the contents have to be copied to so many diskettes. Recent developments in tape cassette backup systems have eased this problem. Some operating systems now include a backup facility designed to transfer the contents of a hard disk to floppy disks or a tape drive.

Some of the capabilities of a backup facility include the ability to transfer (or backup) hard disk files on floppy disks, to transfer (or restore) the files from floppy disks to hard disk, to compare hard-disk files to files on backup diskettes, and to list the files on a backup diskette.

When hard-disk files are backed up on floppy disks, the user has certain options about which files will be transferred. A *hard disk* is typically referenced as if it were a third floppy disk drive. In Exhibit 5.18 the hard disk has been designated as C:.

Exhibit 5.18a shows a backup command which will transfer only the files on the hard disk with a WKS extension to a floppy disk in drive B. The word *changed* is an optional keyword which tells the OS that only files which have been changed since the last backup should be transferred to the diskette.

Exhibit 5.18b shows the backup command that will transfer files with a WKS extension from the floppy disk in drive B to the hard disk. A single file, a group of related files, or all of the files on the floppy disk can be transferred using this type of command.

When files are periodically backed up on floppy disks, the backup files are similar to snapshots. Some of the files on a hard disk will continue to change with time, and soon it may be difficult to determine if a file on a

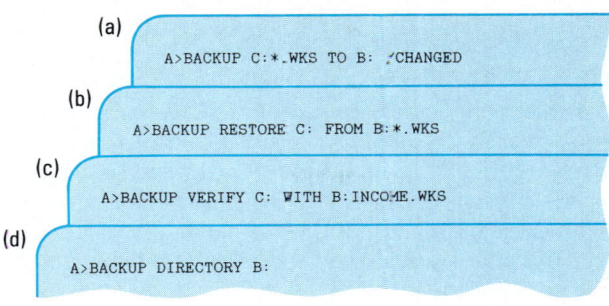

EXHIBIT 5.18
Backup Options

backup floppy disk represents the current version of a hard-disk file. To help a user compare hard-disk files to backup copies on a floppy disk, the backup facility will often include a command similar to that shown in Exhibit 5.18c. The *verify* command will compare the backup file to the file on the hard disk and tell the user if the two files are the same.

A final option included in most backup facilities is the directory option shown in Exhibit 5.18d. The directory option lets the user look at the files on a floppy disk to find a specific one.

SOFTWARE PORTABILITY

The unbundled approach to microcomputer systems has led to a variety of choices for operating systems. We have seen that particular operating systems can be adapted for use on many different microcomputers. In addition, there is not just one operating system available for a particular microcomputer. The IBM PC, for example, can use tailored versions of PC DOS, CP/M-86, and OASIS-16

The critical point is that application programs or software packages, such as word processing and spreadsheets, are designed to be used with a specific operating system. In turn, most operating systems are designed for a particular computer. With some exceptions, the general rule is that application software is not portable. That is, it cannot be assumed that application software designed for one computer system will run on any other brand of computer system. This is true even when the two different computer systems use the same operating system and have identical microprocessors.

At present, the computer industry can be compared to a stereo market, where you would have to know the model of a given phonograph player before you could buy an album to play on it. Perhaps in ten years we will be able to buy or develop software that will run on any computer system.

Finally, many operating systems are now being implemented in **firmware**—permanently coded instructions within a ROM. These so-called software-on-silicon (SOS) chips are also being used to contain translators for high-level languages such as BASIC and FORTRAN. Hewlett-Packard, in its HP75 portable computer, has put a spreadsheet, mathematical programs, and a text formatter in a ROM chip. The SOS chip approach is effective for software that is relatively standard and is free of bugs so that it isn't going to change. It also is a means for distributing an enhanced version of the OS or other application and support software every year or so.

Summary

Application software are programs written to meet the needs of users. *System software* is a series of programs written to simplify the interface between the programmer and the computer hardware. System software is generally composed of an operating system, language translators and utilities, data management, and data communication systems.

The overall purpose of the *operating system* is to control the activities of the computer system. It serves as the traffic cop, directing and managing computer events. In addition, the OS provides a useful interface that allows the user to concentrate on what he or she wants to accomplish rather than on the details of how the computer internally carries it out.

A major difference between operating systems designed for microcomputers and those for mini- and maxicomputers is a *public*, rather than a *proprietary, orientation*. This unbundled approach has led to a variety of operating system choices for use on a specific microcomputer. Operating systems can also be adapted for use on different microcomputers.

While there hasn't been any official committee that has specified industry parameters, several de facto standards for microcomputer operating systems have developed. A *de facto standard* is one that vendors informally accept, generally because it has come to dominate a market segment of the business. For the 8-bit microcomputer, it is the CP/M operating system; for the 16-bit micro, it is the MS-DOS; and for the 32-bit micro, UNIX or OS/2 may become the dominant OS. Many operating systems are now being implemented in *firmware*, permanently coded instructions within a ROM.

Microcomputer operating systems are designed to function with two disk drives (either one hard and one floppy or two floppy), one of which is labeled the default drive. When the computer is *booted*, it looks for the OS on the disk in the default drive and loads it into the primary memory of the computer.

The OS provides many commands which enable the user to maintain diskettes and the files on those diskettes. Files are typically given two names: a file name and a file type. The file type usually indicates what the file is used for.

The FORMAT command lets a user prepare a blank diskette for use by the OS. The DIR command provides a list of the files on a disk. The TYPE command allows a user to display the contents of a file on the screen. The ERASE command deletes a file from a diskette. RENAME lets a user change the name of a file. CHKDSK gives the user information about the use of a diskette's storage space. The COPY command lets a user make copies of a file on the same diskette or a second diskette. The PRINT command transfers the contents of a file to a printer attached to the microcomputer.

An OS often includes advanced features such as a *menu-driven interface* with the user, which allows a user to pick the commands to be executed rather than typing them in. An OS may contain an *editor*, which helps a user create and modify files. An OS usually can create a special *startup file*, containing OS commands, which are to be executed whenever the computer is booted with the diskette containing that file. An OS sometimes can create *subdirectories* below a root directory; the user can then work with a hierarchy of directories. A microcomputer with a hard disk can often take advantage of backup commands in an OS, which allow backup copies of a disk to be made.

A critical point to understand is that application programs or software packages, such as payroll, word processing, and spreadsheet, are designed to be used with a specific operating system. In turn, most operating systems are designed for use with a particular microprocessor. The general rule is that application software is not *portable*. That is, it cannot be used with just any computer system.

Review Questions

1. Briefly describe the functions of the operating system.

2. Explain what *booting* a microcomputer means.

3. Explain how the wildcard character (*) is used in the DIR command.

4. Explain what a startup file is and how it is used.

5. What is an editor?

6. What is a subdirectory?

CHAPTER 6 ■ Word Processing

CREATING A DOCUMENT

DOCUMENT EDITING

- The Cursor
- Moving the Cursor
- Word Wrap
- Correcting a Document
- Deleting Text
- Block Moves
- Searching

DOCUMENT FORMATTING

- Margins
- Indenting
- Centering
- Justification

DOCUMENT PRINTING

DOCUMENT MANAGEMENT

CHOOSING A WORD PROCESSOR

SUMMARY

REVIEW QUESTIONS

Word processors can be used by employees at all levels of a business. Clerks use them to improve productivity when handling all of the documents needed in the daily operations; managers and executives use them to prepare reports and memos.

When a mistake is made using a typewriter, it has to be erased from the paper. If new words or lines need to be added, the entire document has to be retyped. A word processor allows a user to store text electronically rather than typing it directly on paper. The user can make changes in the electronic version of a document and commit it to paper after all editing and revising is complete. Even after a document is printed, it is quite simple to make changes and then have the word processor print a new copy.

With a word processing system, a user can quickly print a document using a few simple commands. If multiple documents are needed, perhaps for letters sent in mass mailings, a single copy can be generated, and the word processor will create the copies, all of which are originals. (With a typewriter, each copy would have had to have been retyped.)

Many word processing vendors also offer very useful "add-on" packages to their word processing software. **Spelling checkers** make use of online dictionaries to locate spelling errors. **Thesaurus programs** provide online lists of synonyms and antonyms. **Style checkers** analyze documents to locate and correct grammar or punctuation errors and to suggest ways of improving writing style. Finally, **mail merge programs** link documents with address lists to "mass mail" letters.

In our discussion of word processors, we will cover five basic functions which all word processors provide: document creation, editing, formatting, printing, and handling.

In this chapter you will learn to do the following:

1. Explain how a document is created.
2. Describe how the contents of a document can be changed.
3. Recognize how word processors format documents.
4. Understand how word processors handle documents.
5. Evaluate and compare various word processing programs.

CREATING A DOCUMENT

A **document** is a written text record of a message, such as a memo, letter, or report. A user enters the text into the computer, which stores the electronic document in its own file on a floppy disk or a hard disk. Before a document is entered, it is given a name so that the user can identify it when he or she wants to use it. The document must be in the primary memory of the computer in order for the user to be able to interact with its contents.

Most word processors distinguish between creating new documents in primary memory and moving existing ones into primary memory to work on them. There are separate commands for each method. Other word processors simply ask the user to name a document, and, if that name does not refer to an existing document, the word processor assumes that the user wants to create a new document under that name.

After the new document has been named, the user can begin to enter the text. Some word processors (like WordPerfect) place the user into the new document automatically after it is named; others (like WordStar) require the user to enter what is called an *EDIT mode* before the text can be entered.

DOCUMENT EDITING

Once the user has entered the EDIT mode, text can be typed on the screen. As long as the document remains in primary memory, the user can move around within the document to look over what has been entered and to correct any mistakes that have been made.

The Cursor

A **cursor** on the screen indicates the user's current position in the document. Typically, the cursor is an underscore character (_) or a rectangle (■) about the size of a character. The user moves through the electronic document by repositioning the cursor, depending on the desired position within the document. Exhibit 6.1 shows the document which will be used in this chapter to demonstrate the various features of word processors. Notice that the cursor is on the *M* in *Mr.* at the beginning of the document.

```
Mr. William Williams
123 Cherry Street
Appleton, OH    44444

January 1, 1989

Dear Mr. Williams:

I would like to apply for your position for a microcomputer
specialist.  I feel that I have many skills which are
appropriate for this job.

     1.  Have worked with microcomputer operating systems.

     2.  Am an expert user of word processors, electronic
         spreadsheets, graphics, data bases, and data
         communications.

     3.  Am well motivated and eager to learn.

I believe that I can be an asset to your organization and I
look forward to hearing from you soon.

                         Sincerely,

                         Sam Samuels

                    Doc 1   Pg 1   Ln   1    Pos 10
```

EXHIBIT 6.1
The Sample Letter As It Appears in the WordPerfect Word Processor

Moving the Cursor

At the most basic level, documents are simply collections of **characters** (letters, numbers, and special symbols). These characters are grouped into words, which are grouped into lines. All word processors allow the user to move in any direction, one character at a time. Many word processors use arrow keys on the keyboard; other word processors still use the procedure of holding the control key down and then pressing one of the letter keys.

In addition to moving through a document one character at a time, many word processors allow for moving a word at a time, a line at a time, and even a screen at a time. There are also special movement keys to jump immediately to the top or bottom of the document. Exhibit 6.2 shows the movement functions implemented in the PFS: First Choice word processor. Word processors like PFS: First Choice take advantage of many of the special keys on a microcomputer's keyboard when executing such cursor movement functions (see Exhibit 6.3).

Word Wrap

It's very frustrating for someone to type a document on a typewriter and realize that the words have gone off of the page. To alleviate this problem, most word processors have a feature known as **word wrap** so that, at the end of a line, the user does not have to press the RETURN or ENTER key to move down to the next line. Instead, he or she simply continues typing, and when a word is typed that goes beyond the right edge of the screen, the word processor automatically moves that word, and the cursor, down to the next line. In essence, the word that is too long for the current line "wraps" around to the beginning of the next line. The only time the RETURN key needs to be used is when a line ends short of the right margin.

In the letter in Exhibit 6.1, the lines at the top and bottom are examples of short lines where the RETURN key has to be pressed. Thus, after the user types *Mr. William Williams*, the RETURN key must be pressed so the cursor will move down to the beginning of the next line where the address needs to be typed. In the body of the letter, however, the user begins typing and doesn't press RETURN until a paragraph ends. A blank line is created by pressing RETURN at the beginning of the line.

Correcting a Document

When creating a document, the user only has to worry about getting all of the words on the screen in the correct order, with the appropriate blank lines necessary to separate the paragraphs and other items from each other. Special spacing, such as indenting, can be accomplished when the document is formatted later. Once a letter is typed, the user can edit it and fix any mistakes which may have been made. Exhibit 6.4 shows what the letter looks like after a user has typed it into the computer. Note that some mistakes have been made and must be corrected before the document can be printed. Although these mistakes are relatively minor, they

EXHIBIT 6.2
The Movement Functions in the PFS: First Choice Word Processor

Press	To move to
Ctrl + Home	Beginning of document
Ctrl + End	End of document
PgUp	Previous screen (Page Up)
PgDn	Next screen (Page Down)
Ctrl + ←	Previous word
Ctrl + →	Next word
↑	Up one line
↓	Down one line
←	Left one character
→	Right one character
Home	Beginning of line
End	End of line

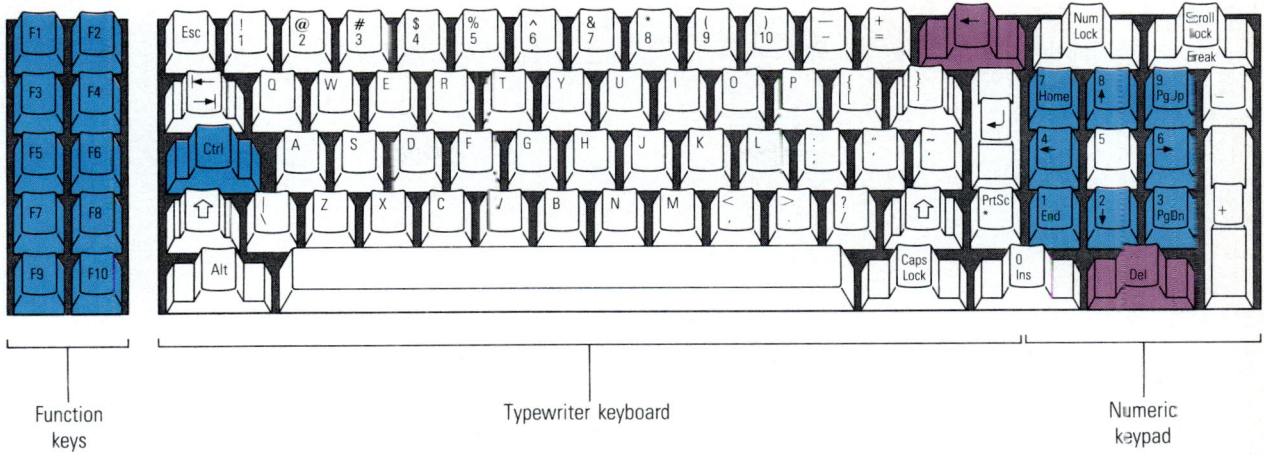

EXHIBIT 6.3
The Keyboard of the IBM PC

Word processors usually use the arrow keys and the *PgUp, PgDn, Home,* and *End* keys to the right when implementing movement functions. On the left side of the keyboard are the *Ctrl* key and the ten function keys (*F1* through *F10*) which are sometimes used in movement functions. The backspace (←) and DELETE keys are used for revising a document.

would necessitate retyping if a typewriter were used. On a computer, the extra letters can be removed, the gaps can be closed up, and the misplaced item can be moved quickly and easily prior to printing a hard copy.

Overtype Mode

When a document's contents need revision, there are two typing modes that can be used for correcting and changing text. The first one is known as the **overtype mode.** Word processors that operate in this mode allow the user to position the cursor on a word and type new characters over the characters that are already in the document. Thus, the new characters replace existing ones.

In order to fix a mistake such as the misspelling of *Cherry* on the second line (see Exhibit 6.5a), the user positions the cursor on the letter *a* and types an *e*. In overtype mode, the *e* replaces the *a*.

```
Mr. William Williams
123 Charry Street
Appleton, OH  44444

January 1, 1989

Der Mr. Williams:

I have would like to appply for your position for a
microcomputer specialist.  I feel that I have many skills
which are appropriate for this job.

     1.  Have worked with microcomputer operating systems.
     3.  Am well motivated and eager to learn.
     2.  Am an expert user of word processors, electronic
         spreadsheets, graphics, data bases, and data
         communications.

I believe that I can be an asset to your organization and I
look forward to hearing from you soon.

                         Sincerely,
                         Sincerely,

                         Sam Samuels

                         Doc 1  Pg 1  Ln 1  Pos 10
```

EXHIBIT 6.4
The Sample Letter with Mistakes

Document Editing   ■   109

EXHIBIT 6.5
(a) Using the overtype mode

```
Mr. William Williams
123 Charry Street
Appleton, OH   44444

January 1, 1989

Der Mr. Williams:

I have would like to appply for your position for a
microcomputer specialist.  I feel that I have many skills
which are appropriate for this job.
```

A mistake such as the spelling of *Dear* as *Der* in the line seven cannot be corrected with the overtype mode. If the user moves to the *r* in *Der* and corrects it, the *r* would be changed to *a,* but there would be no room for the *r* after the *a* because the space between *Dear* and *Mr.* is still needed. What the user really wants to do is insert an *a* between the *e* and the *r*. This requires a second typing mode.

Insert Mode

The **insert mode** creates space so that a letter or word can be inserted in its proper position. The cursor is positioned over a character. A new character is typed and appears in front of the cursor, while the characters to the right of (and under) the cursor move to the right. In Exhibit 6.5b, the user can put the cursor on the *r* in *Der* and type an *a*. In insert mode, the *r* and everything to the right of it is pushed to the right one space as the *a* is inserted between the *e* and the *r*. In this mode, the text that is already in the document cannot be destroyed; it gets pushed to the right and down.

Deleting Text

Deleting, or eliminating, text is a particularly important function on word processors that do not support the overtype mode. Without this ability, there would be no way to remove text from a document once it was entered.

There are varying levels of deletion, just as there are varying levels of movement throughout a document. At the most basic level, there is the elimination of a single character by moving the cursor to that character and then pressing a key or issuing a command to delete. In Exhibit 6.5c, the cursor can be positioned on the extra *p* in the word *apply* and the delete function used.

(b) Using the insert mode

```
Mr. William Williams
123 Cherry Street
Appleton, OH   44444

January 1, 1989

Der Mr. Williams:

I have would like to appply for your position for a
microcomputer specialist.  I feel that I have many skills
which are appropriate for this job.
```

■ 6 Word Processing

```
Mr. William Williams
123 Cherry Street
Appleton, OH   44444

January 1, 1989

Dear Mr. Williams:

I have would like to app ly for your position for a
microcomputer specialist.  I feel that I have many skills
which are appropriate for this job.
```

(c) Deleting a letter

Another character delete mechanism often provided by word processors is the **backspace** (←). This special key is often helpful if the user notices a mistake while typing. The user simply backs up over the mistake, deleting it as the cursor moves backward, and then types in the correct characters. In the sample letter, the extra *p* can also be removed by positioning the cursor on either of the last two *p*'s or the letter *l* and using the backspace key. If the cursor is positioned on the first *p,* the letter *a* will be deleted, since the backspace key deletes the letter to the left of the cursor.

If users want to delete words or entire lines at one time, they can press a key or use a command. Even entire blocks of text can be deleted with a single command. In our example, the word *have* in the first line of the body of the letter can be removed this way by positioning the cursor on the *h* and using the word delete function to take out that entire word (see Exhibit 6.5d). The line delete function can be used to delete the extra line

```
Mr. William Williams
123 Cherry Street
Appleton, OH   44444

January 1, 1989

Dear Mr. Williams:

I have would like to apply for your position for a
microcomputer specialist.  I feel that I have many skills
which are appropriate for this job.
```

(d) Deleting a word

(with the word *Sincerely* on it) at the bottom of the document (see Exhibit 6.5e). As with word delete, the cursor is positioned at the beginning of the line to be deleted before using the line delete command.

Another important feature related to deleting text is the **undelete** function. With the ability to delete whole lines and blocks of text with a single command, it is easy to make a costly mistake by deleting the wrong

```
I believe that I can be an asset to your organization and I
look forward to hearing from you soon.

                          Sincerely,
                          Sincerely,

                          Sam Samuels

                          Doc 1  Pg 1  Ln 26   Pos 41
```

(e) Deleting a line

Document Editing   ■   **111**

thing or changing your mind. Some of the more advanced word processors do not really destroy text; instead, they store the deleted text in designated memory locations, which are used as temporary holding places (usually called *buffers*). If the user did not really want to delete the text, he or she can issue an undelete command that will go to this buffer and bring the deleted text back.

Block Moves

When entering large amounts of text, an end-user may find that a group of words or paragraphs would work better in a different location in the document. Rather than forcing the user to delete the words that are in the wrong place and retype them in the new place, most word processors provide a way to move sections of text. These sections can be as small as a single character or as large as an entire document. They are commonly referred to as **blocks of text.**

The process of moving text around in a document is know as a **block move.** First the beginning and end of the block are marked and a command is issued to remove the block from the document and to put it into a buffer area. Once the block of text is in this buffer, the user moves to the place in the document where the block should now appear and issues another command to place the block back into the document at that new location.

In our example, item 3 has been typed in the wrong place and needs to be moved below item 2. Rather than deleting item 3 and retyping it in the correct location, a user can use a block move to mark it, move it into the buffer, move the cursor down to the blank line below item 2, and put the block back into the text at that location. Exhibit 6.5f shows how the sample letter would appear in WordPerfect after the user had marked the block and begun the *move* command. After selecting one of the options shown in the exhibit, the user moves to the new location of the text and issues another *move* command to retrieve the text back into the document. Exhibit 6.6 shows how the document looks after the letter has been corrected.

Searching

Another common function provided by most word processors is the ability to search for a particular group of characters or words in a document. Most **SEARCH** commands ask what the user is searching for. If the word *expert* was supplied, the SEARCH command would look through the document for the next occurrence of that word and put the cursor there. Usually this search takes place from the current cursor position down through the document. If the word is above the current position in the document, the SEARCH command may fail to find it. A common practice is to first move to the top of the document before issuing a SEARCH command so that the entire document will be scanned, although some word processors search backward through the document.

An available option is the substitution of a special **wildcard character** for parts of the string of characters being searched for. For example, if a user specifies *ex** as the string to search for, the word processor will

```
   3. Am well motivated and eager to learn.
   2. Am an expert user of word processors, electronic
      spreadsheets, graphics, data bases, and data
      communications.
I believe that I can be an asset to your organization and I
look forward to hearing from you soon.
                           Sincerely,

                           Sam Samuels
1 Cut Block; 2 Copy Block; 3 Append; 4 Cut/Copy Column; 5 Cut/Copy Rectangle: 0
```

(f) In WordPerfect, the block of text to be moved is highlighted and the user issues a move command.

locate the first string that begins with *ex*. The * indicates that the user doesn't care what characters follow the *ex*.

Also associated with the search function is a feature known as **search and replace.** In search and replace, the user specifies two strings: a string to search for and a string to replace it once it is located. When the search string is located, the user can decide if it is to be replaced. In addition to a normal search and replace, there is also a **global search and replace** in which every occurrence of the search string throughout the document is replaced; for example, all of the misspellings of *received* as *recieved* throughout the document can be corrected with a single command.

DOCUMENT FORMATTING

Once all of the words have been entered into the document, there is a group of commands that can be used to affect the document's overall appearance. These are usually referred to as **formatting commands.** They include settings for margins, indents, and other characteristics of the document as a whole.

```
Mr. William Williams
123 Cherry Street
Appleton, OH  44444

January 1, 1989

Dear Mr. Williams:

I would like to apply for your position for a microcomputer
specialist.  I feel that I have many skills which are
appropriate for this job.
   1. Have worked with microcomputer operating systems.
   2. Am an expert user of word processors, electronic
      spreadsheets, graphics, data bases, and data
      communications.
   3. Am well motivated and eager to learn.
I believe that I can be an asset to your organization and I
look forward to hearing from you soon.
                           Sincerely,

                           Sam Samuels

                           Doc 1  Pg 1  Ln 1   Pos 10
```

EXHIBIT 6.6

This is the sample letter after the block move and all other corrections have been completed.

Document Formatting

There are two major ways that word processors deal with formatting. Some word processors do not format on the screen but wait until the document is to be printed before putting it into its final form. These types of word processors commonly use what are known as embedded commands to do formatting. Unlike the text of the document itself, the **embedded command** is a message to the word processor telling it how to format the document. It is entered onto the screen and identified as an embedded command using a special symbol (such as beginning with a period) or by its position in the document (such as on a line by itself). The word processor will look for indications that this piece of text is not to be treated like others in the document but rather is to be interpreted as a command. Thus, an embedded command appears on the screen but does not appear in the printed document.

Exhibit 6.7 shows part of our letter in the WordStar word processor, which uses embedded commands for some formatting. For example, the .MT6 at the top instructs WordStar to create a top margin of 6 lines when the document is printed.

The second way of formatting is to format a document on the screen as it is entered so that a user can see exactly what will appear on paper when the document is printed. This kind of formatting is done using commands when the document is created. Then, when it is printed, it will be reproduced on paper in essentially the same format as it appeared on the screen. A word processor which does the formatting on the screen is often said to be **WYSIWYG** (pronounced wizzy-wig), which stands for *What You See Is What You Get*. The exhibits showing our letter in the WordPerfect word processor are examples in which the formatting is done on the screen.

In formatting a document, a user must make decisions about the look of the document—what margins are necessary, whether material should be indented, whether any information should be centered, and whether the text should appear as a block or with a ragged right edge. Word processors can control these procedures more easily than typewriters can.

EXHIBIT 6.7

The WordStar word processor uses embedded commands to do some of the formatting of a document when it is printed. The .MT6 sets a top margin of 6 lines. The .MB6 embedded command sets a 6-line bottom margin, .PL66 sets the page length at 66 lines, and .OP suppresses page numbering.

```
 A:LETTER          P01 L01 C01 Insert Align
                     E D I T   M E N U
     CURSOR       SCROLL        ERASE      OTHER              MENUS
  ^E up         ^W up         ^G char    ^J help           ^O onscreen format
  ^X down       ^Z down       ^T word    ^I tab            ^K block & save
  ^S left       ^R up screen  ^Y line    ^V turn insert off ^P print controls
  ^D right      ^C down   Del char       ^B align paragraph ^Q quick functions
  ^A word left      screen   ^U unerase  ^N split the line  Esc shorthand
  ^F word right                          ^L find/replace again
L----!----!----!----!----!----!----!----!----!----!--------R
.MT6                                                                1
.MB6                                                                1
.PL66                                                               1
.OP                                                                 :
Mr. William Williams                                                <
123 Cherry Street                                                   <
Appleton, OH   44444                                                <
                                                                    <
January 1, 1989                                                     <
                                                                    ^
Dear Mr. Williams:                                                  >
    Display Center   ChkRest ChkWord Del Blk HideBlk MoveBlk CopyBlk Beg Blk1End Blk
    1Help   2Undo    3Undrlin4Bold   5DelLine6DelWord7Align  8Ruler  9Save & 0Done
```

Margins

Word processors provide a variety of commands to control all four margins of the document: top, bottom, left, and right. Some word processors handle margins using embedded commands, while others use a **ruler,** which is a line in the document on which margins can be specified. All text following the ruler is formatted by that ruler. A document can have many rulers, so the margins can be shifted each time a new ruler is introduced or an old one is recalled. Exhibit 6.7 shows a ruler at the top of our letter in the WordStar word processor The top and bottom margins are controlled by the .MT and .MB embedded commands, respectively. The right and left margins are represented by the R and L at the ends of the ruler. The positions of the R and L on the ruler are set with a command from the WordStar menu. On most microcomputer printers there are 85 characters across a page; therefore, one inch is equivalent to 10 characters (most microcomputers use 10 characters per inch as the standard, but 12 characters per inch is also common). This means that the left margin will be 10 characters wide.

There is usually no specific setting to indicate a right margin of 10 spaces. Instead, the right margin is determined by the number of characters in the text line. With 20 spaces needed for margins on each line (10 for the left margin and 10 for the right), 65 characters of actual text can fit on each line.

Another way of determining the right-hand margin is to specify the actual column on the page where the right margin is to be located. In this case the right margin will be 75. The first 10 print positions will be used for the left margin and then 65 additional spaces will be used for text. When the printer reaches the 75th column on the piece of paper, it will move down to the next line. This will leave a 10-space right margin.

An 8½ × 11-inch piece of paper contains 66 lines of type. That is six lines per inch. The user can usually determine the size of the margin at the top of the page by setting the top margin to begin the copy on line seven. That will give an inch margin at the top of the page.

A user may also be able to set a bottom margin directly. If 12 of the 66 lines are needed for margins (6 at the top and 6 at the bottom), there are 54 lines that can accommodate the actual text. Therefore, a user can indirectly set a bottom margin of 6 by setting the top margin at 6 and the number of lines per page at 54. Thus, when the text is printed there will be 6 blank lines at the top, followed by 54 lines of actual text, leaving 6 lines for the bottom margin. Exhibit 6.8 shows a diagram of the typical margin measurements for a microcomputer printer.

Indenting

In our sample letter, items 1 through 3, in the middle of the letter, need to be indented. Some word processors do this by using rulers stored in the text which indicate the position of the left and right margins. By moving the left margin to the right, the text that follows the ruler can be indented. Other word processors use an embedded command to indicate where an indent is to begin and where it is to end. Regardless of the method, the user usually has to indicate where the indent is to begin and then cancel it when the text is not to be indented.

EXHIBIT 6.8
Typical Margin Measurements for a Microcomputer Printer

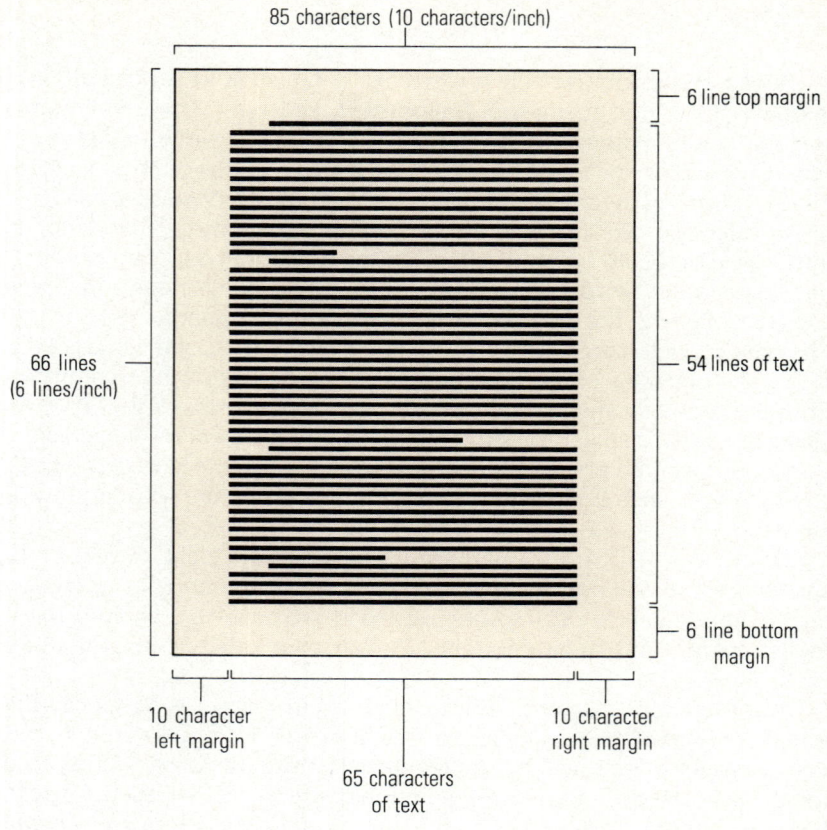

Paragraphs can be indented any number of characters depending on the user's requirements. The word processor must then have some way of deciding where a paragraph begins. Some word processors require that the beginning or end of a paragraph be marked so that it can then tell where to begin indenting. In our sample letter, the paragraph indent would be set to zero.

Centering

Many word processors have a command that centers text. Some word processors even preserve this centering when the margins are changed. For example, if the margins are changed so that the entire line is shorter than it was, the word processor will automatically adjust the centered text so that it is centered in the new line length.

Justification

Most word processors also include commands that remove unnecessary blank spaces created as changes are made in a document. All the user has to worry about is getting all of the text in the document in the right order, and then the word processor worries about getting as many words as it can on a line. With some word processors, the unnecessary blank spaces within a paragraph are not removed until the document is sent to the printer.

Many word processors have the ability to align the right-hand margin. That is, the edges of text on the right are as straight and parallel as those on the left. The text looks like a block. This process is called **justification.** Typical examples of justified text can be found in newspapers or by looking at this textbook. As you may have also noticed, justification is accomplished by inserting some extra blank spaces between the words in the line so that the last word can be pushed out to the right margin.

In word processors which do the formatting on the screen, justification is usually done with a command. Word processors which use embedded commands sometimes have a JUSTIFY command, which can be put at the top of the document.

DOCUMENT PRINTING

As mentioned earlier, some of the formatting commands may be part of the printing process. When a user instructs the word processor to print a document, he or she can specify how the document is to be printed. A user typically has control over such things as the margins used during printing, the number of copies to be printed, how the pages will be numbered, and the line spacing (single- or double-spaced).

Once a user has determined the formatting of the document and any other special settings related to the printing of the document, a simple command transfers the contents of the document to a printer. With a typewriter, making revisions and retyping a document can be very time consuming. With a word processor, a document can be retyped easily with the use of the simple PRINT command. Thus, word processors free a user from worrying about making a costly change and let the user concentrate on creating the best possible document.

DOCUMENT MANAGEMENT

The primary focus of a word processor is the document. A document can be as small as a simple, one-paragraph memo or as large as an annual report. Regardless of its size, the document is the unit of storage in word processors. Word processors usually store each document in a separate file on the microcomputer.

One of the major functions that a word processor must support is the management of the documents it stores. Word processors respond to commands that allow the creation of new documents, the saving of documents on disks, the retrieval of documents from floppy disks or hard disks, the listing of available documents, the deletion of documents, copying, and document renaming.

The two functions used most often are probably the SAVE and RETRIEVE commands. Because most word processors, like most humans, can work on only one thing at a time, only one document can be actively processed in the microcomputer at once. Other documents must be stored in permanent form on disks. Whenever more than one document is being worked on, each, in turn, must be moved into the primary memory of the microcomputer so that the word processor can work on it. When that document is finished, it must be put back on disk before another document is retrieved, because the new document will replace the old one in primary memory. If the old document is not saved in a permanent form on the disk, it will be lost. Thus, documents are constantly being moved in and out of primary memory using RETRIEVE and SAVE commands. Newer word processors, such as WordPerfect, allow users to work on two or more documents at the same time. This allows the user more flexibility if more than one document needs to be edited. Even in this situation, SAVE and RETRIEVE commands are needed to move documents to and from a floppy disk. No matter how many documents can be held in primary memory at one time, they will all have to be moved to a floppy disk to be saved permanently because of the volatile nature of primary memory.

There are two ways that word processors carry out the retrieval of a document from a floppy disk or hard disk. Most word processors make a copy of the document on disk and place that copy into primary memory for the user to work on. As changes are made, they are actually altering the copy of the document rather than the original document. However some word processors do not make a copy of the original document when a retrieval is done. Instead, the user is actally working on the original document, and every change is permanent.

This second approach is much more dangerous because every change is permanent. Word processors which create a copy of the original document allow the user to change the copy and then decide if those changes are to be kept or abandoned. Since the original document on the disk is never changed, the word processor allows the user to destroy the copy in primary memory without changing the original document on the disk.

A word processor which uses a copy of the original document gives a user three ways of saving a document. First, the user has an option which instructs the word processor to destroy the copy of the document in primary memory and, thus, to leave the original document intact on the disk. In this option, the user is instructing the word processor to forget all changes made to the document since the editing session began.

A second option (usually called UPDATE, REPLACE, or REVISE) allows the user to instruct the word processor to replace the original document on the floppy disk with the version of the document in primary memory. Usually the original version of the document is destroyed during this process, and the copy of the document is stored on the disk under the same name as the original.

Some word processors use a slightly different version of this second option in which the original document is not destroyed. Instead, it is placed in a separate file with the original document name but with a special extension (BAK for backup is a common extension). Thus, if the original document was called ORIGINAL.DOC, the copy in primary memory would be placed on the disk under ORIGINAL.DOC and a new file called ORIGINAL.BAK would be created for the storage of the original version. This gives the user another level of protection against accidentally destroying an original document. If the user decides the old version of the document is needed again, it is always available on the disk in the file with the BAK extension. Word processors which make the user work directly on the original document cannot offer this type of protection against accidental alteration of the original document.

The third option available in word processors which use copies of an original document is commonly referred to as *saving*. When the copy is to be moved to a disk for permanent storage, the user can instruct the word processor to store that file under a different name than the name of the original document. This way, the copy is stored and the original is left intact. When this third option is used, the user must give a name for the file under which the document in primary memory is to be stored. Some word processors do not separate this third option from the second. Instead, the user must always supply a name of a file under which the copy of the document is to be stored. If the user wants to update the original document, the file name is the same as that under which the original is stored. If the file name is different, then a new file is created with the copy in it, and the original is left intact under the old name. Exhibit 6.9 illustrates the retrieval of a file and the three options a user has.

CHOOSING A WORD PROCESSOR

Now that you have seen what word processors can do, you should be able to evaluate any word processor with respect to the features it supports and how it accomplishes them. Exhibit 6.10 shows a chart comparing six current word processors.

1. The first factor in choosing a word processor might be price. Word processors can range from $25 to $500 and more. Naturally, the more expensive ones will have more specialized features. Users must decide which features are desired and how much they are willing to pay for them.

2. Some of the features which might be critical to an end-user are also shown in the chart. The memory feature indicates the minimum amount of primary memory the PC must have to run the word processing program.

3. The interface column indicates whether the user can enter commands, pick options from a menu, or both when giving instructions to the word processor.

4. The automatic backup feature refers to the practice of keeping a backup of the original document on diskette so the user can always return to the original version if necessary.

5. With the abort feature, the word processor always stores the results of the last deletion operation in a buffer. Thus, if the user issues a command to delete a paragraph, that paragraph will be stored in a buffer. If the user decides the deletion was a mistake, an UNDO option can be selected to bring the deleted text back into the document.

Primary Memory

Secondary Storage (diskette)

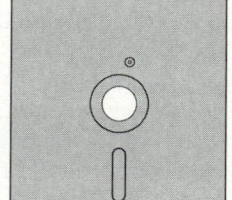

Retrieve

Copy of Original.Doc Placed in Primary Memory.

Original.Doc

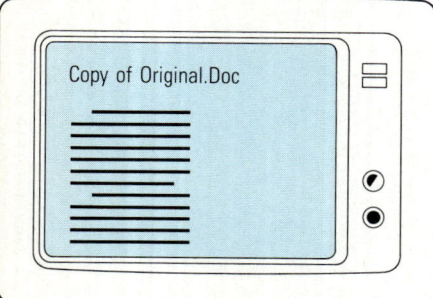

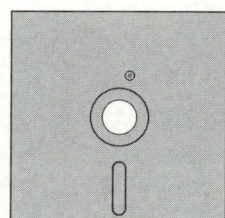

Quit

Copy is Destroyed. Original on Diskette Left Intact.

Original.Doc

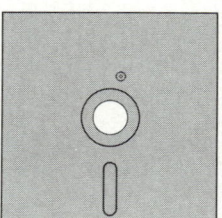

Replace

Copy Replaces Original by Assuming the Same Name as the Original. Original Destroyed or Moved to Backup File.

Original.Doc (copy)

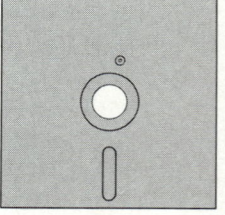

Save

Copy Saved Under Newname. Original on Diskette Left Intact.

Original.Doc
Newname.Doc (copy)

EXHIBIT 6.9
Retrieving and Saving a Document in a Word Processor Which Works with Copies of Original Documents

EXHIBIT 6.10
A Comparison of Six Current Word Processing Programs

	PC-WRITE	PFS: PROFESSIONAL WRITE	MICROSOFT WORD 3.1	WORDSTAR PROFESSIONAL RELEASE 4	OFFICEWRITER 5.0	WORDPERFECT 4.2
Memory (in bytes)	320K	320K	256K	256K	256K	256K
Interface	Both	Both	Both	Command	Both	Command
Automatic Backup	Y	N	Y	Y	Y	Y
Abort	Y	N	Y	N	Y	Y
Format on Screen	Y	Y	Y	Y	Y	Y
Multiple Document	Y	N	Y	N	N	Y
Dictionary	50,000	77,000	85,000	87,000	120,000	115,000
Price	$89	$199	$450	$495	$495	$495

Source: "Beyond the Basics," *PC Week* 4 (April 24, 1987).

6. The format on screen feature indicates whether special formatting, such as boldface or underlined text, is shown on the screen as it will appear in the document when it is printed.

7. The multiple document column shows whether the word processor can edit more than one document at a time.

8. All of the word processors shown in Exhibit 6.10 have spelling checkers. The dictionary column shows the number of words contained in the spelling checker dictionary.

Summary

Word processors deal with documents stored on floppy disks and hard disks. When a document is retrieved, a copy of that document is placed in primary memory, and the user works on that copy.

The contents of a document are changed by editing that document. The word processor allows a user to move a cursor around in the document with various movement commands.

When a user begins entering text into a document, the words will automatically wrap to the next line when they go beyond the right margin. This is known as *word wrap*.

Word processors usually support both an *overtype mode*, where characters can be replaced by typing new characters over them, and an *insert mode*, where characters are always inserted in front of the cursor and the old characters are pushed to the right.

Word processors give users various deletion capabilities, where a character, word, line, or block of text can be deleted.

Text can be moved around in the document by using a *block move* feature. In a block move, the beginning and end of the text to be moved is marked, the text is removed from the document, the user moves to the place where the text is to be moved to, and the block is placed back into the text.

Word processors allow users to *search* through the document for specific words or phrases. A *search and replace* option allows a user to replace a string when it is found. This can be done for a single occurrence of the string or for every occurrence of the string in the document (*global search and replace*).

Document formatting is accomplished in some word processors with *embedded commands*. These commands are used by the word processor to format the document at the time of printing.

Other word processors actually format the document on the screen so that the user can see exactly how it will look at the time of printing.

Some other formatting procedures include setting *margins*, *indenting* sections of text, *centering* words on a line, and *justifying* the right edge.

Documents are put on paper by using a PRINT command. Most word processors provide a command that will let the user preview the printed document on the screen before actually committing it to paper.

When a user ends an editing session, there are three possible options. One option ends the session by destroying the copy of the document in primary memory and leaving the original document on the floppy disk unchanged. The REPLACE option puts the copy in the place of the original document on the floppy disk. The original document is either destroyed or moved to a backup file. The SAVE option lets the user put the copy on the floppy disk under a name different from the original.

Some of the features a user might look for in choosing a word processor include the type of user interface, amount of memory required, and document formatting done on the screen.

Other features might include automatic backup, undeleting deleted text, and the ability to edit more than one document. For word processors with spelling checkers, the size of the dictionary might be an important feature.

Review Questions

1. Explain the difference among the QUIT, REPLACE, and SAVE options for ending an editing session with a word processor.
2. What is the difference between overtype and insert?
3. What is word wrap?
4. Explain how a block move is accomplished.
5. How is the search function in a word processor used?
6. Explain how margins are set in a word processor.
7. What are the normal measurements for margins on a microcomputer printer?
8. What is a ruler? How is it used in indenting text?
9. Explain *justification*.
10. What is an embedded command?

CHAPTER 7 ■ Introduction to Electronic Spreadsheets

INTERACTING WITH A SPREADSHEET
Moving Around
Windows

CREATING A SPREADSHEET
The Control Panel
Labels, Numbers, and Formulas
Entering Labels and Numbers
Entering Formulas
Automatic Recalculation
Ranges
Built-In Functions

EDITING A SPREADSHEET
Editing Cells
Adding and Removing Rows and Columns
Moving Cells

FORMATTING THE SPREADSHEET
Formatting Labels
Formatting Numbers
Changing Column Widths

SPREADSHEET COMMANDS
Menus
The HELP Facility
Global Versus Range Commands
Printing a Spreadsheet
Saving and Retrieving

SUMMARY

REVIEW QUESTIONS

The second major category of microcomputer software that is useful to an end-user is the electronic spreadsheet. Spreadsheets are particularly helpful in financial applications where a large number of figures and formulas need to be organized to ensure accuracy. A typical use for a spreadsheet is in budgeting, which requires reports such as income statements, balance sheets, and budgets. These reports are laid out in columns and rows to create cells. Many of these cells contain labels or headings that indicate what each figure is. Other cells contain data about a company, and some contain figures which result from calculations based on values appearing in other cells on the spreadsheet.

In this chapter you will learn to do the following:

1. Identify the various components of a spreadsheet.
2. Enter labels and numbers into a spreadsheet.
3. Edit the contents of a spreadsheet.
4. Format a spreadsheet.
5. Identify the commands to print and save a spreadsheet.

INTERACTING WITH A SPREADSHEET

The electronic spreadsheet, like its paper ancestor, is simply a large grid of cells that is created by the intersection of columns and rows. Electronic spreadsheets, however, hold many more cells than would be practical on a sheet of paper; the largest ones today contain as many as 32,000 columns and 32,000 rows, giving a user over 1 billion cells to work with. There are, of course, practical limitations to using this many cells, including the memory size of the microcomputer using the spreadsheet and the ability of a user to keep track of so many cells. Most users can get by with less than 1000 cells for most applications.

Naturally, thousands of cells cannot be placed on a computer screen at one time. Approximately 20 rows and 8 columns of most spreadsheets can appear on a screen at one time. The columns are usually labeled with letters of the alphabet (a notable exception is MULTIPLAN, which uses numbers). Since there are only 26 letters, columns from 27 on are labeled AA, AB, AC, and so on. The rows are usually labeled with numbers. Therefore, each cell is referred to by its *address,* which is a combination of the letter of the column and the number of the row that the cell is in. Cell addresses include A1, AC87, and BB2045. Typically, the column letter is first, followed by the row number. Exhibit 7.1 shows what the Lotus 1-2-3 electronic spreadsheet looks like.

Moving Around

When you are using a spreadsheet, your current location will always be represented by the **current cell pointer.** In Exhibit 7.1, the current cell pointer is the rectangular highlight shown in cell A1. This current cell pointer can be moved one cell at a time in any direction by using the arrow keys on the numeric keypad portion of the keyboard (see Exhibit 7.2). There are varying degrees of movement through a spreadsheet, just

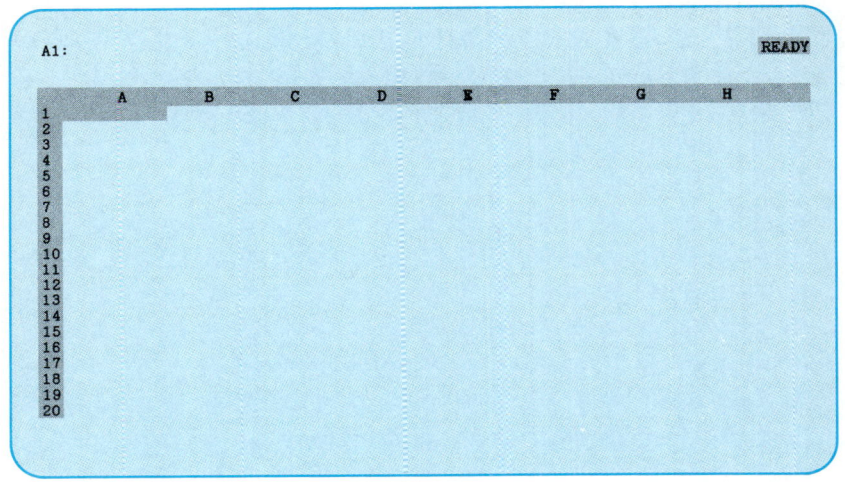

EXHIBIT 7.1
The Lotus 1-2-3 Electronic Spreadsheet

as there are through the text in a word processor. Usually the *PgUp* and *PgDn* keys move the spreadsheet up and down a full screen (about 20 rows). The *Tab* and *Shift-Tab* keys move the screen right and left about 8 columns at a time.

In addition, spreadsheets include a jump feature which allows the user to specify an address of a cell and jump to the part of the spreadsheet containing that cell, making it the current cell. One particular jump that most spreadsheets use is the *home* key. By pressing this key, you can jump immediately to cell A1, which is considered the *home* location in the spreadsheet. More advanced spreadsheets give more complex movement functions, but the ones discussed are typical electronic spreadsheets.

Windows

When interacting with a spreadsheet, an end-user must think of the screen as a window through which the spreadsheet is viewed. For example, Exhibit 7.1 represents a window which shows the top left corner of the

EXHIBIT 7.2
This is the IBM PC keyboard with some of the special keys used by spreadsheet programs highlighted.

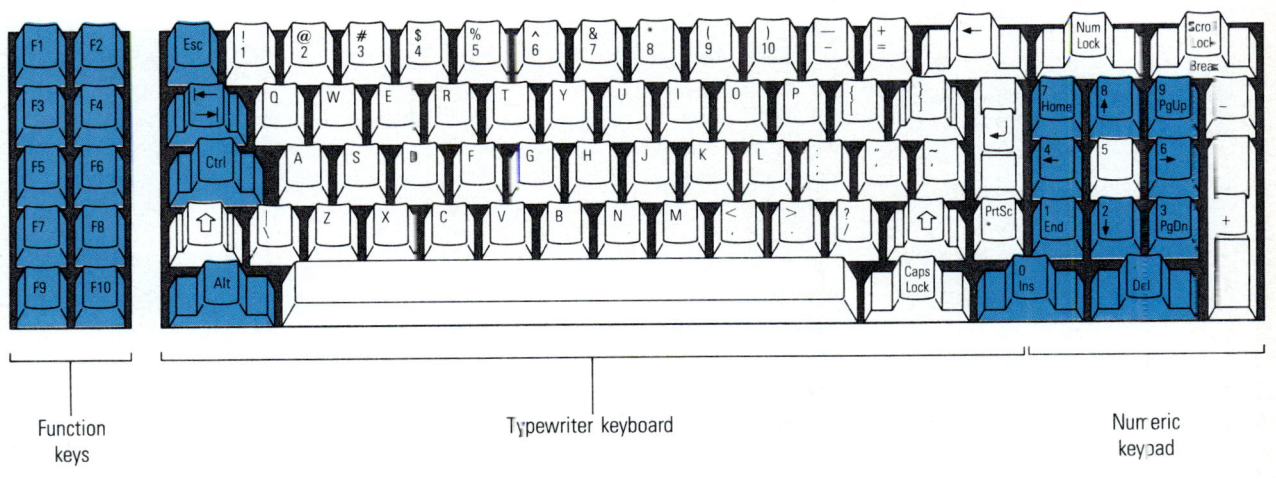

Function keys · Typewriter keyboard · Numeric keypad

Interacting with a Spreadsheet   125

EXHIBIT 7.3
When the cursor moves from cell H1 to I1, column I appears at the right and column A disappears at the left. The window has *scrolled* one column to the right.

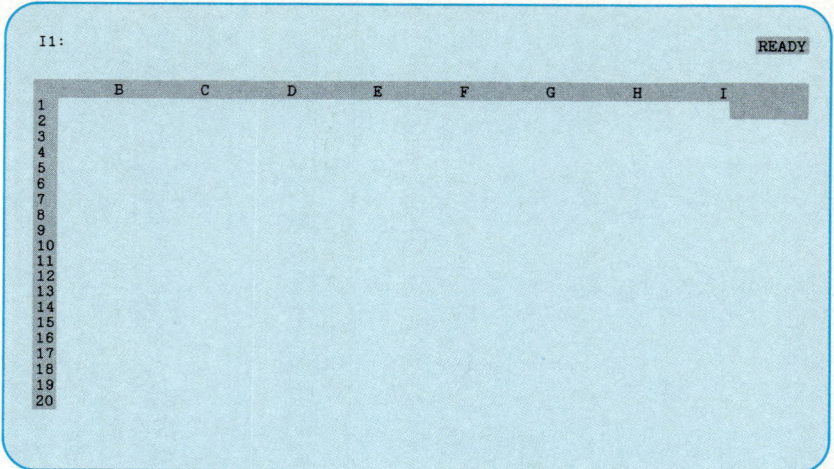

spreadsheet. There are additional columns to the right and additional rows at the bottom which cannot be seen. Even though the additional rows and columns cannot be seen, they do exist.

For example, to see the columns to the right of the screen, a user can move the current cell pointer to the right until it is at the edge of the screen. Exhibit 7.3 shows what the spreadsheet would look like after the pointer is moved into cell I1. Note how column I appears at the right of the screen and column A disappears at the left. In other words, the window has been shifted one column to the right so the new column can be seen. This process of shifting the window in any direction is **scrolling.**

CREATING A SPREADSHEET

A spreadsheet is created by entering data into the cells. In this section, we will look at the many different types of data that can be entered. For purposes of illustration, we will use the sample spreadsheet in Exhibit 7.4, which shows a breakeven analysis.

The Control Panel

In Exhibit 7.4, there are three lines on the screen above the row of column letters. This area outside of the spreadsheet itself is known as the **control panel.** In Lotus 1-2-3 the control panel is at the top, but in other spreadsheets, such as SUPERCALC4, the control panel is at the bottom (see Exhibit 7.5).

The control panel is the place where most of the activity will occur as information is entered into the cells on the spreadsheet. The first line, called the **status line,** shows information about the current cell, such as the current cell address and what is stored in that cell (see the first line of the control panels of Exhibits 7.4 and 7.5).

In addition to the status line, control panels include a **prompt line** (line 3 in Lotus 1-2-3 and line 2 in SUPERCALC4), which is used during

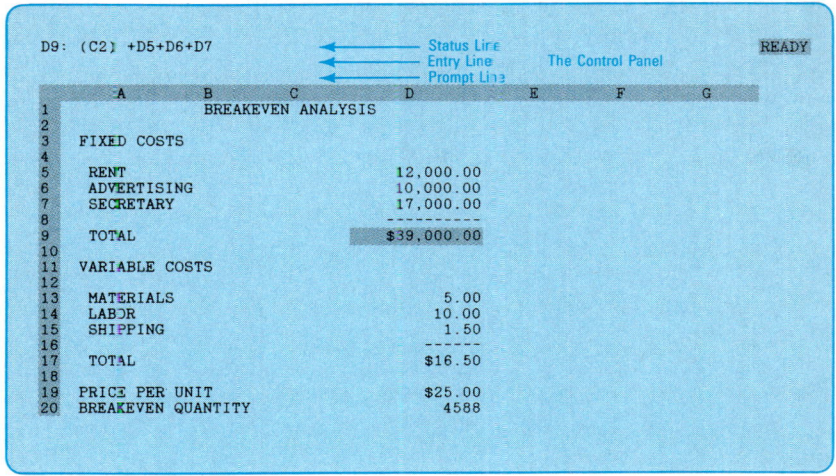

EXHIBIT 7.4

A Sample Spreadsheet Used to Perform a Breakeven Analysis

The three lines above the row of column letters represent the control panel in this Lotus 1-2-3 spreadsheet.

commands and which will display messages to the user (prompts) when commands are being entered. The third line in the control panel is called the **entry line.** Whenever a user types a command or data into a cell, the characters appear on this entry line rather than in the cell on the spreadsheet. This allows a user to edit the information on the entry line before sending it to the current cell to be stored. Lotus has only these three lines in its control panel. SUPERCALC4 adds a fourth line called the **HELP line,** which displays information that may be helpful to the user.

Labels, Numbers, and Formulas

Any entry in a cell on the spreadsheet must be one of three things: a label, a number, or a formula. **Labels** contain alphabetic letters and special characters and cannot be used in mathematical operations. **Numbers** can contain the digits from zero to nine and a period to indicate a decimal place. These numbers can be involved in mathematical operations, such as addition, subtraction, multiplication, and division. A for-

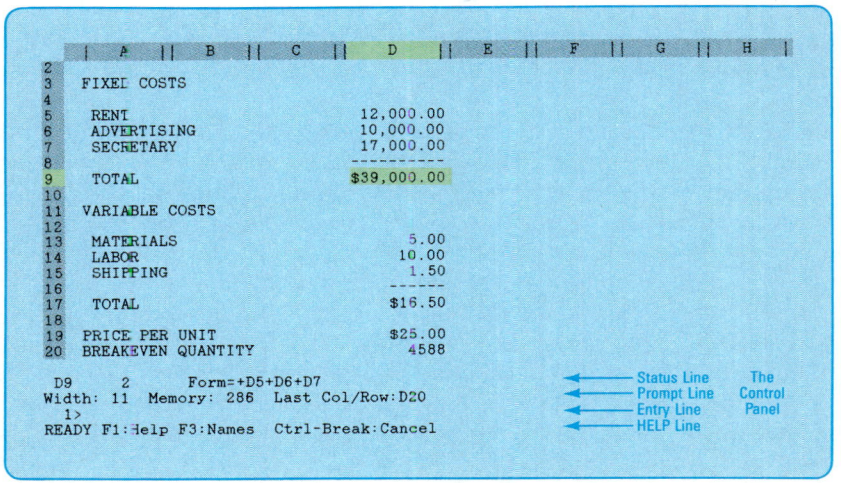

EXHIBIT 7.5

The Breakeven Analysis Shown in the SUPERCALC4 Spreadsheet

The control panel is the group of four lines shown below line 20.

Creating a Spreadsheet

mula is a combination of cell addresses and numbers joined together by mathematical symbols (+, −, *, and /). In Exhibit 7.4, cell A3 contains the label FIXED COSTS. An example of a cell containing a number is cell D5, which contains the number 12000. However, notice the comma and decimal places (12,000.00) in the display. If an entry that is a number can only contain digits and a decimal place, where did the comma come from? Special characters like commas and dollar signs are added to numbers with format commands (see the discussion later in this chapter).

This example illustrates an important concept in spreadsheets: the information displayed in the cell on the spreadsheet is not always the same as what is actually stored in that cell. The number 12000 is stored in cell D5 but on the spreadsheet cell D5 displays 12,000.00. The difference between what is displayed and what is stored also occurs in formulas. For example, cell D9 contains the formula +D5+D6+D7. This formula instructs the spreadsheet to add the contents of cells D5, D6, and D7 and display the result. Thus, when +D5+D6+D7 is stored in cell D9, the number $39,000.00 is displayed in cell D9 on the spreadsheet.

The only way to tell what is actually stored in a particular cell on a spreadsheet is to move the current cell pointer to that cell and look at the status line in the control panel (see Exhibits 7.4 and 7.5). The status line always shows you the actual contents of the cell.

Entering Labels and Numbers

When a user wishes to enter something into a cell on the spreadsheet, the current cell pointer must first be moved to that cell. As indicated earlier, the letters or numbers the user types appear on the entry line of the control panel. When the entry line contains the information to be entered, the user presses the RETURN key, and the information is placed in the current cell.

In addition to entering data into a current cell by using the RETURN key, a user of some spreadsheets (like Lotus 1-2-3) can enter data and simultaneously move the current cell pointer in a certain direction by pressing an arrow key. For example, pressing the right arrow key after information is typed on the entry line will enter that information into the current cell and then move the current cell pointer to the right one cell. This is helpful when, after entering something in the current cell, the user wants to go to the cell to the right to make the next entry. Other spreadsheets (like SUPERCALC4) use the direction of the last arrow key pressed as the direction to move the current cell pointer when an entry is made. This usually gives less control, since RETURN can never be pressed without the current cell pointer being moved. Regardless of how this feature of making an entry and simultaneously moving the pointer is implemented, it can be very useful when making a long series of entries down a column or across a row.

Spreadsheets are programmed to determine whether an entry is to be a label or a number by the first character typed on the entry line. Some spreadsheets treat every entry which begins with a letter as a label. Others require the use of a special **label-prefix character** (usually double quotation marks) to indicate that an entry is to be treated as a label. If the first character of an entry is a number or decimal point, the spreadsheet treats that entry as a number.

Entering Formulas

Like a label or number, a formula is typed on the entry line and then entered into the current cell by pressing the RETURN key. A formula contains numbers and cell addresses which are related by mathematical symbols. The most common symbols include addition (+), subtraction (−), multiplication (*), division (/), and exponentiation (** or ^). A formula can contain only numbers, only cell addresses, or a mixture of both. For example, a cell may contain the formula 18/3. The result of this calculation, 6, will be displayed on the screen in the cell in which this formula is stored. The simplest formula involving a cell address is one which simply sets one cell equal to another. If cell A10 contains the number 56 and the formula +A10 is entered into cell F34, then the value 56 will be displayed in cell F34. A formula in a cell indicates that the cell in which the formula is stored is equal to the result of the calculation. Thus, +A10, stored in cell F34, essentially says F34 = +A10.

Formulas can, of course, be much more complicated than the ones used in the example. For example, cell D20 on the sample spreadsheet in Exhibit 7.6 contains the formula +D9/(D19−D17). (This is seen by checking the status line.) In other words, cell D20 is equal to +D9/(D19−D17). The use of parentheses in this formula brings up an important concept in constructing formulas known as **precedence,** which means that computers perform mathematical operations in a particular order when a calculation is made. First, any exponentiations are performed, followed by any multiplications and divisions, and then all additions and subtractions are performed. Operations at the same level are performed in order from left to right.

Consider our example without the parentheses: +D9/D19−D17. Under the normal rules of precedence, the division of D9 by D19 will be performed first, since divisions are done before subtractions. 39,000 will be divided by 25, giving 1560. Then D17 will be subtracted from that (1560 −15), which is 1545. This is not the correct answer, because the breakeven quantity is calculated by first finding the difference between the total variable costs (D17) and the selling price (D19) and then dividing the

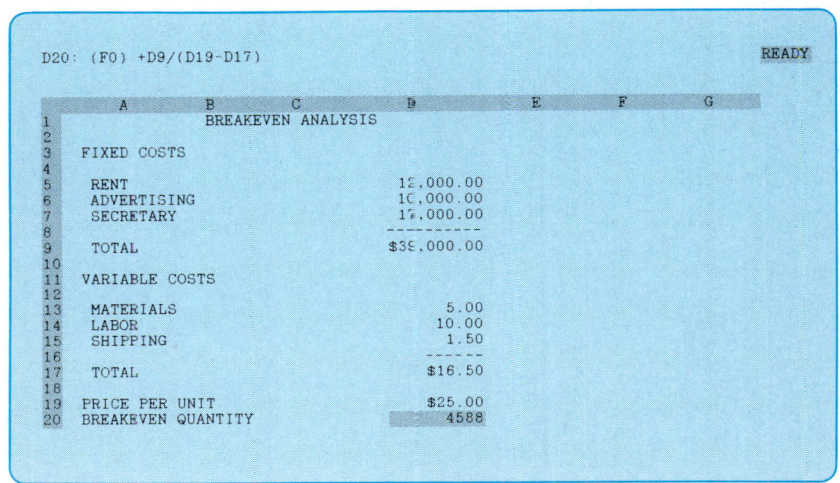

EXHIBIT 7.6
The Breakeven Analysis with the Formula in Cell B20 Displayed on the Screen

fixed costs by that difference. Thus, we want the spreadsheet to calculate the difference between D19 and D17 first and then do the division. When the normal precedence of operations is not desired, it can be overridden by putting the calculations to be performed first inside parentheses, as was done in cell D20 of Exhibit 7.6.

Automatic Recalculation

When a formula involves cell addresses, a change in a cell referenced in a formula causes the result to be recalculated. The formula +D9/(D19−D17) currently displays 4588 in the cell in which it is stored. If the entry in cell D19 were changed from 25 to 30, the number displayed in cell D20 would automatically be updated to 2889. It is as if the spreadsheet is constantly monitoring all of the formulas so that a change in a cell that affects the answer to a formula automatically causes the results of that formula to be recalculated and updated on the screen. Sometimes a change in a single cell can cause a ripple effect throughout the spreadsheet. For example, Exhibit 7.7 shows our sample spreadsheet after the entry in cell D5 is changed from 12000 to 10000. This change causes the total for the fixed costs in cell D9 to change to 37000. Cell D9 is, in turn, used in the formula in cell D20 so that the formula is recalculated and the result changed to 4353.

No matter how complex the formula is, if any of the cells referenced in that formula change, the result is automatically recalculated and the new result is displayed. This automatic recalculation feature makes a spreadsheet extremely useful to managers who can use the results as quickly as they can get them. Using a spreadsheet, a manager can perform a *what if* analysis. The manager can see how an increase in rent by 1000 dollars will affect the breakeven point by simply increasing the rent entry by 1000. The effect of a decrease in labor costs coupled with a simultaneous increase in shipping costs on the breakeven quantity can be determined by simply changing the two entries and watching the spreadsheet do the recalculation.

EXHIBIT 7.7
When the entry in D5 is changed to 10000, the results of the formulas in cells D9 and D20 are automatically recalculated.

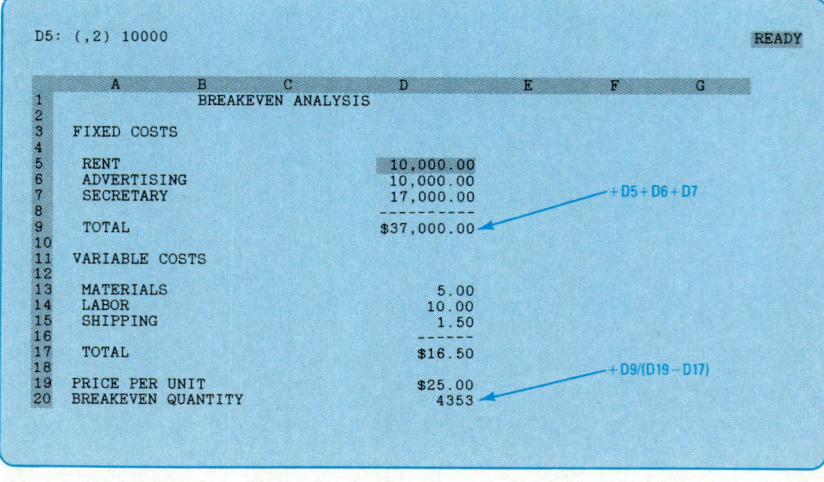

■ 7 *Introduction to Electronic Spreadsheets*

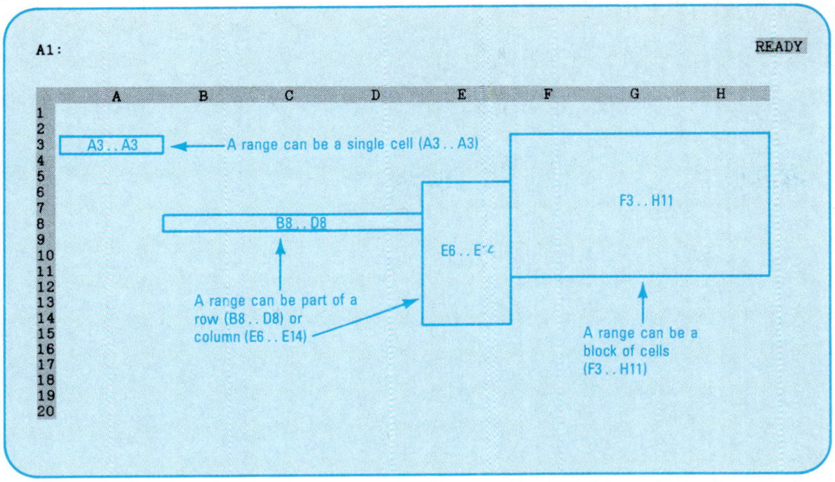

EXHIBIT 7.8
Some Examples of Ranges

Ranges

In spreadsheets it is important to understand the concept of a range before understanding how functions and commands are used. A **range** is simply a continuous group of cells that forms a square or rectangle. It can be used in commands when a user wishes to perform an operation on many cells rather than just one. A range can be as small as a single cell or as large as the entire spreadsheet. A range can be a row or a column; it can be part of a row or part of a column. It can be a block of cells (several columns and rows). A spreadsheet requires that all ranges be identified by a beginning and an ending cell address separated by a special character (usually a period or a colon). Some spreadsheets allow you to assign a name to a range, which can be used in place of the beginning and ending cell addresses. Exhibit 7.8 shows some examples of valid ranges. Notice how each range has a rectangular shape.

Built-In Functions

Spreadsheets provide functions that will perform operations normally accomplished with complex formulas. For example, the +D5+D6+D7 formula in cell D9 was used to add the contents of three cells together. Note that these cells are also the range D5 .. D7 (D5 to D7). In other words, we want to sum up all of the cells in this range. Spreadsheets have a built-in function, called SUM, which will sum up contents of all of the cells in any range. Thus, we could have used SUM(D5 .. D7) to do the same thing as the formula above. The advantage of the SUM function is that it can be used to add the contents of the cells in a range of any size. If we wanted to sum the first 100 cells in column D, we could use SUM(D1 .. D100). This is much more efficient than writing a formula with 100 cell addresses separated by plus signs.

Exhibit 7.9 shows our breakeven analysis with the SUM function used to total the variable costs (see the status line). Note how there is an @ in front of the word SUM. In Lotus, if an entry begins with a letter, it is treated as a label. Thus, if a user entered SUM(D13 .. D15), it would become a

Creating a Spreadsheet

EXHIBIT 7.9

The @SUM function in cell D17 is used to add the contents of all of the cells in the range D13..D15. The (C2) in front of the @SUM function indicates that cell D17 has a currency format with two decimal places (see the discussion of formatting later in this chapter).

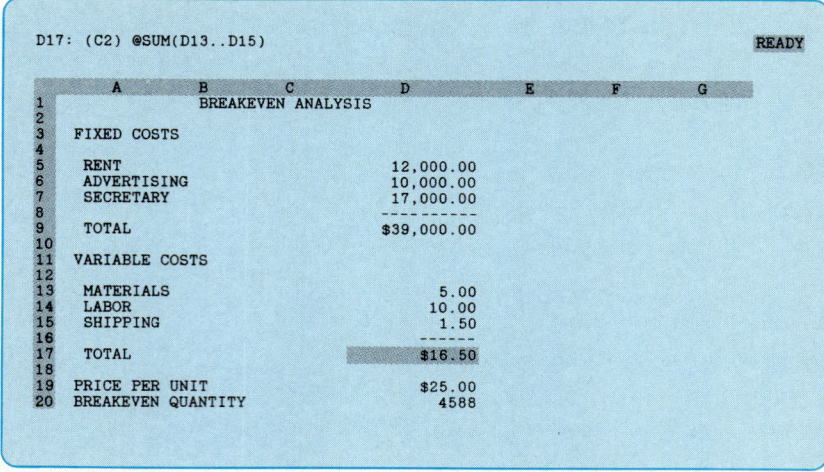

label instead of a formula. To avoid this problem, Lotus begins all built-in functions with an @. Other spreadsheets require a label prefix in front of all labels so that formulas can start with the letter in a cell address or the letter that begins a function name.

Spreadsheets provide many different types of built-in functions for calculations that are mathematical, financial, and statistical. Exhibit 7.10 shows some of the functions provided by most spreadsheets.

EXHIBIT 7.10
Some of the Built-In Functions Available in Lotus 1-2-3

MATHEMATICAL FUNCTIONS

@SQRT(X)	square root
@ABS(X)	absolute value
@LOG(X)	log base 10
@PI	pi
@SIN(X)	sine
@COS(X)	cosine
@TAN(X)	tangent

FINANCIAL FUNCTIONS

@NPV(x,range)	net present value
@PMT(principal,interest,term)	monthly payment
@FV(payment,interest,term)	future value
@PV(payment,interest,term)	present value

STATISTICAL FUNCTIONS

@SUM(range)	total value
@AVG(range)	average
@MIN(range)	minimum
@MAX(range)	maximum
@STD(range)	standard deviation

EDITING A SPREADSHEET

Once entries have been made in the cells of the spreadsheet, a user still has a great deal of control over how the spreadsheet is arranged. The contents of any cell can be changed, new columns and rows can be added, and entries can be moved from one cell to another.

Editing Cells

The simplest way to edit a cell is to replace its contents with something else. Thus, if a user entered *runt* instead of *rent* into cell A5, that user could simply move to A5, type *rent,* and press RETURN. The *runt* would be replaced by *rent*.

All spreadsheets provide an EDIT command or key which lets the user copy the contents of the current cell and put it back on the entry line where it can be altered. Once the entry has been changed, the user can press RETURN, and the revised entry will be placed back in the current cell. This is particularly useful when there is a minor mistake in a long label; typing the whole label over would be inefficient.

When an entry is on the entry line, a spreadsheet will allow editing of that entry by deleting and adding characters to it. Usually the right and left arrow keys can be used to move a cursor across the line. Sometimes the HOME and END keys can be used to jump to the beginning or end of the entry. Some spreadsheets will not allow typing over any characters that are already in the entry, forcing the user to specifically delete any character that isn't wanted. Other spreadsheets have both an insert and an overtype mode, just as some word processors do.

Adding and Removing Rows and Columns

A user can create new cells on a spreadsheet by inserting a new column or row. For example, if a user needs some additional cells to the left of column A, a command can be used to instruct the spreadsheet to create a new column A. When this column is inserted, the entries in the old column A and all of the entries in the columns to the right will be shifted one column to the right. (Exhibit 7.11 shows what the sample spreadsheet will look like after column A is inserted.) The same thing can be done with rows. If a new row 11 is inserted, the old row 11 and all of the rows below it will be moved down one row.

Columns and rows can also be deleted using a command. When a column is deleted, all of the entries to the right of that column are shifted to the left to fill the gap. When a row is deleted, all of the entries below that row are shifted up. Exhibit 7.12 shows the sample spreadsheet after row 18 has been deleted.

It is important to note that when columns or rows are added, some of the numbers and formulas may be shifted into different cells. Spreadsheets are able to adjust all formulas so that their relative locations to the cell addresses in them are preserved. This is known as the *adjustment of a formula,* and it occurs automatically whenever the location of a formula is

EXHIBIT 7.11
When column A is inserted, the contents of the spreadsheet are shifted to the right.

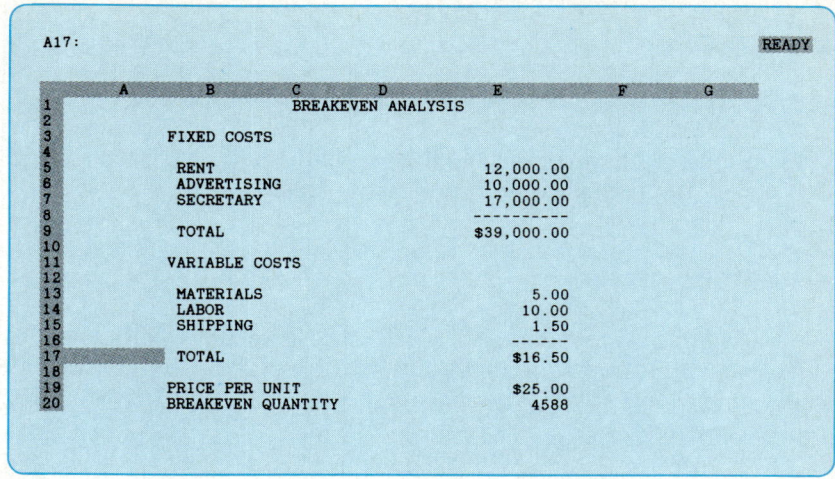

altered by inserting or deleting a column or row. (See the "Adjustment of Relative Formulas" discussion in Chapter 8 for more details.) This adjustment allows the formula to remain correct when columns and rows are inserted or deleted as long as a cell used in the calculation is not deleted.

EXHIBIT 7.12
When a row is deleted, all entries below that row shift up to fill the gap.

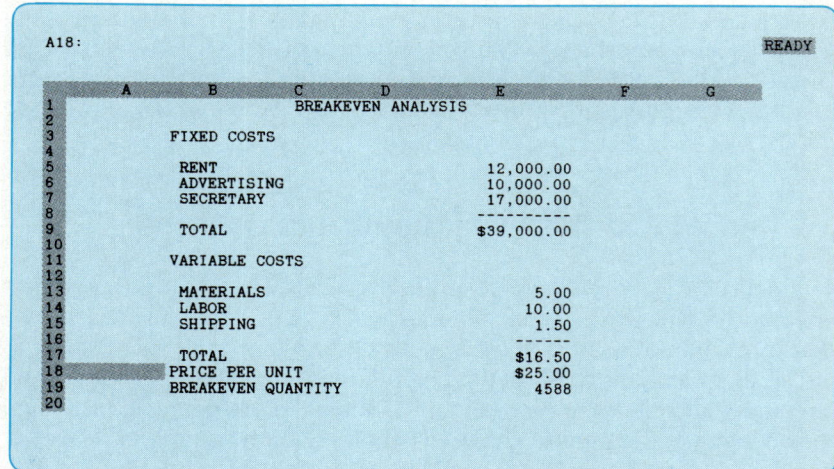

Moving Cells

A user can move an entry from one cell to another using a special MOVE command. The user must supply the address of the cell to be moved and the new address the entry will be moved to. Care must be taken when moving numbers that are used in formulas. If a number such as the 5.00 in cell E13 of Exhibit 7.12 were moved, an error would occur in the formula in cell D17 since it refers to the entry in cell D13. Moving a formula can also cause misleading results, because the addresses in the formula will be altered when its location is changed (see the "Adjustment of Relative Formulas" discussion in Chapter 8). Thus, the MOVE command is most useful in rearranging headings and must be used with great care when numbers and formulas are involved. It should also be noted that the contents of a cell that is the destination of a MOVE command will be destroyed and replaced with the contents being moved into the cell.

FORMATTING THE SPREADSHEET

Formatting is the process of altering the way in which numbers and labels are displayed on the spreadsheet itself. Once a number has been entered into a cell, its appearance can be altered by adding such things as dollar signs and commas. Labels can be moved within a cell to get them to line up any way the user desires.

Formatting Labels

The formatting of labels can be accomplished in two ways. Some spreadsheets provide different label prefixes which can do the formatting. Others give the user control over label formatting in the form of a command. Some spreadsheets use both methods.

Basically, the types of formatting include left-justified, right-justified, centered, and repeating. These formats refer to the displaying of the label in the cell on the spreadsheet. Exhibit 7.13 shows some examples of these types of formatting. The repeating prefix repeats the entry across the cell. The repeating text entry is on the status line, and the cell on the spreadsheet shows how the entry is repeated all the way across the cell.

Formatting Numbers

Some spreadsheets give the user control over the positioning of a number in a cell, just as can be done with labels. Usually right- and left-justify options are available. Other spreadsheets force all numbers to be

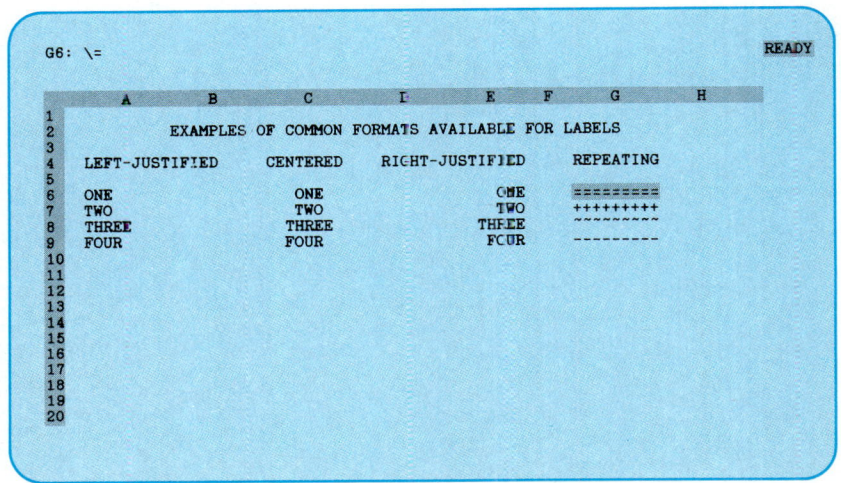

EXHIBIT 7.13
Some Examples of Different Formats for Labels
Note how the repeating text character (\) in G6 causes the dash that follows to be repeated across the cell.

Formatting the Spreadsheet ■ 135

right-justified in order to make the decimal places line up better and to make it easier to read the numbers without making an error.

Many more format variations exist for numbers than for labels. Spreadsheets give various levels of control over the number of decimal places displayed. Dollar signs and commas between thousands can also be displayed. Some spreadsheets offer a percent format and scientific notation. The types of formats available and the amount of control over them vary widely among the different spreadsheet programs. Exhibit 7.14 shows some of the numeric formats available in Lotus 1-2-3.

Changing Column Widths

It is important to realize that the size of a cell on the screen does not place any limitation on the size of the entry that can be placed in that cell. Every cell can hold up to 256 characters regardless of how big it looks on the screen. Its size on the screen is simply the *display width*.

A user can alter the display width of a cell on the screen only by altering the width of a column. In order to keep things lined up, the spreadsheet programs do not allow the width of individual cells to be changed. The width of any column can be set from 1 to 72 by using a column-width command. Spreadsheets have a special way of dealing with entries that are too long to fit in the display width of a cell. If an entry is a label, the characters that will not fit in the cell will overflow into the cells to the right as long as those adjacent cells are empty.

The long title for the sample spreadsheet, BREAKEVEN ANALYSIS, was entered into cell C1 and allowed to overflow into cell D1. As long as the cells to the right remain empty, the label will continue to be displayed. As soon as an entry is made in the cell to the right, the label will be truncated (cut off) at the border between the two cells. Thus, if a long label is put into a cell and it cannot overflow into the cell to the right, then the user must widen the column to accommodate the long label.

Numbers that are too large to be displayed in a cell are treated in a different way. When a number is too long, it would not be good to truncate it and display only the part that fits, because a user will think that the entire

EXHIBIT 7.14
Some Examples of Numeric Formats That Can Be Used in Lotus 1-2-3

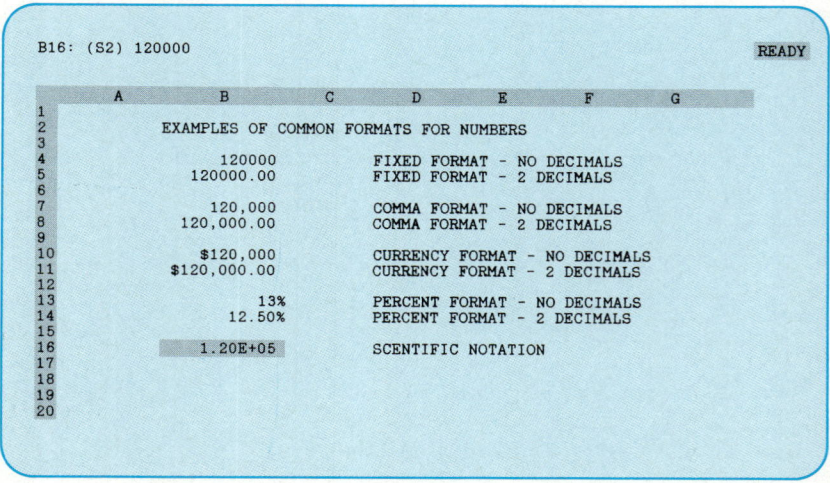

number is being shown. Therefore, when a number is too large, the cell will usually be filled with stars (*) to indicate that a number is in the cell but is too big to be displayed (sometimes < is used). This often occurs when a number is formatted, because a format, such as currency, adds extra characters to the number, which makes it longer. The user's only option, in this case, is to widen the column so that the number can be displayed.

SPREADSHEET COMMANDS

In many places in the preceding discussion, we have indicated that certain functions can be accomplished using commands. In spreadsheets, commands are used to format entries, change the layout of the spreadsheet, print spreadsheets, and work with spreadsheet files. The user tells the spreadsheet when a command is to be entered by typing a special character (usually a slash) in the first position on the entry line. When the slash (/) is typed, the spreadsheet enters the command mode and shows the user menus of commands from which to choose.

Menus

In Lotus 1-2-3, the menu of commands appears on the entry line with the first choice in the menu highlighted, and the prompt line (the third line of the control panel) shows an extended description of the highlighted menu choice (see Exhibit 7.15). A user can choose an option in the menu by moving the highlight with the arrow keys and pressing RETURN to select the highlighted choice. A choice can also be selected by typing the first letter of the option.

As options are chosen, a submenu usually appears for more detailed information needed to complete the command. As a user goes deeper into the hierarchy of menus, it is possible that an incorrect choice might be made. Spreadsheets usually allow a user to back through the various

```
D20: (F0) +D9/(D19-D17)                                          MENU
Worksheet Range Copy Move File Print Graph Data Quit
Global, Insert, Delete, Column-Width, Erase, Titles, Window, Status
        A         B         C         D         E         F         G
 1
 2                    BREAKEVEN ANALYSIS
 3       FIXED COSTS
 4
 5       RENT                         12,000.00
 6       ADVERTISING                  10,000.00
 7       SECRETARY                    17,000.00
 8                                    ---------
 9       TOTAL                        $39,000.00
10
11       VARIABLE COSTS
12
13       MATERIALS                         5.00
14       LABOR                            10.00
15       SHIPPING                          1.50
16                                         -----
17       TOTAL                            $16.50
18
19       PRICE PER UNIT                   $25.00
20       BREAKEVEN QUANTITY                 4588
```

EXHIBIT 7.15

Lotus 1-2-3 displays a menu of commands on the entry line, and the prompt line shows the options available if the highlighted command is chosen.

EXHIBIT 7.16
The SUPERCALC4 Command Menu

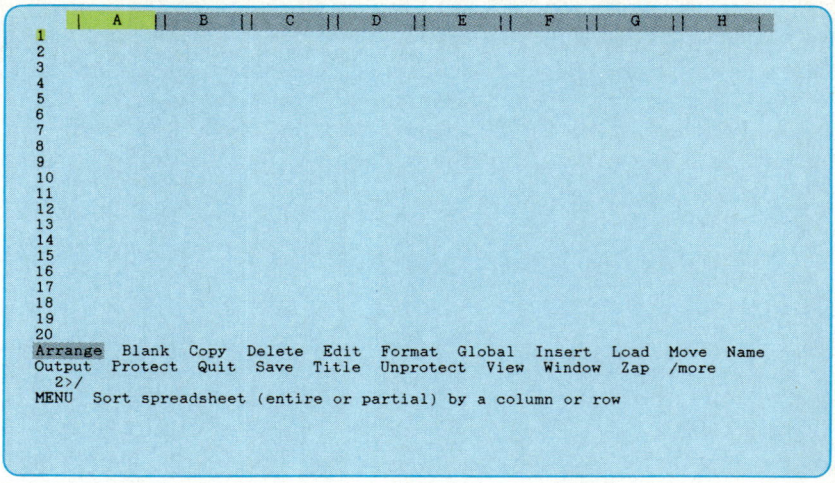

menus by pressing a special key (such as the *Esc* key) to back up to the previous menu.

In SUPERCALC4, typing a slash on the entry line causes the first and second lines to display a menu of choices that represent various commands (see Exhibit 7.16). As with Lotus 1-2-3, the user can select a menu option by moving a menu cursor to the option desired and pressing RETURN or by typing the first letter of the desired option.

The HELP Facility

Spreadsheet programs provide a special **HELP key** (F1 in Lotus 1-2-3 and SUPERCALC4) that can be pressed at any time to get information about using the spreadsheet. Some spreadsheets contain very complex HELP facilities that allow the user to choose among screens that cover almost every aspect of using a spreadsheet. Exhibit 7.17 shows the Lotus 1-2-3 HELP screen in which the user can choose among various topics for which help is available.

EXHIBIT 7.17
In the Lotus 1-2-3 HELP facility, a user can get information about any aspect of creating or using a spreadsheet.

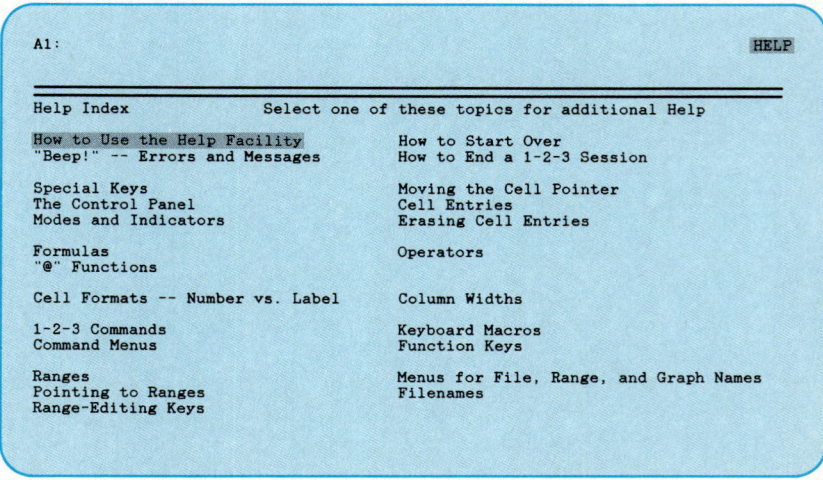

An important feature of the HELP facility is that it is sensitive to what the user was doing before it was invoked. If the user was making an entry, the HELP facility will provide information about how entries can be made. If the user was issuing a print command, the HELP facility will provide information about how the print command works.

When the HELP facility is entered, the spreadsheet disappears so that the HELP screens can be shown. The work the user was doing on the spreadsheet is remembered so that when the HELP facility is terminated, the user is put back to the exact place he or she was before the HELP key was pressed.

Global Versus Range Commands

Most spreadsheets make some type of distinction between *global commands* and *range commands*. This distinction has to do with the amount of the spreadsheet affected by the commands. For example, spreadsheets have a global format command and a range format command. **Global commands** affect all of the cells on the spreadsheet. A user can set the global format for numbers to currency with two decimal places. Conversely, if a user only wanted to change the format of some numbers in a few cells, a **range command** can be used. The user specifies a range over which that format is to take effect.

Other global commands include setting a column width for all columns and choosing a global format for all labels. When a global command is issued, it is important to realize that a global format cannot override a range format. Thus, if the display width of column C is set to 13, a subsequent global column-width setting of 12 will not affect column C. The same thing occurs with numeric and label formats. Those set with a range command are unchanged by a subsequent global command.

Printing a Spreadsheet

Once a spreadsheet has been created, it can be printed on paper at any time. As with word processors, a single command causes the spreadsheet to be printed. Thus, making a mistake is not costly, since the information is stored in electronic form, which can be easily corrected and reprinted.

In a print command, the user must specify a range that represents what is to be printed. The user has complete control over how much of the spreadsheet is printed. As little as one cell or the entire spreadsheet can be printed; the only limitation is that the part to be printed must be a valid range of cells.

PRINT commands give a choice of destinations for a printed document. It can be sent either to a printer or to a file. The advantage of sending the printout to a file is that this file is in electronic form, and it can be incorporated into another file, such as a word processing document. Thus, a user can send a spreadsheet to a file, get into a word processor, and then pull that spreadsheet into a document so it can be used as a table or a figure.

Once the range and destination of the file have been specified, the user also has options about the printing of the range. It can be printed as it is displayed on the screen, or the actual contents of the cells (including formulas) can be listed. Headers and footers can be specified, margins can

EXHIBIT 7.18
An Example of How the Breakeven Analysis Spreadsheet Appears When It Is Printed

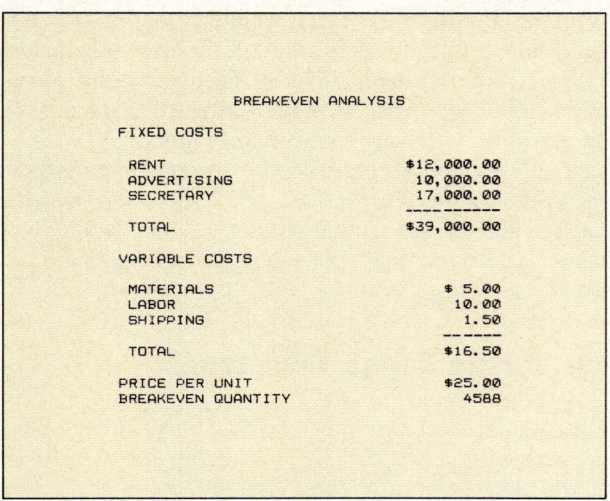

be changed, and even the borders (column letters and row numbers) can be included on the printout (Exhibit 7.18 shows how the sample spreadsheet looks when it is printed, using A1 . . D20 as the range).

Saving and Retrieving

The saving and retrieving of a spreadsheet also involves a spreadsheet command. The program asks for the name of the file to be used. Normally files are assumed to be on drive B, but this can be overridden by specifying the drive letter along with the file name. File extensions are usually omitted because each spreadsheet uses a default extension. For example, Lotus uses a WKS (worksheet) extension, while SUPERCALC4 uses a CAL extension.

When a spreadsheet is saved for the first time, it is simply put into the file named. Some spreadsheets have options during the SAVE command about saving just the values on the screen or saving all the contents of the spreadsheet, including values and formulas.

When a spreadsheet is altered, the user has a choice of saving the new version of the spreadsheet under the original name or under a new name. Usually, the user specifies a file name under both circumstances, and, if the name given is the same as the name of a file already on the diskette, the spreadsheet asks if the new version is supposed to replace the old one.

When a file is retrieved, a copy of the spreadsheet is placed in primary memory where it can be worked on. As with some word processors, this leaves the original spreadsheet intact on the diskette. Therefore, a user can make changes to the spreadsheet in memory but cannot change the original; or a user might retrieve a spreadsheet just to get a look at it and then go on to something else without having to save it. Normally, when a file is retrieved, any spreadsheet currently in memory is destroyed when a new spreadsheet is brought in. There are, however, different ways of retrieving a file. A user can copy all, or part, of a spreadsheet in a disk file into the current spreadsheet without destroying the current spreadsheet. When two spreadsheets are combined in this way, the user indicates where the new spreadsheet is to be merged.

Summary

A spreadsheet is a grid of columns and rows, forming cells that contain labels and numbers.

Electronic spreadsheets can hold many more cells than paper spreadsheets and are much more flexible and powerful because they are stored electronically.

A location on the spreadsheet is usually highlighted by the *current cell pointer.* This pointer can be moved in any direction with arrow keys.

Only a fraction of a spreadsheet can be seen at one time. This *window* of cells can be moved (*scrolled*) with the arrow keys. A user can also move through the spreadsheet a screen at a time in any direction and can use special jump keys to jump immediately to a cell on the spreadsheet.

Most of the activity involved in creating a spreadsheet takes place in the *control panel.* This is usually three or four lines at the top or bottom of a spreadsheet where the user interacts with the spreadsheet being created.

The first line of the control panel is the *status line,* which gives the user information about the current cell.

The control panel also has an *entry line* where entries are typed before being placed into the spreadsheet itself. When something is typed on the entry line, the user can edit that entry until it is correct. When the user presses the RETURN key, the entry is moved from the entry line to the current cell of the spreadsheet.

The third part of the control panel is the *prompt line,* which displays messages to the user during commands. Some spreadsheets add a fourth line, a *HELP line,* to the control panel, which provides help messages for the user.

Both labels and numbers can be entered into cells. Labels are usually preceded by a label prefix, which indicates how the label is to be lined up in the cell containing that label. A spreadsheet can also contain formulas, which are numbers and cell addresses joined by mathematical symbols to represent calculations to be performed.

In a spreadsheet, there is a difference between what is stored in a cell and what is displayed on the spreadsheet. Formulas are stored in cells, but the result of the calculation is what is displayed on the spreadsheet.

A label or number is entered by typing it on the entry line and pressing RETURN. Some spreadsheets allow a user to simultaneously make an entry and move the current cell pointer in some direction.

A formula is entered in the same way as a label or number is. When mathematical symbols are used, there is a specific order in which the calculations will be performed, known as *precedence.* Normally, exponentiation is performed first, followed by multiplication and division, and then addition and subtraction. This order can be altered by enclosing parts of the calculation in parentheses when they are to be performed first.

One of the most important features of a spreadsheet is its ability to deal with formulas containing cell addresses. Using cell addresses instead of numbers allows a user to change the contents of the cells on which the formula is based and have the result of the formula automatically recalculated.

A *range* is any continuous group of cells that can be specified by a beginning and ending cell address.

Spreadsheets provide built-in functions, such as the SUM function, which can add the numbers in a range of cells.

Spreadsheets also have an EDIT function, which allows the user to move an entry from the spreadsheet back onto the entry line for further editing.

Rows and columns can be inserted and deleted from the spreadsheet, and entries can be moved from one cell to another.

Formatting is the process of altering the appearance of entries on the spreadsheet. Labels can be formatted to be left- or right-justified, centered, or repeated. Numbers can be formatted with various numbers of decimal places, commas, and dollar signs. Percent formats and scientific notation are also available.

A cell can contain entries up to 256 characters long. The size of the cell on the spreadsheet itself is simply the number of those characters that will be displayed. The width of any column on the spreadsheet can be changed by the user.

When a label is too long to fit in a cell, it will overflow into the cells to the right as long as they are empty. Numbers that are too long will not be displayed, and the user must widen the column to see them.

Spreadsheet commands allow a user to perform tasks involving the spreadsheet as a whole or involving parts of the spreadsheet. When the command mode is entered, a user receives a menu from which choices can be made.

A distinction is made between global commands and *range commands.* Global commands affect the whole spreadsheet. Range commands affect only cells in a specified range. A global command cannot override a setting made by a range command.

The contents of a spreadsheet can be output to a disk file or to a printer. Any range on the spreadsheet can be printed. The user has options about setting margins, headers and footers, and the way the contents of the spreadsheet will be printed.

When a spreadsheet is saved, it can be stored in a new file, or it can replace a spreadsheet in an existing file. When a spreadsheet is retrieved, a copy of the spreadsheet is placed in primary memory. A user can also retrieve all, or part, of a spreadsheet and merge it with a spreadsheet already in memory.

Review Questions

1. List some problems in other courses you have taken that can be solved by using electronic spreadsheets.

2. Give an example of how the contents of a cell can differ from the display of that cell in a spreadsheet.

3. What is scrolling?

4. Describe the lines in a spreadsheet's control panel. Tell what each is used for.

5. Explain how a manager can use the automatic recalculation feature of a spreadsheet to perform a what if analysis.

6. List some of the built-in functions of spreadsheets.

7. What is the difference between global and range commands?

8. What type of formatting can be done to numbers and labels on a spreadsheet?

9. Explain how precedence affects the way a formula is calculated.

10. How does a spreadsheet handle numbers and labels that are too long to be displayed in a single cell?

CHAPTER 8 ■ Advanced Spreadsheets

COPYING FORMULAS
Adjustment of Relative Formulas
The COPY Command
Absolute Versus Relative Addresses

ADVANCED BUILT-IN FUNCTIONS
The LOOKUP Function
The IF Function
The CHOOSE Function

TEMPLATES
Designing a Template
Cell Protection
Hidden Cells

KEYBOARD MACROS

CHOOSING AN ELECTRONIC SPREADSHEET

SUMMARY

REVIEW QUESTIONS

In addition to the basic features discussed in Chapter 7, spreadsheets contain many advanced features that can make them even more useful for business applications. COPY commands can streamline the process of entering a large number of formulas. Advanced built-in functions, such as the IF function and lookup tables, enable the spreadsheet to determine decision outcomes. Templates can be used to predesign applications so that a user can fill in cells and create a spreadsheet without having to know a great deal about the spreadsheet program. Keyboard macros can be designed to perform common tasks for a user.

In this chapter you will learn to do the following:

1. Determine how formulas can be created using a COPY command.
2. Understand how the IF function and lookup tables work.
3. Discover how a template can be designed and used.
4. Define *keyboard macro* and become acquainted with what it can do.

COPYING FORMULAS

In Chapter 7 we saw how a formula was created by typing it on the entry line and pressing RETURN. All of the numbers displayed in Exhibit 8.1 in the RAISE, NEW SALARY, and YEARLY TAX columns are the results of formulas. This would mean that 36 formulas would have to be keyed in, and the user would have to be sure that all of the cell addresses in every formula were correct to avoid any errors.

Exhibit 8.2 shows the sample spreadsheet with the 36 formulas displayed in the cells where the results of those formulas would normally appear. Observe that the formulas within a column are all similar in nature. For example, the formulas in the RAISE column all multiply the number in the cell to the left by 0.1 (that is, a 10-percent raise across-the-board).

EXHIBIT 8.1
In this sample spreadsheet, all of the numbers in the RAISE, NEW SALARY, and YEARLY TAX columns are the results of formulas.

```
C1: '       PERSONNEL FILE                                          READY

         A           B              C            D          E            F
                                    PERSONNEL FILE
 1
 2
 3       LAST        JOB            CURRENT                 NEW          YEARLY
 4       NAME        TITLE          SALARY       RAISE      SALARY       TAX
 5
 6       JENKINS     CLERK          23,000       2300.00    $25,300      $6,325.00
 7       JONES       FOREMAN        34,000       3400.00    $37,400      $9,350.00
 8       STAMLER     DRIVER         29,000       2900.00    $31,900      $7,975.00
 9       SMITH       MANAGER        45,000       4500.00    $49,500      $12,375.00
10       ASHTON      DIRECTOR       59,000       5900.00    $64,900      $16,225.00
11       BECK        ENGINEER       39,000       3900.00    $42,900      $10,725.00
12       BURSON      BARTENDER      17,000       1700.00    $18,700      $4,675.00
13       DRAKE       BUSBOY         15,000       1500.00    $16,500      $4,125.00
14       BRINKLEY    CASHIER        24,000       2400.00    $26,400      $6,600.00
15       WARD        SALESPERSON    27,000       2700.00    $29,700      $7,425.00
16       STANLEY     SECRETARY      20,000       2000.00    $22,000      $5,500.00
17       JACOBS      MESSENGER      19,000       1900.00    $20,900      $5,225.00
18
19
20
```

EXHIBIT 8.2
The Sample Spreadsheet with the Formulas Displayed
Note how the formulas in each column are similar to one another.

```
A1:                                                              READY
         A            B           C          D         E           F
 1                              PERSONNEL FILE
 2
 3    LAST         JOB        CURRENT                NEW        YEARLY
 4    NAME         TITLE      SALARY      RAISE      SALARY     TAX
 5
 6    JENKINS      CLERK       23,000     0.1*C6     +C6+D6     +E6*0.25
 7    JONES        FOREMAN     34,000     0.1*C7     +C7+D7     +E7*0.25
 8    STAMLER      DRIVER      29,000     0.1*C8     +C8+D8     +E8*0.25
 9    SMITH        MANAGER     45,000     0.1*C9     +C9+D9     +E9*0.25
10    ASHTON       DIRECTOR    59,000     0.1*C10    +C10+D10   +E10*0.25
11    BECK         ENGINEER    39,000     0.1*C11    +C11+D11   +E11*0.25
12    BURSON       BARTENDER   17,000     0.1*C12    +C12+D12   +E12*0.25
13    DRAKE        BUSBOY      15,000     0.1*C13    +C13+D13   +E13*0.25
14    BRINKLEY     CASHIER     24,000     0.1*C14    +C14+D14   +E14*0.25
15    WARD         SALESPERSON 27,000     0.1*C15    +C15+D15   +E15*0.25
16    STANLEY      SECRETARY   20,000     0.1*C16    +C16+D16   +E16*0.25
17    JACOBS       MESSENGER   19,000     0.1*C17    +C17+D17   +E17*0.25
18
19
20
```

Since the twelve formulas in the RAISE column are all very similar, it would seem time consuming and error prone to have to key in each formula separately. Spreadsheets are able to take advantage of this similarity by allowing a user to enter a formula once and copying the formula to other cells requiring one of similar form. Let's look more closely at how spreadsheet programs implement this feature.

Adjustment of Relative Formulas

When a formula is entered into a cell, a spreadsheet program interprets that formula in a special way. Take, for example, the formula + C6 + D6 in cell E6 of Exhibit 8.2. In performing this calculation, the formula treats the addresses C6 and D6 as relative distances from the cell (E6) in which the formula is stored. Thus, C6 is two cells to the left and D6 is one cell to the left of the location of the formula. The formula is, therefore, read by the spreadsheet as "add the entry in the cell that is two cells to the left to the entry that is one cell to the left." All cell addresses in the formula are interpreted as *relative distances* from the location of the formula rather than as *actual locations*.

Since the cell addresses in a formula are stored internally by the spreadsheet as relative distances from the formula, if the formula is moved to a different cell, the actual cell addresses in the formula are altered. In other words, if the formula in cell E6 is copied into cell E7, the formula becomes +C7+D7. This occurs because the cell that is two cells to the left of the formula is now C7, and the cell that is one cell to the left is now D7. This translation of the relative addresses in the formula into the new cell addresses is known as **adjustment.**

When we look at the formula in E6, we see +C6+D6, and when that formula is copied into E7, we see +C7+D7. As far as the spreadsheet is concerned, both cells contain the same formula because the addresses in both formulas are the same relative to where the formula is located. The first address is always two cells to the left of the formula and the second address is always one cell to the left. This adjustment of formulas is automatic when copies of formulas are made and placed into other cells.

Copying Formulas

When formulas in a group have the same relative description, as we have in the last three columns of Exhibit 8.2, a user can enter a formula once and then copy it to the other cells requiring the same type of formula. The spreadsheet will automatically adjust the formula in each cell, thus saving the user a considerable number of keystrokes and cutting down the possibility of errors. Some spreadsheets refer to this creation of new formulas from an existing formula as **copying,** while others refer to it as **replication.** Regardless of its name, this command is probably one of the most powerful features of spreadsheet programs.

The COPY Command

In our sample spreadsheet, only three formulas, one at the top of each column, need to be entered. The COPY (or *replicate*) command can then be used to create the remaining 33 formulas needed to complete the spreadsheet. This command always requires the user to specify two ranges: the location of the formula or formulas to be copied and the place where the copies are to be placed. Thus, to make copies of a formula, that formula must already exist in a cell on the spreadsheet. Exhibit 8.3 shows the formulas entered into the top cell of each of our three columns.

When using the COPY command, a user is not limited to making copies of a formula in a single cell (although this is the way this command will be used most often). Each of the formulas in our example can be copied separately (use the COPY command three times), or all three formulas can be copied with one COPY command. Let's look at both of these possibilities.

EXHIBIT 8.3
In order to make copies of a formula, it must be entered somewhere on the spreadsheet. In this example, the formula for the first employee has been entered.

```
D6: 0.1*C6                                                          READY

         A            B            C           D          E            F
 1                              PERSONNEL FILE
 2
 3      LAST         JOB       CURRENT                   NEW        YEARLY
 4      NAME         TITLE     SALARY      RAISE        SALARY       TAX
 5
 6     JENKINS      CLERK       23,000    0.1*C6        +C6+D6      +E6*0.25
 7     JONES        FOREMAN     34,000
 8     STAMLER      DRIVER      29,000
 9     SMITH        MANAGER     45,000
10     ASHTON       DIRECTOR    59,000
11     BECK         ENGINEER    39,000
12     BURSON       BARTENDER   17,000
13     DRAKE        BUSBOY      15,000
14     BRINKLEY     CASHIER     24,000
15     WARD         SALESPERSON 27,000
16     STANLEY      SECRETARY   20,000
17     JACOBS       MESSENGER   19,000
18
19
20
```

If the formula in D6 is to be copied to cells D7 through D17, the first range (location of the formula) would be D6 or D6 .. D6. (Remember that a range can be as small as a single cell.) The second range (place where

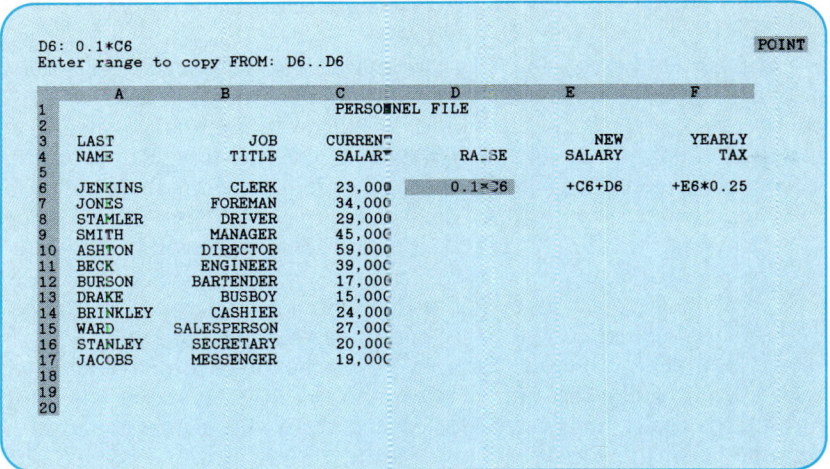

EXHIBIT 8.4

In Lotus 1-2-3, the COPY command first asks the user for the range where the formula to be copied is located. In this case, the range is a single cell—D6..D6.

the copies are to go) would be D7..D17. Exhibit 8.4 shows the first range being specified in the COPY command of the Lotus 1-2-3 spreadsheet and Exhibit 8.5 shows how the second range is specified after the first one is entered. This command fills in the rest of the RAISE column, with each formula being automatically adjusted as it is copied.

A more efficient way of completing the sample spreadsheet is by using D6..F6 as the first range so that all three formulas will be copied. The second range, in this case, is D7..D17. This may seem strange, since we are really trying to fill all of the cells from D7 to F17 with formulas. You must remember, however, that what is being copied in this case is a group of three formulas. The second range is showing where the copies of this three-formula group are to go. Each group of three formulas should begin in a cell in column D; therefore, the second range must be D7..D17.

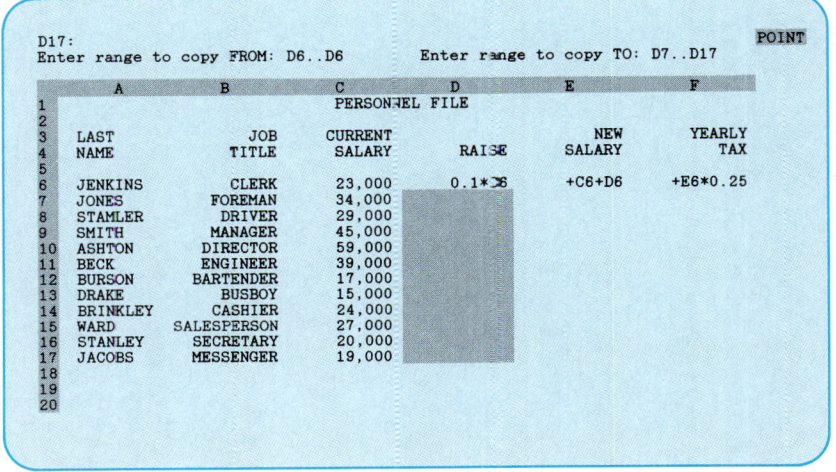

EXHIBIT 8.5

Once the range where the formula is located has been specified, the user must then enter the range that indicates where copies of the formula are to be placed. In this case, the second range is D7..D17.

Copying Formulas

Absolute Versus Relative Addresses

Sometimes the adjustment of a formula is inappropriate for an application. Exhibit 8.6 shows a loan analysis with the formulas in the INTEREST column displayed where the numeric results would normally appear. The formulas multiply the principal in the cell to the left of the formula by the interest rate in cell C2 divided by 12 to convert it from a yearly interest rate to a monthly interest rate. Thus, the formula in cell C11 is +B11*(C2/12). (The actual formula is +B11*$C$2/12. The dollar signs will be explained later in this chapter.)

All of the formulas in the interest column are similar in form; the cell to the left is multiplied by cell C2 and divided by 12. Thus, a user might realistically plan to enter this formula once at the top of column C and then copy it down to the rest of the cells in the INTEREST column. When this formula is copied, however, the reference to C2 will be interpreted as 10 cells up from the location of the formula. Thus, if the +B11*(C2/12) formula is copied from C11 to C12, it will become +B12*(C3/12). The reference to B11 is really "one cell left," and it changes to B12 when the formula is in C12. This is exactly what we need to have happen. Note, however, what has happened to the reference to the interest cell. It has changed from C2 to C3 because the cell that is "10 cells above the formula" is now C3 instead of C2. Ultimately, this will cause an error in our calculations because now the entry in the term cell is being used as the interest rate.

This is an example of an inappropriate adjustment of a cell reference in a formula. The reference to C2 in our formula needs to be *absolute* instead of relative. When a formula is copied, there is a method to indicate when an address is to be absolute. In Exhibit 8.6, you will notice that the formula in C11 is not +B11*C2/12; it is +B11*$C$2/12. The dollar signs in front of the column letter and row number of the C2 reference indicate that it is an absolute cell address which cannot be adjusted if the formula is copied or moved to another location.

Some spreadsheets allow a user to indicate which cell addresses are absolute during the COPY command. The spreadsheet will go through all

EXHIBIT 8.6

In this loan analysis spreadsheet, the formulas have been displayed where the results of these formulas would normally appear.

```
A1: 'PRINCIPAL:                                                       READY

         A              B              C              D              E
 1  PRINCIPAL:                      8,600.00      PRINCIPAL  INTEREST RATE
 2  INTEREST RATE (YEARLY):           14.5%       ==========  ==============
 3  TERM:                              10              0.00         18.0%
 4  MONTHLY PAYMENT:                 $918.18       5,000.00         14.5%
 5                                                10,000.00         13.5%
 6                                                20,000.00         12.0%
 7                                                50,000.00         10.5%
 8                                               100,000.00          9.0%
 9
10  MONTH        PRINCIPAL        INTEREST       PAID ON LOAN    BALANCE
11       1        8600.00      +B11*$C$2/12          814.27      7785.73
12       2        7785.73      +B12*$C$2/12          824.11      6961.63
13       3        6961.63      +B13*$C$2/12          834.06      6127.56
14       4        6127.56      +B14*$C$2/12          844.14      5283.42
15       5        5283.42      +B15*$C$2/12          854.34      4429.08
16       6        4429.08      +B16*$C$2/12          864.67      3564.41
17       7        3564.41      +B17*$C$2/12          875.11      2689.30
18       8        2689.30      +B18*$C$2/12          885.69      1803.61
19       9        1803.61      +B19*$C$2/12          896.39       907.22
20      10         907.22      +B20*$C$2/12          907.22          .00
```

```
    |A||    B    ||   C    ||    D    ||    E     || F |
  1 PRINCIPAL:            8,600.00     PRINCIPAL INTEREST RATE
  2 INTEREST RATE:          14.5%      ========= ==============
  3 TERM:                      24           .00        18.0%
  4 MONTHLY PAYMENT:       $414.95      5,000.00       14.5%
  5                                    10,000.00       13.5%
  6                                    20,000.00       12.0%
  7                                    50,000.00       10.5%
  8                                   100,000.00        9.0%
  9
 10  MONTH     PRINCIPAL    INTEREST  PAID ON LOAN    BALANCE
 11    1       8,600.00      103.92
 12    2
 13    3
 14    4
 15    5
 16    6
 17    7
 18    8
 19    9
 20   10
Source cell C11. Adjust C2 (Y or N)?
Copying to... 12
20>+B11*C2/12
MENU  Confirm adjustment for each cell reference
```

EXHIBIT 8.7

In the SUPERCALC4 spreadsheet, the user can ask the spreadsheet to go through each address in the formula to see whether it is to be adjusted. Here the spreadsheet is asking if the reference to C2 is to be adjusted when the formula is copied. The user should answer N for no.

the cell addresses in the formula one at a time and ask the user if each one is absolute or relative. This has to be done each time the formula is copied. Exhibit 8.7 shows the SUPERCALC4 COPY command asking the user if the reference to cell C2 is supposed to be adjusted or remain absolute. In earlier versions of SUPERCALC, this was the only way to make a cell reference absolute. SUPERCALC4 actually allows the user to use either method of making a cell reference in a formula absolute. Spreadsheets that allow the user to embed characters, such as dollar signs, in a formula to indicate absolute addresses are more flexible, since the addresses are always designated as absolute, and this designation does not have to be made every time the formula is copied. In addition, using characters in front of the column letter and row number allows creation of a **mixed cell address** in which the column letter can be absolute and the row number relative or vice versa.

ADVANCED BUILT-IN FUNCTIONS

Spreadsheet formulas are typically designed to perform only one type of calculation. A formula like +D5+C6 always adds D5 and C6. Some built-in functions allow a user to create formulas which can take on different values depending on what values are in other cells of the spreadsheet. In this section, we will look at three of these functions: LOOKUP, IF, and CHOOSE.

The LOOKUP Function

In Exhibits 8.6 and 8.7, there is a table in the upper-right corner which lists the interest rates for various principals. Cell C2 contains a formula which takes the principal in cell C1 and uses it to *look up* the appropriate interest rate in this table. This process is accomplished using a special built-in function called the **LOOKUP function.**

EXHIBIT 8.8

The Loan Analysis Spreadsheet Showing the LOOKUP Function in Cell C2

This function determines the interest rate by comparing the principal in cell C1 to the principals in the table.

```
                Value looked up    Location of Table    Offset
                C2: (P1) @VLOOKUP(C1,D3..E8,1)                        Lookup table      READY

        A              B                    C                  D                E
 1  PRINCIPAL:                           8,600.00         PRINCIPAL    INTEREST RATE
 2  INTEREST RATE:                         14.5%         ===========  ==============
 3  TERM:                                     10              0.00         18.0%
 4  MONTHLY PAYMENT:                      $918.18        5,000.00         14.5%
 5                                                      10,000.00         13.5%
 6                                                      20,000.00         12.0%
 7                                                      50,000.00         10.5%
 8                                                     100,000.00          9.0%
 9
10   MONTH      PRINCIPAL              INTEREST       PAID ON LOAN       BALANCE
11     1         8600.00                103.92           814.27          7785.73
12     2         7785.73                 94.08           824.11          6961.63
13     3         6961.63                 84.12           834.06          6127.56
14     4         6127.56                 74.04           844.14          5283.42
15     5         5283.42                 63.84           854.34          4429.08
16     6         4429.08                 53.52           864.67          3564.41
17     7         3564.41                 43.07           875.11          2689.30
18     8         2689.30                 32.50           885.69          1803.61
19     9         1803.61                 21.79           896.39           907.22
20    10          907.22                 10.96           907.22             .00
```

Exhibit 8.8 shows the spreadsheet with the LOOKUP function shown on the status line of the control panel. This LOOKUP function compares the value in cell C1 to the value in the principal column of the lookup table (D3 to D8). This column is often called the **comparison column** of the lookup table since it contains the numbers to which the value being looked up is compared.

The LOOKUP function finds the highest number in the comparison column which is as close to the value being looked up without going over it; thus, the function is looking for the principal in the comparison column that is closest to the principal in C1. When the function finds this value in the comparison column, it looks at the cell to the right (in the interest column of the table) and returns that value to the cell with the LOOKUP function in it (C2).

For example, when the LOOKUP function in cell C2 is calculated, it will go to the principal cell (C1) and find the number 8600.00. This number will then be compared to the numbers in the comparison column (D3 to D8), starting with the number at the top of the column. The function will continue down this column until it finds the number that is as close as possible to the principal without going over it. Thus, when 8600.00 is looked up in the comparison column, the LOOKUP function will find that 5000.00 is the closest to 8600.00 without going over it. The LOOKUP function then goes to the right of the cell containing 5000.00 and finds an interest rate of 14.5 percent. This number (.145) is what is returned to cell C2.

The way in which the LOOKUP function is calculated has implications for the construction of the lookup table. First, the values in the comparison column must start with the smallest and increase to the largest value. In addition, the column that is to contain the values to be returned must be in the column immediately to the right of the comparison column. Thus, our lookup table comprises cells D3 to E8. The comparison column is the first column, and the values to be returned are in the next one.

Some spreadsheets have additional options. The LOOKUP function itself can have as many as four components. First, there is the name of the function itself. Some spreadsheets use LOOKUP; others use VLOOKUP for *vertical lookup* and also include an HLOOKUP for *horizontal lookup*. In parentheses after the name of the function are the value to be looked up (or the address of the cell containing that value), the location of the table (its range), and sometimes an **offset value,** that value which lets the function know how many cells it must go to the right of the comparison column in order to find the value to be returned.

In our example, the three values in parentheses were C2 for the value to be looked up, D3 .. E3 for the location of the table, and one for an offset. When defining the location of the table, some spreadsheets (like SUPERCALC4) require that the column of values be the next column to the right of the comparison column. Other spreadsheets allow the column of values to be placed any number of columns to the right of the comparison column. In the example, the offset value is one because the column of values is one column to the right.

The IF Function

The **IF function** allows the user to have a cell adopt one of two values depending on the result of a certain condition. A condition is something that can be either true or false. In a condition, a number or a cell can be compared to another number or cell using the relational operators equal (=), not equal (<>), greater than (>), and less than (<). For example, C4 = 5, C7*4 > 6, D7−D8 <> D5, and 5 < 7 are all conditions that can be either true or false. The general form of the IF function is IF (condition, true, false). For example, Exhibit 8.9 shows @IF (B3 > 2000, 0.1*A3, 0) stored in cell C3. The entries for the true and false part of the function can be numbers, cell addresses, or any valid spreadsheet formula. The IF function essentially lets the user create a cell that can contain two different formulas or values. Which one will be used is determined by whether the condition is true or false. Let's look at the different parts of this IF function. The B3 > 2000 is the condition. It says that whatever is in cell B3 (DEDUCTIONS) should be compared to the number 2000. If B3 is greater than 2000, the condition is true. If it is less than or equal to 2000, the condition is false. The *true* part of the function is the value that the cell containing the IF function will take on when the condition is true. Thus, if

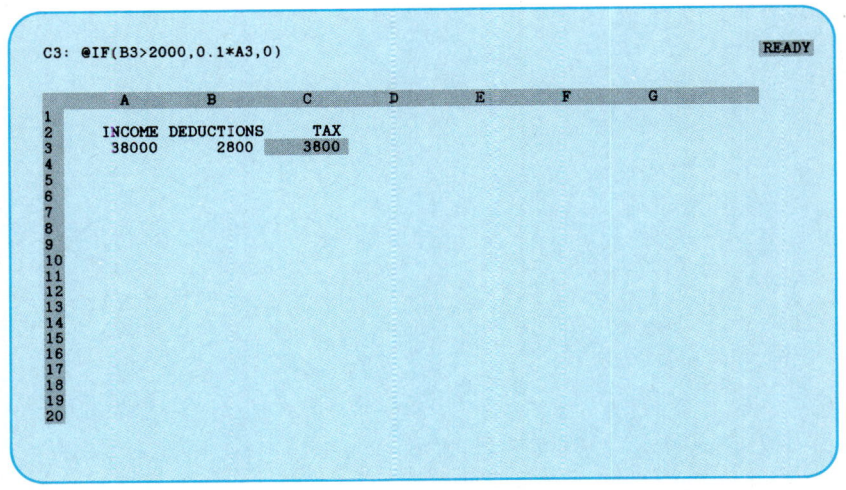

EXHIBIT 8.9

The IF function in cell C3 calculates TAX as either 10 percent of income or zero, depending on what is entered in the DEDUCTIONS cell.

Advanced Built-In Functions

B3 is greater than 2000, cell C3 will take on a value of 0.1*A3. In other words, the tax will be one tenth of the income if the deductions are more than 2000. If the condition is false, the cell containing the IF function (C3) will take on the value in the *false* part of the function, in this case zero.

The CHOOSE Function

The **CHOOSE function** is very similar to the IF function, except that it allows a cell to take on more than just two values. The basic form of the CHOOSE function is CHOOSE (offset, value 1, value 2, ...). Note how there is no condition in the CHOOSE function; the user can list any number of values for the cell containing this function. These can be numbers or formulas. The offset in the beginning of the function is a number or the address of a cell that will contain a number. The number in this cell indicates which of the values listed in the function is to be used. Exhibit 8.10 shows an example of a CHOOSE function. In this example, there are four possible values that the function can take on (1000, 2000, 3500, and 5000). The entry in the INSURANCE TYPE column indicates which of these four values is to be used. If the type is 0, the CHOOSE function will result in 1000; if the type is 3, the result will be 5000. Thus, the values in the function correspond to choices 0, 1, 2, and 3. The value in the TYPE column determines which of those four values will be chosen.

TEMPLATES

When spreadsheets are used in business, there may be a large number of spreadsheets in common among the various divisions and departments in the company. A **template** which has the headings and formulas already filled in can be created so that the user only has to put in the numbers to have a completed spreadsheet. A manager can use such a template to create an application without having to design all of the details of the spreadsheet. In addition, once the template is completed, the manager can use it to do *what if* analyses of data in the resulting spreadsheet.

EXHIBIT 8.10
An Example of the CHOOSE Function

Cells C3 to C7 all contain a CHOOSE function in which the formula can take on one of four values, depending on what number is entered in the corresponding cell in column A.

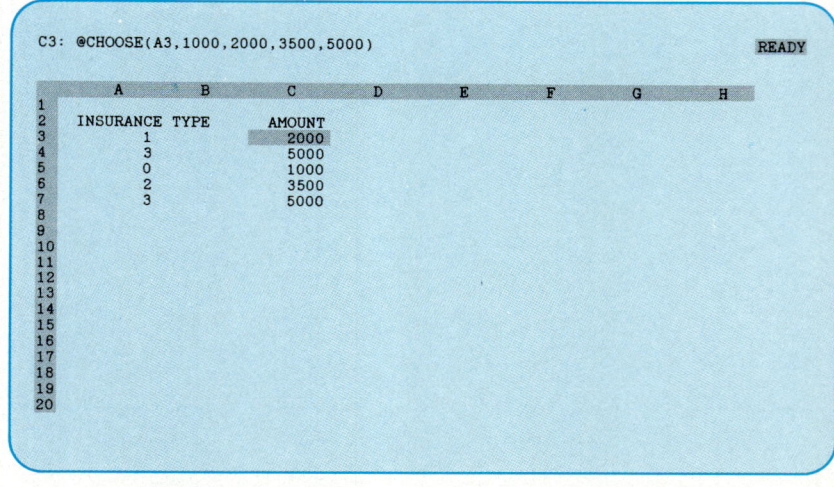

8 Advanced Spreadsheets

Designing a Template

Almost any spreadsheet can be used as a template by leaving blank any of the entries a user can enter. Exhibit 8.11 shows one constructed from the breakeven analysis in Chapter 7. The entries for fixed costs, variable costs, and the price per unit have been left blank. The formulas for totaling the fixed and variable costs, plus the breakeven formula, are there but display zero, since the cells they use are now blank. A user can retrieve this spreadsheet and type in the missing entries. The cells with formulas in them will automatically be recalculated so that, when the user finishes entering numbers, the spreadsheet will be finished.

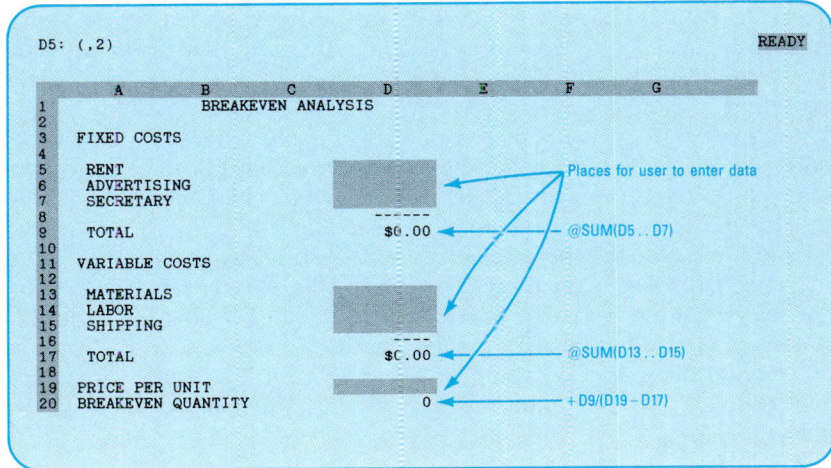

EXHIBIT 8.11
A Template for the Breakeven Analysis
Zeroes are displayed in cells containing formulas. The user enters all of the fixed and variable costs and the price to finish the spreadsheet.

Cell Protection

A **protected cell** is one that will store no other entry than the one that is already there. A spreadsheet allows a user to designate certain cells as protected by using a command; the spreadsheet will allow no other entry to be stored there. The only way something can be entered in a protected cell is if a user knows how to operate the protection command and purposefully unprotects the cell.

In our sample template, all of the cells except D5, D6, D7, D13, D14, D15, and D19 will be protected. This way, the user cannot accidentally erase any of the headings or formulas.

Hidden Cells

Another spreadsheet feature which is useful in designing templates is the ability to hide cells. Some spreadsheets hide an entire column of cells by having the user set that column's width to zero. In this way, intermediate calculations that the user does not have to see can be hidden so that they don't take up space and so that they cannot be easily tampered with. Some spreadsheets also hide single cells by formatting those cells with a special hidden format.

KEYBOARD MACROS

While templates are useful because they reduce design time and minimize the data a user must enter to create a spreadsheet, the user must still know something about the spreadsheet in order to use it effectively. The creation of a spreadsheet can be simplified even more by creating **keyboard macros,** which are cells on the spreadsheet (or sometimes separate files) containing keystrokes used to perform spreadsheet functions. A keyboard macro contains symbols that emulate the keystrokes used when carrying out a particular spreadsheet function. It also contains commands of its own which obtain data from the user, show the user menus from which to make choices, and control the execution of the macro itself. A macro is given a name and can be executed by pressing a single key. In many ways, a macro is like a program that works with the spreadsheet; like a program, it is not something that the casual user might be able to write.

Exhibit 8.12 shows a macro that can be used with our breakeven template. This macro automatically moves to each unprotected cell on the template and asks the user to enter the data. When all of the cells are filled in, the macro shows menu choices that allow the user to print the spreadsheet, save the spreadsheet, enter the numbers again, or quit. The macro shown has been given a special name (/0) which causes it to execute when the file is retrieved. Thus, a user only has to know how to retrieve a file, and the macro will take the user through all of the steps of creating, printing, and saving a breakeven analysis. The user doesn't have to know anything else about the spreadsheet to produce this breakeven analysis.

EXHIBIT 8.12
The macro in the Lotus 1-2-3 spreadsheet prompts the user to enter data into the breakeven template and then displays a menu that allows the user to print, save, re-enter the analysis, or quit the macro.

```
E1: '\0                                                              READY

         E         F                    G              H           I
 1     \0        {GOTO}D5
 2               /XNENTER RENT FIGURE - ~~{DOWN}
 3               /XNENTER ADVERTISING COSTS - ~~{DOWN}
 4               /XNENTER SECRETARY COSTS - ~~{GOTO}D13~
 5               /XNENTER MATERIAL COST PER UNIT - ~~{DOWN}
 6               /XNENTER LABOR COST PER UNIT - ~~{DOWN}
 7               /XNENTER SHIPPING COST PER UNIT - ~~{GOTO}D19~
 8               /XNENTER PRICE PER UNIT FIGURE - ~~
 9               /XMMENU~
10
11     MENU      PRINT                SAVE           REENTER       QUIT
12               PRINT OUT            SAVE FILE      DO AGAIN      STOP
13               /PPRA1.D20~AGPQ      /FS~R          /XGSTART~     /XQ
14               /XMMENU~             /XMMENU~
15
16
17
18
19
20
```

EXHIBIT 8.13
A Comparison of the Features of the Current Spreadsheet Programs

	MEMORY REQUIRED (IN BYTES)	ON-DISK TUTORIAL	MULTIPLE WINDOWS	SIZE	RANGE NAMES	COPY PROTECTION	CELL PROTECTION	FILE PASSWORD	MACRO	PRICE
Framework II	384K	Y	Y	32,000 by 32,000	N	N	Y	N	Y	$695
SUPERCALC4	256K	Y	Y	255 by 9999	Y	N	Y	N	Y	$495
SMART	384K	Y	Y	999 by 9999	Y	N	Y	Y	Y	$895
Symphony	384K	Y	Y	256 by 9999	Y	Y	Y	Y	Y	$695
1-2-3 VER	384K	Y	Y	256 by 8192	Y	Y	Y	Y	Y	$495
Enable	320K	Y	Y	65,025 cells	Y	N	Y	N	Y	$695

Source: Adapted from "Beyond the Basics," *PC Week* 4 (April 21, 1987): 38–39.

CHOOSING AN ELECTRONIC SPREADSHEET

Some of the features that may be important to an end-user when selecting an electronic spreadsheet are compared for six popular spreadsheet packages in Exhibit 8.13. The *Memory Required* column shows how much primary memory a microcomputer must have in order to run the spreadsheet program. *On-Disk Tutorial* indicates if the spreadsheet provides a tutorial disk to help a user learn how to use the spreadsheet. The *Multiple Windows* column indicates whether the spreadsheet can be displayed as multiple windows so a user could see different parts of the spreadsheet on the screen at the same time. *Size* indicates how many columns and rows a spreadsheet has. The *Range Names* feature refers to the ability to assign a name to a range of cells. The user can then refer to those cells by name rather than by cell addresses. The *Copy Protection* column indicates whether the spreadsheet is protected from unauthorized copying. Some users do not like copy protection since it makes authorized duplication, such as making backups, more difficult. However, some software companies want to protect the investment they have made in developing the software. *Cell Protection* indicates if an individual cell can be protected so that it cannot be accidentally erased, and *File Password* indicates if a file containing a spreadsheet can be protected by a password. *Macro* designates whether a spreadsheet allows a user to create programs which contain spreadsheet commands. Finally, *Price* can be an important factor in an end-user's decision of which spreadsheet to buy.

Summary

The process of entering formulas can be made more efficient by using a COPY command. A spreadsheet interprets cell addresses in a formula as relative distances from the cell containing the formula. When a formula is copied to a new cell, those addresses change so that they represent the cells that are the same relative distances from the new formula as the cells in the original formula. This is known as *adjustment*.

The COPY command requires the user to specify a range indicating the location of the formula or formulas to be copied and a range that indicates where the copies of the formula are to be placed.

Spreadsheets also allow users to indicate if a cell address is to be held constant when the formula is copied. A cell address which is not adjusted is known as an *absolute cell address*. The user can either instruct the spreadsheet to ask which addresses are to be adjusted when the formula is copied or can mark the absolute addresses with a special character, such as a dollar sign. This second method allows the user to create mixed addresses in which only the column letter or the row number is held constant when the formula is copied.

LOOKUP functions allow a user to compare a value in a cell against values in a table. The column in the table to which this value is compared is called the *comparison column*. The LOOKUP function finds the value in the column that is closest to the value being looked up without going over it. The function returns a number from the column to the right of the comparison column corresponding to that value.

LOOKUP functions require a user to supply the location of the value to be looked up and the location of the lookup table itself. Sometimes the column of values to be returned can be located more than one column to the right of the comparison column. In that case, the user must supply an offset number.

The IF function allows a user to create a formula that, depending on whether some condition is true or false, can adopt one of two values. In this function, the user specifies the condition to be checked, a formula or value that the cell is to use if the condition is true, and one to be used if the condition is false.

The CHOOSE function allows a user to create a formula that can result in more than two different values. In this function, the user specifies an offset which contains a number that determines which value in a list of values is to be used.

A *template* is a partially completed spreadsheet in which many of the entries are already made. A user can retrieve this spreadsheet and complete it to produce a finished application. The *cell protection* feature of spreadsheets is useful in designing a template in which all of the cells that the user should not alter are protected. *Hidden cells* can also be used on a template to hide columns or cells containing information the user does not have to see.

Keyboard macros are cells or files that contain spreadsheet commands. A macro can be executed by pressing a single key, and all of the spreadsheet functions in the macro will be carried out.

Review Questions

1. Explain how a spreadsheet interprets cell addresses as relative distances from the location of the formula.

2. Explain how the COPY command works and what the two ranges specified in that command are for.

3. Explain the difference between absolute and relative cell addresses.

4. Explain how a lookup table works. How does this affect the way the table must be constructed?

5. What three pieces of information must be specified in a LOOKUP function?

6. Some spreadsheets mark absolute addresses in a formula, while others require that absolute addresses be indicated when the formula is copied. Which method do you think is best? Why?

7. Explain the difference between @IF and @CHOOSE. When would each be used?

8. What is a template? Give a useful application of a template.

CHAPTER 9 ■ Graphics

DATA-DRIVEN GRAPHICS
- Spreadsheet Graphics
- Dedicated Graphics
- Selecting a Graphics Program

ILLUSTRATION GRAPHICS

PRESENTATION GRAPHICS

DESKTOP PUBLISHING
- Creating Publications
- Manipulating Text
- Manipulating Graphics
- Page Layout

SUMMARY

REVIEW QUESTIONS

Everyone has heard that a picture is worth a thousand words. It may also be worth a thousand numbers. Graphics can be used to condense large amounts of data into a simple picture which emphasizes a relationship among the various pieces of data. Graphics software allows an end-user to store and display numeric data in the form of a picture or to create simple drawings using lines and geometric shapes.

In this chapter, we will look at four categories of software that involve graphics. These types of software can be used by an end-user to create and display information graphically. Typically, graphics software is used to display numeric data in the form of a chart or graph, but it also can be used to create pictures that are not numerically oriented. Software used to produce graphs for charting and displaying of numeric data is known as **data-driven graphics** software. Software used to create pictures which are not numerically oriented can be called **illustration graphics** software. A third category of software in which graphics is important is **presentation graphics** software. This type of software is used to display previously created graphs and pictures in a sequence determined by the end-user. A final application of graphics is known as **desktop publishing,** in which an end-user can merge graphics with text to create professional publications.

In this chapter you will learn to do the following:

1. Understand the similarities and differences among pie, bar, and line graphs.
2. Understand the differences between spreadsheet and dedicated graphics software.
3. List some of the features that are important when choosing graphics software.
4. Describe some of the features of illustration graphics software.
5. Identify some of the features of presentation graphics software.
6. Explain the role of desktop publishing software and list some of the features included in these programs.

DATA-DRIVEN GRAPHICS

As indicated previously, **data-driven graphics** software is used to present numeric data in the form of a chart or graph. It is important to remember that graphs are typically used to help a viewer understand the relationship among groups of numbers. An end-user must create a graph that shows that relationship as clearly as possible.

Because data-driven graphics software is used to display numbers in graphic form, it is often incorporated as part of a spreadsheet program. Since spreadsheets already deal with numbers, it is common to have graphics capabilities integrated into the spreadsheet program itself. Graphics software which is incorporated into spreadsheet programs is referred to as **integrated** or **spreadsheet graphics.** There are also many graphics packages which are separate programs. These are referred to as **stand-alone** or **dedicated graphics** because these programs can be used without any associated spreadsheet program and are designed to do

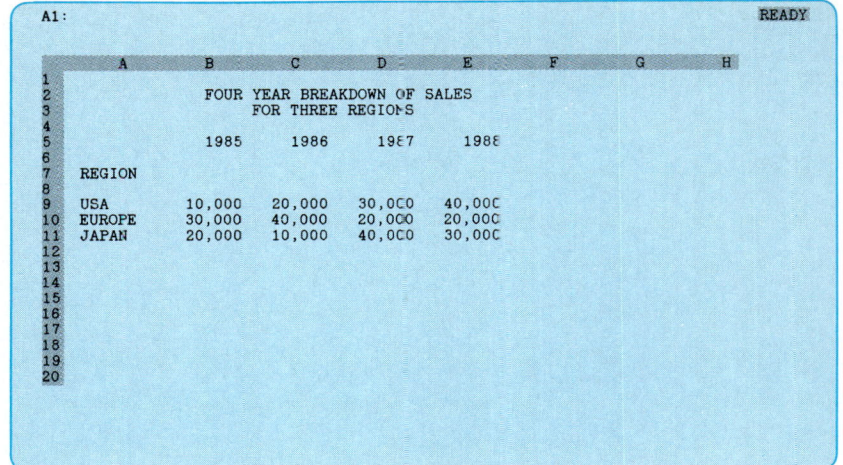

EXHIBIT 9.1
A Lotus Spreadsheet Containing Sales Figures for Three Regions Across Four Years

only graphics. Because the functioning of these two types of data-driven graphics software is slightly different, we will look at spreadsheet graphics and dedicated graphics separately.

Spreadsheet Graphics

Many spreadsheet programs, such as Lotus 1-2-3 and SUPERCALC4, include graphics capabilities. The numbers in the spreadsheet can be graphed on the screen without having to leave the spreadsheet program. The advantage of producing graphs from the numbers in the spreadsheet is that, if the numbers on the spreadsheet change, the graph is automatically updated without any intervention on the part of the end-user. Thus, just as spreadsheets automatically recalculate the results of a formula, a graph is automatically recalculated every time a number in the graph is changed.

Exhibit 9.1 shows a spreadsheet containing some data which will be used to illustrate some of the common types of graphs that can be produced with spreadsheet graphics programs. This spreadsheet shows sales data for three regions (USA, EUROPE, and JAPAN) across four years (1985 through 1988). Using this data, we will create three different types of graphs: a pie chart, a bar graph, and a line graph.

The Pie Chart

Exhibt 9.2 shows an example of a pie chart. Pie charts are a simple form of graph used to show how various values compare to one another across a single category. The exhibit shows how the sales for three regions compared in a single year (1988). In 1988, the sales figures were 40,000 in the USA, 20,000 in EUROPE, and 30,000 in JAPAN. The pie chart shows how much each region contributed to the total sales in 1988 in terms of a percentage. In 1988 the total sales were 90,000. The size of the slices in the pie indicates how much each region contributed to that total sales figure.

EXHIBIT 9.2
A Pie Chart Generated by Lotus 1-2-3

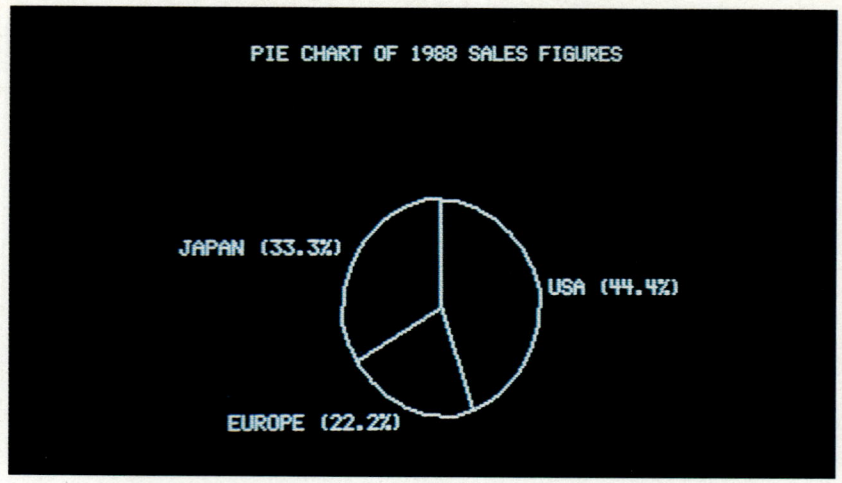

As you can see, the slice corresponding to the USA is largest, since that region accounted for 44.4 percent of the sales, while EUROPE accounted for only 33.3 percent, and JAPAN only 22.2 percent. Note that, when all of the slices of the pie are added together, the result is approximately 100 percent.

In Lotus, this graph could be produced using the /Graph command. Exhibit 9.3 shows the Graph menu with the options used to create graphs. To create the pie chart, a user would select the Type option. This would show another menu of graph types which includes a choice for pie charts. The data to be graphed are selected using the X and A ranges in the graph menu. For a pie chart, the X range would be the cells on the spreadsheet which contain the values for the category across which the data are being compared. In the sample spreadsheet, this would be cells A9 through A11, since we are comparing values across those three regions. The A range would be the sales figures to be graphed. In the pie chart, the 1988 sales figures are being graphed, so the A range would be cells E9 through E11. The Options choice in the graph menu includes an option for graph titles, which could be used to create the title shown over the sample pie chart.

EXHIBIT 9.3
The Lotus Graph Menu
In this menu, the type of graph can be selected, the ranges of data can be specified, the graph settings can be reset, the graphs can be viewed on the screen or saved on diskette, and graph options can be set and named.

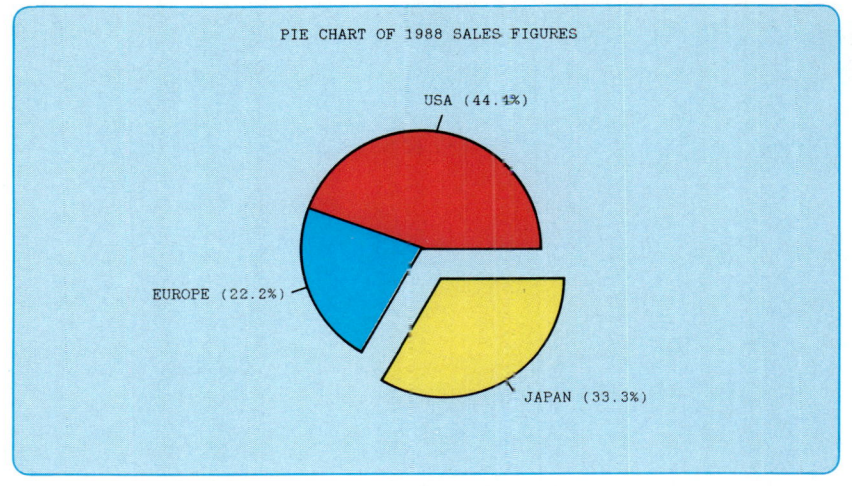

EXHIBIT 9.4
A Pie Chart with One Slice Exploded

In the exhibit, sales figures are being compared for the three regions. Thus, values are being compared across the region category. In a pie chart, you cannot compare values across more than one category because you can only slice the pie in one way. Thus, sales figures could not be shown for more than one year because we are comparing values by region, not by year. If we had wanted to show sales across the year category, then we would have had to show figures for only one region.

With some spreadsheet graphics packages, an end-user can produce a variation of the pie chart known as the exploding pie chart. In an **exploding pie chart,** one or more slices of the pie can be pulled away from the rest to emphasize the data represented by that slice. Exhibit 9.4 shows an example of an exploding pie chart with the slice representing the sales in JAPAN pulled away for emphasis.

The Bar Graph

Exhibit 9.5 shows an example of a bar graph, created in Lotus, showing our sales data. In a bar graph, the vertical line of numbers at the left side is known as the **y-axis.** The y-axis usually shows the measurement scale for the numbers being graphed. In the exhibit, the y-axis shows sales figures, since the numbers being graphed all represent sales. The height of each bar in the graph corresponds to a number on the y-axis which represents the amount of sales. The line of numbers across the bottom of the graph makes up the **x-axis.** The x-axis always represents values for a category across which we are making a comparison. In the exhibit, the values for the year category were used to create the x-axis. The bars represent the sales figures across the various years. The region category could have also been used for the x-axis.

When there is a second category to be graphed, as we have here, values for that second category are represented by different kinds of bars. Our example shows a bar graph with three types of bars represented by different colors. Each bar color represents a value in the region category. If we graphed the data for only one region, we would have had only one bar over each year on the x-axis. Since we are graphing sales figures for three regions, there are three bars over each year on the x-axis.

Data-Driven Graphics

EXHIBIT 9.5
A Bar Graph Created by Lotus 1-2-3

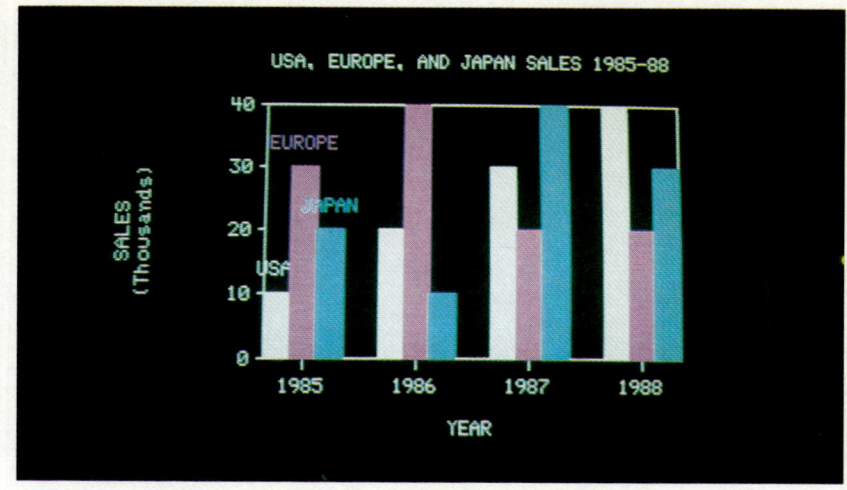

In Lotus, the bar graph in Exhibit 9.5 can be created by using the Type option in the graph menu to choose Bar as the type of graph. Exhibit 9.6 shows the sample spreadsheet, with the ranges needed for the bar graph highlighted. The X range is the cells containing the year values, since years are being displayed across the *x*-axis of the graph. The A range corresponds to the figures for the USA region. The B range is the figures for the EUROPE region, and the C range is the JAPAN figures. As you can see, the number of ranges needed in addition to the X range is the same as the number of values on the second category being graphed. Since we wanted to compare the data across three regions, three ranges were needed to show the data for those regions.

In Exhibit 9.5, there are labels arranged in various places on the graph. Each axis has been given a title, and there is a title over the graph itself. These labels are controlled using the Options choice in the graph menu. Exhibit 9.7 shows the Options submenu in Lotus.

EXHIBIT 9.6
The Sample Spreadsheet with Highlighted Ranges Needed for the Bar Graph

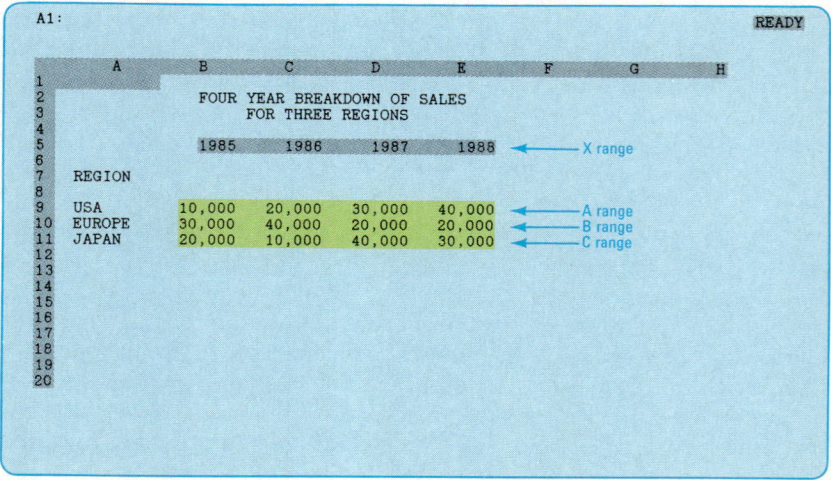

162 ■ 9 Graphics

Various points on each axis are labeled in addition to the label for the entire axis itself. For example, the *y*-axis has the points 0, 10,000, 20,000, 30,000, and 40,000. Spreadsheet graphics programs typically determine the data values shown on the *y*-axis automatically using the maximum and minimum values in the data being graphed. Many programs also give the end-user the ability to manually determine the values displayed on an axis through a process known as **scaling**. A scaling option can be found in the Options submenu in Lotus (see Exhibit 9.7).

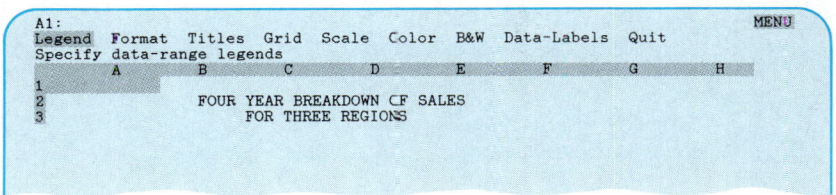

EXHIBIT 9.7

The Options Submenu of the Graph Command in Lotus 1-2-3

Within the graph in Exhibit 9.5 are three labels that are used to identify the three bars. These **data labels** are used to identify the values for the second category being graphed (region) and are also controlled from the Options submenu in Lotus (see Exhibit 9.7).

Other variations on the bar graph include the stacked bar, horizontal bar, and three-dimensional bar. Particular spreadsheet programs may support some or all of these variations. In the stacked bar graph, one bar is shown at each point on the *x*-axis (see Exhibit 9.8a). The height of each bar in the exhibit represents the total sales for all three regions in a particular year. The bar is then divided to show the relative contributions of each region to the total sales in that year. Thus, in the bar for 1985, you can see that most of the sales for that year came from EUROPE, since that region takes up most of the bar for 1985.

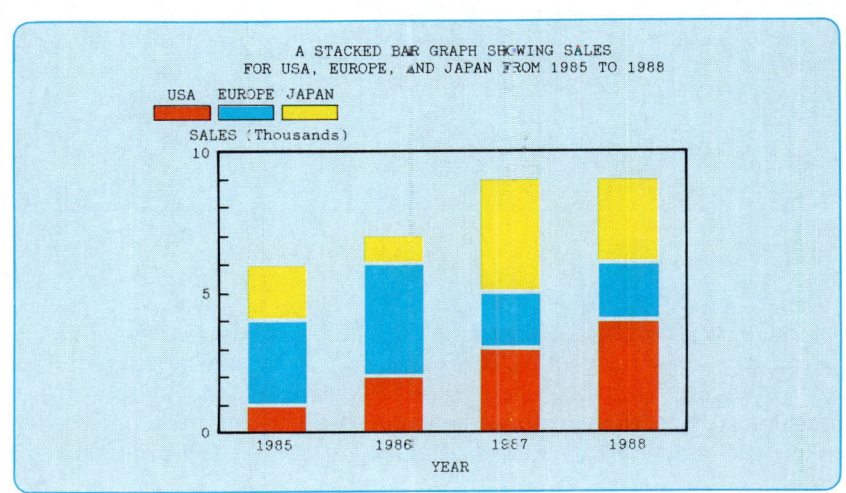

EXHIBIT 9.8a

An Example of a Stacked Bar Graph

Data-Driven Graphics

EXHIBIT 9.8b
An Example of a Horizontal Bar Graph

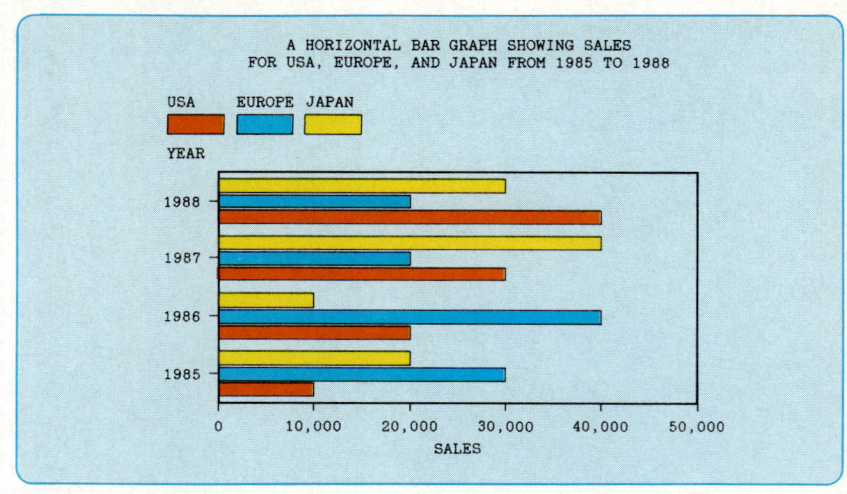

In the horizontal bar graph, the measurement scale for the numbers being graphed is on the *x*-axis, and one of the categories is on the *y*-axis (see Exhibit 9.8b). The bars extend horizontally from the *y*-axis. Three-dimensional bar graphs spread the bars back in a third direction rather than putting them next to each other (see Exhibit 9.8c).

EXHIBIT 9.8c
A Three-Dimensional Bar Graph Showing Sales for Four Stores Across Five Years

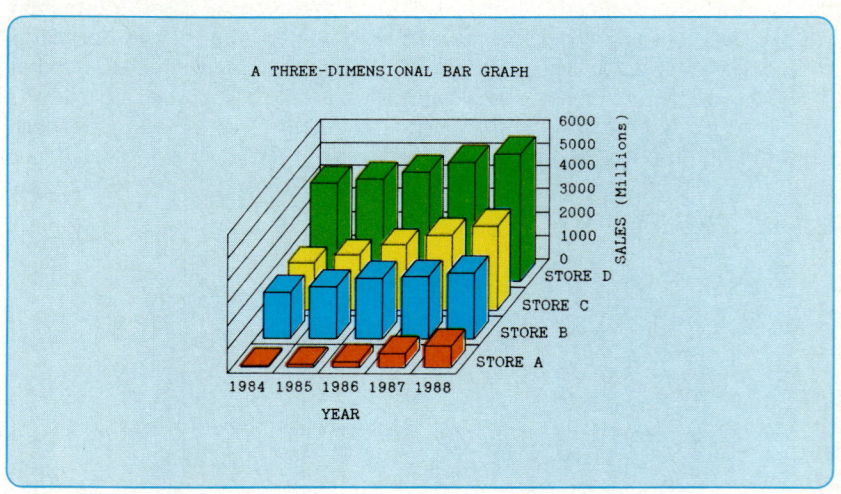

The Line Graph

Like the bar graph, the line graph can be used to compare values across one or two categories. However, instead of using bars to represent each number in the table, a point is placed on the graph in the appropriate position. A line is then drawn to connect the points. When a second category is graphed, each value on the second category is represented by a

164   ■ 9 Graphics

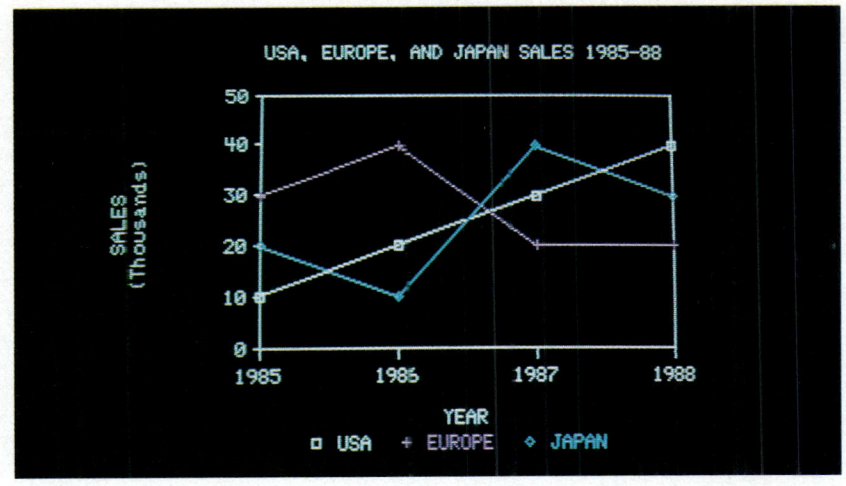

EXHIBIT 9.9
A Line Graph Created by Lotus 1-2-3

different line. Exhibit 9.9 shows a line graph of the sales data for the three regions from 1985 to 1988. The points on each line are in the same positions as the tops of the bars in the bar graph (see Exhibit 9.5), since we are representing the same data in both graphs. Typically, bar graphs are best used to emphasize relative values or amounts. Line graphs are best used to emphasize change over time or trends. In Lotus, the line graph would require similar ranges and options to those of the bar graph discussed earlier. The only change would be that the graph type would now be Line instead of Bar. Exhibit 9.9 also shows the use of a **legend** to identify the lines corresponding to the three regions. A legend performs the same function as a data label. In Lotus, a legend can be created using the Options submenu (see Exhibit 9.7).

Dedicated Graphics

The second source of graphics capabilities available to the end-user comes in the form of dedicated graphics packages. These are programs written specifically to produce graphics. The programs will usually accept data from a variety of sources. A user can enter data to be graphed from the keyboard or can instruct the graphics program to accept data from any text file, including files created by spreadsheets and word processors. Stand-alone graphics programs typically give the user more types of graphs and more control over the parts of those graphs (see Exhibit 9.10). These graphics programs usually provide default formats that allow a user to create graphs quickly. The defaults can be overridden to provide a user with more precise control of the graph, if desired. For example, an end-user can control the placement of text within the graph, the size of the text, and the letter style (or font) of the text. The user can manually control the x- and y-axes. Various types of shading or colors can be used to emphasize parts of the graph.

EXHIBIT 9.10

Stand-alone graphics packages, such as Picture Perfect, give the user complete control over the graphs that are created.

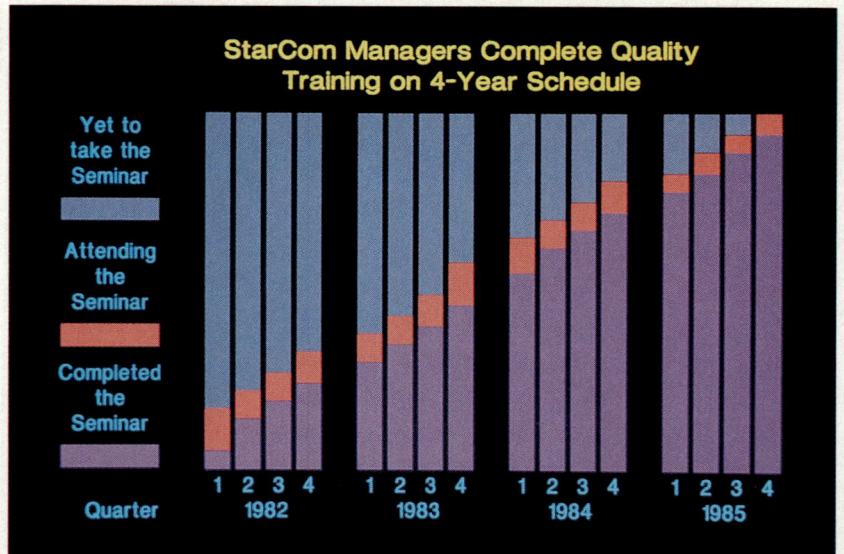
(a)

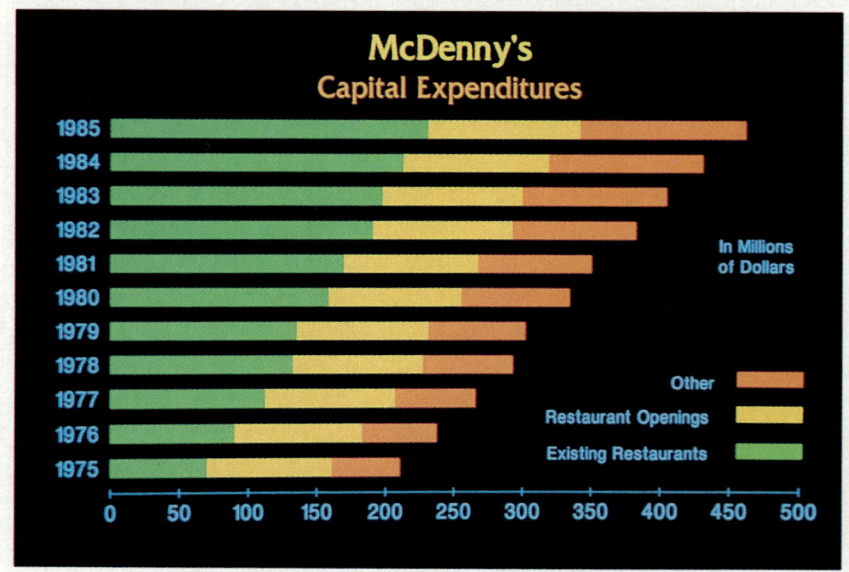
(b)

Exhibit 9.11 shows the main menu from the IBM Graphing Assistant dedicated graphics program. The Get/Save/Remove option in this menu allows a user to save and retrieve graphs as well as import data from other sources, such as spreadsheets and word processors. Data can also be entered directly from the keyboard using the Enter/edit data option. When this option is selected, a screen similar to that shown in Exhibit 9.12 is displayed. At the top of the screen, the user can indicate the type of data used on the *x*-axis. Values on the *x*-axis can be designated as identifiers (labels), numbers, or dates. In the exhibit, I was entered to indicate that the values on the *x*-axis are simply identifiers (or labels). Values were then

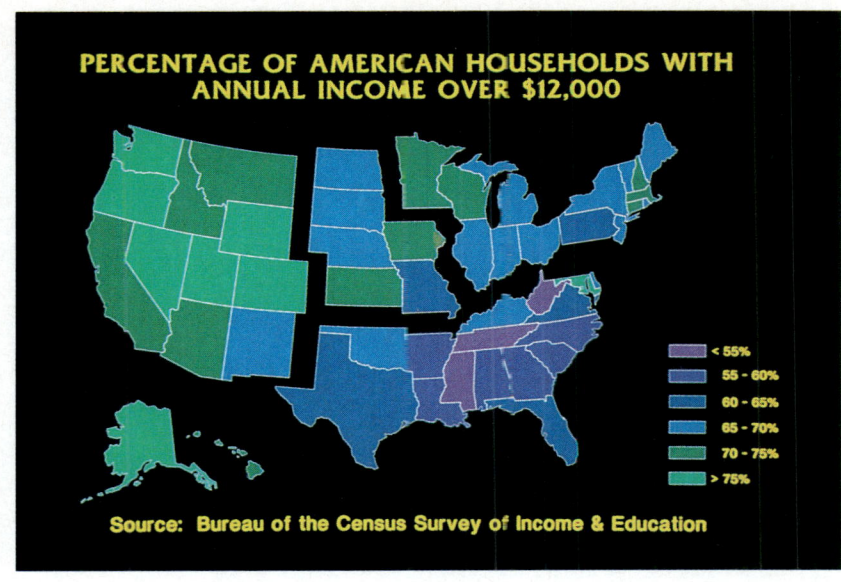

(c)

entered in the X data column of the screen. To graph the second category, region, three groups of data are needed. In the IBM Graphing Assistant, these groups are entered into the columns labeled Graph A, B, and C. The Graph A column contains the data for the USA region, B contains the data for the EUROPE region, and C contains the JAPAN data.

The Define chart option in the main menu can be used to control how the graph is displayed. Choosing this option brings up the screen shown in Exhibit 9.13. On this screen, the type of graph can be specified, and a legend can be created for each group of numbers entered by the user. The user can give a title for the graph, the *x*-axis, and the *y*-axis. The *y*-axis can

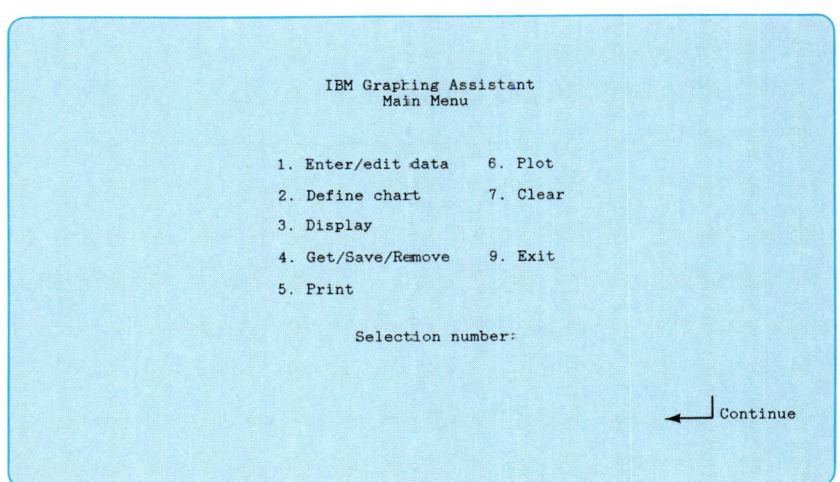

EXHIBIT 9.11
The Main Menu from the IBM Graphing Assistant Program

Data-Driven Graphics

167

EXHIBIT 9.12

In dedicated graphics programs, such as the IBM Graphing Assistant, the end-user can enter data from the keyboard.

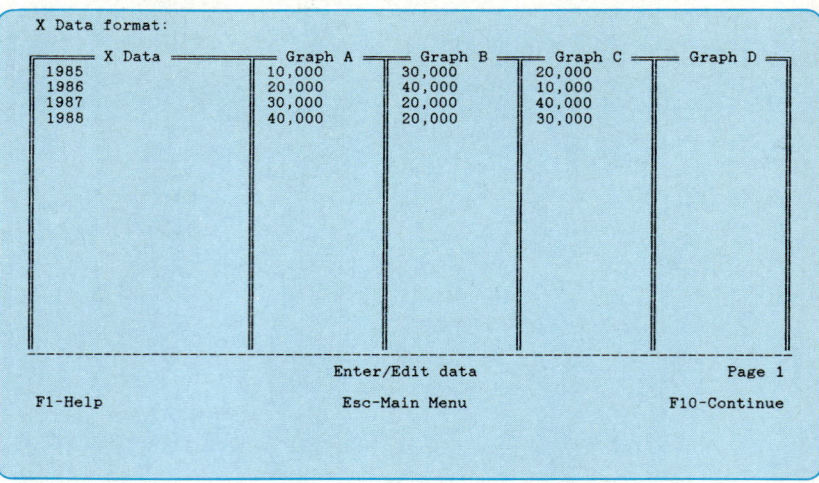

EXHIBIT 9.13
The Define Chart Menu in the IBM Graphing Assistant Program

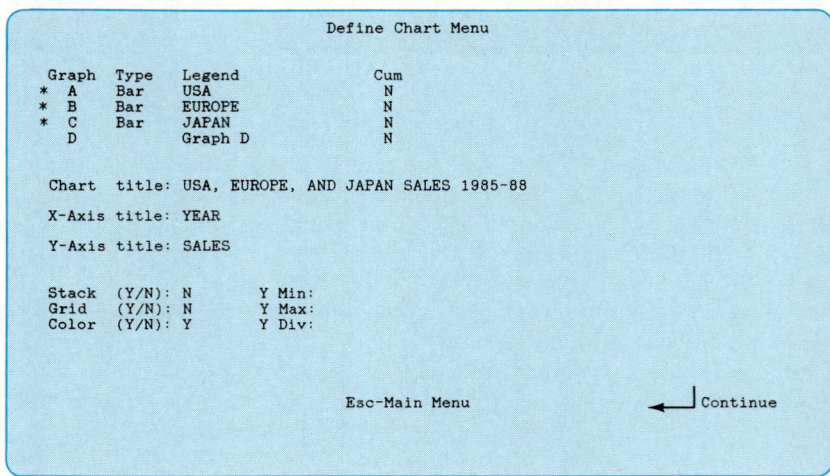

EXHIBIT 9.14
A Bar Graph Displayed by the IBM Graphing Assistant Program

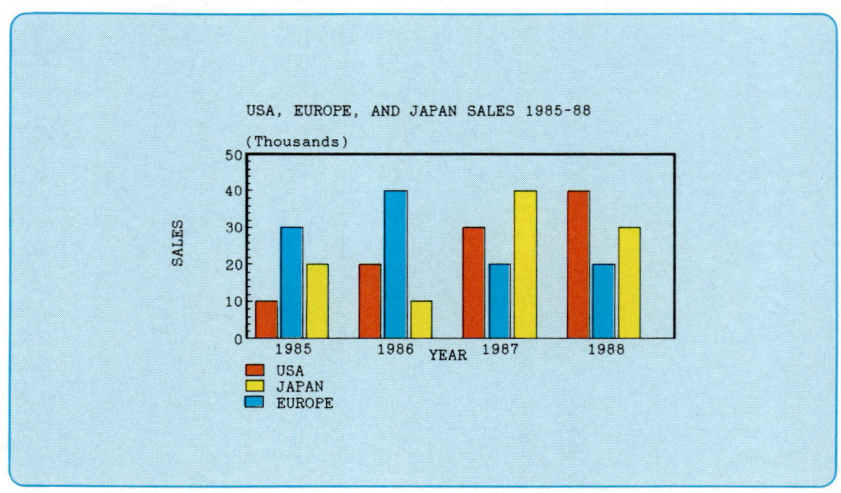

EXHIBIT 9.15
Some Features for Popular Graphics Programs Which Might Be Used in Selecting a Graphics Package

	SPREADSHEET GRAPHICS			STAND-ALONE GRAPHICS					
	Enable	Lotus 1-2-3	SUPERCALC4	Micrograph	Freelance Plus	Harvard Presentation Graphics	PFS:Graph	Picture Perfect	Ener-graphics
Stacked Bar	Y	Y	Y	Y	Y	Y	Y	Y	Y
Exploding Pie	Y	Y	Y	N	Y	Y	N	Y	Y
Fill Patterns	8	6	3	Y	14	12	8	57	8
Legends	Manual	Manual	Manual	Auto	Auto/Manual	Auto/Manual	Auto/Manual	Manual	Auto/Manual
Labels	Manual	Manual	Manual	Auto	Auto/Manual	Auto/Manual	Auto/Manual	Manual	Manual
Manual Axis Control	None	x,y	x,y	None	x,y	x,y	x,y	x,y	x,y
Library Images	0	0	0	0	543	0	0	7	99
Text Styles	9	11	8	1	13	5	1	13	8
Screen Colors	4	4	16	4	13	16	8	9	16
Menu-Driven	Y	Y	Y	Y	Y	Y	Y	Y	Y
Price	$695	$495	$435	$95	$495	$395	$140	$295	$595

Source: Adapted from *PC Magazine* 6 (March 10, 1987): 124–27.

be scaled, and there are options concerning the stacking of bars, the display of a grid over the graph, and the use of color. Exhibit 9.14 shows the bar graph created by the IBM Graphing Assistant using these settings.

Selecting a Graphics Program

Exhibit 9.15 lists some of the common graphics programs available and some of the features that might be important to an end-user. The chart is separated into packages that are integrated into spreadsheet programs and those that are stand-alone. The majority of graphics programs currently on the market allow the user to create the standard pie, bar, and line graphs. It may be important to an end-user to have a graphics package capable of producing other types of graphs beyond the basic types included in most packages. The chart shows which packages can create two special types of graphs which might be important to an end-user: the *stacked bar* and *exploding pie*. The next line in the chart shows how many *fill patterns* the package allows for shading the different parts of the graphs, such as the slices of a pie or the bars in a bar graph. The *legends* and *labels* features in the chart indicate whether the graphics program allows the end-user to manually place legends and labels on the graph exactly as desired or if the program automatically places them. Automatic placement makes the program simpler to use, but it is also less flexible. The *manual axis control* entry shows which axis, if any, can be manually controlled so that the end-user can determine exactly which points will be placed on the axis. The *library images* entry shows how many stored images the program provides for an end-user to copy into a graph. If a graphics program has zero images, it means that the program does not include a library of images. The *text styles* entry shows how many styles of text can be used for the labels and titles of the graph. *Screen colors* shows how many different colors can be on the same graph when it is displayed on a microcomputer's color monitor screen. The *menu-driven* feature indicates if the program allows the user to create graphs by making choices in menus. The final feature of graphics programs which might be important to an end-user is *price*. An end-user must decide if the more advanced features are worth the higher price.

ILLUSTRATION GRAPHICS

Illustration graphics programs are typically used for drawing or painting images, as opposed to graphing numbers. They turn a PC into an electronic drawing board on which a user can "liven up" a graph or create a picture. The arrow keys on the keyboard or special input devices, such as a joystick or mouse, can be used to move a cursor on the screen to create a drawing. The user can call up certain common shapes (such as squares and circles), change the size of those objects, and move them around on the screen. Objects can be erased, shaded, rotated, inverted, stretched, and magnified. Text can be placed anywhere on the screen in different sizes and styles.

EXHIBIT 9.16
A Screen from an Illustration Graphics Program Called PC Paintbrush

These programs are designed so that in a matter of minutes a user can create simple pictures, save them permanently on diskette, and print them out. Many illustration graphics programs include libraries of previously created images that a user can retrieve and include in a drawing. Exhibit 9.16 shows a screen from the PC Paintbrush graphics program. The left side of the screen shows the various tools available for working with the illustration. For example, the paintbrush is currently highlighted in this area, which means the user could begin drawing at this time. To select a tool, the user simply moves a cursor over to this area of the screen and selects the desired option with a click of the mouse button or a special keystroke sequence. Some of the other tools in this area include scissors for cutting and moving parts of the image, a spray can for shading objects, and a roller for filling an object with a color or pattern. The colors or patterns available to the user are shown across the bottom of the screen. In the bottom left corner is an area where the user can select the width of the brush, which determines the width of the lines that can be drawn. Selections can be made in these areas of the screen the same way they are made in the area displaying the tools.

Across the top of the screen is a series of menu choices which allow an end-user to select various options that control what the program is currently doing. These options are selected by moving a cursor over the option desired and selecting it. This causes a **pull-down menu** to be displayed, which contains further options the user can select by moving the cursor to the desired option and pressing the mouse button (or using a special keystroke sequence). In Exhibit 9.16, the Pick pull-down menu is shown. It can be used to manipulate objects on the screen. Other pull-down menus include Style for various text styles and Edit for moving objects around on the screen.

PRESENTATION GRAPHICS

A third category of graphics software is designed to use a PC to display a series of previously created graphs and illustrations. **Presentation graphics** use the PC monitor to display a series of screens as a slide show, with various types of transitions available between the screens that make up the presentation. With a presentation graphics program, a user starts with a series of screens that have been saved in files. In order to create these files, presentation graphics software typically contain a component that allows a user to take a "snapshot" of a screen and save it in a file. Because of their similarity to cameras, these components are often called picture takers or cameras. The picture taker program is started by the user and remains active in the RAM of the computer. The user can then enter any other software, such as a spreadsheet or graphics program. At any time, the user can press a special key sequence to have the picture taker program store the current contents of the screen in a special file. Thus, anything that can be displayed on the screen can be captured in a file.

EXHIBIT 9.17
Some Common Transitions Used in Presentation Graphics Programs
In these examples, the blue represents the old screen and the orange represents the new screen. The arrows indicate the directions in which the new screen is moving.

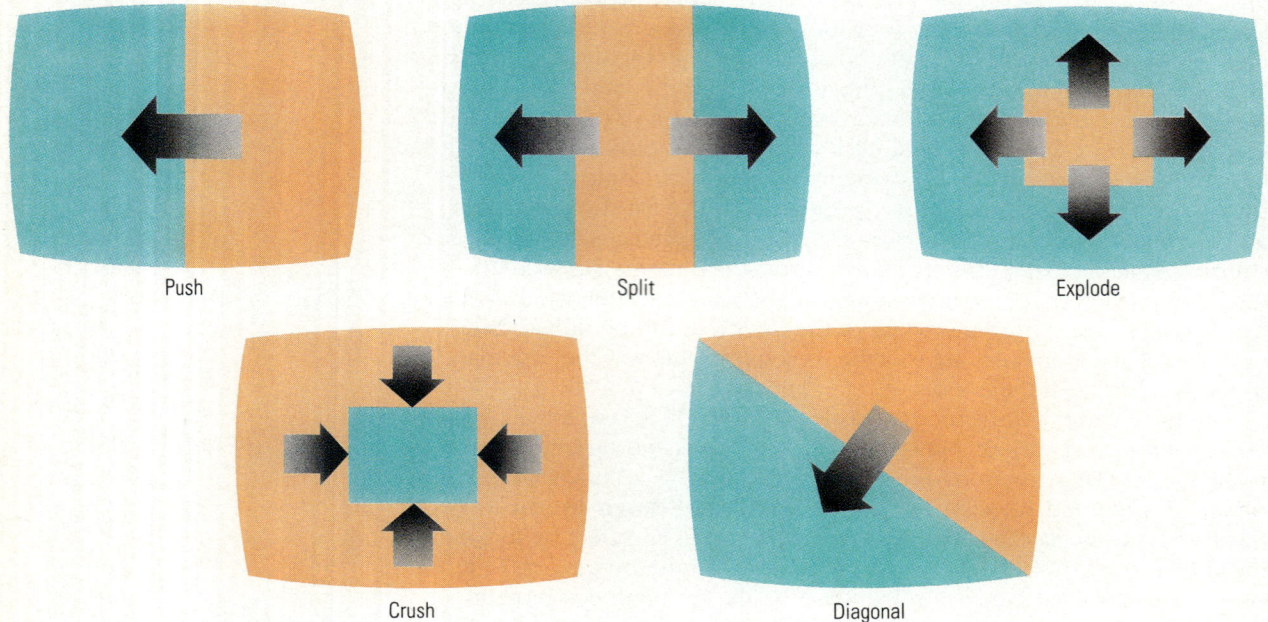

Once the screens needed for a presentation have been saved in files on a diskette, the user can use a story editor program to create a sequence of screens to be displayed. In the story editor, the user simply names the screens within the file or files that have been saved on diskette. The order in which the screens are named determines the order in which they will be displayed.

The user can also pick a transition to be used from one screen to the next. Just as the picture taking program is similar to a camera, the types of transitions available are similar to those used in motion pictures. Exhibit 9.17 shows some of the common transitions that can be used in the PC Storyboard package. The user can have a new picture push the old one off of the screen in any of four directions. The old picture can be split in the middle and move off horizontally or vertically to reveal the new one. The new picture can explode from the center and move out over the old one in all four directions. A crush is the opposite of explode—the new picture comes from the outside and moves over the old one toward the center in all four directions. In diagonal transition, the new picture starts in one corner and moves diagonally to cover the old picture.

Once the sequence of pictures and the transitions between them have been specified, the presentation description is saved on the diskette, along with the files containing the screens used in the story. The user can then run the presentation and have all of the screens displayed in the order specified using the chosen transitions.

DESKTOP PUBLISHING

Desktop publishing software deals with the incorporation of graphics into text. A number of hardware and software developments have been responsible for the increased interest in desktop publishing as an end-user tool. Desktop publishing began with the introduction of Apple Macintosh combined with a laser printer and a special type of software called Pagemaker from Aldus Corporation. Before the introduction of this combination of hardware and software, users had to purchase large, expensive systems to produce high-quality publications.

The Macintosh gives the user a simple interface in which a mouse can be used to move objects on the screen and make selections from menus. This, coupled with the introduction of inexpensive laser printers for microcomputers and software allowing the user to control the placement of text and graphics on a page, have placed control of the publishing process on the user's desktop microcomputer. With this combination of hardware and software at a relatively low cost, users with little training can produce professional-quality publications.

As with other end-user applications, the software is the driving force behind the interest in desktop publishing. Products such as Pagemaker, Ventura, and Frontpage combine simple menu commands, the ability to display pages exactly as they will appear on paper, and the ability to print those pages on high-quality output devices.

Creating Publications

Exhibit 9.18 shows the layout of the Pagemaker page composition program. When a user creates a publication, the master page icons at the bottom are used to specify the general characteristics of the pages. Both left and right master page icons can be used for publications that are to be printed like a book, with left and right facing pages. A user selects one of these master icons using a pointing device, such as a mouse. A user can specify the types of units to be used in the measurements of the page (inches, spaces, centimeters) as well as page size, number of pages, margins, and the use of left and right facing pages. Once the basic layout is specified, the user is presented with a blank page meeting those specifications.

While creating a publication, the user can take advantage of many special features that make it easy to lay out a page. As shown in Exhibit 9.18, rulers can be used to determine page height and column positioning; icons representing all of the pages in the publication appear at the bottom to aid in the selection of the page to be displayed; and various pulldown menus can be used to issue commands.

Manipulating Text

The user can enter text from the keyboard or can import it from word processors such as WordPerfect and Wordstar. Text on a page can be highlighted using the mouse pointer, and the characteristics of the high-

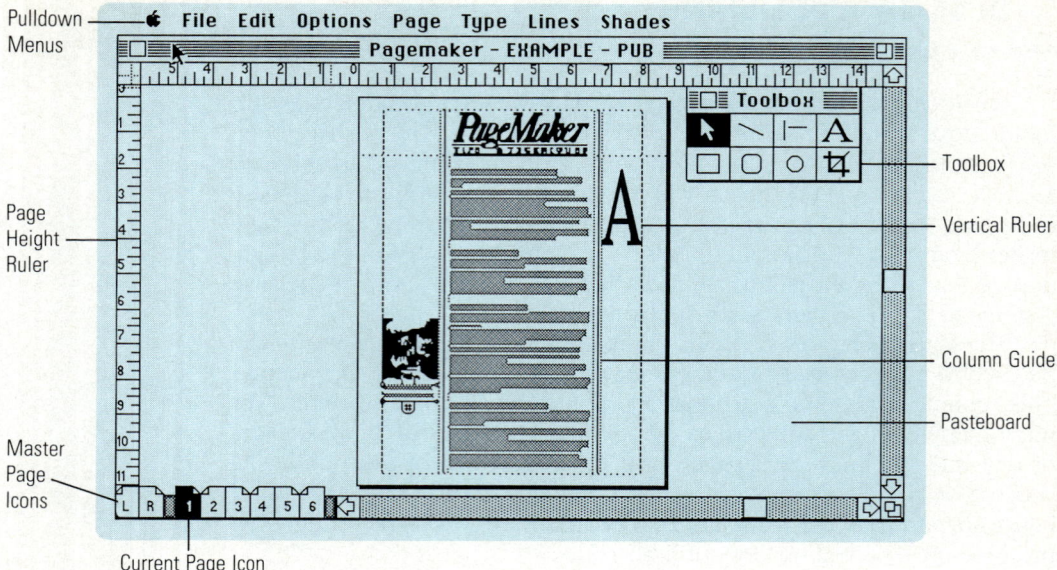

EXHIBIT 9.18
A Representation of the Pagemaker Page Composition Program

lighted text can be adjusted by the user. Pagemaker gives the user over 100 fonts to choose in sizes ranging from 4 to 127 points (one point is 1/72 of an inch). Special type styles, such as bold, underline, italic, superscript, and subscript, are also available. Text can be automatically hyphenated using a dictionary of hyphenations, or the user can be prompted to indicate the position of the hyphen.

Manipulating Graphics

The toolbox in Exhibit 9.18 provides features that allow the user to create simple graphics involving lines, text, and geometric shapes. As with illustration graphics programs, users can specify line thickness, shade objects, position objects, and alter the size of objects. More importantly, Pagemaker allows the user to import graphics from other graphics programs. Graphics can be placed anywhere on the page and adjusted in size as they are imported so they will fit on the page.

Page Layout

When building a page, the user can divide the page into columns, set up headers and footers, control page numbering, and wrap text around graphics. While a page is being constructed, the user can place blocks of text or graphics in the Pasteboard area of the screen (see Exhibit 9.18). These text blocks and graphics can be pasted back onto any page and sized to fit. Perhaps the most important aspect of Pagemaker, and all other page

EXHIBIT 9.19
An Example of a Page Created with Ventura Publisher

composition programs, is that the user sees the page formatted on the screen exactly as it will be printed. To accomplish this, these programs require microcomputers capable of displaying graphics on the screen and laser printers capable of producing high-quality output.

Exhibit 9.19 shows an example of a page that can be created using Ventura Publisher. This exhibit shows how text and graphics can be combined in a single document. Both numerically oriented graphs and illustrations can be placed within the text. The text itself is displayed in many different sizes and styles in multiple columns. This type of software combined with a high-quality laser printer allow an end-user to create professional publications, such as newsletters, without the need for a highly trained graphic arts staff.

Summary

Graphics software can be used to display numeric information in the form of a graph. There are four categories of software involved in the creation and use of graphics: data-driven graphics, illustration graphics, presentation graphics, and desktop publishing software.

Data-driven graphics software displays numeric data graphically. Data-driven graphics software can be separated into software integrated into a spreadsheet (*spreadsheet graphics*) and software that functions independent of any spreadsheet (*dedicated graphics*). Spreadsheet graphics programs can take advantage of the spreadsheet's ability to recalculate numeric results and update the graph as the numbers change.

Common types of graphs include pie charts, bar graphs, and line graphs. *Pie charts* are used to compare values across one category as a percentage of the whole. Each value in the category is represented as a slice of the pie, where the size of the slice indicates the percentage for that value. An *exploding pie chart* lets the user pull one or more of the slices away from the pie for emphasis.

A *bar graph* is used to show how data differ across one or two categories. Values in one category are shown on the *x-axis* with a bar above each value. The height of the bar indicates a value on the *y-axis*, which represents the measurement scale for the numbers being graphed. If a second category is graphed, it is represented by multiple bars over each value on the *x*-axis. Bar graphs may also include a title for the graph and for each axis. *Data labels* can also be used within the graph to label the various bars. A user can also manually set the points shown on each axis through the use of a *scaling* feature. Variations of the bar graph include stacked bar, horizontal bar, and three-dimensional bar graphs.

Line graphs are similar to bar graphs, except that data are graphed as a group of points joined by a line. Line graphs are typically best used for showing trends, whereas bar graphs are best used for showing amounts. In both line and bar graphs, a *legend* can be used to identify the lines or bars.

Dedicated graphics programs typically have more options than those associated with a spreadsheet. Default settings can be used to create a graph quickly or can be overridden to allow the user more flexibility. The user has more control over the placement of text within the graph, over the size of the text, and over the style of that text.

Some of the features important in choosing a graphics program include the types of graphs it can produce; automatic generation of labels and legends; manual axis control; image libraries; number of available text styles, shading patterns, and screen display colors; menu-driven commands; and price.

Illustration graphics programs allow the end-user to create free-form pictures by drawing or "painting" images on the screen. These programs let the user draw objects, move them around, shade them, and manipulate shapes. These images can be printed or stored on diskette for future use.

Presentation graphics programs allow users to sequence a series of graphic images and determine transitions between them. These programs also include software that allows a user to capture a picture of the screen in a file for use in a presentation. Once a presentation is described, the user can call it up, and the images listed in the presentation are displayed with the selected transitions between them.

Desktop publishing software involves the incorporation of graphics into text to create professional-quality publications. Desktop publishing uses page layout software to position text and graphics on a page and to select different text styles and sizes. This software, combined with a laser printer capable of producing high-quality output, allow a user with little training to produce professional-quality publications, such as user manuals and newsletters.

Review Questions

1. List some of the common types of graphs that can be produced with graphics software.

2. Compare graphics software incorporated in a spreadsheet program to stand-alone graphics software.

3. Explain how a pie chart is used to graph data.

4. What is the difference between a bar graph and a stacked bar graph?

5. What are the similarities and differences between a bar graph and a line graph?

6. What would an illustration graphics program be used for?

7. Explain the function of the picture taking software in a presentation graphics program.

8. What are the three components responsible for the interest in desktop publishing?

9. What is the role of pagemaking software in desktop publishing?

CHAPTER 10 ■ Microcomputer Data Bases

THE ROLE OF DATA MANAGEMENT SOFTWARE
THE MICROCOMPUTER DBMS
CREATION AND UPDATING
RETRIEVAL
- Projecting
- Selecting
- Joining
- Sorting
- Performing Calculations

MICROCOMPUTER DBMS FEATURES
- Data Dictionary Features
- Restructuring the Data Base
- Data Base Programming
- Forms
- Natural Language Interfaces
- Report Generators
- Backup and Recovery Features
- Integration with Other End-User Tools

CHOOSING A DBMS
SUMMARY
REVIEW QUESTIONS

Although data base management systems began on large computers, microcomputer versions have grown to become a significant part of the software market. Since most end-users are not likely to be involved with designing and maintaining corporate data bases on mainframe computers, they would more likely use microcomputer data base management systems to design and maintain small personal data bases, which can often be used in conjunction with other end-user tools, such as word processors and spreadsheets. Data kept in a data base can be included in a word processing document or incorporated into a spreadsheet. In this chapter, we will discuss the specifics of data base processing in terms of a microcomputer DBMS. We will also look at some of the common features of a microcomputer DBMS.

In this chapter you will learn to do the following:

1. Understand how a data base is created.
2. Determine what an index is.
3. Explain how data are retrieved with project and join operations.
4. Understand how a criterion is used in the selection operation.
5. Explain how data can be sorted.
6. Ascertain how various values can be calculated when a report is created.
7. Understand some of the features included in a microcomputer DBMS.
8. Identify some of the features that can be important in choosing a microcomputer DBMS.

THE ROLE OF DATA MANAGEMENT SOFTWARE

The primary role of data management software is to provide an easy way to create and maintain files and to retrieve data from those files for use in developing information for users. Considering how data can be organized and also learning more about data management functions are necessary to an understanding of this concept.

A familiar example—a phone book—helps show the basic concepts of data organization. Exhibit 10.1 shows a portion of the Local College phone directory. A collection of related characters forms a **data item,** or **field.** Employee names and phone extensions are examples of data items. An occurrence of all data items is called a **record.** A **file** is a collection of similar types of records. In this particular case, the phone directory file contains the records of all of the faculty and staff members of Local College.

This phone directory file is ordered on the key *employee name.* A **key** is a field that can be used to identify a record. A **primary key** is a field (or fields) that identifies a unique record. Organizations often have to use employee number or social security number as a primary key, since several people may have the same name. The primary key field is often used by data management software to put records into the file in a certain order. You may have noticed that the records in Exhibit 10.1 are in ascending order based on the value in the primary key field (Employee Name).

■ *10 Microcomputer Data Bases*

Employee Name	Job Title	Building and Room Location	Telephone Extension	
ANDAZOLA, Genevieve	Secretary, Financial Aid	1-308	0245	
CARTER, Georgia	Secretary, Student Affairs	1-224	4716	
DUREIN, Martina	Secretary, Counseling and Testing Services	1-110	4235	
EKIZIAN, Olivia	Administrative Secretary, Student Affairs	1-224	4714	
HART, Dr. Joseph T.	Director, Counseling and Testing	1-110B	4234	
JACOBS, Harry M.	Director, Financial Aid	1-308	0244	
JONES, Madelena	Administrative Assistant, Student Affairs	1-224	4715	
SMITH, Rose	Secretary, Admissions and Records	1-104	4823	A record
WELLS, Dr. Janet	Vice-President, Student Affairs	1-224	4713	
YORK, Richard	Director, Admissions and Records	1-104	4822	
Primary key values		Character	Field or data item value	

EXHIBIT 10.1
A File Made Up of Records Ordered by Primary Key

THE MICROCOMPUTER DBMS

Microcomputer DBMSs all have two primary functions: updating and retrieving data to satisfy user requests. This chapter will concentrate on these two functions. The data shown in Exhibit 10.2 will be used for purposes of illustration. Each product listed has a unique identification number called a *product code*. The *product description* indicates what the product is, but it is possible for more than one product to have the same description. A *product group* places the products in categories so that similar products can be stored together in the warehouse. *Stock quantity* shows how many units of a product are currently in the warehouse, and product *price* indicates how much the company paid for the product. This information will be used to show how data can be stored and retrieved using a microcomputer DBMS.

PRODUCT CODE	PRODUCT DESCRIPTION	PRODUCT GROUP	STOCK QUANTITY	PRODUCT PRICE
AZ-247	Keyboard	Computer	200	125.00
DD-397	Turntable	Stereo	45	175.95
XT-222	Hard Disk Drive	Computer	30	945.00
TL-346	Speaker	Stereo	345	39.95
GC-349	Receiver	Stereo	100	275.75
DC-349	Antenna	Television	35	29.99
GK-151	23-Inch B & W	Television	10	349.95
DL-399	Disk Drive	Computer	145	75.00
TK-496	Monitor	Computer	36	39.00
GD-534	Needle	Stereo	340	12.50
AZ-293	IBM PC Keyboard	Computer	200	125.00
99899	IBM PC Computer	Computer	56	2500.00

EXHIBIT 10.2
Product Data Showing Product Codes, Descriptions, Groups, Stock Quantities, and Prices

CREATION AND UPDATING

When creating a data base initially, the fields in each type of record to be stored in a file or files must be defined. Each field is given a name and a maximum length. In addition, fields are assigned a **data type,** which indicates the kind of data to be stored in that field. Common data types include character, integer, and decimal. The **character data** type indicates data in a field to be treated as text; this type cannot be used in any numeric calculations. **Integer data** are numeric but cannot have any decimal values. **Decimal data** are numeric and do allow decimal values. Some data base programs have additional special data types. For example, R:Base System V includes data types such as date, time, and currency. Exhibit 10.3 shows how our product data base is defined in the dBASE III Plus DBMS. Each field in the data base is given a name, a type, a width (length), and the number of decimal places to be kept. In dBASE III Plus, both integer and decimal fields are called *numeric,* indicating use in arithmetic operations. Integer variables are numeric variables without any decimal places, and decimal fields are created by putting in a value in the column for decimal places.

Data base files usually have a primary key to uniquely identify each record and determine the order of the records in the file. Thus, when creating a data base, a user sometimes must choose a field to serve as the primary key. The user can then supply the value of the primary key in the particular record in the data base that is to be retrieved. The primary key for the data in Exhibit 10.2 should be the product code, since that code is unique for each product.

Some data base management systems (like dBASE III Plus) do not require a primary key. Instead the records in the data base can be stored in any order, and that ordering can be manipulated with sorting commands. In other data base management systems, such as R:BASE System V, there is no primary key field, but many fields can be designated as keys by the user. When a field is labeled as a key, an **index** of the locations of the data in

EXHIBIT 10.3
Defining the Fields in the Product Data Base Using dBASE III Plus

```
B:PRODUCT.dbf                                         Bytes remaining:   3953
                                                      Fields defined:       5

    field name   type        width   dec        field name   type   width   dec
  1 PROD_CODE    Char/text      6
  2 PROD_DESC    Char/text     20
  3 PROD_GROUP   Char/text     10
  4 STOCK_QNTY   Numeric        4     0
  5 PROD_PRICE   Numeric        7     2
  6              Char/text


Names start with a letter; the remainder may be letters, digits, or underscore
```

```
       INDEX ON PROD_CODE TO PRODINDEX
           10 records indexed
       FIND GC-349
       DISPLAY
       Record#   PROD_CODE  PROD_DESC      PROD_GROUP  STOCK_QNTY  PROD_PRICE
            5    GC-349     RECEIVER       STEREO         100         275.75
```

EXHIBIT 10.4

In dBASE III Plus, the INDEX command creates an index for the PROD_CODE field called PRODINDEX. A subsequent FIND statement with a value for the product code GC-349 will locate that record. The DISPLAY command shows the located record on the screen.

that field is created. When a user wishes to search for records on the basis of a value in a key field, the index is used to locate records with that value in the key field. Thus, a record can be located by specifying a value in the indexed field for the record that is desired. Exhibit 10.4 shows how an index is created on the PROD_CODE field of our sample data base and how that index is used to FIND a record with a specific product code in the dBASE III Plus DBMS.*

Having the product code as a primary key or an indexed field allows a user to find a record with a specific value in that field without having to scan through all of the records. If, however, a user wants to find a record with a specific value in the description field, all of the records have to be scanned, since they are not ordered on that field. Scanning records can be relatively slow, particularly when a data base contains many records. To speed this process, a DBMS may allow indexes to be created on many different fields in a data base.

Once the structure of the data base is defined, data must be entered into that structure to create the records in the data base. Some data base management systems give a user a blank form containing the names of each field and enough space to enter a value for that field or allow the user to create his or her own form. Other data base management systems simply prompt a user for values, one at a time, until a record is filled in. Exhibit 10.5 shows a form used by dBASE III Plus when a user is in the process of entering data.

EXHIBIT 10.5

dBASE III Plus displays a form for the user to enter the data into when records are entered into the data base.

---

*dBASE III Plus normally uses a menu-driven interface called ASSIST for entering commands. In this system, the user builds a command by selecting pieces of the command from the various menus. This is one of the major differences between dBASE III and dBASE III Plus. With the ASSIST option turned off, dBASE III Plus commands can be entered directly by the user as they are in dBASE III. The dBASE III Plus commands are shown in this text as they would be entered without the ASSIST menus in order to illustrate the commands more clearly and efficiently.

Creation and Updating

Since valuable data are often stored in a data base, the integrity of the stored data becomes very important. Thus, a DBMS provides commands that allow users to *update* the data base. The user can *insert* new records, *change* the contents of records, and *delete* unwanted records. In order to modify record values or delete specific records, a DBMS must also allow a user to retrieve or *get* a single record. This is usually accomplished by requiring the user to supply the record's primary key or the value in an indexed field.

RETRIEVAL

The second major function of a DBMS is the selected retrieval of data to satisfy users' queries. There are five major types of operations that can be involved in producing the desired information: projecting, selecting, joining, sorting, and performing calculations.

Projecting

Projecting is the extraction of a subset of the fields in a data base. When a report is created, a user typically needs only a few of the fields in the data base, so a DBMS allows a user to project only the fields needed for the report. Exhibit 10.6a shows how a projection can be done in the dBASE III Plus DBMS by using the LIST command.

Selecting

In addition to projecting fields, a DBMS also enables a user to select specific records. **Selecting** allows the user to retrieve a subset of the records from a data base. When selecting records, the user must supply a criterion that gives the basis of the selection. A **criterion** is a comparison of a field in the data base to some value or to another field in the data base. For example, Exhibit 10.6b, in the middle of the screen, shows a DISPLAY command in dBASE III Plus that uses a criterion of STOCK_QNTY > 100. This criterion selects records in which the value in the STOCK_QNTY field of each record is greater than 100. This comparison involves a numeric field, but it is also possible to use a character field. For example, WHERE PROD_GROUP = "COMPUTER" would select records with COMPUTER in the PROD_GROUP field (see Exhibit 10.7a). Note how the value is enclosed in quotation marks in a comparison involving a character field. Other possible comparisons include *less than* (<), *not equal to* (<>), *greater than or equal to* (>=), and *less than or equal to* (<=).

Simple criteria can also be joined together to form a more complex criterion using the logical operators *AND* or *OR*. For example, Exhibit 10.7b shows a criterion which joins the criteria used in Exhibits 10.6b and 10.7a with an AND relationship. When two simple criteria are joined with the AND logical operator, *both* criteria must be satisfied for a record to be selected. If the two criteria in Exhibit 10.7b had been joined by an OR

```
LIST PROD_CODE, STOCK_QNTY, PROD_PRICE
Record#  PROD_CODE  STOCK_QNTY  PROD_PRICE
   1     AZ-247         200       125.00
   2     DD-397          45       175.95
   3     XT-222          30       945.00
   4     TL-346         345        39.95
   5     GC-349         100       275.75
   6     DC-349          35        29.99
   7     GK-151          10       349.95
   8     DL-399         145        75.00
   9     TK-496          36        39.00
  10     GD-534         340        12.50
  11     AZ-293         200       125.00

DISPLAY ALL FOR STOCK_QNTY > 100
Record#  PROD_CODE  PROD_DESC         PROD_GROUP  STOCK_QNTY  PROD_PRICE
   1     AZ-247     KEYBOARD          COMPUTER       200        125.00
   4     TL-346     SPEAKER           STEREO         345         39.95
   8     DL-399     DISK DRIVE        COMPUTER       145         75.00
  10     GD-534     NEEDLE            STEREO         340         12.50
  11     AZ-293     IBM PC KEYBOARD   COMPUTER       200        125.00
```

EXHIBIT 10.6
Retrieving Data in a DBMS

(a) In dBASE III Plus, the LIST command projects a subset of the fields for all of the records in the data base.

(b) In dBASE III Plus, the DISPLAY command can be used to perform a selection of records. In this example, the criterion selected only those records in which the STOCK_QNTY field contained a value greater than 100.

```
DISPLAY ALL FOR PROD_GROUP = "COMPUTER"
Record#  PROD_CODE  PROD_DESC         PROD_GROUP  STOCK_QNTY  PROD_PRICE
   1     AZ-247     KEYBOARD          COMPUTER       200        125.00
   3     XT-222     HARD DISK DRIVE   COMPUTER        30        945.00
   8     DL-399     DISK DRIVE        COMPUTER       145         75.00
   9     TK-496     MONITOR           COMPUTER        36         39.00
  11     AZ-293     IBM PC KEYBOARD   COMPUTER       200        125.00

DISPLAY ALL FOR STOCK_QNTY > 100 .AND. PROD_GROUP = "COMPUTER"
Record#  PROD_CODE  PROD_DESC         PROD_GROUP  STOCK_QNTY  PROD_PRICE
   1     AZ-247     KEYBOARD          COMPUTER       200        125.00
   8     DL-399     DISK DRIVE        COMPUTER       145         75.00
  11     AZ-293     IBM PC KEYBOARD   COMPUTER       200        125.00

DISPLAY ALL FOR STOCK_QNTY > 100 .OR. PROD_GROUP = "COMPUTER"
Record#  PROD_CODE  PROD_DESC         PROD_GROUP  STOCK_QNTY  PROD_PRICE
   1     AZ-247     KEYBOARD          COMPUTER       200        125.00
   3     XT-222     HARD DISK DRIVE   COMPUTER        30        945.00
   4     TL-346     SPEAKER           STEREO         345         39.95
   8     DL-399     DISK DRIVE        COMPUTER       145         75.00
   9     TK-496     MONITOR           COMPUTER        36         39.00
  10     GD-534     NEEDLE            STEREO         340         12.50
  11     AZ-293     IBM PC KEYBOARD   COMPUTER       200        125.00
```

EXHIBIT 10.7
Three Criteria Used in Selecting Records

(a) When the criterion involves a character field, the value to be searched for must be enclosed by quotation marks.
(b) The AND operator can be used to join two simple criteria into a single multiple criterion. In this example, a record must have both a quantity greater than 100 AND belong to the COMPUTER product group.
(c) When the OR operator is used to create a multiple criterion, records are selected if they satisfy either of the two parts of the criterion.

operator, the results would have been different (see Exhibit 10.7c). When criteria are joined with an OR, a record is selected if it meets *either* of the two criteria.

Sometimes a report will require a comparison involving more than one field. For example, Exhibit 10.8 shows a criterion in which records are selected when the value in the STOCK_QNTY field is less than that in the

```
DISPLAY ALL FOR STOCK_QNTY < PROD_PRICE
Record#  PROD_CODE  PROD_DESC         PROD_GROUP   STOCK_QNTY  PROD_PRICE
   2     DD-397     TURNTABLE         STEREO          45        175.95
   3     XT-222     HARD DISK DRIVE   COMPUTER        30        945.00
   5     GC-349     RECEIVER          STEREO         100        275.75
   7     GK-151     23 INCH B & W     TELEVISION      10        349.95
   9     TK-496     MONITOR           COMPUTER        36         39.00
```

EXHIBIT 10.8

A criterion can compare values in two fields rather than comparing a single field to a value specified in the criterion.

Retrieval

PROD_PRICE field. In this example, both of the values in the criterion are now coming from fields in the data base instead of just one of the values as before.

Joining

The third DBMS feature involved in producing reports is the **join** function. This function allows two data bases to be combined across a common field. Exhibit 10.9a shows a supplier data base displayed with the CONDOR DBMS LIST command, which contains information about the product a particular supplier carries. If a product data base were created in CONDOR with the same PRODCODE field, the supplier and product data bases could be joined across the common PRODCODE field (see Exhibits 10.9b and 10.9c). This way, information about suppliers and products can be kept in separate files, which can be joined when a particular query requires information from both of them.

EXHIBIT 10.9
The Join Function

(a) The supplier data base contains information about suppliers and contains the same product codes that appear in the product data base.

```
B>>LIST SUPPLIER BY PRODCODE, SUPPID, SUPPNAME
Dataset: SUPPLIER              10 Records
PRODCODE  SUPPID  SUPPNAME
AZ-247    2343    MICROCENTER
DD-397    2222    STEREO STORE
XT-222    3333    COMPUTERWORLD
TL-346    4444    STEREO LAND
GC-349    5555    STEREO LAND
DC-349    6666    TV WAREHOUSE
GK-151    4654    TV WORLD
DL-399    5969    COMPUTRONICS
TK-496    8675    COMPUTECHNICS
GD-534    4099    STEREO SUPPLY
```

(b) The JOIN command in the CONDOR DBMS merges the supplier and product data bases across the common product code field.

```
B>>JOIN B:PRODUCTS B:SUPPLIER MATCHING PRODCODE
Dataset: PRODUCTS              10 Records
Dataset: SUPPLIER              10 Records
Joined       10
Total Records in result set = 10
```

10 Microcomputer Data Bases

```
B>>LIST RESULT BY PRODCODE,PRODDESC,PRODPRICE,SUPPID,SUPPNAME
Dataset: RESULT              10 Records
PRODCODE  PRODDESC           PRODPRICE SUPPID SUPPNAME
AZ-247    KEYBOARD              125.00 2343   MICROCENTER
DD-397    TURNTABLE             175.95 2222   STEREO STORE
XT-222    HARD DISK DRIVE       945.00 3333   COMPUTERWORLD
TL-346    SPEAKER                39.95 4444   STEREO LAND
GC-349    RECEIVER              275.75 5555   STEREO LAND
DC-349    ANTENNA                29.99 6666   TV WAREHOUSE
GK-151    23 INCH B & W         349.95 4654   TV WORLD
DL-399    DISK DRIVE             75.00 5969   COMPUTRONICS
TK-496    MONITOR                39.00 8675   COMPUTECHNICS
GD-534    NEEDLE                 12.50 4099   STEREO SUPPLY
```

(c) The join creates a new data base that contains all of the fields from both the supplier and product data bases. Here the common PRODCODE field is shown along with the PRODDESC and PRODPRICE fields from the product data base and the SUPPID and SUPPNAME from the supplier data base.

Sorting

Typically, the records in a data base do not have to be stored in any particular order; however, when records are to be displayed on a report, it may be more meaningful to have the records sorted by the contents of one or more of the fields. A report involving the products in Exhibit 10.1, for example, might be more useful to a manager if it were arranged by product group. Exhibit 10.10 shows our product data base after it has been sorted.

With a microcomputer DBMS, you can often specify multiple sorts on the same report. In a **multiple sort,** the records are ordered on the basis of more than one field. The first sort order is referred to as a **primary sort order** (not to be confused with the primary key). Any additional sort orders are referred to as **secondary sort orders.**

```
SORT ON PROD_GROUP TO B:GRPSORT
100% Sorted          11 Records sorted
USE B:GRPSORT
DISPLAY ALL
Record#  PROD_CODE  PROD_DESC         PROD_GROUP STOCK_QNTY PROD_PRICE
     1   TK-496     MONITOR           COMPUTER        36        39.00
     2   XT-222     HARD DISK DRIVE   COMPUTER        30       945.00
     3   AZ-293     IBM PC KEYBOARD   COMPUTER       200       125.00
     4   AZ-247     KEYBOARD          COMPUTER       200       125.00
     5   DL-399     DISK DRIVE        COMPUTER       145        75.00
     6   DD-397     TURNTABLE         STEREO          45       175.95
     7   TL-346     SPEAKER           STEREO         345        39.95
     8   GC-349     RECEIVER          STEREO         100       275.75
     9   GD-534     NEEDLE            STEREO         340        12.50
    10   GK-151     23 INCH B & W     TELEVISION      10       349.95
    11   DC-349     ANTENNA           TELEVISION      35        29.99
```

EXHIBIT 10.10
The Product Data Base Sorted on the PROD_GROUP Field in Ascending Order Using dBASE III Plus

A common example of a multiple sort is the campus phone book mentioned at the beginning of this chapter. First, all records are sorted by last name (primary sort order). If two records have the same last name, this primary sort order cannot determine their precise position on the report. The secondary sort order (first name in a phone book) is then used to determine the order of any records which cannot be positioned using the primary sort order alone. Thus, a secondary sort order does not change the order of the records determined by the primary sort order, but rather specifies an order for any records that have the same value in the field used to determine the primary sort order.

When specifying sort orders, a DBMS will also allow a user to specify if a sort is to be ascending or descending. An **ascending sort** would order the records so that the values in the sorted field would go from lowest to highest. A **descending sort** would place the values from highest to lowest. For fields containing character data, the letter A is considered to be the lowest and Z the highest. A DBMS will usually allow the use of different sort orders for the primary and secondary sort orders. Exhibit 10.11a shows an example of a multiple sort with a primary sorting on the PROD_GROUP field and a secondary sort on the PROD_PRICE field. The primary sort is ascending and secondary sort is descending.

Performing Calculations

A final DBMS feature used in producing reports is the capability to perform calculations. It is often desirable to have summary statistics produced for certain fields of a report. Common statistical functions include minimum, maximum, total, count, and average. Usually any or all of these statistics can be produced on the fields in a report which contains numeric data. For example, the DBMS can be requested to produce an average for the STOCK_QNTY field (see Exhibit 10.11b).

A second type of calculation involves the creation of new fields from other fields. For example, if the total value of the inventory on hand is

EXHIBIT 10.11
Sorting and Performing Calculations
(a) Here is an example of a multiple sort with the records sorted on PROD_GROUP (primary order) in ascending order and on PROD_PRICE (secondary order) in descending order. Note how the secondary order sorts only records with the same value in the field used for the primary sort.

(b) In dBASE III Plus, an average can be calculated for a particular field.

```
SORT ON PROD_GROUP/A, PROD_PRICE/D TO B:MULTIPLE
100% Sorted           11 Records sorted
USE B:MULTIPLE
DISPLAY ALL
Record#   PROD_CODE  PROD_DESC           PROD_GROUP  STOCK_QNTY  PROD_PRICE
      1   XT-222     HARD DISK DRIVE     COMPUTER            30      945.00
      2   AZ-293     IBM PC KEYBOARD     COMPUTER           200      125.00
      3   AZ-247     KEYBOARD            COMPUTER           200      125.00
      4   DL-399     DISK DRIVE          COMPUTER           145       75.00
      5   TK-496     MONITOR             COMPUTER            36       39.00
      6   GC-349     RECEIVER            STEREO             100      275.75
      7   DD-397     TURNTABLE           STEREO              45      175.95
      8   TL-346     SPEAKER             STEREO             345       39.95
      9   GD-534     NEEDLE              STEREO             340·      12.50
     10   GK-151     23 INCH B & W       TELEVISION          10      349.95
     11   DC-349     ANTENNA             TELEVISION          35       29.99
AVERAGE STOCK_QNTY
   11 records averaged
STOCK_QNTY
      135
```

needed, the STOCK_QNTY is multiplied by the PROD_PRICE to get a total value for each product. Then these values are summed to get the total value of our inventory (see Exhibit 10.12). On this report, the code, description, group, quantity, and price for each product came from the product data base, and the VALUE field was calculated when the report was created by multiplying the quantity and price for each product.

```
Page No.    1
01/01/80
                        REPORT OF INVENTORY VALUE

PRODUCT   PRODUCT           PRODUCT     STOCK   PRODUCT     TOTAL
CODE      DESCRIPTION       GROUP       QUANTITY PRICE      VALUE
=======   ===========       =======     ======== =======    =====

XT-222    HARD DISK DRIVE   COMPUTER        30    945.00    28350.00
AZ-293    IBM PC KEYBOARD   COMPUTER       200    125.00    25000.00
AZ-247    KEYBOARD          COMPUTER       200    125.00    25000.00
DL-399    DISK DRIVE        COMPUTER       145     75.00    10875.00
TK-496    MONITOR           COMPUTER        36     39.00     1404.00
GC-349    RECEIVER          STEREO         100    275.75    27575.00
DD-397    TURNTABLE         STEREO          45    175.95     7917.75
TL-346    SPEAKER           STEREO         345     39.95    13782.75
GD-534    NEEDLE            STEREO         340     12.50     4250.00
GK-151    23 INCH B & W     TELEVISION      10    349.95     3499.50
DC-349    ANTENNA           TELEVISION      35     29.99     1049.65
*** Total ***
                                                           148703.65
```

EXHIBIT 10.12
A dBASE III Plus Report Showing How a New Field (TOTAL VALUE) Can Be Created from Other Fields in the Data Base
In the example, TOTAL VALUE is equal to STOCK QUANTITY times PRICE. At the bottom, a total is calculated for the TOTAL VALUE field. Totals can be obtained for any numeric field on the report.

MICROCOMPUTER DBMS FEATURES

Microcomputer data base management systems include many features that can make the creating, updating, and retrieval of data easier and more efficient. In this section, we will look at some of these features and how they are used.

Data Dictionary Features

The core of any DBMS is the **data dictionary,** which holds the definitions of all of the fields in the data base. At a minimum, it supports the definition of field names, lengths, and data types. Some data base management systems have a more advanced data dictionary that lets a user determine how the data are stored to prevent some of the errors that may be made during data entry.

The user can sometimes specify maximum and minimum values that can be entered into a numeric field. Exhibit 10.13 shows the product data base being created in the CONDOR DBMS, which lets a user specify minimum and maximum values for a field. If a user does not specify a value for that field when a record is being inserted, the data base management system will automatically fill it in with a **default value,** a value which is specified in the data dictionary.

EXHIBIT 10.13

In the CONDOR DBMS, a user can specify minimum and maximum values for a field as well as the name, length, and type. In addition, default values for each field can be used to enter values in the field if the user leaves it blank.

```
Enter data definitions in the following format:
>FIELD-NAME: FIELD-TYPE, FIELD-SIZE, MIN-VALUE, MAX-VALUE, "DEFAULT-VALUE"
    Choices : (ANJ$N.nR) (1-127 bytes) (1 - 10 digits)  (0-15 Characters)

>1.PROD_CODE:   AN,  6,         0,         6,"            "
>2.PROD_DESC:   AN, 20,         0,        20,"            "
>3.PROD_GROUP:  AN, 10,         0,        10,"            "
>4.STOCK_QNTY:   N,  4,         0,      9999,"            "
>5.PROD_PRICE: N.2,  8,  -9999.99, 99999.99,"            "
>{{ END }}

Definitions OK (Y/N)?
```

Some data dictionaries have a **query** capability, which lets a user get information about the data base from the data dictionary. In dBASE III Plus, for example, the DISPLAY STRUCTURE command will display the current definitions of the fields in the data base (see Exhibit 10.14).

EXHIBIT 10.14

In dBASE III Plus, a user can get information about a data base from the data dictionary by using the DISPLAY STRUCTURE command.

```
     DISPLAY STRUCTURE
     Structure for database : B:PRODUCT.dbf
     Number of data records :     11
     Date of last update    : 01/01/80
     Field  Field name   Type        Width    Dec
         1  PROD_CODE    Character       6
         2  PROD_DESC    Character      20
         3  PROD_GROUP   Character      10
         4  STOCK_QNTY   Numeric         4
         5  PROD_PRICE   Numeric         7      2
     ** Total **                        48
```

Some data dictionaries also provide **password protection** so that only certain users are able to see what is in the data dictionary. Any user can still enter and retrieve data from the data base, but only a user with the appropriate password can change the actual structure of the data base. Some data bases will even let a user protect sets of data in addition to the data dictionary itself. That way not every user has access to all of the data in the data base but only to selected data. Different types of access can also be defined for a specific set of data. Some users may only be able to retrieve information from the data base but not alter the values in the fields. Other types of access important to a user might include the ability to change field values in the data base, add new records to the data base, or delete records from the data base.

Some data base management systems support special data types to be assigned to fields. These include **packed fields,** in which the data are stored in compressed format to more efficiently utilize storage space. For example, blank spaces at the end of text fields might be removed in a field with a packed format so that only the necessary characters are stored. Sometimes special data formats are available for fields in which the user wants to use dates.

Certain types of **integrity controls** are often part of a data dictionary. One which requires a unique primary key for each record in the data base may check to make sure the values in that key field are not duplicated when records are inserted. Another integrity control is the checking of numeric fields to make sure only valid numbers (no text characters or special symbols) are entered.

Restructuring the Data Base

There may be occasions when a data base containing information has a structure which is no longer appropriate because some aspect of the data has been changed. Perhaps a new field needs to be added to the data base or an existing field's length or data type needs to be changed. For example, a field containing a 5-character zip code may need to be lengthened to accommodate the new zip-plus-four zip code.

When a field needs to be lengthened or added to a data base that already has data in it, the data must be rearranged. This rearrangement cannot be accomplished directly by many DBMSs. In such situations, the DBMSs require the user to create a new data base with the correct structure and copy the data from the old data base into the new data base.

Data Base Programming

Normally, when data base operations, such as creating a data base structure, entering data, or producing reports, are performed, a user must enter a series of commands, one at a time; the user must know the exact syntax of each command and enter it correctly. An inexperienced user, not knowing the commands, will have difficulty interacting with the data base. To overcome this problem, a data base program which contains the data base commands necessary to perform a certain task can be written by an experienced user who is familiar with programming. The program can be set up to prompt any user for the information needed to build the commands. In this way, an inexperienced end-user can use the data base without having to understand how the data base commands work. Not only can the procedural commands for data retrieval be used in these programs, but other commands, such as those to create the data base structure and modify the data, may also be included. Thus, in some data base management systems, a user can automate most of the tasks that are performed with the data base.

Another advantage of programming certain data base functions is the automation of tasks that need to be done periodically. Without a program, the commands necessary to produce a particular report have to be entered every time a report is needed. With a program, a single command is used to run a program which produces the report.

Exhibit 10.15 shows a program that can be used in dBASE III Plus to create a report from the PRODUCT data base. This program accesses the PRODUCT data base and sorts it on the basis of both the PROD_GROUP (ascending order) and the PROD_PRICE (descending order) fields. The

EXHIBIT 10.15

This exhibit shows a dBASE III Plus program that prints a report of all of the codes, descriptions, and groups for products with a stock quantity greater than 100. Records are sorted first by product group in ascending order and then by product price in descending order. After this report, an average for the price field is computed.

```
dBASE Word Processor
USE B:PRODUCT                                                      <
SORT ON PROD_GROUP/A, PROD_PRICE/D TO B:SORT1                      <
USE B:SORT1                                                        <
DISPLAY PROD_CODE, PROD_DESC, PROD_GROUP FOR STOCK_QNTY > 100      <
AVERAGE PROD_PRICE                                                 <
```

result of the sort is stored in another data base file called SORT1. The program then accesses this SORT1 data base and selects records that have a value greater than 100 in the STOCK_QNTY field. For the records selected, only the PROD_CODE, PROD_DESC, and PROD_GROUP fields are shown. After this, the program calculates the average PROD_PRICE for all of the records in the data base. Exhibit 10.16 shows what the screen looks like when this program is executed.

EXHIBIT 10.16

When the program in Exhibit 10.15 is run with the DO command, this is what the user sees.

```
DO B:PROG1
  100% Sorted           11 Records sorted
Record#   PROD_CODE  PROD_DESC          PROD_GROUP
      2   AZ-247     KEYBOARD           COMPUTER
      3   AZ-293     IBM PC KEYBOARD    COMPUTER
      4   DL-399     DISK DRIVE         COMPUTER
      8   TL-346     SPEAKER            STEREO
      9   GD-534     NEEDLE             STEREO
     11 records averaged
PROD_PRICE
    199.37
```

10 Microcomputer Data Bases

```
dBASE Word Processor
SET TALK OFF
USE B:PRODUCT
DONE = 'C'
DO WHILE DONE = 'C' .OR. DONE = 'c'
CLEAR
APPEND BLANK
@ 5,5 SAY 'PRODUCT CODE' GET PROD_CODE
@ 7,5 SAY 'PRODUCT DESCRIPTION' GET PROD_DESC
@ 9,5 SAY 'PRODUCE GROUP' GET PROD_GROUP
@ 11,5 SAY 'STOCK QUANTITY' GET STOCK_QNTY
@ 13,5 SAY 'PRODUCT PRICE' GET PROD_PRICE
READ
@ 20,5 SAY 'USE "C" TO CONTINUE,'
@ 21,5 SAY 'RETURN KEY ONLY TO QUIT'
ACCEPT TO DONE
ENDDO
SET TALK ON
RETURN
```

EXHIBIT 10.17

This dBASE III Plus program allows the user to add records to the end of the PRODUCT data base.

A data base programming language also includes sets of commands used to control the program itself: *if* statements so that the program can selectively perform commands, *while* statements to create a loop in the program, and statements to obtain information from the user while the program is running. Exhibit 10.17 shows a dBASE III Plus program which uses some of these programming features to create a program that allows a user to add records to the PRODUCT data base.

In this program, the SET TALK OFF command causes the display of all commands on the screen to be suppressed while the program is running. The SET TALK ON at the bottom reverses this setting. The program then accesses the PRODUCT data base and initializes a variable called DONE to the value C. Then a loop begins at the DO WHILE statement and continues as long as the DONE variable remains equal to C. Inside the loop, the program first uses CLEAR to blank out the screen and then uses APPEND BLANK to put a blank record on the end of the PRODUCT data base.

Next the program uses the @ command to position the cursor on the blank screen and print a heading for the user to see. For example, the first @ command displays PRODUCT CODE on row 5, column 5 of the screen and then obtains information to be put into the PROD_CODE field of the record. After all of the headings have been placed in the appropriate positions on the screen, the READ command pulls up the blank record appended to the PRODUCT data base and allows the user to type values into the variables listed in the @ statements. Once all of the variables have been filled in, two more messages are displayed, and the ACCEPT command receives the answer that the user types from the keyboard and puts it into the DONE variable. The ENDDO sends the program back to the DO WHILE, where the contents of the DONE variable are checked again to see if the user typed C at the end of the loop. If DONE is not equal to either an upper- or lowercase C, then the loop stops and the program does SET TALK ON and then RETURNs to where the user was before starting it.

Exhibit 10.18 shows what this program displays on the screen when it is run. A user only needs to know how to start the program in order to use it to add records to the PRODUCT data base.

EXHIBIT 10.18
When the program in Exhibit 10.17 is run, this is what the user sees on the screen.

```
PRODUCT CODE 9989
PRODUCT DESCRIPTION IBM PC COMPUTER
PRODUCE GROUP COMPUTER
STOCK QUANTITY   56
PRODUCT PRICE 2500.00



USE "C" TO CONTINUE,
RETURN KEY ONLY TO QUIT
```

Forms

Many microcomputer DBMSs allow the user to create customized forms that can be used when working with the data in the data base. Once a form is created, it can be used to enter data, edit data already stored, and display data on the screen. With a DBMS form design facility, the user has control over how the data will be shown on the screen rather than being forced to see the data the way the DBMS was designed to show it. Exhibit 10.19 shows a form being designed in the R:BASE System V DBMS for our product data base. Each *S* on the form indicates the start of a field and the *E* following each *S* indicates the end of the field.

EXHIBIT 10.19
In R:BASE System V, a user can create a customized form for entering, editing, and displaying data.

```
Product Code:      S      E     Description:  S                    E
Product Group:     S        E
Product Price:     S      E
Quantity in Stock: S  E
```

Natural Language Interfaces

Another advanced feature included in some DBMSs is a natural language interface. A **natural language interface** lets a user retrieve data with simple, Englishlike commands. For example, the R:BASE 5000 DBMS contains a natural language interface called CLOUT that allows the user to pose a question more as he or she would in talking with an associate, rather than by using formal commands. Thus, a first query using CLOUT can be posed as follows: "Give me the names of all persons with sales of more than $100,000 one year ago." Without CLOUT, the query would take this form: SELECT Name, Sales from Annual Sales WHERE Sales greater than 100,000 AND Year equals 1987.

The CLOUT software package has been programmed to look for key words in a sentence. In our query, these would be *names, sold, 100,000,* and *one year ago.* CLOUT keeps track of key words and their synonyms that have been defined to the system. These are used to determine the meaning of the query and to select appropriate relationships and data items. In the example, *names* can mean persons, people, salespersons, and last names. CLOUT builds a profile of common user terminology. If it cannot match a key word to a synonym, it is programmed to ask the user to give another word or to select from several choices that are probable synonyms.

Report Generators

Some data base management systems give a user special facilities, called **report generators,** to create reports that are to be printed on paper. Report generators are very similar to query facilities, since they are both designed to retrieve information from a data base and display it for the user. The major difference between report generators and query facilities is that the records retrieved by report generators are formatted so that they can be printed on paper instead of being displayed on screens.

Because the destination of the output from report generators is paper rather than a screen, report generators include settings for such mechanics as margins and line spacing to control how the reports are printed. Exhibit 10.20 shows a screen from the dBASE III Plus report generator in which a user can specify a heading for each page of the report and determine settings for report characteristics, such as margins.

Report generators also make it easy for users to get totals and subtotals for values in various fields. Subtotals can be computed for each of the

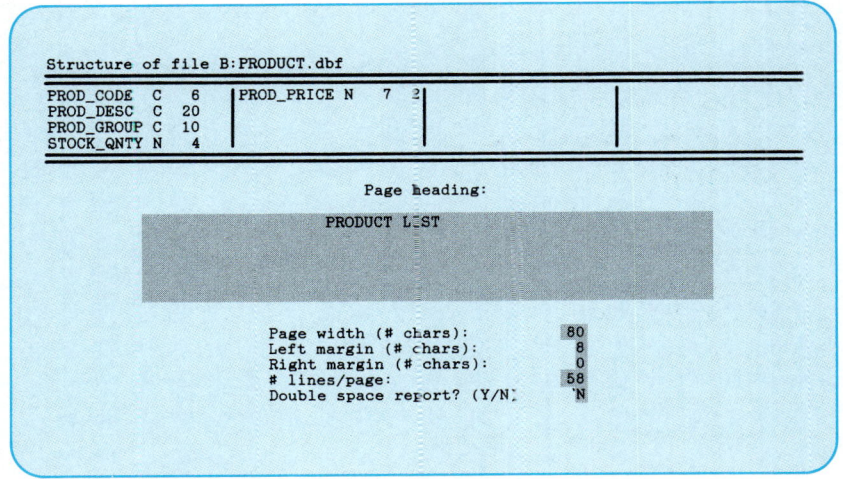

EXHIBIT 10.20

In the dBASE III Plus report generator, the user can specify a heading for the report as well as settings.

Microcomputer DBMS Features ■ 193

groups in the PROD_GROUP field. Finally, most report generators give users control over the labels associated with the data being retrieved. If a field is called PROD_CODE, it doesn't mean that PROD_CODE has to be the name for the column showing that information on the report. Exhibit 10.21 shows a dBASE III Plus report that has been produced using some of the options already described.

Backup and Recovery Features

When important data are stored in a data base, the ability to keep that data safe from accidental loss is crucial. In microcomputer data base management systems, backup and recovery features are often lacking. They are, however, no less important for data stored on a microcomputer than for data stored on a mainframe computer. Some of the more advanced microcomputer DBMSs, such as R:BASE System V, have specialized backup and recovery commands. For example, in R:BASE System V, a user can issue a simple command to backup not only the files containing the data but also any files used to store the structure of the data base.

An obvious, but often overlooked, backup procedure is keeping one or more duplicate copies of diskettes containing data base files. If the original is ever damaged, a backup copy can take its place.

Deleting a record is often a simple procedure, and accidental deletion may occur easily. Some data base management systems do not actually erase the information in a deleted record, but rather simply mark that record as deleted so that it is not printed on reports or queries. If a record has been unintentionally deleted, the process can be reversed simply by removing the mark.

EXHIBIT 10.21
A dBASE III Plus Report Showing How Subtotals and Various Field Headings Look When the Report Is Produced

```
Page No.        1
01/01/80
                                                PRODUCT LIST

PRODUCT    PRODUCT              PRODUCT         STOCK         PRODUCT
CODE       DESCRIPTION          GROUP           QUANTITY      PRICE
=======    ============         =======         ========      =======

** GROUP TOTALS COMPUTER
AZ-247     KEYBOARD             COMPUTER             200      $ 125.00
99899      IBM PC COMPUTER      COMPUTER              56       2500.00
XT-222     HARD DISK DRIVE      COMPUTER              30        945.00
DL-399     DISK DRIVE           COMPUTER             145         75.00
TK-496     MONITOR              COMPUTER              36         39.00
AZ-293     IBM PC KEYBOARD      COMPUTER             200        125.00
** Subtotal **
                                                              $3809.00

** GROUP TOTALS STEREO
TL-346     SPEAKER              STEREO               345      $  39.95
GC-349     RECEIVER             STEREO               100        275.75
DD-397     TURNTABLE            STEREO                45        175.95
GC-534     NEEDLE               STEREO               340         12.50
** Subtotal **
                                                              $ 504.15

** GROUP TOTALS TELEVISION
GK-151     23 INCH B & W        TELEVISION            10      $ 349.95
DC-349     ANTENNA              TELEVISION            35         29.99
** Subtotal **
                                                                379.94

*** Total ***
                                                              $4693.09
```

Integration with Other End-User Tools

Some data base management systems give users methods of moving data between DBMS files and files used by other end-user tools such as word processors and spreadsheets. This data transfer can be performed in either direction. The data existing in spreadsheets and documents can be used as input into a data base; conversely, the output from a data base in the form of a report can be incorporated into a spreadsheet or document.

All such transfers of data cannot be accomplished directly because spreadsheets, word processors, and data base management systems usually store data in different formats. Fortunately, these end-user tools can usually transfer data into an intermediate format which they all can then use.

Spreadsheets can create and read from files which are stored in DIF (Data Interchange Format) formats. Some data base management systems can also create and read from files in this format.

The common format for word processors is the ASCII text file. Some word processors store documents directly in ASCII, while others use special formats that include symbols for formatting documents in addition to the ASCII characters that make up the text. Some data base management systems can read data from text files if there is some way for the data to be divided into fields. Sometimes the data can be put into a text file so that the data for each field are on a separate line. This is often referred to as **column formatting**. Another common method of dividing the data in a text file into fields is to separate the data with commas. This is usually called **comma formatting**. Exhibit 10.22 shows examples of both of these formats.

The problem of translating information into a common format before it can be transferred between two different end-user tools can be solved by using recently developed **integrated software**. An integrated end-user program combines all of the features of word processors, spreadsheets, and data base management. Because it is all one program, all of the data are stored in the same format and can be easily transferred among the various end-user tools in the integrated program. Integrated software will be discussed in more detail in Chapter 12.

```
Column Format

AZ-247
KEYBOARD
COMPUTER
200
125.00


Comma Format

AZ-247,KEYBOARD,COMPUTER,200,125.00
```

EXHIBIT 10.22
When a text file is used to add data to a data base, it usually must be in either column or comma format so that the DBMS can tell where the fields are separated.

EXHIBIT 10.23
A Comparison of Seven Current Microcomputer DBMS Programs

	DATAFLEX	dBASE III PLUS	R:BASE SYSTEM V	KNOWLEDGEMAN II	REFLEX	CONDOR	PC-FILE 'N REPORT
Memory Required (in Bytes)	256K	256K	512K	512K	384K	128K	96K
Menu-Driven	Y	Y	Y	Y	Y	Y	Y
Help Screens	Y	Y	Y	Y	Y	Y	Y
Query Language	Y	Y	Y	Y	N	Y	Y
Procedural Language	Y	Y	Y	Y	N	Y	N
Passwords	Y	Y	Y	Y	N	N	N
Encryption	N	Y	Y	Y	N	N	N
Maximum Number of Fields	255	128	800	255	250	127	99
Maximum Field Size	255	254	4096	65,535	254	127	67
Maximum Records	16 million +	1 billion	DISK SPACE	1 billion	65,520	65,535	DISK SPACE
Price	$995	$695	$700	$595	$149.95	$495	$59

Source: Adapted from "Beyond the Basics," *PC Week* 4 (April 21, 1987).

CHOOSING A DBMS

There is a large number of data base products for microcomputers. At the upper end are the expensive, full-featured products, such as Microrim's R:BASE System V and Aston Tate's dBASE III Plus, used primarily in business. There are also many inexpensive data base products, such as PC-FILE 'N REPORT and REFLEX. The more expensive products often provide advanced features such as query and programming languages, report generators, and integrity and security features.

Exhibit 10.23 compares some of the current DBMS products available for microcomputers. The features an end-user might find important when choosing a DBMS include the amount of *primary memory* a microcomputer must have to be able to run a data base program, an indication of whether the DBMS is *menu-driven,* and if it gives users *help screens* whenever the user requests them. Another feature that might interest an end-user is whether the DBMS has a *query language* in which a user can issue simple commands to get data out of the data base. An end-user may also want a *procedural language,* which can be used to write programs that carry out data base functions. *Passwords* for protecting files and *encryption* of data might also be important in the decision of which DBMS to buy.

With a DBMS, the capacity of the data base in terms of the maximum *number of fields* and the maximum *size of a single field* should be considered. In the *maximum records* column of Exhibit 10.23, the words *disk space* indicate that the maximum number of records in a data base depends only on the amount of disk space available for storing them. As with all other software products, *price* may be a major factor.

Summary

The way in which data are arranged is termed *data organization*. Letters, numbers, and symbols are called *characters*. A collection of related characters forms a *data item*, or *field*. An occurrence of all data items is called a *record*. A *file* is a collection of similar types of records. A *primary key* is a data item that has a unique value that can be used to identify a single record.

A DBMS has primarily two purposes: storing data and retrieving data. When a data base is created, all of the fields must be named, given lengths, and given a data type. Possible data types include *character, integer,* and *decimal.* Character fields contain text, which has no numeric value. Integer fields store numeric data with no decimal places, while decimal data allow decimal places.

A microcomputer DBMS may require a primary key to be declared so the records can be ordered on the basis of that field. A DBMS may also allow the creation of an index on any field or fields in the data base. An index allows the user to search through the data base for a value in any field that has an index set up for it.

When data are entered, a DBMS may give the user a form with blank areas that can be used to enter values for each field. Alternatively, the DBMS may prompt the user for a value for each field, one at a time, until the entire record is built.

A DBMS includes commands to insert new records, update records, delete records, and get specific records from the data base.

Data retrieval involves five functions: *projecting, selecting, joining, sorting,* and *performing calculations.* In projecting, a subset of the fields is retrieved. In selecting, a subset of the records is retrieved based on a criterion. A simple criterion usually compares values in a field to a value specified in the criterion. Any record having a value in the field which satisfies the criterion is retrieved. Multiple criteria can be built by joining simple criteria with an AND or OR relationship. A criterion can also involve a comparison of one field to another rather than one field to a value in the criterion itself.

The join function allows two sets of data to be merged across a common field. Sorting allows the user to order the records on the basis of one or more fields. The first field the sort is based on gives the records a *primary sort* order. A *secondary sort* orders any records that have the same value in the field used for the primary sort order (secondary sort order). Primary and secondary sorts can be either *ascending* or *descending*.

When producing a report, a user can perform a number of calculations. Summary statistics, such as totals and averages, can be computed for the records that are retrieved. New fields can be created by manipulating existing fields mathematically.

A DBMS contains many features in addition to those used in data retrieval which make the interaction with the data base more efficient. The data dictionary may allow *maximum, minimum,* and *default values* for fields. Sometimes a user can display information about the entries in the *data dictionary*. Some data dictionaries are *password protected* and allow the files of the data base to be assigned various levels of protection. Special data formats, such as packed fields and date fields, are also sometimes available.

A DBMS may provide features that allow a user to change the structure of the data base. This usually involves creating a new data base and transferring the data from the old structure to the new.

A DBMS may include programming capabilities in which a program can be written with the data base commands used to create the data base, enter data, and retrieve information. There are usually commands, similar to those in traditional programming languages, which allow the user to construct a program that can make decisions, perform loops, and get data from the user when the program is running. Some DBMSs allow users to create customized forms for entering, editing, and displaying data.

Report generators are similar to query facilities in that the information retrieved is formatted for printing rather than displayed on the screen. A user can make margin settings, create headings, and obtain totals and subtotals for the report.

Backup and recovery features are often lacking in microcomputer data base management systems. A good practice is to keep backup copies of diskettes containing data base files. In addition, some data base management systems allow a user to recover the accidental deletion of a record. In these systems, the record is not actually deleted; the DBMS simply marks it as unused. This allows the record to be unmarked if it is accidentally deleted.

Some data base management systems allow a user to import data from word processors or spreadsheets or export data to them. This usually requires that the data be transferred into an intermediate format common to both end-user tools. Integrated packages are making this process much easier.

Some of the features of a microcomputer DBMS which might be important to an end-user include the amount of memory required, whether the DBMS is menu-driven, and whether there are help screens available. A user might also need a query language or a procedural language to process data. Other features include the ability to protect data with passwords and do data encryption. Some important considerations in buying a microcomputer DBMS are price, the maximum number of fields allowed, the maximum size of a single field, and the maximum number of records in the data base.

Summary

197

Review Questions

1. Explain the meaning of the terms *field, record,* and *file* as they are used to describe the data in a data base.

2. What is a data type and what are the differences among the three most common data types?

3. Explain the difference between sorting and indexing. What are the advantages of each?

4. When would projecting and selecting be used to retrieve data? Give examples.

5. What is a criterion? Give an example of a simple criterion and a multiple criterion.

6. Explain the difference between the AND and OR logical operators.

7. What is the difference between a primary and a secondary sort order?

8. Describe some of the calculations which can be performed when a report is produced with a DBMS.

9. What is one of the advantages of having the capability of programming a data base?

10. If you were going to purchase a microcomputer DBMS, what are some of the features you would consider important?

CHAPTER 11 ■ Data Communication

DATA COMMUNICATION FUNDAMENTALS
- External Data Paths
- Telecommunication Fundamentals

LOCAL AREA NETWORKS
- Topology

ROLE OF COMMUNICATION SUPPORT SOFTWARE

USING A MICROCOMPUTER IN DATA COMMUNICATION
- Terminal Emulation
- Sending and Receiving Files
- Accessing Information Utilities

USING CROSSTALK TO COMMUNICATE WITH THE SOURCE

CHOOSING A COMMUNICATION PROGRAM

SUMMARY

REVIEW QUESTIONS

In this chapter we will discuss the hardware and communication software needed to send data between two computers. The computers may be directly attached in the same building complex or located across the country. In this chapter, you will learn to do the following:

1. Explain the differences in hardware and software needed to transmit data between the computer and both local and remote terminals.
2. List and describe the transmission media that are used in telecommunication and local area networks.
3. Explain why the telephone network is used as the primary way to communicate data between remote sites.
4. Describe what a local area network is and the major functions it serves.
5. Specify the additional features an operating system must have in order to function as communication support software.
6. Describe three uses of microcomputers in data communication.

DATA COMMUNICATION FUNDAMENTALS

The movement of data from one location to another is called **data communication.** The types of communication hardware and support software that are necessary to move that data depend primarily on the distance involved. To move data within the computer itself, or to and from peripherals within a radius of a hundred feet, the only hardware needed are comparatively simple cables, and the only software needed are the standard operating systems.

If the peripherals are several miles away, or across the country, a telecommunication network, such as the phone system of AT&T, must be used to move data. **Telecommunication** refers to the transmission of data over long distances. This task requires extensive communication hardware and communication software; however, data communication doesn't always occur over long distances. Recently, many organizations have realized the advantages of communicating data between microcomputers and shared peripherals within an office building. Such computer systems, called **local area networks,** require a moderate amount of communication hardware and software. In developing an understanding of what sending and receiving data involves, we will begin by discussing the fundamentals of data communication. With that background, we will then discuss the role of communication support software.

External Data Paths

In a typical microcomputer system, external data paths include the connections between input and output devices, such as monitors, disk drives, and printers, that are used to send or receive data. These connections are often accomplished using special kinds of cables (see Exhibit 11.1). The cables that link a microcomputer to its input and output device are called **transmission media.**

EXHIBIT 11.1
Special cables are used as transmission media to send and receive data between the computer and its input and output devices.

There is a printer cable linking the CPU and the printer; similarly, most microcomputer systems also have a disk cable and a monitor cable. Let's look a little more closely at these cables. The CPU uses digital signals to communicate 1s and 0s. Typically, high voltage represents a 1 and low voltage represents a 0.

Data bits can be sent down the cable in a **serial** fashion, which means that one bit is sent after the other, or data can be transmitted in a **parallel** fashion, in which the eight bits that represent a character are sent simultaneously on eight parallel data paths. For distances less than 100 feet, parallel data transfer can be economically accomplished. One way of doing this is with flat-ribbon cables. The outlet where the cable is plugged into the computer is called an **input/output port.** The number of devices that can be connected to a computer is a function of the number of I/O ports (see Exhibit 11.2).

EXHIBIT 11.2
Serial and Parallel Data Transfer

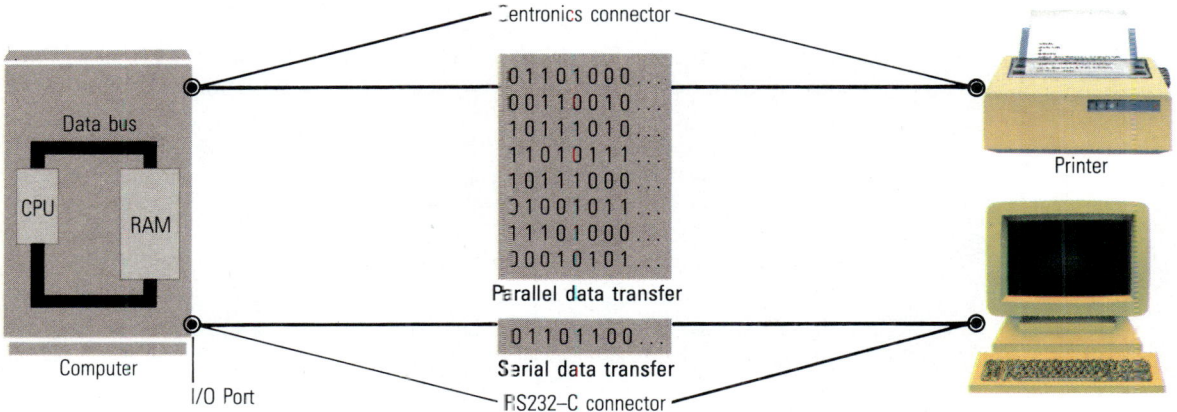

Data Communication Fundamentals

Serial and parallel connections require different types of I/O ports. The two de facto standards for microcomputers are called RS232-C and Centronics. For serial data transfer, the de facto standard is the RS232-C (Recommended Standard number 232, version C). It was developed by the Electronics Industries Association. The parallel standard is based on the connection used on the commercially successful Centronics printer, which popularized this approach to data transfer.

Telecommunication Fundamentals

So far, we have discussed data communication for stand-alone computer systems with local peripherals. How can data be transmitted to and from remote computers located in different buildings or in other regions of the country? Telecommunication, the transmission of data over long distances, is needed for these tasks. Conceptually, telecommunication uses the same principles as local data communication. The cables used for local communication, however, are not effective for long distances.

There are two basic limitations to cables. First, there is a limit to the distance that data can be transferred over a cable, due to loss of signal strength. The electrons moving down the cable meet resistance, similar to what we recognize as friction, which causes the signal to diminish. In addition, there is background noise in the cable and its surrounding environment. The signal strength has to be loud enough to be differentiated from the noise. Just as, in talking to someone in a noisy restaurant you have to talk more loudly to be heard above the din, for distances greater than several hundred feet *repeaters* are needed to amplify the electronic signal to overcome electrical resistance and background noise. A second problem is finding a place to physically put all of those cables. As more computers were added, computer owners would have to string new cables themselves.

One way to avoid this tangle is to use what has been the primary means of remote voice communication—the telephone system. It is, after all, in place and working very well in North America. Since almost every workplace and home has a telephone, electrically connecting one location to another is as simple as dialing the appropriate phone number and hooking the appropriate type of interface unit between the telephone and the computer. However, there is one major problem with using this system. The telephone network, which was invented and first built in the early 1900s, was designed for voice communication, not for data communication. It is, in fact, slow and inefficient for transmitting data. To overcome these disadvantages, telecommunication now uses microwave communication channels, either land-based or satellite.

Carrier Signals

The human voice is made up of complex sound patterns that are combinations of sound waves. Like the music on a stereo, these patterns are composed of bass (low frequency) and treble (high frequency) sound waves. In addition to different frequencies, sound waves have varying amplitudes, or heights, that we hear as loud and soft sounds. These types

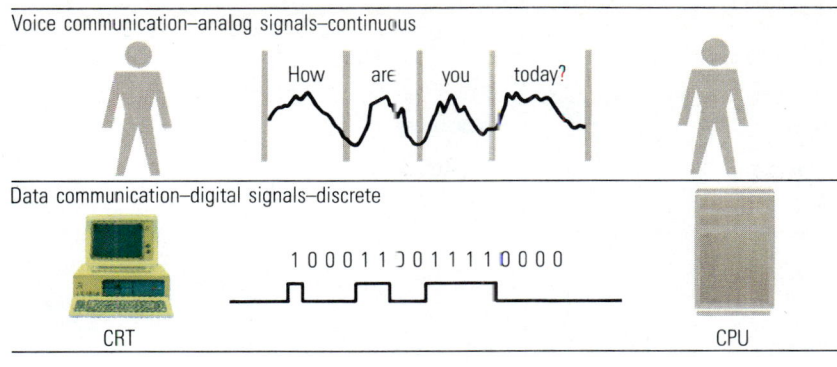

EXHIBIT 11.3

Voice and Data Communication Differences

People use their voices to communicate. The sounds they make are continuous analog wave patterns. In contrast, computers communicate data by the use of discrete digital signals.

of continuous sound waves are called **analog signals.** In contrast, the computer is limited to processing a discrete pattern of 1s and 0s, called **digital signals.** Digital signals are generated by on/off or high/low electrical signals. Exhibit 11.3 shows the difference between analog and digital signals.

The basic challenge, then, is to use the existing telephone network, which was designed to transmit analog signals, to transmit digital data. The solution is a hardware device that converts digital signals to analog signals. This device, called a **modem,** places a digital stream of data on top of an analog carrier signal.

A **carrier signal** is the basic analog signal used to transmit data over telecommunication lines. In a *modulating* process, this basic signal is modified by slight changes to either its amplitude or frequency to represent data. At the other end of the telephone line, a *demodulating* process occurs in which another modem is used to separate the digital data (1s and 0s) from the carrier signal. Thus, the term *modem* refers to a device that can *MOD*ulate and *DEM*odulate signals.

The frequency of the carrier signal partially determines the speed, or **data rate,** of a telecommunication link. This speed is usually measured in bits per second (bps). For example, a rate of 300 bps means that 300 data bits can be transmitted each second. Frequencies are stated in cycles per second (cps) or Hertz (Hz), in honor of one of the pioneers of electromagnetic theory.

To understand the relationship between carrier frequency and data rate, look at Exhibit 11.4. The amplitude of the carrier wave is increased to signal a 1 and left unchanged to signal a 0. If the amplitude is increased or not increased just once each cycle, then the speed of transmitting data is directly related to the frequency of the carrier signal. For a carrier wave with a frequency of 3000 cps, each cycle's change/no change in amplitude signals a 1 or a 0, meaning that 3000 bits can be transmitted each second. When the amplitude can change once per cycle, then bps is equal to the **baud rate,** a term derived from the name of Émile Baudot, a pioneer in data communication. Thus, 300 baud are often referred to as 300 bps. The speed of modems is frequently described as 1200 baud or 9600 baud. For higher rates, engineers have devised ways to transmit several bits per cycle. In these cases, using bps and baud interchangeably is incorrect.

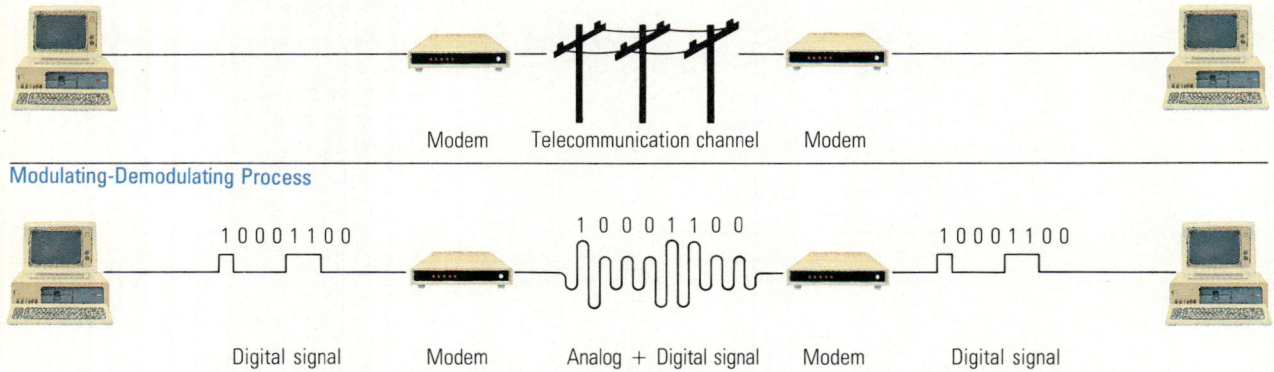

EXHIBIT 11.4
Data Communication Over a Telecommunication Channel

The discrete digital signal from the computer is placed onto an analog carrier wave by the modem. At the other end of the telecommunication channel, a modem demodulates the carrier signal and sends the digital information to the computer.

There are two basic types of modems. One type is connected to the computer via a cable and to the telephone line via a standard phone jack. The other type of modem is the acoustic coupler, which is also attached to the computer by a cable. The body of the acoustic coupler contains molded rubber cups in which a telephone headset is cradled. The acoustic coupler converts bits of data into high- and low-pitched sounds that are "spoken" into the telephone mouthpiece. Thus, it provides an acoustic connection between the computer and the telephone line. The advantage of the acoustic coupler is its portability. Its disadvantage is the amount of noise transmitted, which results in higher error rates. Exhibit 11.5 shows each type of modem.

EXHIBIT 11.5
Types of Modems

One type of modem connects to the computer via a cable and to the telephone line via a standard phone jack (far right photos). The second type of modem, the acoustic coupler, cradles a telephone headset in molded rubber cups and connects to the computer via a cable (above).

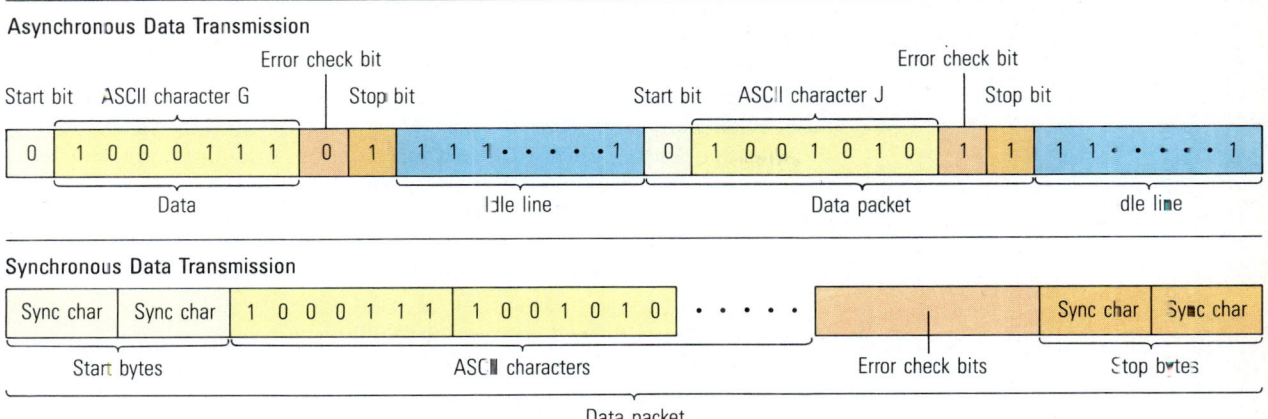

EXHIBIT 11.6

Asynchronous and Synchronous Data Transmission

In asynchronous data transmission, individual characters are sent. In synchronous data transmission, blocks of characters are sent. Data packets shown include start, stop, and error check information.

Data Packets

In order to send data in a telecommunication network, start and stop information, origin and destination information, and error check bits must be added to the encoded data to form a **data packet.** These added data bits are used to aid in sending and receiving data, to check for errors, and to route messages through a network of computers. The contents of a data packet are affected by the way data are transmitted. Data can be transmitted in either the asynchronous or synchronous mode. Exhibit 11.6 shows the differences between these two modes.

In the **asynchronous mode,** sometimes abbreviated **async,** one character is transmitted at a time. The data packet contains a start bit to let the receiving unit know that a character is to follow; it also contains the bits representing the encoded character. The most popular code used in telecommunication is the seven-bit ASCII. Next is an error check bit and a stop bit. The error check bit is used to make sure the data received were not garbled during transmission. The stop bit is used to signal the receiving unit that the complete character has been sent. This simple mode of transmission does not use origin and destination bits; thus, it is used only for single-point-to-single-point transmission.

In asynchronous transmission, the commonly used error check method is a parity bit. A **parity bit** is an extra bit that makes the sum of bits representing a character either even or odd. In an even parity system, the sum of bits is even. For example, in ASCII, the letter G is encoded as 1000111. Since the number of 1s is already an even number (4), the eighth bit is a 0 to give 10001110. Although the parity bit scheme cannot catch all errors, such as some double errors, its ability to catch most transmission errors has made it a standard feature.

The net result of adding start, stop, and error check bits is that each data packet contains 10 bits to transmit a single character via asynchronous transmission. Thus, a 1200 baud (bps) modem would be able to send about 120 characters each second. Asynchronous transmission is especially appropriate for low-speed data communication, such as a person working at a computer. When compared to a computer, most people are relatively slow to enter data and to respond.

The **synchronous** or **sync mode** of data transmission is used when large volumes of data are to be sent and speeds of thousands of characters per second are needed. In the synchronous mode, a block of hundreds of characters is sent in the data packet rather than on a character-by-character basis. Each block is preceded by a sync byte or bytes to signal the start of the message and is followed by an error check code and an ending sync byte or bytes. In synchronous transmission, the most common error check code is called **Cyclic Redundancy Checking (CRC).** This complex algorithm calculates a value by placing a different weight on each bit. Through this method, most transmission errors can be detected.

The synchronous mode might be used when the contents of a file are to be sent from a central computing facility to a remote site for printing. The obvious advantage of this mode is its speed and the reduced transmission costs for a given amount of data. Its disadvantages are the complexity and expense of the timing devices needed to synchronize transmission.

Communication Channels

A **communication channel** is a path along which data can be transmitted between the sending and receiving devices. Typically, in telecommunication, the communication channel is a telephone line, but it can also be a land microwave or a satellite link. These channels, regardless of the medium used, can be classified as operating in the simplex, half-duplex, or full-duplex mode.

A **simplex channel** can transmit data in only one direction. While this is the cheapest mode, it has very limited use in telecommunication applications. However, it is now starting to be used in certain types of local area networks, which will be discussed later in this chapter.

A **half-duplex channel** can transmit data in either direction, but only one way at a time. This is the most common mode and is used for data communication between the user at the terminal and the CPU. The user types in data, which are transmitted over the communication channel to the CPU. The CPU processes the data and then uses the same channel to respond to the user at the terminal.

A **full-duplex channel** allows data to be transmitted in both directions simultaneously. This is analogous to trucks carrying goods in both directions on a two-lane highway. For high-speed communication between computers and peripherals or computers and computers, this more costly communication method is warranted.

LOCAL AREA NETWORKS

An emerging form of data communication that is bypassing the telephone network can be found within the business office itself. A system of electronic pathways that connects various communication devices is called a **network.** When a network is confined to a building or office complex, it is called a **local area network** or **LAN.** LANs serve new needs based primarily on the evolving uses of microcomputers.

When professionals first purchased microcomputers, the attraction was stand-alone processing capability that enabled people to increase their individual productivity. A professional's equipment included a printer and, often, hard disk capability as well With more and more people in organizations wanting their own microcomputers, it became evident that it was too costly to equip each user with a printer and hard disk capability. Ways of sharing expensive peripherals were explored.

As more users got their own microcomputers, they wanted to share data and information electronically. Instead of using word processing software to write a memo on a micro and a printer to produce a hard copy output to send through office mail, why not just send a message electronically to the appropriate microcomputer? A co-worker could then read the memo and send a response electronically. This process is called *electronic mail*.

In addition, users realized the advantages of allowing only authorized access to important data files stored on other microcomputers. For example, assume the company accountant had developed such files and stored them in the hard disks of his or her microcomputer. If the vice-president of finance could electronically transfer a copy of that data to his or her microcomputer's hard disk, then that data could be used as input to an electronic spreadsheet for use in future planning.

Microcomputer users also realized they needed access to the data base held in the company's main computer, which might be a mini- or maxicomputer. If those data could be downloaded to microcomputers, users could be sure they were using the latest information in preparing accurate reports and projections. Once this link was established, the next step in the process would be to provide the means for downloading software programs.

Another emerging objective in many organizations is the connection of computer equipment manufactured by different vendors. As organizations purchased microcomputer equipment during the late 1970s and 1980s, different departments usually bought different kinds of computer systems. Department A got IBM PCs, Department B went with Apples, and Department C acquired Datapoints. As long as microcomputers were used as stand-alone units, this wasn't a major problem. However, once organizations needed to share resources or information electronically, the realization that computers from different vendors weren't compatible caused significant problems. In theory, LANs can overcome these incompatibility problems. So far, though, there has been limited success in connecting highly different computer systems.

The future importance of LANs becomes clearer in light of studies that show 70 to 80 percent of an organization's communication takes place within a local area. Most of that communication now occurs through written correspondence (interoffice mail) or voice conversation (intercom telephone network or face-to-face meetings). The projection is that LANs will replace most written and voice communication within an organization and open exciting new ways of exchanging ideas.

Topology

The term *topology* refers to the patterns formed when hardware devices are connected to form a network. The three most common network topologies used with LANs are the star, the bus, and the ring. Exhibit 11.7 shows each of these topologies.

EXHIBIT 11.7
Three Common Network Topologies

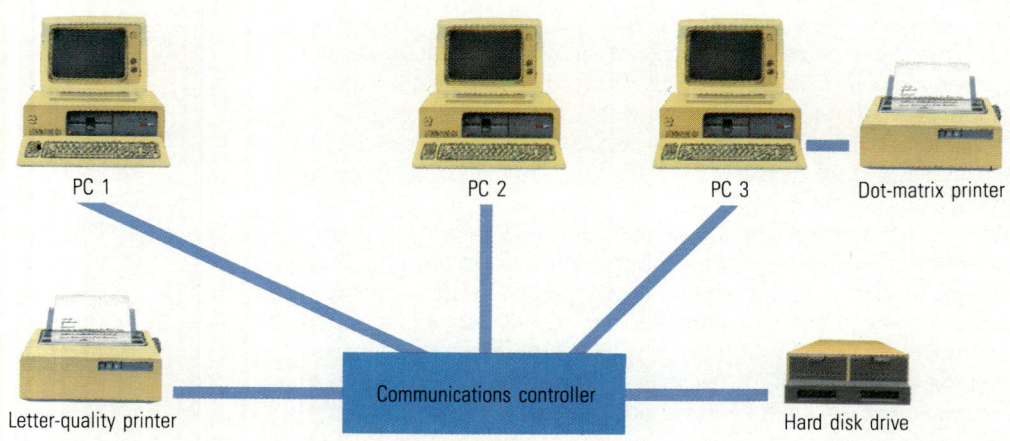

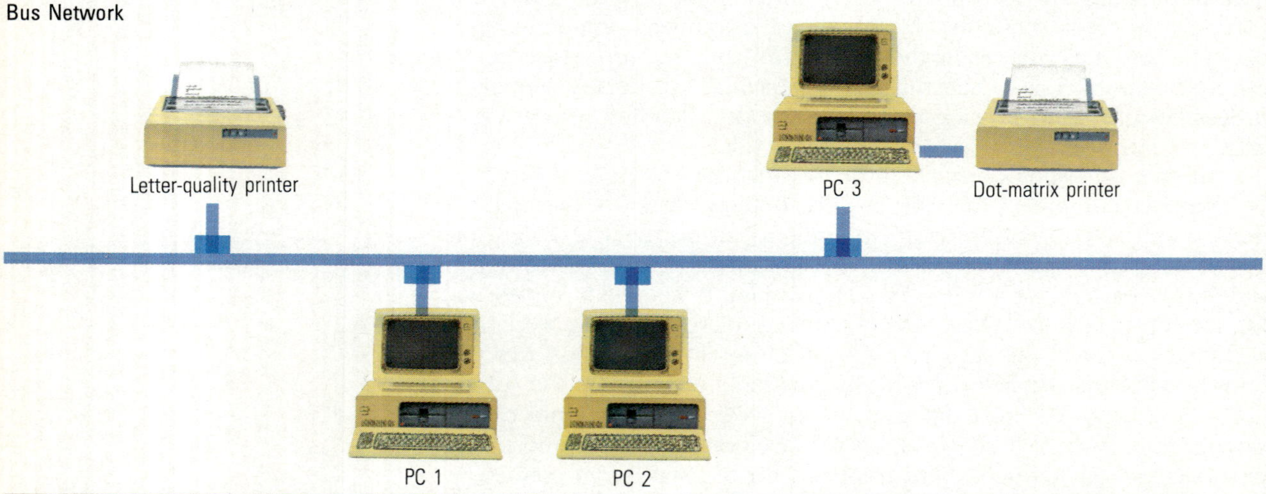

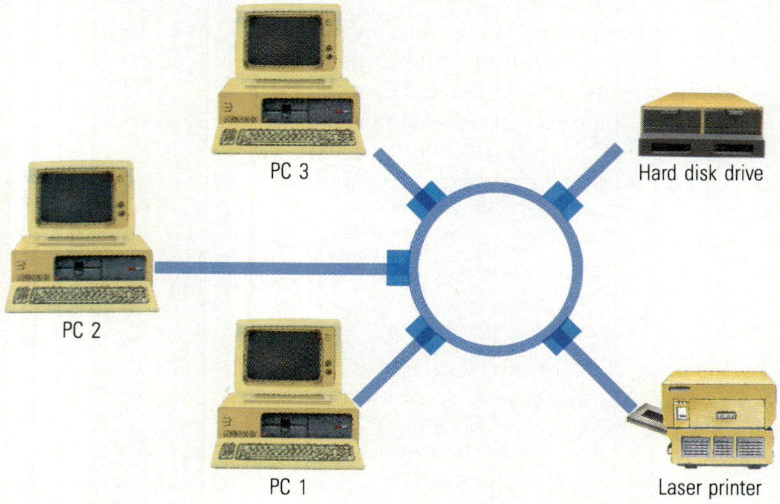

In the **star network topology,** each device is connected to a central unit. Any communication between one device and another goes through the central unit. The exhibit shows a typical configuration using microcomputers and peripherals. Each device is directly connected to the central communications controller, which is a microcomputer containing the interface cards and software to manage all data communication in this network. If a user at microcomputer PC 2 wants to print out a memo on the letter-quality printer, microcomputer PC 2 sends that request to the network controller. This central controller notifies microcomputer PC 2 when that task is complete.

With the **bus network topology,** each device is connected to a common cable. Each component must have its own interface device. This is usually a circuit board or card, which plugs into one of the expansion slots. The card contains the hardware and software necessary to access the network. All communication takes place on the common cable or bus. The data are sent down the bus and are available to all devices. Each message must contain information identifying the destination device.

With the **ring network topology,** each terminal is connected to two others, forming a circle or ring. All communication between terminals follows a clockwise or counterclockwise pattern. The message goes from terminal to terminal until the designated device is reached.

ROLE OF COMMUNICATION SUPPORT SOFTWARE

Now that we have examined the considerations involved in data communication and local area networks, let's look at the role that communication support software plays. In this section, we will discuss three of the major functions that **communication support software (CSS)** must provide: protocols, error detection and correction, and security.

The first function of the CSS is to handle a protocol. A **protocol** is a set of rules and procedures used for transmitting data between two hardware devices in a network. For example, before data can be exchanged between two computers, the following must be established: Are the data to be sent asynchronous or synchronous? What format will the data packet be in (start and stop bits) and what kind of error-checking method is being used (parity or CRC)? Unfortunately, there are many different protocols in use today, with no universally accepted standard. Consequently, it is not always possible to communicate between any two computers. However, as in other facets of the computer field, a small number of protocols are emerging as de facto standards.

In a previous section, we discussed the use of the parity and CRC methods of detecting errors in data transmission. With both methods, the CSS detects an error and responds with a signal to the sending computer to retransmit the complete message. This form of error control ensures a high accuracy rate but can require a significant amount of retransmission. The error rates are a function of the type of media used. Regular voice-grade lines have the highest error rates.

In those situations where high security is needed for transmitting sensitive organizational data across telecommunication paths, **data encryption** techniques can be used. These convert the data to be transmitted into a scrambled form. Unauthorized users who might somehow get to the data, but don't know the encryption key, would get meaningless data. Encryption keys must be very sophisticated schemes so they can't be easily deciphered. However, the underlying concept is not complicated. A simple encryption key could be to add 3 to each number and to descend 3 letters for each alphabetic letter.

Using this simple encryption key, the data would appear as shown:

the data   5 A T   6 1 1
the encrypted data   8 D W   9 4 4

The decryption process is just the reverse. Subtract 3 from each encrypted number and ascend 3 letters.

USING A MICROCOMPUTER IN DATA COMMUNICATION

A major use of the microcomputer has been as a personal computer. That is, a person at home or at work does his or her computing tasks on a stand-alone machine. As users become more sophisticated in their use of personal computers, they sometimes want to connect their computers to larger computers for special applications or to other microcomputers to exchange data. To facilitate this, data communication equipment, such as a modem, is added, allowing the microcomputer to communicate with other computers in addition to doing stand-alone computing.

When a microcomputer is equipped with communication capabilities, there are three primary functions that it can perform for an end-user: terminal emulation, sending and receiving files, and accessing information utilities.

Terminal Emulation

When a microcomputer is used to access a large mainframe computer, that microcomputer is performing a task known as **terminal emulation,** which means that the microcomputer is taking on the characteristics of a certain type of terminal. Different mainframe computers expect terminals to communicate in certain ways. Thus, a terminal attached to one mainframe may not have the same characteristics as a terminal attached to another mainframe. When a microcomputer is used in terminal emulation, it must have some way to alter its communication characteristics so that they match those of a normal terminal on the particular mainframe computer.

The actual hardware connection of a microcomputer to a remote mainframe is accomplished by attaching the microcomputer to a modem. In order to alter its communication characteristics, a microcomputer uses a communication program which allows terminal emulation. During this process, the communication program must match the communication characteristics of the microcomputer to those of a terminal on the remote computer system. As we saw earlier in this chapter, there are many variables which can be involved in the communication between computers. A communication program that allows terminal emulation lets the

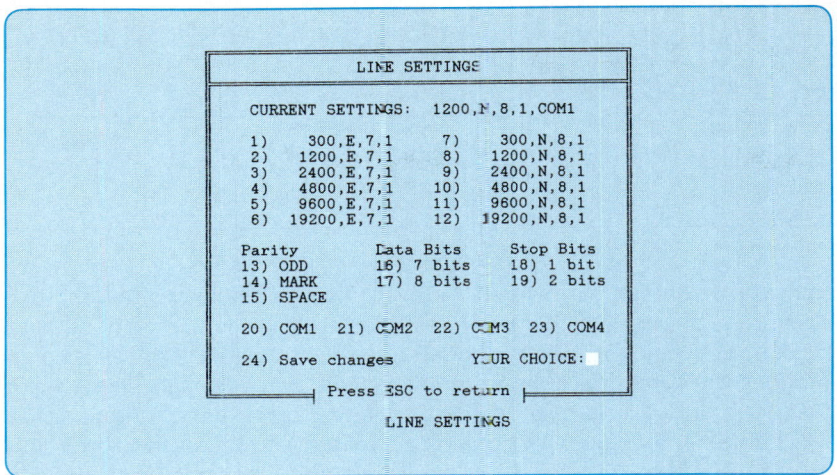

EXHIBIT 11.8
A Screen from the PROCOMM Communication Program
The screen shows the communication settings at the top and allows the user to change them with the menus at the bottom. Parameters include baud rate, parity, type (duplex), and the stop bit to be used (stop).

user determine the characteristics which will govern the communication parameters of a microcomputer with a remote computer. Some of these characteristics include baud rate, type of parity (odd or even), and type of channel (simplex, half-duplex, or full-duplex). Exhibit 11.8 shows a screen from the PROCOMM program which includes some of the terminal emulation options.

A communication program often allows a user to create command files, which are groups of communication settings and commands. A command file can be written to set up a microcomputer to emulate a specific type of terminal and then establish a link by dialing the number of a remote computer. Once these settings and commands are stored in a command file, the user can execute that file with a single command to perform all of the commands, saving the user a large number of keystrokes.

Sending and Receiving Files

Much end-user computing today occurs on microcomputers and is described as **stand-alone use.** That is, the microcomputer users create and use private data bases.

One of the first complaints voiced by business professionals about stand-alone end-user computing is the time they spend entering data. This is particularly frustrating when the data being entered are stored in a mainframe data base or on someone else's microcomputer. Requests soon arise to electronically capture these data.

One way to electronically share data files is to link microcomputers through a LAN. Then a user working with an end-user tool on one microcomputer can access data files that have been organized specifically for the tool and stored on any of the other microcomputers attached to the LAN.

Communication programs currently available give end-users the capability to establish a link between a microcomputer with a modem and another microcomputer with a modem by using telephone lines as the communication channel. When a communication program establishes a

A Microcomputer in Data Communication ■ 211

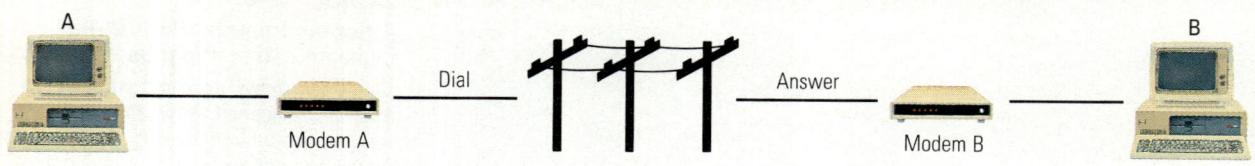

EXHIBIT 11.9
Transferring Files Between Microcomputers

If microcomputer A wishes to connect with microcomputer B, it must use a communication program to instruct its modem (A) to dial the number of microcomputer B. Microcomputer B's modem must be turned on and set up to answer the phone using a communication program running on microcomputer B.

link with a remote computer, it must use the phone line to link the two computers. If the microcomputer has an acoustic modem, the phone must be dialed by hand in order to connect into the phone line. With an internal modem, the communication program can talk to the modem directly and instruct it to dial a number by sending signals down the phone line, as a touch-tone phone does when dialing a number. Communication programs give users various options for using a modem to dial numbers. One has the remote computer dialed automatically **(autodial).** Some programs provide a directory of phone numbers that the program can choose from. A communication program may provide automatic redialing of a number that was busy or that was somehow cut off. When a user calls another microcomputer, the remote PC must have a modem that is set up to answer the incoming call. Some communication programs will automatically answer the incoming call so another user can access the microcomputer remotely (see Exhibit 11.9).

Once the microcomputers are linked across the phone line, an end-user can transfer information between the two computers. Usually the microcomputer that was instructed to dial the phone is referred to as the **local** computer. The microcomputer that answers the incoming call is called the **remote** computer. Some communication programs provide users with commands that can transfer a file from the remote microcomputer to the local microcomputer **(downloading)** or from the local microcomputer to the remote microcomputer **(uploading).**

Communication programs usually make a distinction between two types of files during the transfer process. Files containing documents from word processors and files containing source programs written in a computer language, such as BASIC, are **text files.** These files contain characters which need to be in a form (ASCII) that humans can read. Computers, however, cannot process instructions written in English and must have those instructions translated to binary before they can be executed. Thus, **binary files** are those containing programs whose instructions have been converted to binary. In fact most of the software packages provided to users on floppy disks, such as word processing and spreadsheet programs, are in binary formats so that computers can execute the programs directly.

As we saw in the discussion of data packets, data are sent in groups of 10 bits, each of which represents a single character. The middle 8 bits are used to represent the character (7 bits of data plus a parity bit). This is the representation used in text files. It is also possible to transfer files which are already in binary (zeros and ones) form. In a binary file, there are still 10 bits, but the middle 8 bits are data (no parity is used). Because of this difference, the communication program must know what type of file is being transferred in order to interpret the bits correctly.

When files are transferred, a protocol can be used to help ensure an error-free transmission. The most widely used error-checking protocol on microcomputers is called *xmodem*. With the xmodem protocol, data are sent in blocks of 128 bytes, and error checking is accomplished with the **checksum method.** The sender of the data includes a checksum at the end of the 128 bytes of data, which is the sum of all 128 bytes. When the receiver gets the 128 bytes, it performs its own checksum and compares it to the one sent along with the data. If the sums are the same, then transmission continues; otherwise, the receiver asks the sender to send the block again. This process continues, one block at a time, until the whole file has been sent and verified. As this example implies, when a protocol is used to ensure error-free transmission, both the sender and receiver must be capable of running the same protocol.

Accessing Information Utilities

A microcomputer with communication capability can be connected to another microcomputer with the same capability. The two microcomputers can then send information between them, as is done in a local area network. An **electronic bulletin board,** where users can leave messages, information, and even useful programs for one another, is often established on a microcomputer running special software. The microcomputer is linked to a phone line with a modem and is capable of answering incoming calls automatically. A user using a microcomputer with a communication program can call the microcomputer with the bulletin board. He or she can read the messages and transfer the programs from the bulletin board's microcomputer to his or her own microcomputer. The only cost for accessing a bulletin board is the charge for the phone call. Exhibit 11.10 shows a screen from the Scott, Foresman bulletin-board system in which instructors can get information about topics related to the teaching of computer information system courses.

Some specialized mainframe computers are operated by *information utility companies*. These companies sell access to information data bases to users. Three of the largest information utilities are The Source, Dow Jones News/Retrieval Service, and CompuServe. Users are charged a fee to

EXHIBIT 11.10
The Scott, Foresman Bulletin Board

```
PLEASE MAKE LIBERAL USE OF THE HELP OPTIONS AVAILABLE ON THIS
BULLETIN BOARD.  YOU CAN SELECT "H" FOR HELP AT VIRTUALLY ANY
TIME BY SIMPLY PRESSING THE "H" KEY AND THEN PRESSING THE RETURN
(OR ENTER) KEY.
*****************************************************************
CHANNEL-ONE MAIN MENU

A ? at any prompt gives more HELP.
N) ews Center
M) essage system   ( 0 new ones)
F) ile transfer           ( 0 new ones)
P) rofile
O) ptions
S) ystem description & ordering
H) elp!  (or use H x, where x=letter)
G) OODBYE

Please [Enter] your selection :
```

A Microcomputer in Data Communication

EXHIBIT 11.11
The CompuServe information utility offers a user many different types of services.

```
CompuServe

CompuServe Information Service

1 Home Service
2 Business & Financial
3 Personal Computing
4 Services for Professionals
5 The Electronic Mail (tm)
6 User Information
7 Index

Enter your selection number,
or H for more information:
```

subscribe to the system and for the amount of time they are connected to the system over a communication line. These utilities provide users access to large data bases containing information on such things as the stock market, encyclopedias, and abstracts from journals and magazines. Exhibit 11.11 shows a screen containing the services provided by CompuServe.

USING CROSSTALK TO COMMUNICATE WITH THE SOURCE

Now that you have learned some of the potential communication applications of microcomputers, let's look at a specific example involving the concepts you have learned. In this example, the Crosstalk communication program is used to connect a microcomputer to an information utility known as The Source.

Before using a communication program, an end-user must have a microcomputer with a modem. The communication characteristics of the modem are controlled by a set of switches (called *dip switches*) which are located inside the modem. Usually the modem comes with the switches set correctly for most uses. If you are unable to establish a communication link, it is possible that the modem switches are incorrectly set for the specific application you are trying to perform. Thus, there may be circumstances in which you will have to consult the modem's manual to make sure all of the switches are set correctly for your specific application.

Once the modem is attached to the microcomputer, you must run the communication software. With Crosstalk, you simply boot the microcomputer with DOS and type XTALK at the DOS prompt. The status screen shown in Exhibit 11.12 is displayed once the Crosstalk program has been loaded. In order to begin communicating with a remote computer, you must make sure that the values under the communication parameters section are correct for the computer with which you are attempting to communicate. In Crosstalk, each of the values on the screen can be altered by typing the first two letters of the parameter you wish to change, followed by the new value.

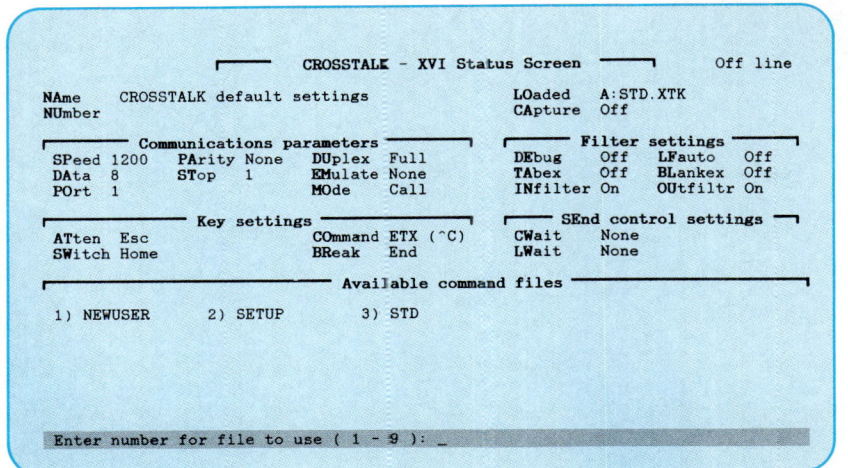

EXHIBIT 11.12
The Crosstalk Status Screen

Once the parameters are set, you must enter a phone number for the remote computer you are calling and a name for that computer. These two pieces of information appear as parameters in the top left area of the Crosstalk status screen. These two parameters can be changed in the same manner as any of the other communication parameters. For example, the phone number can be set by typing NU, followed by the number to be dialed. Once the number and name of the computer being called have been entered, the Crosstalk GO command can be entered to have Crosstalk dial the phone through your modem using the number you have entered.

After Crosstalk has dialed the number, it will automatically connect your microcomputer with the remote computer when that remote computer's modem answers your incoming call. If the phone of the remote computer is busy, Crosstalk will tell you and offer to redial the number for you. You can even tell Crosstalk to redial the number repeatedly at regular intervals until a connection is made.

Near the bottom of Exhibit 11.12 is a section which lists the available command files. A command file is simply a group of Crosstalk commands that sets up the parameters in Crosstalk for a communication session. The STD command file contains the default setting for Crosstalk. When the Crosstalk program is run, the commands in this file are used to set the default values for all communication parameters. In the top right corner of Exhibit 11.12 under the *LOaded* parameter you can see that Crosstalk has automatically loaded the settings in the STD command file to give Crosstalk its initial settings for the communication parameters shown.

The SETUP command file can be used to alter the contents of the STD command file. This SETUP file can be loaded by typing LO SETUP to change the value for the *LOaded* parameter to SETUP. When this command file is loaded, it will ask you a series of questions about your modem and certain communication parameters. Your answers to these questions are used to alter the contents of the STD command file.

As an alternative to always setting communication parameters one at a time when you use Crosstalk to call a remote computer, you can use the NEWUSER command file to have Crosstalk prompt you for the parameters and build a command file which contains all of the necessary settings. You

EXHIBIT 11.13

In Crosstalk, command files can be created for any of the services listed.

```
Choose a service to set up:

A - The Source
B - CompuServe
C - Delphi
D - Dow Jones News / Retrieval
E - Newsnet
F - The Official Airline Guide
G - MCI Mail
H - LEXIS/NEXIS
I - AT&T Mail
J - VU/TEXT
K - A system running Remote
L - Another PC running Crosstalk or Transporter
O - Other service not listed above

X - Exit from this program


Please choose a service:
```

can save these settings in a new command file under a name of your choosing. The next time you wish to communicate with that remote computer, you can tell Crosstalk to load that command file, and all of the settings will be made automatically. Exhibit 11.13 shows the screen that appears when you load the NEWUSER command file.

In Exhibit 11.13 are listed many common information utilities as well as choices for communication with other microcomputers. To create a command file for connecting to The Source, you would simply enter the letter *A*, which corresponds to that service. Crosstalk will prompt you to enter the local TELENET number that you wish to use for dialing into The Source. Once you enter the number, you will be prompted to the baud rate at which you wish to communicate (usually 1200), your Source account number, and your account password.

Once you have answered these prompts, Crosstalk will build a command file called SOURCE.XTK (see Exhibit 11.14). When you load this command file, Crosstalk will set up the communication parameters as they are shown in Exhibit 11.14, dial the number you have entered, and automatically sign onto The Source using your account number and password.

As was shown in Exhibit 11.13, Crosstalk can create a command file to be used for communicating with many different information utilities and remote computers. This particular example demonstrates how a communication program can simplify the process of performing communication functions with a microcomputer. With programs such as this, end-users can handle their own data communication without having to become communication experts.

CHOOSING A COMMUNICATION PROGRAM

Now that you are familiar with some of the general functions and characteristics of communication programs, you have a basis for determining how well a particular communication program meets a user's needs. Exhibit 11.15 compares six of the programs currently available for the IBM PC. This exhibit shows the amount of primary *memory* required and the

```
┌─────────────── CROSSTALK - XVI Status Screen ───────────────  Off line
│ NAme   The Source (via GTE Telenet)       LOaded   C:NEWUSER.XTK
│ NUmber                                    CApture  Off
│ ┌─────── Communications parameters ──────┐ ┌──────── Filter settings ────────┐
│ │ SPeed AUTO  PArity None  DUplex Full   │ │ DEbug    Off   LFauto    Off    │
│ │ DAta  8     STop   1     EMulate None  │ │ TAbex    Off   BLankex   Off    │
│ │ POrt  1                  MOde  Call    │ │ INfilter On    OUtfiltr  On     │
│ └────────────────────────────────────────┘ └─────────────────────────────────┘
│ ┌────────── Key settings ──────────┐  ┌──── ZDDDD SEnd control settings ────┐
│ │ ATten Esc    COmmand ETX (^C)    │  │  CWait    None                      │
│ │ SWitch Home  BReak   Emd         │  │  LWait    None                      │
│ └──────────────────────────────────┘  └─────────────────────────────────────┘
│
│ Your setup for The Source is now complete.
│
│
│ Would you like to call The Source now? ▮
```

EXHIBIT 11.14
The Crosstalk Status Screen Showing the Parameter Settings for the Source Command File

number of disk *drives* a microcomputer must have to be able to use the communication program. In a *menu-driven* communication program, the various settings, such as baud rate and parity, can be selected by the user from a menu. The *bps rate* column in the exhibit shows the maximum communication speed supported by each program.

The *auto dialing* column indicates if the communication program can instruct an internal modem to automatically dial a specified number. *Auto answer* refers to the ability of the program to automatically answer an incoming call from another computer's modem, and *auto redial* indicates if the program can be instructed to automatically redial the last number if a busy signal is obtained. The *phone directory* feature of some programs allows storage of a directory of numbers which the program can be instructed to dial. The *command file* option indicates if the program allows a user to store sets of communication settings for various terminals and recall them when they are needed. The exhibit also shows which communication programs support *terminal emulation* and *data encryption*. Finally, the *price* of the program is indicated.

EXHIBIT 11.15
A Look at Six Popular Communication Programs for the IBM PC

	PC-DIAL	BLAST	SMARTCOM II	PC-TALK III	IBM ASYNCH COMM PROGRAM	CROSSTALK XVI
Memory Required (in Bytes)	128K	64K	192K	64K	64K	128K
Driver Required	1	2	1	1	1	1
Menu-Driven	Y	Y	Y	N	Y	Y
BPS RATE	9600	19.2K	2400	9600	9600	9600
Auto Dialing	Y	Y	Y	Y	Y	Y
Auto Answer	Y	Y	Y	Y	N	Y
Auto Redial	Y	Y	N	Y	Y	Y
Phone Directory	N	Y	Y	Y	N	Y
Create Command Files	N	Y	Y	Y	N	Y
Terminal Emulation	N	Y	N	N	Y	Y
Data Encryption	N	Y	N	N	Y	N
Price	$29	$250	$149	$35	$60	$195

Summary

The movement of data from one location to another is called *data communication*. The types of communication hardware and support software necessary to move those data differ, depending primarily on the distance involved. The hardware linking computers are called *transmission media*.

With a microcomputer, the transmission medium is generally a cable. The cable hooks to the computer at an *input/output port*. The number of devices that can be connected to a computer is a function of the number of I/O ports. A serial connection requires a different type of I/O port than does a parallel connection.

Telecommunication is the transmission of data over long distances. The telephone voice network uses continuous frequency waves called *analog signals*. In contrast, the computer is limited to processing a discrete pattern of 1s and 0s called *digital signals*. A *modem* is a device that converts digital patterns to analog signals and allows the sending of computer data over telephone lines. A *carrier signal* is the basic signal used to transmit data over telecommunication links and is modulated by slight changes to its amplitude or frequency to represent data.

The *data rate*, or *speed*, of a telecommunication link is the amount of data that can be sent per time period. It is measured in bits per second (bps). To be able to send data in a telecommunication network, start and stop information, origin and destination information, and error check bits must be added to the encoded data to form a *data packet*.

In the *asynchronous* mode of data transmission, one character at a time is sent over the communication link. The *parity bit* method of error checking is used primarily with async. With the *synchronous* mode, a block of characters is sent. Here, the most commonly used error-checking method is *Cyclic Redundancy Checking (CRC)*.

A *communication channel* is the transmission medium that links the sending and receiving devices. Typically, in telecommunication, the channel is a telephone line, but it could also be a microwave or satellite link. A *simplex* channel can transmit data in only one direction. A *half-duplex* channel is one in which data can be transmitted in either direction but only one way at a time. In a *full-duplex* channel, data can be transmitted in both directions simultaneously.

A system of electronic pathways that connects the various communication devices is called a *network*. When that network is confined to a building or an office complex, it is designated as a *local area network*. It serves new needs that are based primarily on the evolving uses for microcomputers.

The major functions that communication support software provide are protocols, error detection and correction, and security. A *protocol* is a set of rules and procedures used for transmitting data between two hardware devices in a network.

In those situations where high security is needed for transmitting sensitive organizational data across telecommunication paths, *data encryption*, a technique for converting data into a scrambled form, can be used.

With communication programs capable of supporting *terminal emulation*, microcomputers can function as terminals for remote mainframes.

Communication programs allow a user to determine the communication characteristics of the microcomputer so that it can function as a terminal on almost any remote system. Groups of settings for a particular type of terminal can be stored in a command file, which can later be recalled. Communication programs also allow end-users to link microcomputers in order to transfer files from a local microcomputer to a remote microcomputer (*uploading*) or from the remote microcomputer to the local microcomputer (*downloading*). Both text and binary files can be transferred. Typically, a transfer is done using a protocol to reduce errors. The most common protocol used with microcomputers is called *xmodem*.

Communication programs are often used to connect a microcomputer with another microcomputer containing an electronic bulletin board. Another common application is in the accessing of information utilities.

Review Questions

1. Distinguish between data communication and telecommunication.

2. Explain the difference between serial and parallel transmission of data bits.

3. The Zenon Corporation desires a means of transmitting data from remote terminals in each of its several regional branches to the mainframe located at corporate headquarters. A consultant has told them they must use the telephone communication network. Why? What alternatives are available?

4. How does a modem overcome the problems involved in the use of telephone lines for the transmission of data?

5. What is a data packet? Explain the difference between the asynchronous and the synchronous modes of transmission.

6. Explain the LAN concept. Why are such systems increasing in popularity?

7. What is meant by the term *topology*? Briefly describe the three most common topologies in use.

8. What is terminal emulation?

9. What is the difference between a text file and a binary file?

10. Explain how the *xmodem* protocol works.

CHAPTER 12 ■ Advanced End-User Software

END-USER COMPUTING
A Crisis in Business Computing
The Solution: Very High-Level Languages and Microcomputers

MULTIPURPOSE TOOLS
Integrated Software
Software Integrators
Desktop Organizers

ADVANCED END-USER TOOLS
QUERY Facilities
Report Generators
Financial Modeling
Statistical Analysis
Project Management

PROMOTING AND MANAGING END-USER COMPUTING
Information Center
Personal Computer Support Center

SUMMARY

REVIEW QUESTIONS

The growth of business computing in many organizations has outstripped the capabilities of computer staffs. Other organizations, particularly smaller firms, cannot afford a skilled computer staff. Today, however, many business professionals are developing their own computer applications using microcomputers. Even if you do not pursue an information systems career, you may well find youself "programming" during your professional life. In this chapter, you will learn to do the following:

1. Explain what end-user computing is.
2. Describe two approaches by which software vendors are providing business professionals with multipurpose end-user tools.
3. Explain what desktop organizers are.
4. List some of the features of very high-level languages.
5. Give some examples of specific very high-level languages.
6. List the two types of facilities used in promoting and managing end-user computing.

END-USER COMPUTING

Throughout Part Three we have looked at a variety of tools that allow end-users to create their own applications rather than having to rely on a traditional data processing center. End-user computing has developed as a response to the crisis facing most traditional data processing centers involving the inability to meet the growing demand for applications on mainframe computers.

A Crisis in Business Computing

Business computing had reached a crisis in the mid-1970s for many firms. A "new breed" of business professional, one aware of the potential of computers, was beginning to enter the work force. As a result, requests for new information systems projects increased. However, the computer staffs in most firms were hard pressed just to keep the existing computer applications running smoothly. Creating applications on large mainframe computers is complex and requires trained professional programmers. Thus, creating an application in the mainframe environment is usually costly and time consuming.

The backlog of "postponed" information systems projects was growing larger and larger. In some firms, this backlog was talked about in terms of "man-centuries" of systems development. (One man-century of work would keep a single systems analyst or programmer busy for 100 years.) It was not that unusual for a marketing manager, for example, to be told that the sales reporting system being requested would be scheduled for development in three or four years. As you might expect, the marketing manager was not very happy—such reports were needed now, not three or four years in the future. This **visible backlog** was actually small compared to the **invisible backlog** of projects that were needed but never proposed.

In small firms, the situation was even worse. Most small firms could not employ many, if any, programmers. As a result, they had to meet most of their information needs through software packages. This caused few problems with standard computer applications, such as accounting and inventory control. However, when a small business wished to go beyond these standard applications, few options existed.

The Solution: Very High-Level Languages and Microcomputers

Two advances in computer technology provided the solution to this crisis. First, very high-level languages began to be developed in the mid-1970s. These programming languages are easy to learn but are designed to handle a specific type of information processing problem. By using these very high-level languages, some business professionals began to develop their own information systems.

Very high-level languages make good **end-user tools** for three reasons. First, a business professional who knows little about software development can begin to produce useful information in a few hours. Second, to a large extent, the business professional describes what is to be produced, rather than the detailed information processing steps actually required. Third, the business professional need not know much about the computer's operating system. In short, the business professional can focus on the problem being solved, rather than on the details of program development.

The second advance was the microcomputer, which was developed in the late 1970s. The use of microcomputers in business has mushroomed during the 1980s. A driving force behind this growth has been the large number of quality business software packages, many of which are suitable for end-user computing. Today, very high-level languages are available to all business professionals, and end-user computing has become commonplace in many firms.

End-user computing offers two obvious benefits to a business—information systems can be developed quickly and inexpensively, and the application backlog is reduced. Two less obvious benefits are even more important. First, better information systems often result. Second, business professionals are more apt to use an information system that they have developed.

End-user computing, to be effective, must be well managed. Appropriate end-user tools in the form of very high-level languages must be made available, and users must be trained in their use. As you might expect, some end-user tools are more appropriate for certain types of information problems than are others. Furthermore, users need to be able to access data already captured and stored in a firm's computer systems.

MULTIPURPOSE TOOLS

It should not surprise you that the five common types of end-user tools are basically the same as the five personal computing software packages discussed in preceding chapters. Personal computing *is* end-user computing. Thus, word processors, spreadsheets, graphics, data bases, and communication programs are the most common microcomputer end-user tools in use today.

A current trend involves providing a business professional with access to a number of these tools at the same time. The idea is to allow a business professional to process a set of data in a variety of ways without having to regularly exit to the operating system and begin a new program.

Why might this be useful? Consider how nice it would be if you could build a spreadsheet model using data stored in a data base, produce some charts from the spreadsheet results, and then embed the charts in a report you were preparing. Data would need to be entered only once. Even better, any changes that occurred to data items in the data file would automatically "perk" through the information outputs you had created—the spreadsheet model, the charts, and the report.

Software vendors are using two basic approaches to provide such multipurpose tools: integrated software and a software integrator. We will describe each and also introduce you to another multipurpose tool, the desktop organizer.

Integrated Software

The intent of **integrated software** is to allow users to apply a very similar set of commands to manipulate data without having to enter any data item more than once. The information processing functions most commonly included in integrated software packages are spreadsheets, word processors, business graphics, and data management. Each tool can be displayed in its own window on the screen, and data values can be moved from one window to another.

EXHIBIT 12.1
Integrated software packages base all tools on one major tool. In the case of Lotus 1-2-3, spreadsheet, graphics, and data management functions all spring from an underlying master spreadsheet.

Adaptation of Figure 1, p. 74. Reprinted by permission of *PC World* from Volume 2, Issue 11, October 1984, published at 501 Second Street, Suite 600, San Francisco, CA 94107.

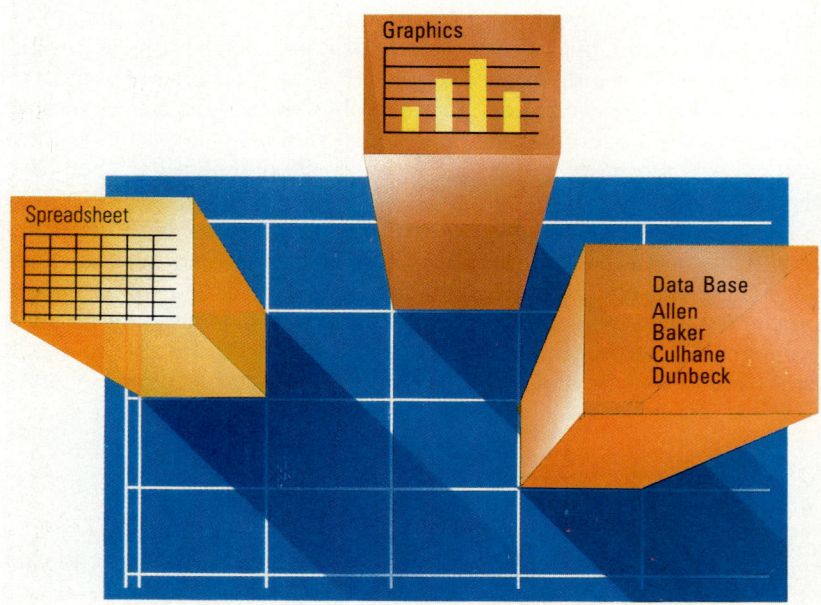

12 Advanced End-User Software

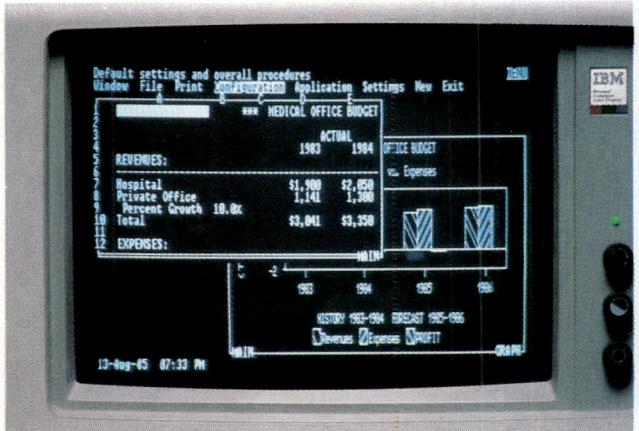

EXHIBIT 12.2
Shown here is a display screen from Symphony, an integrated software package.

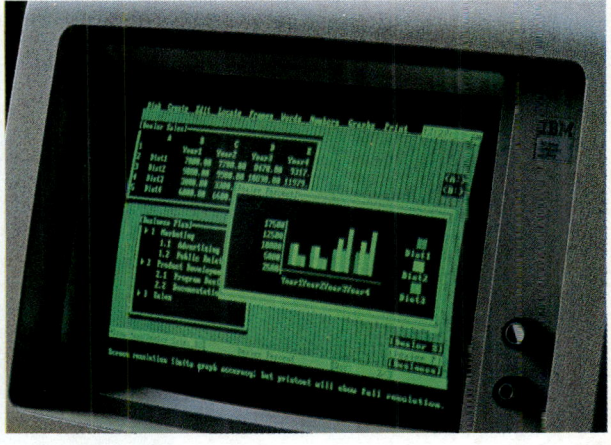

EXHIBIT 12.3
Shown here is a display screen from Framework, integrated software organized in "frames" that can contain a spreadsheet a graph, or an outline of these elements.

The first successful integrated software package was Lotus 1-2-3, which combines spreadsheet modeling, business graphics, and data management. As shown in Exhibit 12.1, Lotus 1-2-3 uses a master spreadsheet to organize data elements. Two of the newer integrated packages are Symphony and Framework (see Exhibits 12.2 and 12.3). Symphony, which added word processing and communication capabilities to Lotus 1-2-3, is still organized around a master spreadsheet. Framework is organized around the concept of a "frame," which can hold an outline, a spreadsheet, a data base, or other frames.

As all of the functions of integrated software must fit within the computer system's primary memory, these functions are generally slower and less capable than those provided with single-purpose software packages. Still, a capability to easily move data back and forth between different functions is very desirable to a business professional who regularly makes use of these functions.

Some software vendors are taking another approach with integrated software. Rather than placing multiple functions within a package, they are developing "families" of single-function tools that can share data files (see Exhibit 12.4). While this approach does not produce a set of tools as tightly integrated as Lotus, Symphony, and Framework, the individual packages are often faster and more sophisticated.

Software Integrators

The second approach for providing business professionals with a set of multipurpose tools is through a **window manager** that sits between the tools and the operating system. Window managers allow users to execute a number of applications at the same time, to view each application in its own window, to change the size of the windows, and to move data values between the windows.

Multipurpose Tools

EXHIBIT 12.4
Rather than offer multiple tools within a single tightly integrated software package, a family of single-purpose packages can provide a user with a loosely integrated set of end-user tools. Each package can read data files created by other family members.

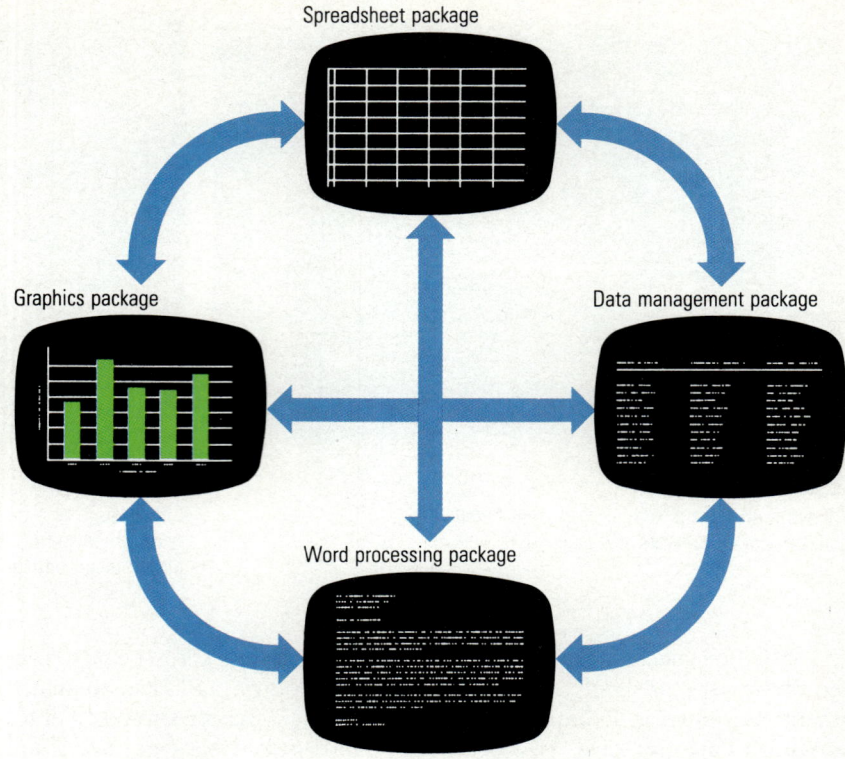

What distinguishes these system integrators from integrated systems is that they work with single-purpose tools. Thus, users have the best of both worlds—they can work with powerful single-purpose tools or a favorite tool but still integrate their end-user applications.

Certain system integrators require that the single-purpose tools be modified to run under the system integrator (see Exhibit 12.5); others, however, can work with any tool (see Exhibit 12.6).

Because the technology is relatively new, window managers have not been that successful. Fitting applications into windows strains the speed and capacity of today's microcomputers. They require microcomputer systems with hard disks and large amounts of primary memory but are still relatively slow. As the technology improves and microcomputers become even more powerful, window managers are likely to achieve the success that was initially predicted for them. The new IBM Personal System/2 PCs announced in mid-1987 represent the first PCs with enough speed and power to make window managers a viable end-user tool. The OS/2 operating system for the new PCs will include windowing capabilities directly in the operating system.

Desktop Organizers

When managers begin to spend a large portion of their time working with microcomputer end-user tools, interruptions that take them away from their microcomputers can be frustrating. Often the smaller the interruption, such as making a phone call or writing a memo, the greater

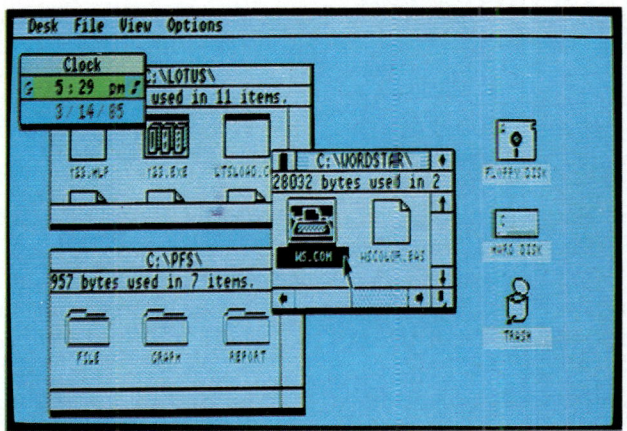

EXHIBIT 12.5
With some window managers, application software must be specially modified if it is to execute within the operating system.

EXHIBIT 12.6
With other window managers, application software does not have to be modified to execute within the operating system.

the frustration. **Desktop organizers** are integrated packages that allow a business professional to juggle several tasks without having to leave the big tasks that are executing on their microcomputers.

These software packages share a number of traits (see Exhibit 12.7). First, they replace common office tools, such as Rolodex files, calendars, notepads, calculators, telephones, and alarm clocks. Second, they stay in the background of other applications, waiting to pop up in a window only when triggered by the user. Finally, they are inexpensive. Many are priced in the $50 to $100 range.

Why are desktop organizers becoming so popular? The main reason is that they fill a real need of many business professionals. Desktop organizers handle the little tasks that recur throughout a manager's workday, thus increasing on-the-job productivity. They also keep these tasks and the associated paperwork in one place, rather than scattered all over a manager's desk and office.

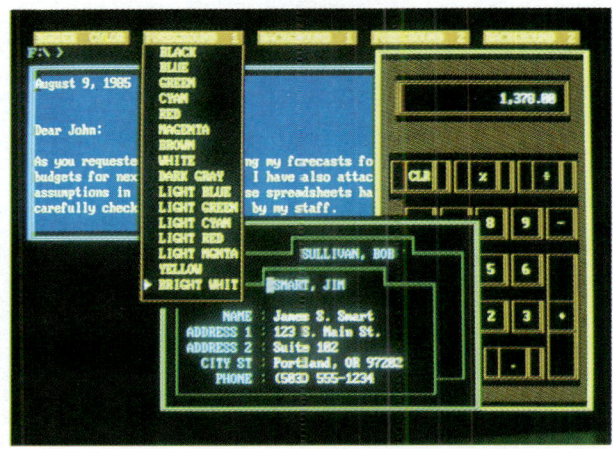

EXHIBIT 12.7
Desktop organizers can execute a number of useful functions, such as performing calculations and retrieving addresses.

Multipurpose Tools

ADVANCED END-USER TOOLS

Very high-level languages make it possible for end-users to create applications. They can also be used to make programmers more productive. In addition to handling procedural statements like traditional programming languages, very high-level languages often include various productivity features that can further simplify the process of building an application to solve a problem. These features include QUERY facilities, report generators, financial modeling, statistical analysis, and project management. In this section, we will look at these features and some of the current products that provide these types of capabilities to end-users.

QUERY Facilities

A **QUERY facility** allows an end-user to make simple requests for data. It is most commonly found in a very high-level language that works with data stored by a data base management system (see Chapter 10). A QUERY facility is useful for one-time requests to retrieve data from a data base when no application exists that can retrieve the particular data in the way the user wants it. A QUERY facility usually allows a user to use a *nonprocedural language,* in which the user specifies *what* data are to be retrieved rather than *how* they are to be specifically retrieved. The QUERY facility determines if PROJECT, SELECT, or JOIN operations are needed to obtain the data requested and then retrieves the necessary data from the data base. Some QUERY facilities even allow users to enter and update data in the data base in addition to simply doing retrievals.

Because QUERY facilities use nonprocedural, Englishlike commands, users with little or no programming experience can retrieve data. There is, however, a great deal of variation in the ease with which inexperienced end-users can formulate queries. Exhibit 12.8a shows a query written for the QUERY facility of a typical very high-level language which is marketed as easy-to-use. Some QUERY facilities have begun to allow users to enter queries in free-form English rather than requiring them to use specific key words to perform certain operations. For example, INTELLECT (by Artificial Intelligence Corporation) can interpret commands written in English by matching words against its own internal dictionary. Exhibit 12.8b shows the same query and the data retrieved by INTELLECT as a result of that query.

EXHIBIT 12.8
Variability in the Way a Query Can Be Written
(a) A query written in a QUERY language that is marketed as easy-to-use

```
LIST BY REGION (83-ACT-SEP-SALES),
SUM (83-EST-SEP-SALES), (SUM(83-ACT-SEP-SALES)
- SUM (83-EST-SEP-SALES)), (SUM(83-ACT-SEP-SALES)
- SUM (83-EST-SEP-SALES))/, (SUM(83-ACT-SEP-SALES)
IF REGION = 'EAST' OR REGION = 'WEST'
```

```
FOR THE EASTERN AND WESTERN REGIONS HOW DID ACTUAL SALES FOR
LAST MONTH COMPARE TO FORECASTS?
RESULT:
           MAY 1983    MAY 1983
           ACTUAL      FORECAST
   REGION  SALES       SALES        CHANGE      % CHANGE

   EAST    2820        2000         820         41.00
   WEST    3180        2800         380         13.57
```

(b) The same query written in INTELLECT and the data resulting from that query

Report Generators

QUERY facilities typically give a user little control over the way data are displayed on a screen. If a user has some special formatting needs beyond the standard formatting, he or she can use a **report generator,** a facility which lets a user create printed reports by using nonprocedural statements to obtain summary information and format the printed output. A report generator is usually designed to handle the more formal formatting and special needs involved with producing paper reports for use by managers. It includes features such as report headings and subheadings, page headings and subheadings, column positioning, automatic page numbering, and automatic totals and subtotals. Typically, an end-user can manipulate these formatting features by making choices in menus or by issuing a few simple commands. Exhibit 12.9a shows an example of the NOMAD2 LIST command, which produces the table with subtotals and totals shown in Exhibit 12.9b.

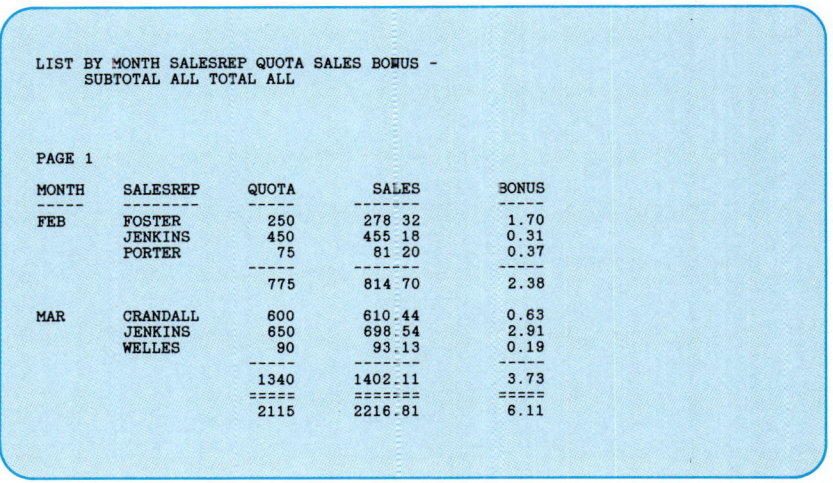

EXHIBIT 12.9
An Example of Report Generation
(a) The NOMAD2 LIST command with totals and subtotals

(b) The table with subtotals produced by the NOMAD2 LIST command

Advanced End-User Tools

A very high-level language can produce graphs as well as tables for reports. Many types of graphs can be created, including pie charts, bar graphs, scatter diagrams, and line graphs. If a user does not specify the type of graph needed, the report generator will determine what graph type is most appropriate for displaying the data requested. As with the reports themselves, graphs can usually be created with a few simple commands.

Financial Modeling

Some very high-level languages are designed to perform a specific type of application. One such application is **financial modeling,** which lets an end-user build models of financial situations which can be used to solve problems. IFPS (by Execucom Systems, Inc.) can handle more complex financial applications than spreadsheet programs such as Lotus 1-2-3. Exhibit 12.10a shows the statements a user enters to create the projected income statement in Exhibit 12.10b. These statements define the relationships between variables involved in the model. IFPS lets a user perform a *what if* analysis by specifying conditions rather than changing the base model, as would be required with a spreadsheet program. Exhibit 12.10c shows how a *what if* analysis can be performed by specifying a new relationship between cost of goods sold and sales. IFPS automatically answers this query by displaying the new model in Exhibit 12.10d.

In addition, IFPS can specify goal-seeking situations in which, for example, the desired net income in a model can be stated as $100,800. The IFPS model will automatically modify the sales variable to determine what is required to generate that profit amount. IFPS can also generate management report templates which can be loaded with different sets of data. This is very useful for corporate financial officers who want a common way to compare accounting data from various divisions. IFPS applications include

EXHIBIT 12.10
An Example of *What If* Corporate Planning
(a) A user can state a problem in a financial modeling language . . .

```
MODEL INCOME STATEMENT VERSION

 10 COLUMNS YEAR 1-YEAR 5
 20 SALES = 400000. 1.12 * PREVIOUS SALES
 30 GROSS PROFIT = SALES - COST OF GOODS SOLD
 40 COST OF GOODS SOLD = 60 * SALES
 50 TOTAL EXPENSES = FIXED EXPENSES + INTEREST PAID
 60 FIXED EXPENSES = 25000. 1.08 * PREVIOUS FIXED EXPENSES
 70 DEBT LEVEL = 80000
 80 INTEREST PAID = .0925 * DEBT LEVEL
 90 TAX LIABILITY = 48 * PROFIT BEFORE FEDERAL INCOME TAX
100 PROFIT BEFORE FEDERAL INCOME TAX = GROSS PROFIT -
    TOTAL EXPENSES
110 NET INCOME = PROFIT BEFORE FEDERAL INCOME TAX -
    FEDERAL INCOME TAX LIABILITY
END OF MODEL
```

```
?SOLVE
ENTER SOLVE OPTIONS
?ALL
                      YEAR 1      YEAR 2      YEAR 3      YEAR 4

SALES                 400,000     448,000     501,780     561,971
GROSS PROFIT          160,000     179,200     200,704     224,788
COST OF GOODS SOLD    240,000     268,800     301,056     337,183
TOTAL EXPENSES         32,400      34,400      36,560      38,893
FIXED EXPENSES         25,000      27,000      29,160      31,493
DEBT LEVEL             80,000      80,000      80,000      80,000
INTEREST PAID           7,400       7,400       7,400       7,400
TAX LIABILITY          61,248      69,504      78,789      89,230
PROFIT BEFORE FEDERAL
   INCOME TAX         127,600     144,800     164,144     185,896
NET INCOME             66,352      75,296      85,355      96,666
```

(b) . . . to create the projected income statement.

```
?WHAT IF
WHAT IF CASE 1
ENTER STATEMENTS
?COST OF GOODS SOLD = .70*SALES
?SOLVE
ENTER SOLVE OPTIONS
?ALL
*****WHAT IF CASE 1*****
1 WHAT IF STATEMENTS PROCESSED
```

(c) By performing a *what if* analysis . . .

```
                      YEAR 1      YEAR 2      YEAR 3      YEAR 4

SALES                 400,000     448,000     501,780     561,971
GROSS PROFIT          120,000     134,400     150,528     168,591
COSTS OF GOODS SOLD   280,000     313,600     351,232     393,380
TOTAL EXPENSES         32,400      34,400      36,560      38,893
FIXED EXPENSES         25,000      27,000      29,160      31,493
DEBT LEVEL             80,000      80,000      80,000      80,000
INTEREST PAID           7,400       7,400       7,400       7,400
TAX LIABILITY          42,048      48,000      54,705      62,255
PROFIT BEFORE FEDERAL
   INCOME TAX          87,600     100,000     113,968     129,699
NET INCOME             45,552      52,000      59,233      67,443
```

(d) . . . IFPS automatically answers the query and displays the result.

Advanced End-User Tools

cash flow projections, lease versus purchase comparisons, risk analysis, budgeting, and return-on-investment decisions.

Statistical Analysis

Some very high-level languages are designed to allow an end-user to create applications that require statistical analysis. For example, SAS (by SAS Institute, Inc.) is a statistical analysis tool that lets an end-user perform complex statistical analyses such as regression analysis, analysis of variance, and discriminant analysis, using simple, Englishlike commands. These operations are incorporated into ready-to-use procedures so an end-user doesn't have to be a statistician to produce the required analysis.

Results can be obtained and put into a report by issuing a few simple commands written in a nonprocedural language. SAS also has sophisticated graphics capabilities that display statistical results. Exhibit 12.11a shows the SAS commands needed to generate the results in Exhibit 12.11b.

EXHIBIT 12.11
Performing a Statistical Analysis
(a) These SAS statements produce the output shown in Exhibit 12.11b.

```
PROC MEANS MEAN MIN MAX;
    VAR AGE, CLAIMS, PREMIUM;
    BY DEPT;
```

(b) The MEANS procedure determines the mean age in each department and the dollar amount of insurance premiums versus claims paid.

```
                K & G Supply Company
              Medical Insurance Analysis
           for Year Ending December 31, 1984

  VARIABLE         MEAN         MINIMUM         MAXIMUM
                                 VALUE           VALUE
  ------------------- DEPT=Accounting ---------------------
  AGE               45            18              72
  CLAIMS           941            17            5025
  PREMIUM         1175           864            1596
  -------------------- DEPT=Marketing ---------------------
  AGE               41            18              65
  CLAIMS          1088            27           60310
  PREMIUM         1128           864            1596
  -------------------- DEPT=Customer Service ---------------
  AGE               44            18              72
  CLAIMS           942            27            4484
  PREMIUM         1144           864            1596
  -------------------- DEPT=Production ---------------------
  AGE               35            18              60
  CLAIMS           943            31           38516
  PREMIUM         1113           864            1596
  -------------------- DEPT=Shipping -----------------------
  AGE               37            18              61
  CLAIMS           884            31            2479
  PREMIUM         1097           864            1596
  -------------------- DEPT=Human Resources ----------------
  AGE               42            18              72
  CLAIMS           946            24            5334
  PREMIUM         1215           864            1596
```

Project Management

A final type of very high-level language designed to perform a specific type of application is the project manager. A **project manager** involves step-by-step planning of a project in which tasks are scheduled and resources are allocated to finish an entire job on schedule. It involves identifying potential schedule problems, tracking progress, and optimizing cost/time/resource trade-offs. The project is divided into tasks of various durations, which are linked together in a relationship that shows which tasks are dependent on other tasks. Therefore, the planned costs for each task can be budgeted and compared to actual costs as the project progresses.

The Harvard Total Project Manager provides end-users with seven different tools for managing a project. An end-user can monitor cross-project resource allocation, perform cost and schedule tracking, create a "roadmap" of the project, set up a schedule with minimum slack or negative slack, and divide the project into subprojects. Exhibit 12.12 shows an example of the type of graphical display used in the Harvard Total Project Manager.

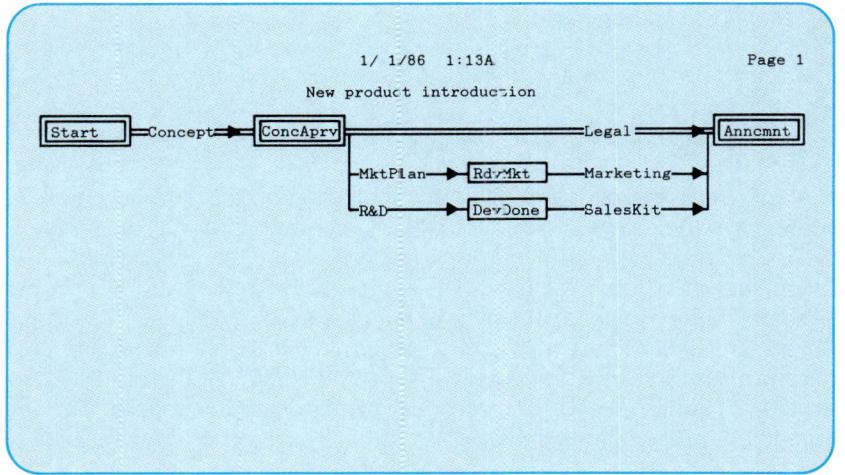

EXHIBIT 12.12
Project Management Software
The Roadmap is the one feature that no project manager can do without. It allows the project manager to keep the big picture in sight.

PROMOTING AND MANAGING END-USER COMPUTING

End-user computing can provide numerous benefits to a business. By actively promoting and managing end-user computing, a firm can increase the benefits it receives and prevent the disruptive and expensive mistakes of inappropriate use by end-users.

A good way to begin is to set up a facility that is staffed by end-user computing specialists who first train and then support business professionals in their computing efforts. Such a facility is usually termed an **information center** when it is directed toward mainframe end-user computing and a **personal computer support center** when it is directed toward microcomputer end-user computing. We will adopt these terms here.

Information Center

The primary objective of an information center is to give business professionals access to mainframe data bases through mainframe end-user tools. The following services are typically provided:

access to and training with end-user tools,

access to terminals,

assistance in accessing and storing data,

advice on how particular business problems might best be solved through end-user computing,

assistance in using end-user tools, and

maintenance of catalogues of available data and previously developed end-user applications.

Personal Computer Support Center

There are two main objectives in establishing most personal computer support centers: to help business professionals acquire microcomputers for their offices and homes and to prevent the uncontrolled influx of microcomputers into a business. The first objective is achieved by encouraging business professionals to experiment with and then use microcomputers. The second is achieved by limiting the variety of microcomputer hardware and software being used in a firm. It is difficult for a business to provide its employees with a high level of microcomputer support without identifying microcomputer hardware and software products that are recommended by the personal computer support center.

As with information centers, personal computer support centers typically offer a wide range of services:

helping employees select and purchase microcomputer hardware and software,

arranging discount purchase programs with microcomputer vendors,

training employees in the use of microcomputers,

keeping employees informed about new microcomputer products,

consulting with employees on their microcomputer applications,

helping employees access and download mainframe data bases,

maintaining catalogues of all developed microcomputer applications, repairing microcomputer hardware, and

providing supplies and replacement parts.

Personal computer support centers take a variety of forms. Some firms with information centers simply add these activities to those already given the information center staff: others separate the two facilities for managing end-user computing. Some personal computer support centers in large businesses have staffs of twenty or more people; others are staffed by one or two people. Some small firms make these duties a part-time assignment for a single employee.

Summary

Business computing reached a crisis in the mid-1970s as the *visible* and *invisible backlogs* of new information systems projects grew very large. Two advances in computer technology, very high-level languages and microcomputers, provided many business professionals with *end-user tools* that enabled them to develop some of their own computer applications. In this way the era of end-user computing began.

End-user computing has a number of benefits. Information systems are developed quickly and inexpensively. The application backlog is reduced. Better information systems often result. Finally, users are more apt to use an information system that they have developed.

End-user computing must be well managed. Appropriate tools must be made available. Users must be trained in their use. Moreover, users must be able to access data already stored on a firm's computer systems.

A current trend with today's end-user tools is to provide a business professional with access to a number of tools at the same time. There are two basic approaches for providing multipurpose tools: *integrated software* and *software integrators*.

With integrated software, users apply similar sets of commands to manipulate data with a variety of end-user tools without having to enter any data item more than once. Each tool can be displayed in its own window on the screen, and data values can be moved from one window to another. While integrated software is very useful, the tools provided with these packages are generally slower and less powerful than those of single-purpose software packages.

With software integrators, a *window manager* that sits between single-purpose end-user tools and the operating system allows users to execute a number of applications at the same time, to view each application in its own window, to change the size of the windows, and to move data values between the windows. Fitting a number of applications into windows does strain the speed and capacity of today's microcomputers. Thus, software integrators tend to require hard disks and a large amount of primary memory, and they are still relatively slow.

A recently introduced integrated software package is the *desktop organizer*. This package provides the business professional with a number of tools to handle the small tasks that occur throughout a manager's workday, replacing Rolodex files, calendars, notepads, calculators, telephones, and alarm clocks. One of the best features of desktop organizers is that they stay in the background of other applications, popping up only when triggered by the user.

Very high-level languages provide users with many tools for improving productivity and making the creation of applications to solve problems easier and more efficient. Very high-level languages require fewer commands to accomplish certain tasks than traditional programming languages, and they often include other features, such as QUERY facilities, report generators, financial modeling, statistical analysis, and project management.

A QUERY facility lets an end-user retrieve data by using *nonprocedural* commands to describe *what* data is to be retrieved rather than *how* it is to be retrieved. Some QUERY facilities allow users to write queries using Englishlike commands.

Report generators are designed to help users format data that is to appear on printed reports. Using simple commands, an end-user can create headings, number pages, and position columns easily and quickly. Some report generators also allow the end-user to present the data graphically.

Some very high-level languages are designed to help end-users create specialized types of applications. Some very high-level languages let the user do financial applications in which a financial model can be created and then used to perform *what if* analyses. Other very high-level languages are specifically designed to help end-users perform statistical analyses. Project managers let end-users create, and then track, complex scheduling applications by using menus and simple commands.

A very good way to manage end-user computing is to provide a facility with end-user tools that is staffed by end-user computing specialists to train and support business professionals. Such a facility is usually termed an *information center* when it is directed toward mainframe end-user computing and a *personal computer support center* when it is directed toward microcomputer end-user computing.

Review Questions

1. Briefly explain the causes and significance of the business computing crisis of the mid-1970s.

2. How has computer technology provided solutions to the business computing crisis?

3. Briefly describe the concept of integrated software. What advantages does such an approach offer?

4. What is a software integrator? How does this approach differ from integrated systems?

5. Briefly explain the concept of desktop organizers. Why have such programs become popular?

6. Give examples of end-user tools that can do specific tasks across many different applications. Then give examples of those that are used for a specific class of applications.

7. What two approaches may a firm adopt to manage end-user computing? How are the two distinguished?

8. Briefly describe the purpose and services of an information center.

APPENDICES

APPENDIX A ■ The History of the Computer

THE COMPUTER AGE
    The First Generation: 1951–58
    The Second Generation: 1959–63
    The Third Generation: 1964–70
    The Fourth Generation: 1971–Present

COMPUTER TECHNOLOGY TRENDS

SUMMARY

REVIEW QUESTIONS

The Dawn of the Computer Age

The Beginning of Information Processing

500 B.C.	The abacus is invented.
A.D. 100	Paper is invented.
A.D. 1458	Johann Gutenberg invents the printing press.

Calculating Machines Are Invented

1642	Blaise Pascal develops the mechanical calculator.
1676	Gottfried von Leibnitz improves Pascal's calculator.
1801	Joseph Jacquard invents an automated loom "programmed" by punched cards.
1822	Charles Babbage develops the Difference Engine.
1833	Babbage outlines plans for the Analytical Engine, a general-purpose computer.

Office Automation Begins

1837	Samuel Morse applies for a patent on his telegraph.
1844	Morse transmits the first telegraph message.
1867	Christopher Sholes begins his work on the typewriter.
1873	E. Remington & Sons acquires Sholes' typewriter and successfully markets it.
1876	Alexander Graham Bell invents the telephone.

Automated Data Processing Begins

1878	James Ritty develops the cash register.
1879	Thomas A. Edison invents the incandescent light bulb.
1885	Dorr E. Felt develops a key-driven calculating machine.
1890	Herman Hollerith develops an electromechanical tabulating machine to count the 1890 census.

continued

Today's computer technologies and uses reflect centuries of far-fetched ideas and persistent hard work by many people. Often, these curious inventions were not immediately recognized as important or practical. For example, John Mauchly's plan to develop the first general-purpose electronic computer was not taken seriously—until a young army officer named Herman Goldstine saw this bizarre idea as a solution to a critical problem for the United States during World War II.

Tracing the history of the computer is useful for many reasons. First, it reveals the close connection between advances in computer technology and the real-world problems these advances solved. Second, it introduces the fascinating men and women who conceived and developed the computer's marvels. Third, it will increase the understanding of computer systems in use. Finally, this history illustrates a number of the issues and trends important to a productive use of computers in business today.

THE COMPUTER AGE

Computer technology has gone through many changes since 1950. Exhibit A.1 shows the impacts of these advances on business computing. Had automobile development paralleled the computer's development, today's luxury cars would cost $50, travel at 700 miles per hour, and get over 1000 miles per gallon. These changes are often divided into **computer generations,** based on the main electronic component used. The first generation of computers (1951-58) used the vacuum tube, while the second generation (1959-63) used the transistor. In the third generation (1964-70), integrated circuits, or "chips," were introduced. In the fourth generation (1971-present), the chips have become smaller and more complex. We will discuss these computer generations in the remainder of this Appendix.

The First Generation: 1951–58

The vacuum tube was the primary electronic element used in first generation computers. These early computers, while useful, were still quite unreliable. Vacuum tubes generated so much heat that water cooling was necessary. Even with these cooling systems, computers were in constant need of repair. The bigger a computer was, the more tubes it had, and the sooner it would fail.

Despite these technological obstacles, the computer industry was beginning to take shape. Remington Rand delivered the first UNIVAC 1 to the U.S. Bureau of the Census in 1951. This marked the first time an electronic computer had been built for a data processing application rather than a military one. By 1952, the Census Bureau had obtained three UNIVACs, which displaced much of the punched-card equipment that IBM had sold the Bureau. IBM was forced to take a hard look at this new data processing technology. Thomas Watson, Jr., IBM's new president, directed

EXHIBIT A.1

This table shows performance differences for representative computers from each succeeding computer generation. In each case, the computer system is handling the same data processing problem.

GENERATION	COST TO PERFORM THE PROBLEM	PROCESSING TIME
1	$15.00	6 Hours
2	2.50	45 Seconds
3	.50	30 Seconds
4	.20	5 Seconds
4½	.05	1 Second

IBM toward electronic computers and away from electromechanical punched-card equipment.

The use of the UNIVAC 1 by the Columbia Broadcasting System (CBS) to project the winner of the 1952 presidential election brought the electronic computer to the attention of the American public. On election eve, the UNIVAC projected that Eisenhower would win by a landslide. Because all of the experts had predicted a close election, Remington Rand's staff thought there was an error in the computer program. They stalled CBS and began to make changes to the program. When they had "improved" the program to the point where Eisenhower would win by only a slim margin, the projection was released to CBS. By 11:00 P.M., voting results indicated an Eisenhower landslide! When this story spread, the computer's image as an electronic "brain" was formed.

A third important event of this period was an antitrust action by the U.S. Department of Justice against AT&T. In 1956, AT&T was barred from having anything to do with the computer market. However, this did not prevent the company from using or making computers for its own use.

Hardware

First generation computers used vacuum tubes for data storage in ALU and CU circuits, as well as in primary memory. By the end of this era, the faster magnetic cores were being used for primary memory. Data and programs were entered most often by punched cards; computer output was produced either on cards or on paper. Cards were the primary form of secondary storage, but, by the end of this time period, magnetic tapes were commonly used for secondary storage.

Work to improve the transistor continued throughout the 1950s. Much of this effort was funded by the American government, which used electronics in the Cold War and in the space program. Transistor manufacturing was still more art than science, however, and engineers of the day, trained to use vacuum tubes, were slow to switch to transistors. After using the larger vacuum tube, working with transistors was rather like doing surgery on the head of a pin; but by 1958, advances in transistors were bringing the first computer generation to an end.

Another important technical event took place in 1958. The leading electronic circuit technology at that time stacked components on top of

---

1896   Hollerith leaves the Bureau of the Census to form his own company. This firm eventually becomes IBM. Guglielmo Marconi invents the radio.

1911   Hollerith's successor at the Bureau of the Census, James Powers, forms another company to sell punched-card equipment. This firm eventually merges with Remington Rand.

1914   James F. Smathers invents the electric typewriter.

1914   Thomas Watson, Sr., joins Hollerith's firm.

1915   Coast-to-coast telephone communication first takes place.

1930   The electric typewriter becomes a commercial success.

The General-Purpose Computer Is Developed

1930   Vannevar Bush develops a large-scale mechanical computer at MIT.

1937–38   George Stibitz and Samuel Williams at Bell Labs develop a small electronic computer using telephone relays as the basic electronic component.

1937–44   Howard Aiken develops an electromechanical computer at Harvard University.

1939   John Vincent Atanasoff and Clifford Berry of Iowa State College develop a small special-purpose vacuum tube computer.

1941–45   Alan Turing and other British scientists develop the Collossus, a large special-purpose electronic computer.

1943–46   J. Presper Eckert, Jr., and John William Mauchly develop the ENIAC, the first large general-purpose computer, at the University of Pennsylvania.

continued

The Computer Age

1944	John von Neuman, working on the plans for the ENIAC's immediate successor, defines the basic computer architecture to be used for the next forty years.
1946	Eckert and Mauchly form their own company to build and market the UNIVAC computer.
1947	William Schockley, Walter Brattain, and John Bardeen invent the transistor at Bell Labs.
1950	The Whirlwind computer is built at MIT.

one another, like dishes, with connecting wires running up through holes cut in the components. Jack Kilby at Texas Instruments wondered if it would be possible to build an entire circuit within a single piece of material rather than stacking the components. His research led to the development of the **integrated circuit.** A few months later, Robert Noyce at Fairchild Semiconductor also developed an integrated circuit along with a greatly improved manufacturing method.

Software

First generation computers had very skimpy, if any, operating systems. Instead, a human operator loaded a stack of cards containing a program and data, which were processed as a batch. Military computers, such as the SAGE air defense system, led to new systems software able to handle remote data entry and to link computer systems together in networks.

The major software advances involved programming languages. All computers are directed by **machine language** instructions. Each instruction takes the form of a series of **binary digits.** The very first computers, such as the ENIAC, were actually directly programmed in machine language, which was very difficult and time consuming. By the early 1950s, though, most programming was being done in **assembly languages,** in which abbreviations replaced the binary digits of machine language. Assembly language programs are then "translated" to machine language instructions by systems software known as an **assembler.** Because these abbreviations are easier to remember and use than binary digits, programming is much easier. Both machine and assembly languages require programmers to work at the level of a computer's electronic circuitry. Programmers have to understand both the problem they are solving and details about computer hardware.

Prior to 1954, all programming was done in either machine or assembly language, and programmers rightly regarded their work as a complex, creative job. These programmers, in general, were convinced that programming could not be automated. Simply too many shortcomings in the hardware had to be overcome by programming skill. As a result, the cost of programming was usually as great as the cost of hardware.

EXHIBIT A.2

Shown here are differences among machine language, assembly language, and high-level language. The task used to illustrate these different forms of programming is the addition of one variable to another variable.

LANGUAGE FORM	LANGUAGE TRANSLATION
MACHINE LANGUAGE 011011 0110 011100 0111 110001 0110 100 010101 0110	No translation is needed.
ASSEMBLY LANGUAGE FX B FY C ADA X Y STA B	These assembly language statements must be translated into machine language. Each assembly language statement will translate into one machine language statement.
HIGH-LEVEL LANGUAGE LET B = B + C	This BASIC statement must be translated into machine language. This one BASIC statement will translate into four machine language statements.

A The History of the Computer

In 1954, a group of IBM scientists led by John Backus began work on the design of a **high-level programming language** for scientific computing. This design was called **FORTRAN**, short for *Formula Trans*lation. With high-level programming languages, program instructions are directed toward the problem being solved rather than the computer on which the program is run. As a result, a single program instruction may represent a series of machine language instructions. As you might expect, programming with a high-level language is not only easier, it is much faster. Exhibit A.2 illustrates some differences among machine, assembly, and high-level programming languages. The drawback of high-level languages is that they have to be "translated" into machine language. This is performed, as shown in Exhibit A.3, by a systems software program called a **compiler**.

When FORTRAN first became available, many programmers refused to use it. They did not believe that a compiler could produce efficient machine language versions of their programs. Luckily, the FORTRAN designers had anticipated this reaction. Their primary goal in developing FORTRAN was to produce an efficient machine language translation. This early decision was a major factor in FORTRAN's success and aided the rapid acceptance of high-level programming languages in general. FORTRAN was available by 1956 and in general use by 1957. By the end of the 1950s, over 200 other high-level programming languages had been developed.

Uses and Users

All earlier computing had involved scientific or large-scale computing. Within this first generation of computers, however, business computing began. By the end of the 1950s, many large firms had begun to develop their basic transaction processing systems, such as payroll, billing, and inventory control.

The first firm believed to have used an electronic computer for business applications was J. Lyons and Sons, a chain of British tea shops. Some of the employees actually built the firm's computer! The firm's computer group broke away to become *ICL,* short for International Computers, Limited, which today is Europe's leading computer manufacturer.

The First Generation 1951–58

1951	The UNIVAC 1 is delivered to the U.S. Census Bureau.
1952	Thomas Watson, Jr., becomes president of IBM.
1953	J. Lyons and Sons, a chain of British corner tea shops, builds its own electronic computer.
1954	General Electric Company becomes the first private firm in the U.S. to take delivery of a computer, a UNIVAC 1.
1954	John Backus of IBM begins designing FORTRAN, the first high-level programming language.
1955	IBM begins delivery of its 705 business computer.
1955	The SAGE air defense system is installed.
1956	Grace Hopper develops a business-oriented programming language, FLOW-MATIC.
1956	John McCarthy at MIT begins to design LISP, the first programming language aimed at artificial intelligence applications.
1956	AT&T is barred from competing in the computer industry.
1958	Jack Kilby at Texas Instruments builds the first integrated circuit.

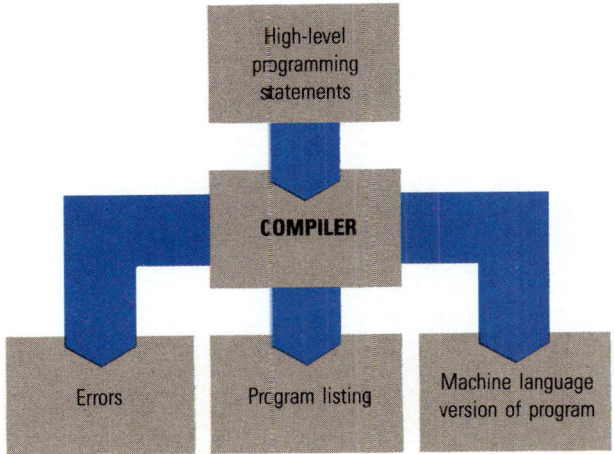

Exhibit A.3

A systems software program called a *compiler* translates programming statements written in a high-level language to the instructions that will actually run on the computer system.

The Computer Age

The Second Generation 1959–63

1959 IBM introduces a transistorized computer, the IBM 1401.

1960 Grace Hopper and others design the COBOL programming language.

1960 Digital Equipment Corporation introduces the PDP-1, the first minicomputer.

1960 The Rand Corporation develops the first interactive computing system.

1961 IBM begins working on the System 360 family of computer systems.

1962 The Telstar communications satellite is launched.

1962 IBM and American Airlines develop the SABRE reservation system.

1963 John Kemeny and Thomas Kurtz develop the BASIC programming language.

1963 IBM begins to design the PL/1 programming language.

In the United States, General Electric was the first firm to purchase an electronic computer.

IBM's development in 1955 of the very successful 705 series of business computers proved to be an important milestone in the history of computers. IBM had finally caught up to, and even surpassed, Remington Rand's electronic computers.

First generation computer users were not computer scientists. None existed! These first users were scientists, engineers, and business people who saw the advantage of using computers and taught themselves to write the necessary programs. **End-user computing,** in which computer users develop their own information systems, flourished out of necessity. The increasing complexity of computer systems soon discouraged this early era of end-user computing.

The Second Generation: 1959–63

The appearance in 1959 of the first **transistorized computer systems** launched the second generation of computers. The continuing trend toward smaller, faster, more reliable, and less expensive computers was started. One year later, Digital Equipment Corporation, or DEC, introduced the first minicomputer, the **PDP-1.** The first minicomputers differed from regular computer systems in a number of ways. Not only were they smaller, they were built to serve special purposes. They were very rugged, unlike their predecessors, and could function in harsh surroundings, with fewer climate controls needed. Also, they were less expensive. With these improvements, computer systems began to be used in new environments, such as laboratories and factories. Thus, the minicomputer not only opened up new markets for electronic computers, but it also introduced the computer to new uses and users.

The IBM System 360 Series played an important role in the history of computing.

A   The History of the Computer

Telstar led the way to the communications satellite.

Two other events in this era were to greatly affect the future of business computing. First, IBM began work on its **System 360 Series** of computers, an immense project that would represent one of the most important events in the history of computing. Second, the launching of **Telstar** led the way to the communications satellite. This meant that business information processing was no longer "tied" to earth. Just as the telephone enabled firms to operate nationwide, communications satellites allowed firms to operate worldwide.

Hardware

Although second generation computers used transistors for most processing circuitry, magnetic cores were still used for primary memory. Most data and programs were entered into the computer from magnetic tape. Often, however, data would first be punched on cards and then copied onto tapes to speed data entry. Similarly, output was often directed to tape to be printed onto paper later. While magnetic tapes were the most common secondary storage devices, magnetic disks did appear toward the end of this era.

Software

The first real operating systems appeared during this second generation of computer development. Besides improving computer system efficiency, these operating systems brought about new forms of data processing, such as interactive processing, real-time processing, and time sharing. With **interactive processing,** users could carry on a dialogue with the computer. With **real-time computing,** events could be captured and processed as they occurred. With **time sharing,** many people could use a computer system at the same time. For example, the SABRE reservation system, developed by IBM and American Airlines, allowed reservation

The Computer Age

clerks to interactively review or update a flight's data file as reservations were being made.

Developments in programming languages also occurred. First, the U.S. Department of Defense sponsored a meeting to develop a business-oriented programming language that could be used by all of its agencies on different computers. This resulted in the design of the *Common Business-Oriented Language*, better known as **COBOL.** Second, two professors at Dartmouth College, John Kemeny and Thomas Kurtz, wanted to make computing available to all Dartmouth students. To achieve this, they needed an interactive programming language that was easy to learn and easy to use. Their work resulted in the *Beginner's All-purpose Symbolic Instruction Code*, or **BASIC.** Finally, IBM began to develop a programming language able to handle both scientific and business data processing. At this time, scientific programs were written in FORTRAN, and business programs were written in COBOL. Few programmers knew both languages. This project resulted in the design of **PL/1,** or *Programming Language One*.

Uses and Users

All types of businesses were now using electronic computers for transaction processing. Some information reporting systems were being developed to provide managers with useful information from the growing data bases being created by these transaction processing systems.

Even though information systems were now common in many firms, not many employers actually came in contact with a computer. Data were usually recorded on paper and sent to the computer department for processing. Similarly, output was distributed by the computer department to users. Only computer specialists worked directly with the computer.

Computer systems had already become too complex for most users. Users explained their needs to programmers, who then developed application programs. Most programmers and other computer specialists obtained their computer skills from "on-the-job training," usually through the military. Colleges and universities had not yet begun to offer degrees, or even many courses, in computer science or information systems.

The Third Generation: 1964–70

In 1964, IBM introduced the six computers that made up the System 360 series of computer systems. These six computers used designs similar enough to allow a program written for one machine to run on another. The computers differed mainly in the capacity of their primary memory. At the same time, IBM introduced another 150 related products. The impact of these innovations on the computer industry was tremendous. First, the "life" of a computer system was extended, since a firm buying a System 360 computer could "grow" into larger members of the series as its information processing needs increased. More importantly, firms could make this move without rewriting their software, an enormous saving of both time and money. This was a powerful incentive to choose and continue to use IBM equipment. Second, the operating system became the key component of a computer system. With software controlling all aspects of a computer's operation, efficiency improved and failures were less frequent. As a result, firms became more willing to depend on computer systems to handle all of their information processing needs.

Three other events important to business computing occurred during this era. First, the development of the **magnetic tape Selectric typewriter** made it possible for typists to store and retrieve documents. This was a major step toward today's **word processing systems,** and it opened the office market to electronic computers. Second, DEC's success with its **PDP-8 minicomputer** spurred other firms to enter the minicomputer segment of the computer industry. Finally, responding to possible U.S. Department of Justice antitrust actions, IBM "unbundled" its software. IBM previously charged customers a single price for its computer systems, which were made up of IBM hardware and IBM software. Other hardware vendors believed this unfair because they could not compete with IBM in developing both hardware and software. Joining the protest, software vendors, such as Computer Sciences Corporation, argued that there were few incentives for IBM's customers to purchase non-IBM software. Perhaps the competing vendors' protests were justified, because, after IBM unbundled its software, many new hardware and software products did appear.

Hardware

By 1964, some of the transistors and magnetic cores had been replaced by integrated circuits. In these **solid-state devices,** an entire circuit was fabricated within a single wafer, or chip, of a semiconductor material, such as silicon. A **semiconductor's** ability to conduct electricity can be made to vary, depending on the chemicals that are permanently added to it. With solid-state circuitry, computer systems were even smaller, faster, more reliable, and less expensive. CRTs were being used for input and output, and the magnetic disk gained importance as a secondary storage medium. These changes reflected the continued growth of interactive business computing.

Software

Operating systems continued to grow in power. Both interactive and remote business computing were now common. More programming languages were also developed. For example, IBM developed **RPG,** or *R*eport *P*rogram *G*enerator, to aid small businesses switching from punched cards to electronic computers. With a minimum of training, a small firm's employees could duplicate the firm's existing data processing procedures on a small computer system. In 1971, Nicholas Wirth developed the **Pascal** language, named in honor of Blaise Pascal. This was the first programming language to use **structured programming** concepts.

Uses and Users

Data input and output were now being performed by clerical employees rather than computer specialists, and the result was faster processing and fewer errors. It makes sense that a purchasing clerk entering a purchase order is more likely to catch an error than someone knowing little about the items being ordered. Also, information systems were being integrated, meaning that the outputs of some information systems became

The Third Generation 1964–70

1964	IBM introduces the System 360 series of computer systems.
1964	IBM introduces the magnetic tape Selectric typewriter.
1964	IBM introduces the RPG programming language.
1965	DEC introduces the PDP-8 minicomputer.
1968	Computer Sciences Corporation becomes the first software company to be listed on the New York Stock Exchange.
1969	IBM "unbundles" its software from its hardware.
1970	Nicholas Wirth develops the Pascal programming language.

The Computer Age

The Fourth Generation 1971–Present

1971	Ted Hoff of Intel develops the first microprocessor, the Intel 4004.
1971	Lexitron introduces a CRT-based word processor.
1973	Xerox develops the Smalltalk, the first "user-friendly" software.
1974	Intel develops a general-purpose microprocessor, the Intel 8080.
1975	MITS, Inc., develops Altair, the first commercially successful personal computer.
1975	Paul Allen and Bill Gates form Microsoft Corporation.
1975	The U.S. Department of Defense sponsors the effort to design the ADA programming language.
1976	Gary Kildall forms Digital Research to sell CP/M, the first commercially successful microcomputer operating system.
1976	Wang introduces a multiuser word processing computer system.
1976	Michael Schrayer develops Electric Pencil, the first microcomputer word processing software.
1977	Steven Jobs and Steven Wozniak form Apple Corporation.

continued

the inputs to other information systems. For example, an order entry system might have access to stock levels maintained by an inventory control system. A manufacturing scheduling system might have access to stock levels maintained by an inventory control system and the equipment statuses as registered by a shop floor control system. Finally, a wide range of information reporting systems was being developed at this time to support a firm's managers and other professional employees.

With interactive computing, users began to regain a more direct relationship with the computer, which had been lost during the second generation of computer development. However, the increased complexity of computer and information systems now limited direct user involvement to input and output tasks. Application design and development, along with computer management and operation, remained the responsibility of computer specialists.

It wasn't until this time that college and university graduates could obtain degrees in computer science and information systems. Computing literacy was beginning to take root, and computer education was not limited to colleges and universities. Elementary and high schools began to introduce students to computing. A new computer user/specialist was emerging. Many of the major events of the fourth generation of computers would be led by people who, having grown up with computers, found computing to be a natural and positive force in their lives.

The Fourth Generation: 1971–Present

Instead of having one simple electronic circuit in a silicon chip, **large-scale integration (LSI)** technology places many circuits within a single chip. During this fourth generation of computing, LSI technology has improved to where first hundreds, then thousands, and now hundreds of thousands of electronic components are manufactured as a single chip. The term **very large-scale integration (VLSI)** is used when referring to these very high chip densities. With LSI and VLSI technologies, computers have become even smaller, faster, more reliable, and less expensive.

The Magnetic Tape Selectric Typewriter

A The History of the Computer

The Intel 4004 Microprocessor

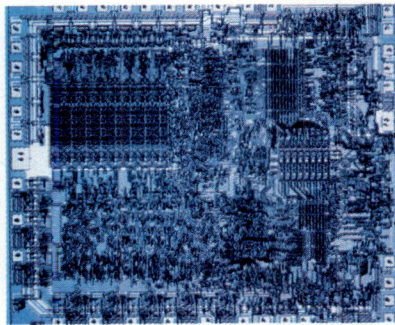

The Intel 8080 Microprocessor

A key achievement of this fourth generation of computers was the development in 1971 of the microprocessor. In the summer of 1969, Busicom, a now defunct Japanese calculator manufacturer, approached Intel with a contract to design a set of chips for a new family of calculators. At least twelve chips were required in Busicom's initial plans. Ted Hoff, Jr., was assigned to the Busicom project. Hoff, who used a PDP-8 in his design work, wondered why the electronics for the calculator were more complex than those in the PDP-8.

Working with fellow engineers Frederico Faggin and Stan Mazor, Hoff whittled the twelve chips down to four, one of which, the **Intel 4004 microprocessor,** contained all of the logic and control circuits. By today's standards, the 4004 was very primitive. Its development, nonetheless, did reshape modern electronics and the computer industry. Intel's earliest microprocessors, the 4004 and the 8008, were designed for special purposes. In 1974, Intel developed the **Intel 8080,** a microprocessor suited for general-purpose computing.

MITS, Inc., a small New Mexico instrument firm, soon developed the first commercially successful microcomputer, the **Altair.** Electronic computers suddenly became affordable. Although the price of a single Intel 8080 chip was close to $400, MITS bought them for less than $100 and was able to sell the Altair in kit form for as little as $439.

But the microcomputer did not become a household word until Steven Jobs and Steven Wozniak formed Apple Corporation in 1977 to build and sell **Apple II** computers. Apple microcomputers were used by many hobbyists and educators but by relatively few business professionals. The world of business had not yet accepted the microcomputer.

Tandy Corporation's **TRS-80 Model II** opened the business world to the microcomputer in 1979. Two years later, the **IBM PC** met with overwhelming acceptance by business, and the microcomputer market exploded. The acceptance of the IBM PC by the business community resulted in its becoming the de facto standard for microcomputing for businesses. The recent announcement that expansion boards holding an 80286 microprocessor could be fitted onto Apple Corporation's latest computers, the **Macintosh SE** and the **Macintosh II,** suggests that the de facto standard is now official.

Managers and professionals are beginning to depend on microcomputers to the same degree that businesses rely on larger computer systems. Portable microcomputers, beginning with the **Osborne I** and

1979	Dan Bricklin and Dan Fylstra develop VisiCalc, the first electronic spreadsheet.
1979	Seymour Rubenstein of MicroPro develops WordStar, the first commercially successful microcomputer word processing software.
1979	Tandy Corporation introduces the TRS-80 Model II, the first commercially successful business microcomputer.
1980	The U.S. Department of Justice deregulates the communications industry.
1981	IBM introduces its personal computer, the IBM PC.
1981	Adam Osborne introduces the Osborne 1, the first portable microcomputer.
1982	The U.S. Department of Justice drops its antitrust suit against IBM.
1983	The U.S. Department of Justice allows AT&T to compete in the computer industry.
1983	Apple introduces the Lisa microcomputer.
1984	Apple introduces the Macintosh microcomputer.
1985	Founders Steven Jobs and Steven Wozniak leave Apple Corporation.
1985	Expert systems and other applications software packages applying artificial intelligence concepts appear.
1986	IBM introduces its "laptop" computer, the PC convertible.
1986	Intel introduces the 80336 chip, the 32-bit microprocessor for MS-DOS microcomputers.
1986	Compaq introduces the Deskpro 386, the first MS-DOS microcomputer to use the 80386 chip.
1987	Apple introduces the Macintosh SE and the Macintosh II.
1987	IBM introduces the PS/2 family of microcomputers.

The Computer Age

The Intel 80386 Microprocessor

The Apple Macintosh II

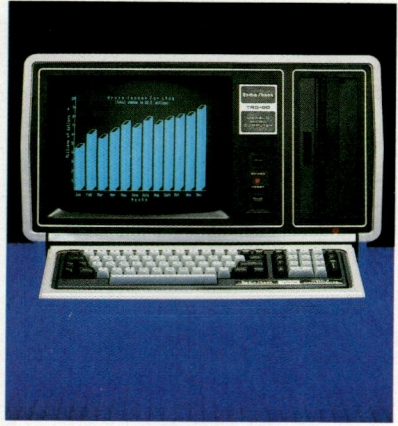
The TRS-80 Model II

The IBM PC

Compaq I, and laptop computers, beginning with the **Workslate,** allow employees to take their computers with them when attending meetings or visiting customers and clients. Still, it wasn't until IBM introduced its own laptop computer, the **PC Convertible,** that the laptop computer began to be accepted by business. Today, very little, if any, computing power is "lost" when using a portable such as the **Compaq Portable III** or a laptop such as the **Toshiba 3100.**

The appearance of microcomputers using 32-bit microprocessors, such as Motorola's **68020** chip and Intel's **80386** chip, are finally enabling microcomputers to operate software in a fashion similar to larger computer systems. Among the first 32-bit microcomputers are Compaq's **Deskpro 386,** Apple's **Macintosh II,** and IBM's **PS/2 Model 80.** However, the main impact of IBM's PS/2 family of microcomputers, which spans the full range of **Intel** processors, will likely be the ease with which it can be integrated with a business' departmental and mainframe computer systems, thus truly "closing the loop" in business computing. Another impact, although not as significant, is the use of 3¼-inch disk drives in the PS/2 microcomputers, which should provide the momentum for finally moving the microcomputer industry to adopt this better (that is, smaller, more durable, greater disk capacity) technology.

While hardware advances brought about the microcomputer, it was the usefulness of its software that thrust the microcomputer into the business world. Electronic spreadsheet and word processing software provided immediate and significant benefits to business users. As a result, **VisiCalc** was largely responsible for many Apple II sales to businesses, and **Lotus 1-2-3** had much to do with the early success of the IBM PC.

Another key development in the computer industry relating to software was the merging of the office systems and computer systems industries. This merger moved slowly, as firms selling word processing systems

AT&T announces its entry into the computer industry.

The Apple Macintosh SE

added electronic components to their products. Many of the early office automation firms, such as Wang, now sell general-purpose computer systems, and a broad range of office automation software is available on computer systems of all sizes. This merging of related technologies continues today, with both desktop publishing and business graphics becoming increasingly common on microcomputers. If anything, this movement to place most office-related functions on microcomputer workstations will continue at an even faster rate with the 32-bit microcomputers.

An Office Computer System by Wang

The Computer Age ■ **249**

The IBM PS/2 Family

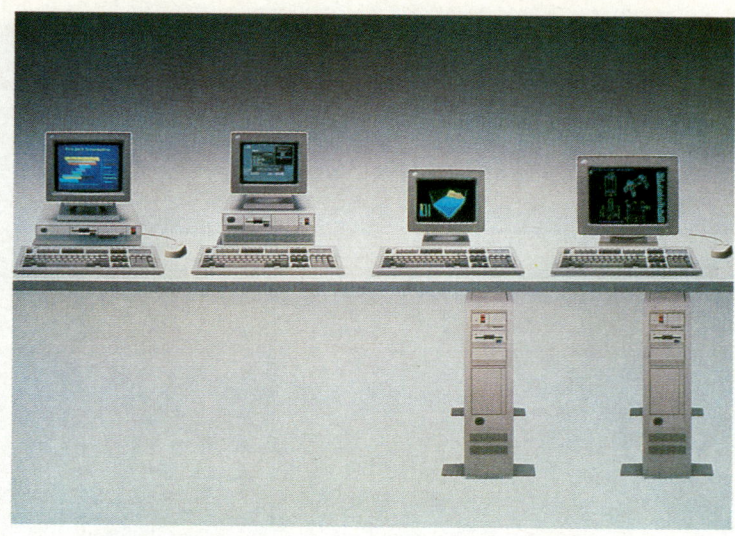

The Toshiba 3100

The Compaq Portable III

Hardware

With VLSI technology, computer processor speeds and primary memory capacities have greatly increased. Computers of all sizes are getting smaller and more powerful, enabling an increasing amount of business processing to be "distributed" to smaller computers located in offices, warehouses, plants, desks, and briefcases. While a variety of input and output devices are used, CRT input and paper output still remain the major means of entering and receiving information. Magnetic disks are the most common secondary storage device; however, optical disks promise to gain increased usage as this technology continues to improve and as appropriate applications are identified.

Software

The operating systems on today's larger computers are extremely sophisticated. Microcomputer operating systems, such as Digital Research's **CP/M** and Microsoft's **MS-DOS,** are comparable to those on second generation computers. With primary memory sizes and processor speeds increasing, more powerful microcomputer operating systems, such as AT&T's **UNIX,** have appeared. **OS/2,** the operating system announced by IBM as part of the PS/2 family of microcomputers, promises to move microcomputer operating systems into those available on third generation computers, such as IBM's 360 family of mainframe computers.

While microcomputer operating systems have lagged behind those available on larger computer systems, most advances in applications software have been led by microcomputer software. Microcomputer software is much more "user friendly" than maxicomputer or minicomputer software. The early research on Xerox' Smalltalk project, for example, was used by the designers of Apple's **Lisa** and **Macintosh** microcomputers, but not by software designers for any of the larger computer systems. Microsoft's **Windows** system integrator software package, which has a user interface design similar to that of Apple's products, has been selected by IBM to serve as the "Presentation Manager" within the OS/2 operating environment. One possible outcome of this decision is that this user interface may now become a standard across applications and operating environments for all of IBM's computer systems.

Another software issue of importance has been the development of the **ADA** programming language Just as the U.S. Department of Defense sponsored the design of COBOL to reduce the costs of military data processing, the skyrocketing costs of weapons systems software motivated the Department of Defense to sponsor another design effort in 1975. This new language, named after Charles Babbage's friend and colleague, Ada Augusta Lovelace, is modeled after the Pascal programming language. It is too early to tell whether ADA will become as important to business computing as COBOL became.

Finally decades of academic research in the area of artificial intelligence began to bear fruit. Software packages that provided *natural language* input and output began to appear. Also appearing were software packages that provided *expert systems,* which mimicked the experience, knowledge, and insights of human experts by incorporating the rules used by them in solving problems.

Uses and Users

Computer-based information systems now handle all aspects of business activities. Many firms have become totally dependent on their computers. In these firms, business transactions are often automatically handled through information systems. The increasing use of decision support systems means that many key business decisions are also being made on the basis of computer output. It seems the computer has a place in a corporate boardroom, as well as in an accountant's office.

Improvements in both systems software and applications software have allowed users to become involved with all aspects of business computing. Employees are performing their day-to-day tasks with or through a computer system. Managers and other professional employees are working with spreadsheet, file management, and graphics software to design and develop computer applications without the aid of computer specialists. Managers are buying hardware and software and then managing the computer operations in their own departments. Computer specialists today are becoming true experts who work only on the complex aspects of business computing.

COMPUTER TECHNOLOGY TRENDS

Three technological trends recur throughout the computer's history:

1. The time between the development of a new technology and its practical use is becoming shorter.
2. Computer systems are becoming more intelligent.
3. Computer technology is being made available to more people.

Each of these trends is important for a number of reasons.

As new computer technologies become useful shortly after their development, businesses and their employees face increased pressures. They must keep abreast of new technical developments, and they find themselves having to adjust to technical change on a fairly regular basis.

Intelligent computers are increasingly able to perform more and more of a business' information processing tasks. Many routine tasks can now be handled without human assistance, and more sophisticated tasks are also being trusted to the computer. Business policies on how to best use computers, including when to create human-computer information processing teams, need to be rethought more frequently.

As computer systems become less expensive and easier to use, a larger portion of a firm's employees are becoming computer users. This change affects hiring, promoting, and even career paths for employees. Personnel policies should be revised to reflect this trend.

Summary

The vacuum tube was the primary electronic component used in *first generation* computers. Vacuum tubes were used for the computer system's processing and storage circuitry. Data input was through cards, and data output was produced on either paper or cards. By the end of the first generation, *magnetic core* was used for primary memory, while *magnetic tapes* were used for secondary storage. The major software advance that occurred with first generation computers was the development of *high-level* programming languages, such as *FORTRAN*. Business computing was just getting underway. As few computer specialists were around at this time, most computer use was performed directly by the users themselves.

The *transistor* was the primary electronic component used in *second generation* computers. These small, but reliable, electronic devices led to the development of new electronic hardware, including the *minicomputer* and the *communications satellite*. Second generation computer systems used transistors for processing circuitry, magnetic cores for memory, and magnetic tapes for data input, output, and secondary storage. The first operating systems appeared, and with them *interactive processing, real-time computing,* and *time sharing*. More high-level programming languages were developed, including *COBOL, BASIC,* and *PL/1*.

While business computing had now become commonplace, management applications were just beginning. Computer specialists began to handle most data processing activities.

The *integrated circuit* became the primary electronic component used in *third generation* computers. Solid state circuitry was used for processing circuits and for primary memories, *CRTs* served as input and output devices, and *magnetic disks* gained importance as secondary storage. The operating system was the dominant component within a computer system at this time, as it controlled most operations. Other high-level programming languages were introduced, including *RPG* and *Pascal*. Business information systems were *integrated* through the use of common input and output data files. Management applications were now routine. Computer users, while not directing data processing operations, frequently handled input and output tasks. Most information processing activities, however, remained the domain of computer specialists, who were now being trained in colleges and universities.

Large-scale integration (LSI) and *very large-scale integration (VLSI)* are the primary electronic components of *fourth generation* computers. Hundreds of thousands of electronic circuits now reside on a single silicon chip. The most important electronic device developed has been the *microprocessor*, which led to the development of the *microcomputer*. While microcomputer hardware and operating systems have lagged behind those of larger computer systems, *user friendly* microcomputer applications software has begun to lead the software industry. Computer-based information systems now handle all aspects of business activities. Computer users are again involved with all aspects of business computing.

Review Questions

1. On what are the various computer generations based? Briefly trace the four computer generations.

2. Briefly trace the advances made in programming languages from the early use of machine languages to the present.

3. What major events occurred during the second generation of computers?

4. Briefly describe the most significant developments of the third generation of computers.

5. What development ushered in the fourth generation of computers? What was the significance of this development?

6. Why do applications for a new technology tend to lag behind its appearance? What characteristics mark its first successful use?

7. Briefly discuss the three trends that have recurred throughout the technological history of the computer.

APPENDIX B ■ Selecting a Microcomputer

Like many students, Brent Hogan is a busy person. A second-year student at a community college, he intends to transfer to a four-year university and complete a bachelor's degree in business. He hasn't declared a major yet and is attempting to finish his general curriculum and basic introductory courses, including one on the use of computers. Brent also works part-time delivering auto parts and supplies twenty hours a week. Clearly, Brent has little free time to shop for a computer.

And yet, Brent is beginning to think a microcomputer could actually save him time. One reason he is considering a microcomputer is that everyone else, it seems, is considering buying one. The computer course, television, magazines, friends, and relatives have all made him aware that

■ B Selecting a Microcomputer

anyone can own and operate a microcomputer. A friend of his, a computer science major at a nearby university, bought one last year, and his uncle, a writer on the East Coast, got one for Christmas.

As Brent sits at his desk struggling to type a paper, he remembers his computer text's discussion of word processing and the demonstration his professor arranged. He also remembers his uncle's delight with word processing and the ease with which he can write, revise, and print almost perfect final drafts. Brent also suspects that some of his accounting assignments would be easier to do on a microcomputer.

A few years ago, neither college students nor even most small businesses could consider such a purchase; but now Brent has seen advertisements for microcomputers priced at around $1000. He has saved $800 and is willing to spend it—if it will make his life easier and help him at school. Certainly, the ads promise that a microcomputer can do this. But before he spends his money, Brent wants to be sure.

By now, you may be eager to buy a microcomputer of your own. Yet, at the same time, you may also be unsure of yourself. Should you buy a microcomputer? If so, what kind? Through the following discussion, we want to show you how to use some systematic techniques to simplify your decision. We'll be following Brent through his decision-making process, but the same techniques can easily be applied to your own decision.

Brent plans a career in business, and he values the logic that goes into the development of computer systems, but he is not sure how to apply this logic to his own decision. Does he need to prepare elaborate plans and forms? He decides to ask his friend Amy, who is a computer science major, for help. Amy plans to become a systems analyst, and she just bought a microcomputer last year.

Brent Amy, I need some advice. I think I need a microcomputer, but I don't know where to begin. How do I go about deciding whether I should buy a microcomputer and what kind I should buy?

Amy Your information processing needs probably aren't as complicated as those of most businesses. You may not need to use all of the tools a computer professional would use in making a choice. Start with a project definition. What do you expect from a microcomputer? Or, to put it another way, what kinds of problems do you think a microcomputer could solve for you?

Brent That's easy. My biggest problem is typing. I had four papers to write last term, and typing them—without mistakes—took as long as writing them. I tried a typing service once, but I won't do that again. I had to give them the draft four days before the actual deadline, and they still made mistakes. Some were my fault, but I still had to pay $1.50 a page.

Amy Let's make a list. Problem number one is typing. What else?

Brent Accounting. I think that will be my major, but the homework is driving me crazy. In most of the assignments, I have to prepare sample ledger entries or financial analyses on a spreadsheet. Some figures are given as part of the assignment, and then I have to calculate the figures that should appear on other parts of the spreadsheet. Usually, the figures are related by formulas like "profit = revenue − costs." Often I have to show what happens to the other figures when one basic figure, like revenue, is changed. Make a change—or mistake—in one entry and it always seems to affect other entries. I use up a lot of pencil erasers.

Selecting a Microcomputer

Amy Okay, problem two: mathematical calculations. An electronic spreadsheet should help you there. Are you taking any other courses that use a lot of calculations?

Brent Not right now, but I will probably take more accounting and finance courses in the future.

Amy It's smart to try to anticipate your future needs. You really need to plan for them, as well as for the present; but let's finish with your present needs. Anything else?

Brent I keep thinking that I can use the terminals in the computing center. The problem is that I can never get a terminal when I am free. Working part-time really limits the hours I can go to the center. We had an orientation tour of the facilities, but I still need help in using them. The few times I tried to work at the center, I couldn't finish my assignment. If I had my own microcomputer, I could start whenever it was convenient, stop in the middle to go to work, and work as long as I needed to finish an assignment. That would really help.

■ "I think I need a microcomputer, but I don't know where to begin."

Amy Yes, it does. I like having my own microcomputer. I used to spend a lot of nights waiting in line at the computing center, so I know what you go through. It seems problem number three is schedule and convenience, both important if you want to go to school and hold down a part-time job. Anything else?

Brent I sure could have used a microcomputer last spring, when I was in charge of the alumni run. It was chaotic! I was up until 3 A.M. addressing mailers, and then I had to organize the entries. I'll probably be asked to help with it again. Could word processing be used in a situation like that, or do I need some sort of data management software?

Amy That's hard to say right now. Let's just list it as problem four: mailing list and organizing entries. Anything else?

Brent Not right now, but I know I will have other problems in the future. I'll be applying to four-year schools soon and some of them require autobiographies and essays. If I had word processing software, maybe I could write one autobiography and just use it again and again. Then I will have to write a résumé. Actually, I'm thinking I might try to get a better job next semester and I will need a résumé for that, too. And when I start my job, I know that having experience on a microcomputer will be a plus. I might want to have my own microcomputer at home, just in case I take a job with a small firm or don't have a microcomputer at the office. I guess this is the point where I start to get confused. If I just had to buy a microcomputer for now, I think it would be relatively simple, but I don't know for sure what my major will be or even where I will be working next year.

Amy In some ways, selecting a microcomputer for your own use is more complicated than developing an information system for a major corporation. You want to use the microcomputer to accomplish some very different tasks, and each task is like a different information system; but don't worry—that's the beauty of computers. They are general-purpose machines. Change the software, and you change the information the computer can produce. With the right software, one microcomputer can meet all of your needs now and maybe even in the future.

I had trouble planning for the future, too. Since computers are going to be my career, I needed a powerful computer, but at a reasonable price. Because prices keep dropping every year, I really wondered if I should wait. The best advice I got was to weigh the benefit of having the microcomputer to use now against the money I might save if I waited. I decided to buy, and I haven't regretted it.

Okay, let's sum up your "project definition." You need a microcomputer to solve four problems: typing papers, mathematical calculations, schedule/convenience, running club mailing list and organizing entries. For the future, you have "complete college applications, write and revise résumé, use on job."

Brent I know that I can probably find a microcomputer that will solve my problems, and I know I will use it. That just leaves the big question: can I afford to buy it?

Amy Some of the microcomputers cost a few hundred dollars, but many are awkward and slow for anything other than games or educational software. The kind of software you need may not even be available for the less-expensive microcomputers. Other microcomputers are as powerful as minicomputers, but their prices are usually over a thousand dollars and often closer to three thousand; and you may want to buy peripherals, like a printer or modem. How much money do you have to spend? We could make out a statement of your finances. I know that helped me.

Brent I'm ahead of you there. I've been looking at this a lot lately. I can come up with over $1400 in cash, counting my tax refund, but that would totally deplete my emergency fund. I don't think I want to leave myself that low, but I've been thinking. I doubt that I can get a loan from a bank, but my church has a credit union, and so does the auto parts store. My savings are split between those two places. Usually, credit unions are pretty good about giving low-interest loans to members. Of course, if my parents cosign, I might be able to get credit from a computer store, but I'd rather not do that. I might be able to get a loan from my uncle. He said he would help me if I ever needed it, and this might qualify.

Amy You might also ask at your school. One of the reasons I chose my computer was that my school was offering a student's discount on a model that met my needs.

Brent I'll do that, and, as a last resort, I could make a down payment and pay something each month. So it looks like I might be able to afford a microcomputer. For right now, let's assume I can. What next?

Amy Next, you prepare a list of requirements. List the functions you need a microcomputer to perform for you; but before you do that, you need to get some more information. I can save you some work by telling you that word processing and electronic spreadsheet software will probably meet most of your current needs. You need to do some reading and ask questions to make sure. Also, you'll find that there are lots of word processing packages and good spreadsheet packages. Each of them offers slightly different functions. You'll have to decide which functions are important to you.

One place you might start is your computer textbook. In looking through the table of contents I see that it has a lot of relevant information about microcomputers. For example, Chapter 2 and Part Three both describe the most popular types of microcomputer software packages used in business.

You can also check some other sources. One good source of free advice is microcomputer owners. Another is your school. Even though the computing center is always busy, sometimes they offer seminars on choosing a microcomputer. My school did. If nothing else, the computing center gives you the chance to experiment with various brands of software and hardware. You'll want to do this before you make a final decision.

Another advantage of the campus computer center is that it may have resources usually available only to computer professionals. For example, our computer center subscribes to two services that rate hardware and software: Datapro Research and Auerbach. These services are expensive, but they publish books, newsletters, and updates regularly. I had to make an appointment to use them, but they did help.

Brent You keep mentioning software. I don't have the microcomputer yet!

Amy Remember, the software determines what the microcomputer can do for you. You have to find out what software can do to help you solve your problems.

Brent So where do I look, besides the text and maybe the computing center?

Amy You might get more relevant information from some of the computer magazines, especially the advertisements. *Personal Computing, Popular Computing,* and *Business Computer Systems* are good because they're somewhat general. Other magazines are written for owners of particular computers, like *PC World* for IBM PC owners, *Compute* for Commodore owners, *Macworld* for Macintosh owners, and *A+* for Apple owners. I can lend you some of my issues, if you want them, or you can check at the library. Read some of the product reviews to get an idea of what professional computer reviewers look for, and study the ads to see what's available. You might also look for the annual and quarterly buying guides some of these magazines offer. They list all possible types of products with information about their features, requirements, and prices. The features are what you are interested in right now.

It's a good idea to check the *Readers' Guide to Periodical Literature* for articles that have appeared in general-interest magazines, like *Consumer Reports.* Articles written for a general audience sometimes give you a better overview of available features than articles written for specialized audiences. Another source is the *Business Periodicals Index.*

After you do some reading, you need to talk to other people. Ask micro owners what was important to them when they chose particular software. Or better yet, ask them what they don't like, and why. Most micro owners love to talk about that sort of thing. Another strategy is to go to a computer store. Tell the sales representative you think you want to buy a microcomputer and see what kinds of questions you are asked.

■ **B** Selecting a Microcomputer

Brent Won't a sales representative be biased? What if I ask the wrong questions?

Amy Sales representatives may be biased, but a good computer store will try to meet your needs; and, if the personnel aren't helpful before you buy, they probably won't be helpful after you give them your money. Don't worry about asking the wrong questions, either. When you are making a large purchase, there are no wrong questions. Let's get together in another two weeks. You'll have had time to do some research and we can go over your list of requirements and your system design.

Brent Wait a minute—how do I design a system?

Amy The requirements describe the functions you need to perform. For example, you need to type four papers. So the function you require is easy correcting of typing mistakes. You might also want a program that can proofread your paper. Maybe you organize your paper as you write it and find that you want to reorder whole paragraphs. Then that is a function you need. Think about organizing the alumni run, and the other things you do for the running club. For instance, will you be mailing the newsletter and special announcements to members and alumni? The body of the letter or newsletter stays the same, but the name and address on each copy changes. So, addressing a mailing would be a function you'd require. Another function you might need is the ability to print papers and mailing labels.

When you are ready to do your systems design, you will translate the functions you require into the capabilities offered by existing software. The type of software you will need will show you the type of hardware you will need to buy. For example, all software requires a minimum amount of primary memory, and some software requires two disk drives. These hardware requirements will play a major part in your choice of a microcomputer. Some functions will translate directly into hardware requirements. For example, the ability to print means you will need a printer. These general software and hardware requirements make up your systems design. When you are ready to acquire your system, you'll be trying to choose among specific software packages and microcomputers.

Brent By then I should know what I really need. Thanks for your help, Amy.

> "Your goal now is to get an idea of what software and hardware are available."

Brent asked the questions and did the research Amy had suggested. They met again, as arranged, two weeks after their first meeting.

Brent Amy, I think you'll be impressed. I have both a list of requirements and a system design down on paper. I still have some questions, though. You said I would probably need word processing and a spreadsheet, and I think you're right. I'm still not sure what kind of software I need to handle the running club work. A data base management system would be nice, but a mail merge package that will let me maintain a list of names and addresses, plus some additional information like standings, might work just as well. Most packages would either let me print out the list by itself, on mailing labels for the running club newsletter, or combine the names and addresses with a form letter to produce a customized letter. This could come in handy when I start applying to other schools or looking for a job after I graduate. Other than finding out about mail merge, it took me over a week to reach the conclusion you came to in five minutes: I definitely need word processing and an electronic spreadsheet. So please tell me, what did I gain?

Amy A lot, Brent. By now, you are a lot more confident about the ways a microcomputer can help you, and you are able to make a more realistic prediction of how much you will have to spend for a microcomputer—software and hardware—that will meet your needs.

Brent So, this is a good time to review my requirements and system design.

Amy Right. You should do that on your own, because from this point; the decisions become pretty personal. I can give you my opinion, but when it comes to spending hard-earned cash, you'll want to do it your way. This is where all of your effort begins to pay off. You will still have to do some research, but it will be more specific than before. You went to your textbook, to magazines, to buyers' guides, and to computer stores just to get an idea of what was available. Now that you have a sense of what is available and what you need, you're ready to narrow your options. You're ready to evaluate specific features and prices.

Brent Actually, I started forming some opinions this past week, but the problem comes when I try to put the pieces together. One word processing package might sound good, but it is not available for the microcomputer I thought I wanted. Where do I start?

Amy Always start with your software. I brought along a software checklist that helped me when I started seriously shopping. You might find it helpful.

Brent How does it work?

Amy As you can see, I made out a separate sheet for each type of software package I thought about buying. One of the entries you need to pay special attention to is the brand and model of microcomputer the package is offered for. This fact will have a big effect on your choice of a microcomputer. Ditto for the operating system required.

Brent Does that mean that I can choose any computer whose ads say it uses the "right" operating system for my software?

Amy Not necessarily. Because of legal restrictions, manufacturers often have to make minor changes to their products. These changes may cause software to perform differently, or not at all. This is what makes compatibility such a tricky issue for microcomputer buyers. There are at least a couple of ways to deal with this problem, though. First, you can buy the brand of microcomputer the software was written for. Second, you can identify the software you want and ask a computer store to demonstrate the software on the brand of microcomputer that is supposed to be compatible.

Brent So the software decisions I make start to limit some of my hardware choices.

■ **B** Selecting a Microcomputer

Software Package Comparison Sheet

	A	B	C	D
Offered for which micros?				
Operating system?				
Memory requirements?				

Ease of use
    Reputation
    Personal experience				

Support
    Documentation
    Telephone hot line?
    Training? (free?)				

Special features				
Related packages				
Total price of software and support				

Amy To some extent, yes. Some of the most popular software packages are available for a number of microcomputer brands and for the two most popular operating systems, CP/M and MS-DOS. Getting back to the software checklist, minimum primary memory requirements are an important consideration. Some programs are very powerful, but they need a lot of primary memory; and primary memory is something you need to consider when you select a microcomputer.

Brent Since all of the software reviews give this information, I expect I can do a lot of shopping in the comfort of my own home. What about the software shopping list entry, "Ease of use: reputation and personal experience"?

Amy You can judge a software package's reputation from reviews and from talking to users; but to decide if you like the software, you have to try it. This means going to the campus computer center or back to the store to see if it has the software you are considering. You won't be able to take the software home or use it for an unlimited amount of time, but most stores will help you try a particular software package.

Brent To save time, I expect I should narrow my choices down to two or three packages before I ask for any demonstrations. When I get to that point, what should I be looking for?

Selecting a Microcomputer

Amy Several things. First, look over your list of requirements to get an idea of the functions you will be using most often. Experiment with them. To use some functions, some software packages require that you hit several keys in sequence. Others require only one or two keystrokes. The difference may not seem significant until you spend several hours at your micro. After the third hour, you may appreciate the more convenient package.

Also, look at the way the software uses menus and commands. A menu saves you the labor of memorizing commands and options. Some software packages always show the menu. Others let you call up the menu only when you need it.

Brent I think I would want the menu there all the time.

Amy At first, you may. Most menus take up a significant portion of the screen, however. Once you learn some of the commands, you may decide you want to see more of your document or spreadsheet and not the menu. Look at the commands the software package uses, too. To save space in memory, most of the commands are made up of two or three letters. These commands should use mnemonics, memory cues that help you learn the commands, so you don't need the menus. For example, pressing a special key called the control key and the "d" key might tell the microcomputer to "delete" a character, word, or paragraph. If you memorize the command, you save the time spent giving the command for a menu and waiting for it to appear; and the sooner you learn the commands, the sooner you will feel comfortable with your software. That means that you will be able to concentrate on the problems you expect the micro to solve, not on the hardware and software.

Brent So once I learn the package, I should be able to do more in less time. How much time should it take to learn a software package?

Amy It depends on you and the support you get from the manufacturer, the store, and other users. Be sure you look at the documentation when you take your "test drive." Some software packages now include tutorials with simple lessons to show you the basic functions. Others offer a telephone hot line to technical experts that will talk you through specific problems. Some stores will include a free orientation lesson in the price of a microcomputer purchase, while other stores charge for the lesson.

Brent So the time to investigate this is before I buy?

Amy Definitely. A final entry on the software checklist concerns features. For example, some word processing packages can handle footnotes and others cannot. You will have to rate this particular feature as essential, preferable, or optional. If you want to, you can assign each feature a numerical value and compare the software package scores.

Brent So I could make out a checklist entry for each package and then compare them side by side. Then I could arrange a test drive of just the packages that scored above a certain number. What does "related packages available" mean?

Amy When I was shopping for software, I wanted to look at some of the "integrated packages," like Lotus 1-2-3. An integrated package combines the equivalent of several software packages in one package. I changed the entry to "related packages available" when I found out that some software companies offer add-on packages. For example, WordStar has been a top-selling word processing package for years. You can also buy a related proofreading program called SpellStar, a related spreadsheet called Calc-Star, and a related mail merge program called MailMerge. The advantage is that you can add packages as your budget allows and still have the convenience of knowing that your word processing package can print a spreadsheet in the middle of a page, if you need that capability.

Brent I might. I definitely know I am on a tight budget. I see you have some entries for comparison shopping. I've been looking at price all along. The mail-order houses seem to offer lower prices, but is it a good idea to order from them?

Amy It depends. There are a couple of issues to consider. One is the kind of support you need versus the kind of support the software company offers. Mail-order houses don't charge as much as retail stores, but they don't offer the same kind of support either. Another issue to consider is the fact that some retail stores will offer you a lower price if you buy the software bundled with the hardware.

You might also want to look into "user-supported software" or "public domain software." In the early days of microcomputers, almost everyone wrote and shared programs. Some software developers carry on that tradition. They will send you their program on a diskette and, if you like it, either ask you to send a modest sum or to buy their manual explaining how to use the program.

Brent That could really save me money. Some of the programs are really expensive, and I know that software companies prohibit users from borrowing programs from one another.

> ∴ "Once you've selected your software, you will know your hardware requirements."

Amy I can see their point. Some of these software packages take thousands of hours and many people to develop. They have a right to make money from their investment. The important point is that you need to choose software that will be valuable to you, and the value of software depends on the functions it performs for you. You may find a very inexpensive program that does everything you need.

Brent So once I've selected software that meets my needs, I'll be ready to "acquire" my hardware. I can see now that the software I choose will affect my hardware choices.

Amy That's right. Once you've selected your software, you will know your hardware requirements. In some cases, the software you choose will limit your hardware options to machines that use a particular operating system, such as CP/M or MS-DOS. In a few cases, the same software package may be offered in slightly different versions for different operating systems. Choosing can be hard. There are literally thousands of software packages available for each of the most popular microcomputer operating systems.

Brent Since I'm going to major in business, am I limited in the kind of machine I buy?

Selecting a Microcomputer

Amy Not at all. Some business-oriented software packages are available for almost every type of microcomputer. You might also consider portable computers, or laptop computers, or even notebook computers. These computers were designed for business professionals who are away from their offices. Most of these types of microcomputers are less expensive than the typical microcomputer, which can crowd the top of a desk. Some of the portables include a small monochrome monitor or CRT, a generous amount of primary memory, two disk drives, and a keyboard in a case that weighs around 35 pounds. The advantage is that you do not need to buy a monitor or disk drives, since these are included in the package. The disadvantage is that the manufacturer chooses these peripherals for you.

Brent So I need some way to systematically compare microcomputers.

Amy True. Here is another chart that helped me. I used it to compare the price of a basic microcomputer plus the options I needed. In some ways, buying a microcomputer is like buying a car. On some models, a certain

Microcomputer Comparison Sheet

	A	B	C	D

Basic price
    Retail
    Discount				

Primary memory
    RAM capacity
    Price				

Disk drives
    Number
    Storage capacity
    Optional? Price?				

CRT
    Monochrome/color
    Optional? Price?				

Printer
    Speed
    Quality
    Price
    Flexibility				

Other items needed?
    Modem? Price?
    Mouse? Price?				

Total price of hardware configuration				

feature may be standard. On other models, the same feature may mean an additional cost. When you buy a computer, the little extras can add up fast. For example, most microcomputers will let you expand the size of memory up to certain limits, but that is an additional expense.

Brent Price is certainly important to me. I've been watching the newspaper for sales. How do I know a price is a good one?

Amy One way is to know the manufacturer's suggested retail price. Another is to check the advertisements that mail-order houses run in the computer magazines. These can be a good reference, although most mail-order houses do not offer the kind of support I know I need. Also, some manufacturers and stores will combine or bundle a microcomputer with certain software packages. If you happen on the right combination, you can save a lot of money this way.

Brent That's good to know. What should I know about choosing a monitor?

Amy First, is the price of the monitor included in the price of the microcomputer? If it isn't, you may have to spend another two to four hundred dollars. Some microcomputers are designed to use a television set as a monitor, but there are drawbacks if you plan to use the microcomputer for complex applications. Second, you need to decide if you want a color or a monochrome monitor. A color monitor is good if you want to do elaborate graphics or play games. Some users feel that a monochrome monitor, whether it is green or amber, is easier on their eyes, however. The important issue here is choosing a monitor you will be comfortable with. After all, you may spend a lot of time staring at your spreadsheets.

The same goes for the keyboard. In most cases, you don't have a choice in the keyboard. For example, some keyboards are built into the housing of the computer itself. Other keyboards are attached to the computer processor by a coiled cord. This feature lets you move the keyboard to a convenient distance from the computer itself. Some keyboards tilt, which also makes them easier to use for long periods. Another useful feature is special keys for moving the cursor around the screen. Without cursor control keys, you may have to hit two or three separate keys. Some people like to use a mouse to do the same thing. A mouse, which is standard on the Macintosh, is a little boxlike control on rollers. Roll the mouse to the left and the cursor moves to the left. Some keyboards offer an entire bank of special keys, called the function keys, which can be used just to enter commands, not data. For example, pressing a single function key may issue the same command as three letter keys pressed in succession. Again, these are matters of convenience.

Brent What I'm interested in is the numeric keypad, the separate bank of keys that is laid out like the keyboard of a calculator. I'm sure I want this feature on my microcomputer. What about a printer? A computer is of no use unless I can print the results of my spreadsheet.

Amy The printer was an important issue for me, too. I decided I was facing one basic question: did I need a dot matrix printer or a letter quality printer? Dot matrix means that each letter is formed of small dots, like the time and temperature signs outside a bank. A letter-quality printer works more like a typewriter, but it is usually slower and more expensive than a dot matrix printer. An issue you'll want to consider is the width of your

printer carriage. My printer accepts paper that is 8½ inches wide, but you may need a printer that accepts wider paper if you are going to be printing spreadsheets. In any case, your research will show you which features are available and important to you. Then you'll be able to make a decision.

Of course, you might be able to save some money by not buying a printer. If your equipment is compatible, you may be able to use a printer at your school's computing center. At my school, any student can use the computing center equipment to print a document for a small hourly charge and an additional charge per page. I printed a term paper for about five dollars.

Another purchase you need to plan for is supplies, like diskettes and fanfold paper. You need to have plenty of diskettes so that you can make backup copies of all of your original software and important data files. You probably know that a backup should always be on a separate diskette, just in case something happens to your original. You can save some money by purchasing some of these supplies by mail through discount houses.

Brent I'm not certain just when I'll buy software and a microcomputer, but I think I have some good ideas for implementing my system. The main task of systems implementation is training and starting to use the new system. After all, I'll have researched training while I am researching my possible purchase, so it should be easy to get my computer system operating.

Amy I hope so. You really should allow lots of time to familiarize yourself with the software and the microcomputer. Sometimes I think computers are governed by Murphy's Law: "If anything can go wrong, it will." If you are hurrying or trying to meet a deadline, the chance you will make mistakes increases. And some mistakes can erase a lot of hard work.

Even if you do buy a microcomputer and printer, don't give up your typewriter. If your printer breaks down, your typewriter is a good backup. Also, you'll need your typewriter to fill out application forms. This is almost impossible to do with a microcomputer and printer.

Brent So I'm still facing the big decision: to buy or not to buy?

Amy No major purchase decision is easy. Anyway, if you have more questions, you can always get answers by checking either your textbook or magazines, or by asking a sales representative at a computer store.

Major purchases are never easy, but Amy helped Brent see how a systematic approach could simplify his decision. We work with computers and are aware of the important role the microcomputer has played and will continue to play in the information society.

GLOSSARY/INDEX

A

Ablative method: Method of recording data in which a hole is burned into the disk surface with a laser beam, 81
Absolute address, 148-49
Access time: Amount of time it takes from the point of requesting data until the data are retrieved, 79
Accounting: Financial transactions involved with business activities, 29
Accounts payable: Business activity of paying suppliers, 28
Accounts receivable: Business activity of receiving and processing customer payments, 28
Adjustment, of relative formulas, 145
Aldus Corporation, 173
Algorithms: Step-by-step instructions given to a computer that lead to the same result every time, 48
Alphanumeric: Presented in the form of letters, digits, and special characters, 69
Alphanumeric printers, 73
    character formation, 73-74
    character transfer, 74-75
    characters printed at a time, 75-76
ALU. *See* Arithmetic-logic unit (ALU)
Analog signals: Type of continuous wave pattern, 203
Apple Macintosh, 173
Applications software: Programs that can perform specific user-oriented tasks, 12
Arithmetic-logic unit (ALU): Unit that contains the electronic circuits that perform data processing operations, 10, 49
Arithmetic operations: Operations such as addition, subtraction, multiplication and division, 17
Arrow keys: Keys used to facilitate the movement of the cursor, 66
Artificial Intelligence Corporation, 226
Ascending sort, 186
ASCII (American Standard Code for Information Interchange), 55
ASCII text files, 195
Asynchronous mode: Means of transmitting data one character at a time, 205
AT&T, 200
Autodial, 212
Automatic recalculation, 130

B

Backlog: Waiting list, 220
Backspace key, 93, 111
Backup: Duplicate set of computer-readable data or equipment that is used only when the original data or equipment is damaged, lost, or destroyed, 102-3
Balance sheet, 29
Band print mechanism: Print mechanism used in computer printing, 74
Bar graph, 161-64
Baudot, Émile, 203
Baud rate: Term used in telecommunication to describe the data rate, 203
Belt print mechanism: Print mechanism used in computer printing, 74
Bidirectional printer: Printer which prints right to left and then left to right, 75-76
Binary files, 212
Binary number system: Number system that is limited to the use of 1 and 0; it corresponds to the two-state nature of the computer system, 54-55
Bit: Smallest piece of data, 54
Bit density: Measurement of bits in terms of the number of bits per inch, 78-79
Bit-map display: Display in which each individual pixel is addressable, 70
Bubble method: Method of recording data in which the optical disk surface is heated by a laser beam until a bubble forms, 82
Buffer, 112
Built-in functions, 131-32
Buses: Electronic highways inside a computer used to send signals between functional units, 60
Business computing, 26
  for accounting, 29
  for buying and selling, 28-29
  cost-benefit analysis of use of, 43-45
  crisis in, 220-21
  decision support system in, 32-33
  information reporting systems, 32
  interaction between information systems in, 33-34
  for manufacturing, 27
  for office work, 29
  personal computers in, 35-45
  reasons for growth of, 24-25
  transaction processing cycle, 31-32

Business graphics: Software that transforms primary memory into an electronic drawing board, 38-39
Business professional: Employee who holds an information occupation that requires judgment, such as manager, planning analyst, legal specialist, or engineer, 35
Bus network topology: Network pattern formed when each hardware device is connected to a common cable, 209
Byte: Combination of bits that may be used to represent a character, 55

C

Calculations, performance of, 186-87
Carrier signal: Basic analog signal used to transmit data over telecommunication lines, 202-4
Cartridges, 83-84
Cassette tapes, 84
Cathode-ray tube (CRT): Terminal screen using cathode-ray tube technology to display a visual image, 69-70
Cells: Points of intersection between rows and columns in an electronic spreadsheet, 36
  hidden, 153
  protection of, 153
  in a spreadsheet, 124
Centering, of text, 116
Central processing unit (CPU): Computer hardware that interprets and executes program instructions; it consists of the control unit and the arithmetic-logic unit, 10, 25, 49
Centronics, 202
Chain print mechanism: Print mechanism used in computer printing, 74
Character data, 180
Checksum method, 213
Chip: Silicon materials(s) containing electronic circuitry, 3
CHKDSK command, 98
CHOOSE function, 152
Circuit boards, 57
Clock: Support device by which events in a computer can be sequenced, 60
CLOUT, 192-93
Color monitor: Monitor that uses a triad of red, green, and blue phosphor dots to display various colors: RGB monitors use three electron guns—one for each color, 70
Column formatting, 195
Comma formatting, 195
Command-line operating system, 100
Commands, 94
  CHKDSK, 98
  COPY, 98-99
  DIR (directory), 95-96
  ERASE, 97
  FORMAT, 94-95
  PRINT, 99-100
  RENAME, 97
  TYPE, 97
Communication channel: Path along which data can be transmitted between the sending and receiving devices, 206
Communications software: Software that electronically links a personal computer to another computer system, 40-41
Communication support system (CSS), role of, 209-10
COMPAQ, 72
Comparison column, 150
Composite video monitor: Monitor that uses one electron gun to turn on the appropriate combination of red, green, and blue phosphor dots within each triad to display color, 70
CompuServe, 213
Computer: Set of electromechanical and electronic devices designed to process information signals, 9. *See also* Microcomputer; Personal computer
  capabilities of, 14-21
  problem solving with, 48-49
Computer literacy: An understanding of what computers are, how computers work, and what computers do, 6
  progress in achieving, 26
Computer processing, 49-51
Computer processor: Main component of a computer system, consisting of the central processing unit (CPU) and primary memory, 10-11
Computer-readable form: Form with data that can be captured quickly and accurately, 16
Computing literacy: Ability to use the computer as a tool to enrich personal and professional life, 2-5, 6-7

Control panel, 126-27
Control unit (CU): Unit that contains the electronic circuits that direct and coordinate the processing activities, 10-11, 49
COPY command, 98-99, 146-47
Copying formulas, for electronic spreadsheets, 144-49
Cost-benefit analysis of business computing, 43-45
CP/M operating system, 90
CPU. See Central processing unit (CPU)
Criterion, 182
Crosstalk, use of, to communicate with The Source, 214-16
CRT. See Cathode-ray tube (CRT)
Current cell pointer, 124
Cursor: Blinking symbol that shows where the next entered character will appear, 107
   moving, 108
Cyclic Redundancy Coding (CRC): Error check code often used in synchronous transmission, 206

D

Daisy-wheel print mechanism: Print mechanism used in computer printers in which each "petal" contains an embossed character, 74
Data: Symbols used to represent facts, events, or things, 9
   coding, for computer use, 51, 54
   output of, 43
   storage and retrieval of, 18-19, 42-43
Data base: Integrated collection of data items that can be retrieved in any combination necessary to produce needed information, 32
Data base management system (DBMS): System that allows the programmer to access data by specifying only the data items that are needed, 178-98
   forms, 192
   natural language interface, 192-93
   programming, 189-92
   restructuring, 189
Data communication: Movement of data from one location to another. See also Telecommunication
   carrier signals, 202-4
   choosing a program for, 216-17
   communication channels, 206

communication support software, 209-10
data packets, 205-6
external data paths, 200-202
local area networks, 206-9
using Crosstalk in, 214-16
using a microcomputer in, 210-14
Data dictionary: Complete description of the characteristics of a data base, 187-89
Data-driven graphics, 158-59
   bar graph, 161-64
   dedicated graphics, 165-69
   line graph, 164-65
   pie chart, 159-61
   spreadsheet graphics, 159
Data encoding schemes, 55
Data encryption: Technique for converting data into a scrambled form, 209-10
Data field: Collection of related characters, 19
Data file: Organized set of related data items, 19
Data General DG/One, 72
Data input, 14-16, 41
Data item: Collection of related characters, 178
Data labels, 163
Data management software: Support software used to provide an easier way for a programmer to create and maintain files and to retrieve data from them, 178
   choosing, 196
   creating, 180-81
   joining function, 184
   for the microcomputer, 179, 187-95
   performing calculations, 186-87
   projecting, 182
   retrieval of files, 182-84
   selecting function, 182-84
   sorting function, 185-86
   updating files, 182
Data packet: Means of sending data in a telecommunication network; start and stop information, origin and destination information, and error check bits are added to the encoded data, 20-21, 205-6
Data processing, 17-18, 42
Data rate: Speed of telecommunication link, 203
Data record: Complete set of data describing each item, such as a part, an employee, or a customer, for which data is being stored within a data file, 19

Data transfer rate: Rate at which data can be transferred between peripheral and primary memory, 79
Data types: General classes of data that are processed by computer systems in particular ways, 180
Dataword length: Number of bits of data that can be retrieved from memory each machine cycle, 59
dBASE III Plus, 180, 181, 193
Decimal data, 180
Decision support system: System that allows management to produce management reports in an *ad hoc* fashion, 32-33
Dedicated graphics, 158-59, 165-69
De facto standard: Standard informally accepted by vendors, generally because it has come to dominate a market segment of the business, 90
Default drive, 92
Default value, 187
Descending sort, 186
Desktop computers: Computer system small enough to fit on a desktop, 4
Desktop organizers: Integrated software that allows a business professional to juggle several small tasks simultaneously with a larger task, 224-25
Desktop publishing: Design and production of stylized documents that combine text and graphics using a personal computer and laser printer, 158, 173
   creating publications, 173
   manipulating text, 173-74
   page layout, 174-75
Digital Research, CP/M operating system, 90
Digital signals: Discrete pattern of impulses generated by on/off or high/low electrical signals to represent 1s and 0s, 203
Dip switches, 214
DIR (directory) command, 95-96
Disk drive: Input device that reads data from or transfers data to a disk or diskette, 11, 61
Diskette: Small, flexible mylar plastic disk coated with magnetic oxide; diskettes are available in a variety of physical sizes, all of which are designed to be removable, 77, 80-81
Document, 106
   correcting, 108-9
   deleting text from, 110-12
   editing, 107-13

   formatting, 113-17
   management, 117-19
   printing, 117
Dot-addressable display: Display in which each individual pixel is addressable, 70
Double-density diskette: Diskette on which data are recorded at twice the normal density, 80
Double-sided diskette: Diskette on which data can be recorded on both the top and bottom surfaces, 80
Dow Jones News/Retrieval Service, 213
Download: Transfer of data from a larger computer to a smaller computer, 40, 212
DVORAK keyboard: Alternative keyboard where the most frequently used keys are placed in the home row and arranged for efficient use of both hands, 65

E

EBCDIC (Extended Binary Coded Decimal Interchange Code), 55
Editors, 100-101
Electrically Erasable Programmable ROM (EEPROM): Chips that can be modified through the use of electrical signals without removing them from the computer, 59
Electromechanical devices: Computer hardware built from both electronic and electromechanical parts, 9
Electronic bulletin board, 213-14
Electronic mail: Process of sending messages electronically from one microcomputer to another, 207
Electronics Industries Association, 202
Electronic spreadsheet: Software that divides a terminal screen into a table of rows and columns, with a means of performing the mathematical calculations involved in answering "what if" questions, 36, 124
   adding and removing rows and columns, 133-34
   automatic recalculation, 130
   built-in functions, 131-32
   changing column widths, 136-37
   CHOOSE function, 152
   choosing, 155
   commands, 137-40

control panel, 126-27
copying formulas, 144-49
creating, 126-32
editing, 133-35
formatting, 135-37
formulas, 127-28
HELP facility, 138-39
IF function, 151-52
keyboard macros, 154
labels, 127, 128-29, 135
LOOKUP function, 149-51
menus, 137-38
moving around, 124-25
moving cells, 134-35
numbers, 127, 128-29, 135-36
printing, 139-40
ranges, 131
saving and retrieving, 140
templates, 152-53
windows, 125-26
Embedded command, 114
End-user, 8
End-user computing: Development of one's own information system by a computer user, 220
  advanced tools in, 226-31
  crisis in business computing, 220-21
  desktop organizers, 224-25
  financial modeling, 228-30
  integrated software, 222-23
  multipurpose tools in, 221-25
  project management, 231
  promoting and managing, 231-33
  QUERY facilities, 226
  report generators, 227-28
  software integrators, 223-24
  statistical analysis, 230
End-user tools: Software packages used in end-user computing, 195
  integration of, 195
Erasable Programmable ROM (EPROM): Chips that can be modified through the use of ultraviolet light, but they must be removed from the computer to do so, 58-59
ERASE command, 97
Expansion slots: Built-in brackets for holding additional circuit boards, 57
Exploding pie chart, 161, 169
External data paths, 200-202

F

Field, 178
File: Collection of similar types of records, 91, 178
File management: Software that transforms secondary storage into an electronic filing cabinet, 39
Fill patterns, 169
Financial modeling system: End-user tool that can perform financial analyses that are far too complicated for an electronic spreadsheet, 228-30
Firmware: Permanently coded instructions within ROM, 57, 103
Flat-panel displays, 71-73
Floppy disk, 11. *See also* Diskette
Format, of document, 38
Formatting commands, 94-95, 113-14
Formulas, 127-28
  entering into spreadsheet, 129-30
Framework, 223
Frontpage, 173
Full-duplex channel: Communication path that allows data to be transmitted in different directions simultaneously, 206
Function keys: Keys used to provide means of commanding certain common tasks in one step, 66

G

General ledger system, 29
Global commands, 139
Global search and replace, 113
Golf ball print mechanism: Print mechanism used in computer printing, 74
Graphics: Pictures or graphs depicting information, 69, 158
Graphics programs, 158
  selecting, 169-70
Graphics terminals, 76-77

H

Half-duplex channel: Communication path that can transmit data in two directions, but only one way at a time, 206
Hard copy: Permanent form of the information that is being displayed on a computer screen, 11, 69
Hard disks: Rigid aluminum platters coated with a magnetic oxide; they come in different physical

sizes and have significantly different storage capabilities, 11, 77, 79-80, 102-3
Hardware: Devices that physically enter, process, store, retrieve, and deliver data and information, 9, 10
   advances in, 24
   computer processor, 10-11
   input devices, 11
   output devices, 11
   secondary storage devices, 11
Hardware maintenance: Technical work involving repair or service of equipment, 44
Harvard Total Project Manager, 231
HELP key, 138-39
Hexadecimal number system: Number system that uses sixteen symbols, 55
Human-computer interface, 64-65

I

IBM
   Graphing Assistant, 166, 167, 168, 169
   PC, 90
   Personal System/2 PCs, 224
IF function, 151-52
Illustration graphics, 158, 170-71
Income statement, 29
Indenting, 115-16
Information: Meaning given to a set of data, 9
Information center: Facility with end-user tools that is staffed by end-user computing specialists who first train and then support business users, 232
Information occupations, 5
Information processing cycle: Stages of input, processing, storage, retrieval, and output, 14
Information reporting systems: Systems that process raw data to produce summary reports that are useful to managers, 32
Information society: Society in which the collection, processing, and distribution of information is the primary source of wealth and work, 2
Information system: System that processes data to produce information, 9. *See also* Management information system (MIS)
   creator role in, 13-14
   user role in, 13
Information utilities, accessing, 213-14
Initialization, 94

Ink-jet technology, 76-77
Input devices: Devices used to move data and information into the primary memory, 11, 14-16, 49, 64-65
   alternatives to keyboards, 66-69
   keyboards, 65-66
Input/output port: Outlet where a peripheral cable is connected to the computer; serial and parallel communication require different types of I/O ports, 201
Insert mode, 110
Integer data, 180
Integrated circuit: Complete electronic circuit contained within a single piece of silicon material, 3
Integrated graphics, 158
Integrated software: Software that combines a number of personal computing tools into one software package, 41, 195, 222-23
Integrity controls, 189
INTELLECT, 226
Intelligence: The apparent capability to act in an informed manner, 5
Interface devices: Devices used to coordinate the flow of electrical signals between two hardware units, 57, 61
Inventory: Supply of goods held in reserve, 28-29
Invisible backlog: Nonvisible waiting list, 220

J

Join function, 184
Joystick, 61, 170
Justification: Spacing that produces fixed paragraph borders, 116-17

K

K: Abbreviation for kilobyte, or 2^{10}, or 1024, bytes, 58
Key: Field that can be used to identify a record, 178
Keyboard: Device for entering data, 61, 65-66
   alternatives to, 66-69
Keyboard macros, 154
Kilo: Prefix that means approximately 1000; in computer usage, 2^{10}, or 1024, 58

L

Label-prefix character, 128
Labels, 127, 169
   entering into spreadsheet, 128
   formatting, 135
Language translator: Program that translates the Englishlike program instructions of a high-level language, such as BASIC or COBOL, into the binary code language of the machine, 89
Laser printers, 77
Legend, 165, 169
Library images, 169-70
Line graph, 164-65
Liquid crystal display (LCD) technology: Technology in which a thin layer of liquid crystal molecules are put between two sheets of glass; when voltage is applied to the liquid crystal in a specific cell, the material turns opaque and blocks light, resulting in a black square, 72-73
Load: Enter the appropriate instructions into the primary memory of a computer, 50
Local area network (LAN): Communication network for transferring data between microcomputers and shared peripherals within a building complex, such as an office or factory, 200, 206-7, 211
   topology, 207-9
Local computer, 212
Logic operations: Complex relational operations, 17
LOOKUP function, 149-51
Lotus 1-2-3, 25, 140, 159, 160, 162, 223

M

Magnetic disk: Rigid metal (hard disk) or flexible plastic ("floppy") disk coated with magnetic material used to store data in the form of magnetic bit patterns, 11, 77-81
Mail-merge programs: Software that links documents with address lists to "mass mail" letters, 106
Management information system (MIS): System that provides managers with information, enabling them to make better decisions and improve job performance, 29, 31
   decision support system, 32-33
   information reporting system, 32
   interaction in, 33-34
   transaction processing system, 31-32
Management report: Information presented to managers to aid them in planning and controlling work activities, 32
Manual axis control, 169
Manufacturing: General term for assembling and delivering completed products, 27
   computer applications in, 27
Margins, 115
Marketing: Business activity that decides what products to offer to consumers and then creates a demand for those products, 28
   computer applications in, 28
Media: Material used to input data into the computer, 11
Menu: List of options available on the computer, 137-38
Menu-driven operating system, 100, 170
Microchip: Silicon material containing electronic circuitry, 3
Microcomputer: Complete computer system built using relatively few microelectronic components, 4, 11. See also Computer; Personal computer
   architecture of, 56-61
   business uses of, 221
   data base management system for, 179, 187-95
   operating systems for, 89-94
Microdiskettes, 81
Microelectronics: Miniaturization of electronic circuits and components, 2-3
   advances in, 3-5
Microprocessor: CPU implemented on a single silicon chip, 3, 59
Microprocessor chips, 3, 59-60
Microsecond: One millionth of a second, 18
Millisecond: One thousandth of a second, 18
Modem: Communication device that enables computer equipment to send and receive digital data over the analog telephone network by using modulation and demodulation techniques, 203, 211-13, 214
   types of, 204
Monochrome monitor: Monitor that can display only one color, such as green or amber, on a black background, 70

Motherboard: Large circuit board containing a collection of chips, generally including the CPU chip and RAM and ROM chips, 57
Mouse: Hand-sized box used to control the cursor and to select functions by moving it around the desktop, 67, 170
MS-DOS (Microsoft Disk Operating System), 90
Multiple sort, 185
Multitasking: Operating system that allows for concurrent tasks, 90

N

Nanosecond: One billionth of a second, 18
Network: Electronic pathway that connects various communication devices, 206
   topologies, 207-9
Numbers, 127
   entering into spreadsheet, 128
   formatting, 135-36
Number system: Method of presenting numbers, 54
Numeric data items: Data that can be mathematically manipulated, 180
Numeric keypad, 66

O

Octal number system: Number system that uses eight symbols, 0 through 7, 55
Office work, 29
Offset value, 151
Operating system (OS): Set of programs that controls and manages the activity of a computer system, 12, 88
   advanced features in, 100-103
   for microcomputers, 89-94
Optical disk, 81-83. *See also* Videodisc
Optical Memory Newsletter, 83
Osborne I, 72
Output devices: Devices used to move data and information out of the primary memory, 11, 49, 69
   cathode-ray tube displays, 69-70
   flat-panel displays, 71-73
   graphics printers/plotters, 73-77
   visual display, 69-73
Overtype mode, 109-10

P

Packaged software, 25
Packed fields, 189
Pagemaker, 173, 174
Parallel transmission, 201
Parity bit: Extra bit that makes the sum of bits representing a character either even or odd; it provides a check for errors that may have occurred during data transmission, 205
Password protection, 188-89
PCDOS (Personal Computer Disk-Based Operating System), 90
PC-FILE 'N REPORT, 196
PC Paintbrush Graphics, 171, 172
Peripheral devices: Devices that are added onto the computer processor, 10
Peripheral interchange program (PIP), 98-99
Personal computer: Computer meant to be used by an individual, 4, 35. *See also* Computer; Microcomputer
   business use of, 35-45
Personal computer support center: Facility with end-user tools that is directed toward microcomputer end-users, 232-33
Pie chart, 159-61
Pixels: Picture elements on a visual display device that can be illuminated, 69
Plotter: Output device that is specialized to produce graphics, 11, 77
Point-of-sale (POS) terminals: Electronic cash register terminals, found in retail operations, that can optically scan merchandise codes, record sales, and process transactions, 59
Precedence, 129
Presentation graphics: Tables, charts, and pictures used in reports, 158, 171-72
Presentation graphics software, 158
Primary key: Field that identifies a unique record, 178
Primary memory: Device that provides temporary storage for all data and information being processed; also the software that directs such processing, 10
Primary memory chips, 57-59
Primary sort order, 185
PRINT command, 99-100
Printer: Device, similar to a typewriter, that uses pa-

per as its output medium, 11, 61
Procedural language, 196
Program: Set of instructions that directs a computer in processing information, 6. *See also* Software
Programmer: Individual who designs and develops computer programs, 14
Projecting, 182
Project manager: Manager responsible for planning and coordinating the tasks to be performed in a systems development project, 231
Prompt: Simple instruction displayed on the computer screen that tells the user what to do next, 93
Prompt line, 126-27
Protected cell, 153
Protocol: Set of rules and procedures used for transmitting data between two hardware devices in a network, 209, 212-13
Pull-down menu, 171
Purchasing: Term for business function of buying and selling, 28

Q

Quad density diskette: Diskette in which data are recorded at four times the normal density, 80
Query, 188
QUERY facilities, 226
Query language: Software that enables end-users to create data bases and then retrieve data to answer specific questions, 196
QWERTY keyboard, 65

R

RAM (Random Access Memory): Memory in which instructions or data can be written into or data can be read out of and transferred to the CPU for processing as needed, 57
Range commands, 139
Ranges, 131
Raster scan: Process of moving a beam of electrons across a screen to create brighter (on) or darker (off) points, 69
R:Base System V, 180, 194, 196
Read/write memory. *See* RAM (Random Access Memory)
Record: A collection of all related data items, 178

REFLEX, 196
Relative address, 148-49
Relative formulas, adjustment of, 145-46
Remote computer, 212
RENAME command, 97
Replication, 146
Report generator: Software that enables users to interactively define data files, to enter and manipulate data, and to produce reports, 193-94, 227-28
Resolution: Measure of the number of pixels that can be addressed on the screen, 70
Retrieve: To access data for use in producing desired information, 118
Return, 93
RGB (red, green, and blue) monitor: Monitor that uses three electron guns to produce color, one gun for each of the red, green, and blue phosphor dots within a triad, 70
Ring network topology: Pattern used to connect hardware devices in which each terminal is connected to two others, 209
ROM (Read Only Memory): Memory that can be used only to read data or written instructions that have been permanently loaded onto a chip, 57
Rothchild, Edward, 83
RS 232-C, 202
Ruler, 115

S

SAS, 230
SAS Institute, Inc., 230
SAVE command, 118
Scaling, 163
Screen colors, 170
Search and replace function, 113
SEARCH command, 112-13
Search time: Time it takes for the requested data to rotate under the read/write head, 79
Secondary sort orders, 185-86
Secondary storage: All information storage devices other than primary memory, usually refers to devices that use removable media, 11
Secondary storage devices, 11, 77, 79-80
  cartridges, 83-84
  cassette tapes, 84

diskettes, 80-81
hard disks, 77
magnetic disks, 77-81
optical disks, 81-83
Seek time: Time it takes to position the read/write head over the desired track, 79
Selecting function, 182-84
Semiconductor: Device that can be made to serve as a conductor or as an insulator, depending on conditions, 57
Semiconductor chip technology, 56-57
Serial transmission, 201
Silicon Valley, 3
Simplex channel: Communication path that can transmit data in only one direction, 206
Single-density diskette: Diskette in which data are recorded at normal density, 80
Single-sided diskette: Diskette in which data are recorded only on the top surface, 80
Soft copy: Temporary copy of the output, such as a visual display or computer voice output, 69
Software: Programs (sets of instructions) that direct the operation of computer hardware, 9, 12
  advances in, 24, 25
  applications, 12
  attractions of packaged, 25
  portability of, 103
  systems, 12-13
Software integrator: Software package that integrates multiple independent application packages, 223-24
Software maintenance: The process of fixing software errors and keeping an information system up-to-date, 45
Sorting function, 185-86
Source, The, 213
  using Crosstalk to communicate with, 214-16
Spelling checkers: Software that makes use of online dictionaries to locate and correct spelling errors, 106
Spreadsheet graphics, 158, 163. *See also* Electronic spreadsheet
Stacked bar graph, 169
Stand-alone graphics, 158-59
Stand-alone use: Microcomputer use involving no access to other computer systems, 211

Star network topology: Pattern in which each device is connected to a central unit, 209
Startup files, 101
Statistical analysis, 230
Status line, 126
Style checkers: Software that analyzes a document to locate and correct grammar or punctuation errors, 106
Subdirectories, 101
SUPERCALC4, 140, 149, 159
Supervisor: Set of programs that handles the overall management of the tasks being conducted by the computer system, 88
Support units, 60-61
Symphony, 223
Synchronous mode: Means of data transmission used when large volumes of data are to be sent, 206
Systems analyst: Individual who defines the information processing needs of a business, department, or person, 14
Systems designer: Individual who devises a hardware/software design to meet the information processing needs of a business, department, or person, 14
System software: Programs written to act as an interface between an application program and the computer, 12-13, 88
  role of, 88-89

T

Telecommunication: Transmission of data over long distances, 202
  carrier signals, 202-5
  communication channels, 206
  data packets, 205-6
Template: Predetermined pattern, representing each character in a specified font style, 152-53
Terminal emulation, 210-11
Texas Instruments, 68
Text files, 212
Text manipulation operations: Operations such as inserting, deleting, and moving characters, words, and text, 17
Thesaurus programs: Software that provides an online thesaurus, 106

Thimble print mechanism: Print mechanism used in computer printers, 74
Transaction: Single business event, 31
Transaction processing system: System used to record, process, and manage data about everyday business activities, 31
Transistor: Electronic component that functions as a semiconductor, 56
Transmission media: Different types of links that can be used in a network to form data paths, 200
TYPE command, 97

U

Undelete function, 111
UNIX operating system, 90
Uploading: The sending of data that have been captured and initially processed on a microcomputer to a data base maintained on a larger computer system, 212
Utilities: Programs that have been written to accomplish common tasks, such as sorting records or copying disk files to magnetic tape for backup, 89

V

Ventura, 173, 175
Verification, 94
Very high-level languages: Nonprocedural programming languages, 221
Videodisc: Also called optical disk; optical technology used with laser disk systems to provide a very high-capacity medium for storage of data, text, audio, and video images, 81-83
Video monitor: Input device consisting of a keyboard for data entry and a TV-like screen for data presentation, 61
Visible backlog: Visible waiting list, 220
Voice recognition system: System in which the spoken word is converted into electrical signal patterns that are compared to a voice template, 67-69
Volatile RAM, 58

W

Wildcard character, 96, 112-13
Winchester technology: Technology in which a hard disk is sealed inside a hermetic (airtight) container, 80
Window: Function that allows the computer's disk display screen to be divided into separate areas or boxes, 125-26
Window manager: Software that allows the user to create a number of applications at the same time, to view each application in its own window, to change the size of windows, and to move data values among windows, 223-24
WordPerfect, 173
Word processor: Software that transforms a terminal screen into "sheets of paper" to be written on electronically, 37-38, 106
  choosing, 119, 121
  creating a document, 106-7
  document editing, 107-13
  document formatting, 113-17
  document management, 117-19
  document printing, 117
WordStar, 173
Word wrap, 108
WYSIWYG, 114

X

x-axis, 161
XENIX, 90
Xmodem protocol, 212-13

Y

y-axis, 161

Glossary/Index

ACKNOWLEDGMENTS

PHOTO CREDITS

Positions of photographs are shown in abbreviated form as follows: top (T), bottom (B), center (C), left (L), right (R), clockwise (CW). Unless otherwise acknowledged, all photos are the property of Scott, Foresman and Company.

Cover
Computer Support Corporation, Dallas, TX, (214) 661-8960

Chapter 1
3L Courtesy Fairchild Camera and Equipment Corporation **3R** Courtesy National Semiconductor Corporation **6TL** Yoav Levy/Phototake **6TR** John McGrail/Wheeler Pictures **6CL** Joe McNally/Wheeler Pictures **6CR** Paul Conklin **6BL** Tom Pantages Photo (Courtesy MIT Experimental Music Lab) **6BR** Dan McCoy/Rainbow **11** Courtesy of International Business Machines Corporation **14** Courtesy Hayes Microcomputer Products Inc. **15CW** Hank Morgan/Rainbow **15CW** Bohdan Hrynewych/Southern Light **15CW** Peter Angelo Simon/Phototake **15CW** Richard T. Nowitz/Phototake **15CW** © Dawson Jones **15CW** Dan McCoy/Rainbow

Chapter 2
26ALL Courtesy Lotus Development Corporation **37** Courtesy Quadram Corporation **38T** Courtesy Software Publishing Corporation **38BL** Courtesy Software Publishing Corporation **38BC** Courtesy Apple Computer Inc. **38BR** Phototake **39** Courtesy Apple Computer Inc. **40L** Courtesy Software Publishing Corporation **40R** Courtesy Lotus Development Corporation

Chapter 3
56L Roberto Broson **56R** Thom O'Connor **59T** Margaret C. Berg/Berg & Associates **59B** Joel Gordon Photography **60L** Milt & Joan Mann/Cameramann International, Ltd.

Chapter 4
64L Peter Angelo Simon/Phototake **64R** © Dawson Jones Inc. **65** Courtesy Keytronic Corporation **66** Courtesy Hewlett-Packard Company **70L** Courtesy Zenith Data Systems **70C** Joe McNally/Wheeler Pictures **70R** Courtesy Ashton-Tate **71T** Courtesy Apple Computer Inc. **71BL** Courtesy of International Business Machines Corporation **71BR** Courtesy of International Business Machines Corporation **72ALL** Courtesy Data General Corporation **74** Joel Gordon Photography **75** John McGrail/Wheeler Pictures **76L** Milt & Joan Mann/Cameramann International, Ltd. **76R** Courtesy Hewlett-Packard Company **78L** Bob Glaze/Artstreet **78R** Courtesy Apple Computer Inc. **82L** Courtesy IOMEGA Corporation **83T** Courtesy Hitachi America, Ltd. **83B** Courtesy Drexler Technology Corporation **84** © Dawson Jones Inc.

Chapter 5
92 Courtesy Digital Corporation

Chapter 9
166ALL Courtesy Computer Support Corporation **167T** Courtesy Computer Support Corporation **170** Courtesy Z-Soft Corporation **175** Courtesy Xerox Corporation

Chapter 11
201T Gus Schonefeld/Berg & Associates **204TL** Don and Pat Valenti/Hillstrom Stock Photos **204TR** Courtesy Hayes Microcomputer Products Inc. **204B** Courtesy Hayes Microcomputer Products Inc.

Chapter 12
223L Milt & Joan Mann/Cameramann International, Ltd. **223R** Courtesy Lotus Development Corporation **225TL** Courtesy Digital Corporation

Acknowledgments

225TR Courtesy Digital Corporation
225B Courtesy Polytron Corporation

Appendix A
242 Courtesy IBM Archives **243L** NASA **243R** Courtesy AT&T, Bell Labs **246** Courtesy IBM Archives **247ALL** Courtesy Intel Corporation **248TL** Courtesy Intel Corporation **248TC** Courtesy Apple Computer Inc. **248TR** Courtesy Radio Shack, A Division of TANDY Corporation **248B** Courtesy Chemical Bank **249T** William Strode **249C** Courtesy Apple Computer Inc. **249B** Courtesy Wang Laboratories, Inc. **250T** Courtesy of International Business Machines Corporation **250C** Courtesy Toshiba America, Inc. **250B** Courtesy Compaq Computer Corporation

LITERARY CREDITS

27 reprinted from the June issue of Modern Office Technology, and copyrighted 1984 by Penton/IPC, subsidiary of Pittway Corp. **36** adapted from Figure 3 in "Personal Computers in the Eighties" by Greggory S. Blundell, *Byte*, January 1983, p. 171. Copyright © 1983 McGraw-Hill, Inc., New York 10020. All rights reserved. Reprinted by permission. **68** reprinted with permission, *High Technology Magazine*, February 1985. Copyright © 1985 by Infotechnology Publishing Corporation, 214 Lewis Wharf, Boston, MA 02110. **222** adaptation of Figure 1, p. 74. Reprinted by permission of PC World from Volume 2, Issue 11, October 1984, published at 501 Second Street, Suite 600, San Francisco, CA 94107.

JUN 0 5 1989